ML

THE FUTURE OF THE UNITED STATES GOVERNMENT

Toward the Year 2000

THE FUTURE OF THE UNITED STATES GOVERNMENT

Toward the Year 2000

Edited by HARVEY S. PERLOFF

Prefaced by Daniel Bell

A REPORT FROM THE COMMISSION ON THE YEAR 2000 OF THE AMERICAN ACADEMY OF ARTS AND SCIENCES

George Braziller NEW YORK

Published simultaneously in Canada by
Doubleday Canada, Limited.

For information address the publisher:
George Braziller, Inc.
One Park Avenue
New York, N.Y. 10016

Standard Book Number: 0-8076-0609-x

Library of Congress Catalog Card Number: 74-148732
First Printing
Printed in the United States of America

CONTENTS

III

UNITED STATES WORLD RESPONSIBILITIES

IV

SOCIAL CHANGE AND ADAPTABILITY OF GOVERNMENTAL INSTITUTIONS

V

THE FUTURE OF NATIONAL GOVERNMENTAL INSTITUTIONS

VI

THE FUTURE OF URBANISM AND OF UNITED STATES FEDERALISM

FOREWORD

Daniel Bell

This volume, edited by Harvey S. Perloff, is the fruit of a working group of the Commission on the Year 2000 of the American Academy of Arts and Sciences. The Commission was formed in October 1965 in an effort to stimulate thinking about long-range social questions. Its members had for some time felt that American society was ill-prepared to deal with social issues because there was no mechanism to anticipate them. If we could pool the ideas of the Commission's thirty-eight members—and, later, of the more than two hundred individuals participating in the discussions of the work groups—we could begin to identify relevant social questions that society would have to confront in the next three decades.

In this attempt, there was no effort to evade the problems of the present. As I wrote in the first working paper: "The future is not an overarching leap into the distance; it begins in the present. . . for in the decisions we make now, in the way we design our environment and thus sketch the lines of constraints, the future is committed." As I pointed out further:

> This is the premise of the Commission on the Year 2000. It is an effort to indicate now the future consequences of present public policy decisions, to anticipate future problems, and to begin the design of alternative solutions so that our society has more options and can make a moral choice, rather than be constrained, as is so often the case when problems descend upon us unnoticed and demand an immediate response.

The first efforts of the Commission were published, in mimeographed form, in five volumes of working papers and transcripts; eventually three thousand sets of these volumes went to individuals in universities, government, and business who were interested in the details of the Commission's work. A selection from these volumes was published as the Summer 1967 issue of *Dædalus,* with the title "Toward the Year 2000: Work in Progress," and the response was gratifying. Eventually more than 100,000 copies of that issue were sold for individual and school use. A hard-cover edition was published by Houghton Mifflin, and later a paperback edition was brought out by Beacon Press. In addition, material from Volumes II and IIa of the working papers, contributed by a special group at the Hudson Institute, was revised by its principal authors, Herman Kahn and Anthony J. Wiener, and published independently by Macmillan as *The Year 2000*.

Following the first phase of the Commission's activities, nine working groups, each directed by a different chairman, were set up to explore in greater detail the problems identified by the Commission. In addition to the group on Government, under the leadership of Harvey Perloff, the other groups, and their chairmen, are: Values and Rights, Fred C. Iklé; Intellectual Institutions, Stephen R. Graubard; The Life Cycle, Kai Erikson; The International System, Stanley Hoffman; The Social Impact of the Computer, Robert M. Fano; Science and Society, Franklin Long and Robert S. Morison; Business Institutions, Martin Shubik. These groups met in extended sessions in two- and three-day conferences each. Detailed transcripts have been mimeographed and some of these are available at the office of the Academy. Their findings and conclusions will be reflected in the final report of the Commission which will be made in 1972.

Since the formation of the Commission on the Year 2000 five years ago, "futurology" has become a worldwide movement, with different groups in a dozen different countries. There is an international association, *Futuribles,* under the leadership of Bertrand de Jouvenel, of the Faculty of Law at the Sorbonne, one of the first men to initiate the idea of studying the future. There have been international congresses in Oslo and Kyoto. A World Future Society flourishes in Washington and publishes a bimonthly, *The Futurist.* The Institute for the Future, headed by Olaf Helmer, now has its headquarters in Middletown, Connecticut, to conduct systematic studies using the Delphi technique, which Helmer and Norman Dalkey pioneered at the Rand Corporation. Work on technological forecasting is carried out systematically by the U.S. Navy and Air Force, as well as by half a hundred corporations. An international journal, *Futures,* is published by Iliffe Science and Technology Publications in England, and another journal, *Technological Forecasting,* is put out in America by the Elsevier Publishing Company. All of this attests to the seriousness of the effort.

With all this, the question is still raised: Can you "predict" the future? Or, as the question is put at this stage: How do you predict the future? In fact, both questions are inaccurate, on two counts. First, no one claims the ability to "predict," if only because the prediction sometimes acts as its own falsification, since the statement of a problem may unleash efforts to deal with it, as in the case of overpopulation or of food shortages. One does not predict a future state of events; one tries to anticipate and identify problems. Second, there is no such entity as *the* future. There are many possible futures, and one can try to identify the alternative lines of possibility based on the kind of problem one is wrestling with.

There are by now many techniques of anticipation or forecasting. The philosophical basis for such efforts has been laid down by Bertrand de Jouvenel in his seminal book *The Art of Conjecture* (New York: Basic Books, 1967). The Delphi technique, which is a method of validating the forecasts of expert opinion, has been elucidated by Olaf Helmer in *Social Technology* (New York: Basic Books, 1966). Erich Jantach made a comprehensive survey of technological forecasting for the O.E.C.D., in Paris in 1967, and James Bright has edited a comprehensive compendium on the subject, *Technological Forecasting for Industry and Government* (Englewood Cliffs, N.J.: Prentice-Hall, 1968). Otis Dudley Duncan has published a review of "Social Forecasting: The State of the Art," in *The Public Interest* (number 17, Fall 1969). And François Hetman has provided a useful bilingual dictionary of terms and methods, *The Language of Forecasting* (S.E.D.E.I.S., Paris, 1969).

Social forecasting, in which the Commission on the Year 2000 is engaged, is an especially refractory undertaking. Economic forecasting at least has the advantages of systematic time series and a comprehensive model of the economy. Technological forecasting tries to identify the physical constraints that inhibit the development of new processes or the parameters of existing processes (for example, speeds of aircraft, memory capacities of computers, and the like). But social forecasting has different realms and boundaries.

In general, there have been three methods of social forecasting. One is simply the analytical identification of future social problems. For example, it takes very little expertise to point out that in the next decade housing will be a crucial social problem. One need only take simple demographic projections (thirty million additional people in the next decade), the present housing stock and its rate of deterioration, and the rate of housing starts. We know that we will need at least two million *additional* housing units a year, over and above the stock of our previous decade; in the first year of the decade, we were at least half a million shy of that goal, and there are indications that we may continue to fall short. Through the same kind of reasoning (demographic projections, estimated demand, and estimated supply), we know that health care will intensify as a social problem. Yet all this, as a method, is rather ad-hoc and fragmentary. We can identify specific areas, but we cannot show how they relate to one another.

A second method is to extrapolate existing social trends for which we have time series. Population estimates and internal migrations are prime examples of this method. Other examples are various kinds of consumer demands. More generally, using opinion polls and other survey techniques, we can chart the frustrations of subgroups of the population (for example, the blacks) and anticipate new social demands. The inherent difficulty with extrapolation is that these are simple projections, and projections do not take into account "system breaks" (such as the spectacular rise of agricultural productivity after 1940, and the accelerated migration of people away from the farms in the 1950's), exogenous variables, or outside interruptions.

A third method is to construct a model of the society in which the relevant independent variables and their dependent functions are identified. The difficulty with the sociological models extant is that they are either simply classificatory or morphological, and give no clues as to what initiates what.[1] One can gauge the difficulty of constructing a sociological model when one learns that in the Brookings Econometric Model of the United States there are, initially, thirty-six sectors and several hundred interacting variables to deal with in order to obtain the equations that allow for quarterly forecasts.[2]

The method we have adopted in the Commission on the Year 2000 stands between the extrapolation of social trends and the creation of a model of American society. It is an effort to identify *relevant structural changes* that will create new *social frameworks*, which set the boundaries of social action out of which social problems emerge. The change from a rural America to an urban America was one such major structural change that framed the problems of American society in this century. This was, at the start, an agrarian society. The major political institutions and the administrative structure of the country were framed to deal with agrarian questions. The industrialization of the society, which began in the 1870's and 1880's, started to reshape the map of America. With the appearance of the automobile, especially in the 1920's, a huge spatial reworking of America—particularly the rise of the suburbs—began. If one looks at such an early effort at social forecasting as the volumes *Recent Social Trends,* which were published under the direction of William F. Ogburn in 1932, it is clear that the implicit framework of their research and discussions was the changeover to a metropolitan America. Their identification of relevant social problems emerged out of that framework.

The working papers of the Commission on the Year 2000 that I prepared for *Dædalus* sought to identify three structural changes that provide the settings for social action in the present and also in the next thirty years. This was not an effort to sketch a picture of total social change in the United States. To do so, one would have to include, at one end of the spectrum, changes in culture and in values, and, at the other, changes in the economy and in technology. Framing all these are the political actions, such as the Vietnam war, which at crucial moments provide turning points for the society. The "prediction" of political events—given their volatility and the strategic problem of the character of political leadership—is, for reasons spelled out in the volume *Toward the Year 2000,* the most difficult and refractory of all. Our effort, however, is to deal with structural contexts, which change relatively slowly and whose direction, we believe, can be charted. From an analysis of such structural changes one can deduce a whole array of more focal social questions.

The three structural changes in the United States—going back thirty years and going forward another thirty—are the creation of a national society, a communal society, and a postindustrial society. It is the simultaneous and interacting nature of these structural changes that, beyond the more surface elements of the Vietnam war and the race issue, forms a set of social problems for the United States.

In this foreword I can only briefly identify the nature of these changes.

The National Society

The United States has for the first time become a national society. It has long been a "nation," in that it has had a national identity and a national symbolism. But it is only in the last thirty years, because of the revolution in communication and transportation—the rise of national network television, coast-to-coast telephone dialing, simultaneous publication of national newsweeklies, jet transport across the country in five hours—that the United States has become a national *society* in the fundamental sense that changes taking place in one section of the society have an immediate and repercussive effect in all others.

Three broad problems can be identified as a consequence of the emergence of a national society:

(a) *Social problems have become national in scope.* Just as the New Deal, in the 1930's, had to grapple with the problem of a national economy—and create institutions for the regulation and management of the economy—so the Great Society has had to deal with a national society in welfare, education, health, housing, and environment. The institutions we set up now will shape our lives for the next thirty years, just as the regulatory mechanisms of the last thirty—the Securities and Exchange Commission (SEC) for finance, the National Labor Relations Board (NLRB) for collective bargaining, the Council of Economic Advisors for employment policy—shaped the present economic structure.

(b) *The inadequacy of the present administrative structure.* In a national society, what is the rationale for a structure with fifty quasi-sovereign states, each with tax powers resting on varied and often inadequate tax bases? What is the rationale for the present crazy-quilt pattern of townships, municipalities, counties, and cities, plus the multifarious health, park, sewage, and water districts? The functioning of any society necessarily depends on the efficiency of its administrative structure. In the United States that structure is largely out of step with the needs of the times.

(c) *The rise of plebiscitary politics.* The ease with which tens and even hundreds of thousands of people can pour into Washington, D.C., within a forty-eight-hour period makes the national capital a cockpit for mobilization pressures in a way that this society has never before experienced. The problems of violence are underlined by such mobilization tactics, and the role of army, national guard, and police in demonstrations has already proved to be a new and difficult problem for the polity to deal with.

Since political conflicts are bound to multiply in the next decades—in part because of the multiple social problems we must face, in part for the structural reasons indicated below—the change to mobilization politics becomes a source of strain for the entire political system.

The Communal Society

The emergence of a communal society derives from two factors: the growth of nonmarket public decision making, and the definition of social rights in group, rather than individual, terms. In scale both changes are distinctly new on the American scene, and both pose new kinds of problems for the society.

(a) *Public Decision Making.* By nonmarket public decision making, I mean problems that have to be decided by public authorities, rather than through the market. The layout of roads, the creation of jetports, the planning of cities, the organization of health care, the financing of education, the cleaning up of the environment—these are all public concerns and become the subject of public debate. Often, they have to be settled by public decision.

There are two reasons for this. First, the items that need to be purchased are public goods, not divisible among individual consumers. No one can buy his share of clean air or clean water in the marketplace; everyone must use communal mechanisms to deal with pollution. Second, there is an increase of *externalities,* which are side effects, usually social costs that are borne by the public or by individuals as a result of activities generated by firms or municipalities. The regulation of externalities—deciding who should bear the costs, and in what proportions—is a political matter.

The rise of nonmarket public decision making inevitably increases community conflicts. The virtue of the market is that it disperses responsibility. When a decision is made by the multiple choice of thousands of consumers acting individually in a marketplace, if a product does not sell, or there is a shift in taste, or if a firm fails because it did not anticipate market changes, no single group, other than the managers of the firm itself, can be saddled with the responsibilities of failure. But when decisions are public and political —the location of a housing project, or a jetport, or the path of a highway—the decision points are visible, and the consequences can be readily assessed; one knows whose ox will be gored. One knows, too, where to go fight: City Hall. Thus the very shift from the market to public decision making becomes a structural source of increased conflict in the society.

(b) *Group Rights.* Increasingly, social claims on the community are made on the basis of membership in a group, rather than individually. We see this, of course, in the demands of the blacks. The demands for preferential hiring, special quotas, and compensatory education are made as group demands. What this leads to, as we have seen in the New York City school situation, is a conflict of rights. The reigning principle is that heads of schools be chosen on the basis of merit and achievement; the blacks demand that in schools where black children are in the majority, the principals be chosen on the basis of color, bypassing the existing merit lists if necessary. The nature of tragedy, as Hegel pointed out long ago, is not the conflict between right and wrong, but between right and right. And there are no unambiguous grounds of adjudication.

In the coming years the demand for group rights will widen in the society because social life is increasingly organized on a group basis. The need to work out philosophical legitimations and political mechanisms to adjudicate these claims is a necessary task in the period ahead.

The Postindustrial Society

The postindustrial society has a double aspect. There is, first, the fact that we have changed from a goods-producing to a service society. Today almost 60 percent of the labor force is in services. By 1980 almost seven out of ten persons will be in the service category.

More importantly, the nature of the postindustrial society is such that a new principle of change becomes the fulcrum of social organization: the fact that invention and innovation derive increasingly from the codification of theoretical knowledge.[3] This is preeminently the case in the relation of science to technology; it is demonstrable in the management of the economy through the application of theoretical principles to policy.

The nature of the postindustrial society is such that the chief requirements for advancement are education and skill, and for that reason the university has become the gatekeeper of place and privilege in the society. The problems of the postindustrial society involve the husbanding of "human capital," which is the scarcest resource in such a society. It requires a more coherent organization of research endeavor, and poses great problems for the social organization of intellectual institutions.

More generally, the emergence of a postindustrial society poses political problems. The mode of decision making in a postindustrial society is inevitably technocratic, based on criteria of optimization, maximization, and functional efficiency. Increasingly this comes into conflict with populist and political feelings. The relation between technocratic and political decision making will thus be one of the chief problems of the postindustrial society.

Structural problems are somewhat susceptible to forecasting, for the issues do not arise overnight, and they are a long time in working themselves out. But structural changes have meaning only within the framework of values, for ultimately it is the value system which decides whether or not these changes are to be facilitated or inhibited.

A public philosophy, to use Walter Lippmann's phrase, legitimates values and guides social policy. Our crucial problem is the inadequacy of the public philosophy we have inherited and the need for new conceptions. And this is, rightly, the heart of Mr. Perloff's introductory essay, which framed the work of his group.

There was a closely related consideration—the question of the governmental and political structure of the society. Administrative problems may seem dull and hackneyed beside the tension, glamour, and conflict of politics. Yet, if politics decides policy, administration has to carry it out; and if this is done poorly or inefficiently, the best policies in the world will have little effect in making the intended changes. This dual emphasis permeates the volume edited by Mr. Perloff.

The basic fact about the American system is that while we have a modern technology and economy, ours is an antiquated Tudor polity with a patchwork system of jurisdictions and sovereignties. What we have is not decentralization but disarray. The major problem in the years ahead will be to define the effective size and scope of the appropriate social units for coping with the different levels of problems: what should be decided and performed on the neighborhood, city, metropolitan, and federal levels.

This combination of philosophical inquiry, social anticipation, analytical definition, and normative design has been the focus of the work group under the direction of Mr. Perloff. I think it makes a unique book.

Harvard University

NOTES

1. See, for example, Bertram D. Gross, "The State of the Nation: Social Systems Accounting," in *Social Indicators,* ed. Raymond A. Bauer (Cambridge, Mass.: M.I.T. Press, 1966), pp. 154–272; and Robin Williams, "A Model of Society—The American Case," in *A Great Society?*, ed. Bertram D. Gross (New York: Basic Books, 1968), pp. 32–58.

2. The Brookings Quarterly Econometric Model of the United States, eds. Dusenberry, Fromm, Klein, and Kuh (Chicago: Rand McNally, 1965). The present model uses 150 equations. The authors write of their future intentions: "In all, we plan to have a model with approximately 32 sectors on the production side. Thus we shall have 32 wage rate equations, 32 production functions, 32 hour equations, 32 price equations and 32 final demand regressions. These changes alone will add approximately 150 equations to an already large model. Corresponding to these changes on the side of production, we shall make similar decompositions on the side of final demand. We would want 32 investment functions in order to build up 32 series on capital stock for the 32 production functions. We would also need 32 depreciation equations. The final demand regressions will be improved if we make these and similar decompositions of other types of final demand. Foreign trade, consumption and inventories will

probably be further decomposed. . . . We shall probably end up with a system of approximately 300 to 400 equations . . ." (pp. 31–32).

3. I have written of the postindustrial society in a number of essays. The most comprehensive statement can be found in my monograph, "The Measurement of Knowledge and Technology," in *Indicators of Social Change*, ed. Eleanor Sheldon and Wilbert Moore (New York: Russell Sage Foundation, 1968).

PREFACE

Harvey S. Perloff

The essays in this volume are concerned with the problems of American government in the year 2000, or rather with issues that will require attention over the next three decades. Actually, if most of the proposed changes in outlook and structure are not realized long before the year 2000, the United States will be in trouble. But the rubric 2000 has forced us to reach toward the future in a problem area—that of governmental change—often characterized by approaches adequate only for the solution of yesterday's problems.

This book is a product of Phase II of the work of the Commission on the Year 2000 of the American Academy of Arts and Sciences, an effort that the Chairman, Daniel Bell, aptly described as having "a touch of extraordinary imagination and daring, and also of preposterousness." Behind the idea of the Commission was the proposition that a society as interdependent as ours should undertake some form of systematic anticipation, of thinking about the future.

After the initial discussions of the Commission in 1965 and 1966, nine working parties were set up to explore in greater detail the problem areas mapped out by the Commission. In 1967, I was asked by Mr. Bell to organize a group that would concern itself with the future of American government, the problems it can be expected to confront, and the adequacy of its structure to deal with these problems.

The first group to meet—on May 25–27, 1967—began to speculate about the future of government in the United States, highlighting subjects that seemed worthy of detailed attention and suggesting individuals who might bring special insights to the selected themes. Members of the groups had already been polled—using a modified Delphi technique—about the social problems they thought would dominate governmental attention at the turn of the century. In line with that technique, ideas about such problems began to be changed and refined through interaction. Additional persons were invited to the second meeting (November 10–11, 1967), and the discussion was much enriched. Several informal memoranda were prepared by participants for this meeting, and these added structure to the discussion. The circle continued to widen for the third and fourth meetings (April 25–27 and May 16–18, 1968), in which first-draft papers prepared by members of the group were discussed. The commentaries on the papers were frank and to the point, and helped to define areas of disagreement as well as agreement.

Even at this stage we continued to identify significant subject gaps, and in the last phase—the preparation of the volume for publication—we invited Martin and Margy Meyerson and William Capron, who had not taken part in the earlier discussions, to contribute papers. Clearly, intellectual "circles" are never completed or rounded; the reader will undoubtedly notice major gaps that remain.

While interest and expertise in certain key themes were major criteria in the selection of the working groups, diversity of background was equally important. From the beginning an effort was made to achieve some sort of balance between governmental practitioners and scholars (the latter from a range of disciplines), and among persons who had had experience at the international, national, and subnational levels, in both the legislative and the executive branches (we were not successful on the judicial side), and who were in business as well as in government.

The fact that so many members of the group were currently in government or had had substantial governmental experience in the past greatly influenced both the discussions and the essays, and gave them a practical rather than a theoretical cast. While philosophical and normal considerations set the framework for the effort, the issues that received the greatest attention were not those of political philosophy, but those of public policy, politics, and public and private institutions.

In undertaking its task, the Working Group had before it the highly valuable reference points established by the Phase I work of the Commission on the Year 2000. These included the many cogent questions raised by members of the Commission and certain propositions framed by Daniel Bell, sketching significant structural changes that had originated in the past generation and that would be playing themselves out in the next. The impact of these changes on government in the United States was a matter of continuing concern for the group. The explorations by Herman Kahn and his associates at the Hudson Institute of "alternative futures" and projections of basic time series were very helpful.[1]

The work of the group was centered on two main questions: what are the most significant problems and critical issues that government in the United States will have to face in the future; and what changes in institutions and processes will have to be made to enable government to cope effectively with these problems and issues, which will at the same time provide adequate scope for the expression of individual and group values? These questions formed the main structure of the discussions and papers that make up the present volume.

NOTE

1. Herman Kahn and Anthony J. Wiener, *The Year 2000: A Framework for Speculation on the next Thirty-Three Years* (New York: Macmillan Co., 1967).

ACKNOWLEDGMENTS

I particularly wish to thank John Manley of the Political Science Department of the University of Wisconsin for his trenchant editorial advice. I have also benefited greatly from the editorial comments of John Voss, Harold Orlans, James D. Barber, H. Field Haviland, Jr., Kenneth L. Karst, Murry L. Schwartz, Myra Kassel, and James L. Sundquist, as well as from suggestions from my wife, Mimi.

I undertook the organization of the enterprise and carried out most of my editorial tasks while associated with Resources for the Future, Inc. I deeply appreciate their support and encouragement.

John Voss of the American Academy of Arts and Sciences nursed the activities of the Working Group from the beginning and helped greatly in every phase of the effort. His contribution went far beyond the call of duty. Pearl Bell provided invaluable assistance in the preparation of the volume for publication. I wish to express my appreciation to the Carnegie Corporation for its support of the Conference which led to this publication.

HARVEY S. PERLOFF

THE FUTURE OF THE UNITED STATES GOVERNMENT

Toward the Year 2000

INTRODUCTION: THE FUTURE OF THE UNITED STATES GOVERNMENT; A FRAMEWORK FOR DISCUSSION[1]

Harvey S. Perloff

Changes in technology, in population, and in world affairs are Janus-like in their impact: they bring both hopeful possibilities for the future and disturbing problems. The potentialities of such changes may not always be fully grasped, but the big problems, those with political dynamite, the government cannot overlook. Those big problems that can be identified in current trends provide a logical starting point for speculation about the future of American government.

I Societal Problems

From today's vantage point four groups of problems will be of primary concern to the government at the turn of the century (and in most cases even earlier):

1. PRESSURES ON THE INDIVIDUAL

Many discernible trends—fantastically rapid technological changes, increases in population and movement, the implications for American citizens of American world responsibility, and the growth of a "meritocracy" (with talent and achievement, particularly educational achievement, becoming the primary bases for stratification)—tend to make the individual feel besieged. There are many dangers. A man may find himself inadequately prepared for the available jobs or threatened by early skill obsolescence. He may be frustrated by his inability to grasp opportunities because of various forms of social prejudice. He may be unable to direct his own career line and life style because of high and continuing military demands. He may be deprived of privacy in an era when technology makes invasion of privacy childishly simple and when the information needs of government and business are great.[2] Or, he may find himself disoriented in a world of new values associated with affluence and leisure.

Such problems challenge the adequacy of existing conceptions of human rights and individual welfare. We need new means of maintaining traditional personal safeguards under new and difficult conditions, and of establishing an appropriate balance between personal freedom on the one hand and social order on the other.[3]

2. DANGER OF DETERIORATION OF THE INTERNAL COHESION OF SOCIETY

The report of the National Advisory Commission on Civil Disorders (March 2, 1968) has pointed out, "Preserving civil peace is the first responsibility of government. Unless the rule of law prevails, our society will lack not only order but also the environment essential to social and economic progress." Threats to internal cohesion come from many sources: (a) the failure to heal racial divisions rapidly enough; (b) a growing gap between rich and poor, with racial overtones, in an increasingly affluent society; (c) racial divisions maintained through segregated housing; (d) mounting violence and crime in the cities; (e) growth of the extreme right and left owing to fear of the rate and form of social change; (f) disagreements about America's role in world affairs and about the draft; and (g) a possible conflict between a relatively small group of overworked technicians and decision makers and a large group of consumers who are needed only marginally within the productive system.[4]

3. DETERIORATION OF THE ENVIRONMENT AND MASS POLITICS: NUMBERS AND THE CHANGE OF SCALE

Growing population and increasing urbanization will further strain our natural and man-made environment as well as individual life. We are already plagued by air and water pollution, the loss of open space near urban areas, intolerable noise, irritating and time-consuming traffic congestion, especially in intercity movement—in airlanes, airports, and highways—in short, by the enormous strain of high-density living. It all seems destined to get worse. And it is ironic that one leaves the congestion of the city only to find a similar situation in overcrowded camping grounds.

Government will have to adjust to the fact that we are now an urban nation, that our major problems are national in origin and scope, and that all our urban communities are intimately tied into a national system of cities. The needs of highly interdependent urban regions cannot be met by local government units designed for a simpler, more constrained rural era. Policies must take into account the location of people, industries, and communities; we must learn the new political art of planning for efficiency and livability in cities of every size and kind.[5]

Large numbers and changes in scale may also greatly influence the tone and style of politics. Mass society may give rise to mass politics. Where decision making is centralized, disaffection might readily explode into violence against decision centers.

4. DOMESTIC STRAINS OF WORLD RESPONSIBILITY

America has come into a role of world leadership at a time when it is denied the political and military means that were open to former world leaders, such as the Romans or the British, and when nuclear weapons can mean worldwide destruction. America's world responsibilities have created many domestic problems. There is an increasing drain on resources needed for personal and national uses, and a related growth in the power of the military establishment. There are mounting tensions among domestic groups because of different reactions to foreign affairs (also a key threat to the internal cohesion of our society). Internal dangers multiply as the gap widens between an affluent America and large parts of the world that are poor, crowded, and that very likely will have nuclear capabilities.

Somehow we will have to find political means for relating the United States to the emerging world order and for evolving a workable domestic consensus for an effective foreign policy.[6]

II Philosophical Bases for Governmental Policy and Action

If American government is to cope effectively with future problems, it must reevaluate the philosophical bases for governmental policy and action, and reformulate organizational and operational principles. Governmental philosophy has not kept pace with other changes in our society, and this imbalance could have a devastating impact. In the political realm, major changes in the philosophical or value bases of governmental action can be as significant as major technological breakthroughs. As Leonard Duhl suggested during the discussion of the Working Group, "The future will be shaped by the outcome of the struggle of competing values. . . . What the future will be like is, therefore, at bottom a political question."

Clearly, our society can go in several quite different directions in the future. We cannot predict the future, but we *can* come to understand the choices ahead of us and can throw light on measures that might point us in a hopeful direction. Because of the vast technological changes and the remarkable productive achievements of the post-World War II era, we are facing a major choice in values, and the next thirty years will be greatly affected by our choices.

Behind the seeming chaos of changing American government policy and action during the past century lie certain philosophical themes that have strongly influenced the style of government action, as well as the relationships between the government and the citizen, among the different levels of government, and between the United States and the rest of the world. At the center there has been an overriding concern for national economic development, running parallel to a concern for individual rights, resulting in a widely accepted idea that individual initiative and entrepreneurship are the keys to national economic progress. Government was to provide the legal framework and infrastructure for individual and corporate endeavor. Equality of opportunity, as well as the protection of personal and property rights, was essential to the maintenance of an open society and the fair distribution of the growing product. Within the context of this concern for national economic expansion and for the "natural rights" of man, government was to be decentralized; the provision of basic social services was left to the states and localities, as was control over voting and the protection of various civic rights. Overseas, American citizen, business, and national "rights" were to be protected; no nation or group of nations could be permitted to upset a balance of powers.

Before the Depression of the 1930's, the American Dream meant the capacity of the individual to make his own way if freed from the shackles of government bureaucracy. Governmental activities were limited; for example, expenditures for civil functions by all levels of government amounted to some 6 percent of the Gross National Product at the turn of the century and about 9 percent toward the end of the 1920's (the federal government accounted for less than 20 percent of total public civil expenditures).[7] But the 1930's, owing to an economic depression unprecedented in intensity and duration, brought about drastic changes in the concept and practice of government in the United States, and a powerful change in social and political philosophy. Economic considerations dominated politics more than ever, but now the federal government was expected to cope with the economic crisis and the urgent relief needs because private institutions had retreated and state and local finances were crippled.

The centralizing impact of the Depression was strongly reinforced by World War II (between 1940 and 1944 federal spending increased tenfold, from $10.1 billion to $100.5 billion), and later by the Korean and the Vietnamese wars, with federal defense expenditures at the end of the 1960's running at an annual level of $80 billion. Paying little attention to the logic of intergovernmental relations, the federal government pumped a hodgepodge of financial aids into the troubled state and local governments, while overlooking their basic incapacity to handle the problems of a rapidly changing nation.

After World War II, the promotion of corporate and national prosperity that had dominated American politics and policy for such a long time had substantial success. By the end of the 1960's, the G.N.P. had soared beyond the $900 billion mark, and the per-capita income was by far the highest in the world; the United States had become a self-consciously affluent nation. Three-quarters or more of American families lived, in terms of creature comforts, at a level that would have pleased a medieval prince.

But this achievement also revealed the inequities of American life, despite the long-standing acceptance of the concept of equal opportunity and the protection of civic and private-property rights. For all the private and corporate affluence, the quality of life in American cities and rural backwaters left much to be desired. War, cold and hot, had become a prop of the much-vaunted prosperity, and seemingly of the American way of life. A centralized government seemed to move further and further away from the people affected by its decisions, and the question "Who's in charge here, anyway?" was asked more and more frequently.

If the dominant features of our inherited socio-political philosophy proved to be inadequate for the problems of the 1960's, they are likely to be even more so for the coming decades. Quite different national philosophical principles must be defined, from which a new set of national goals and priorities will evolve.

By the end of the 1960's, the search for new goals and priorities had begun, led, not unexpectedly, by the most disadvantaged in the society—those who had formerly been left out of the American Dream—and by the young of all races and income levels, who, growing up in a period of unprecedented affluence, were not content with material prosperity alone. The new era called for new definitions—of human rights, of human development, of human dignity, a new view of the quality of life—and a new style of governmental activities.

1. HUMAN RIGHTS AND INDIVIDUAL DEVELOPMENT

Over the years it has become apparent that the "natural rights of man," the keystone of our inherited political philosophy, provide too narrow a base for the relation of government and citizen in a nation no longer concerned single-mindedly with economic expansion. It does not provide enough weight for the well-being of the disadvantaged, as President Franklin D. Roosevelt realized when he suggested expanding individual rights to include freedom from fear and freedom from want. More recently, the revolts of the 1960's have underlined the fact that the dignity of the individual is at the core of social relations and extends substantially beyond formal civil rights. In the future, there will surely be movements to establish the *right* to a job, the *right* to a minimum income, and the *right* to maintain a sense of human dignity.

Among the new rights of the individual is a concern for his capacity to realize his full potential. Thus, Senator Walter Mondale, in proposing a new Council of Social Advisers (parallel to the Council of Economic Advisers) to focus the nation's attention on its social problems, wisely titled his bill the "Full Opportunity Act," while a Panel on Social Indicators, working under the auspices of the Department of Health, Education, and Welfare between 1967 and 1969, defined its central theme as *the realization of the full potential of each individual.* Going beyond the notion of equal opportunity, this theme accepts genetic and cultural differences among individuals. All men are not created equal as far as the capacity to take advantage of opportunity in a given setting is concerned. "Equalizers" for the genetically or culturally disadvantaged must be provided so that they *can* realize their full potential, no matter how limited or brilliant it may be.

Clearly we must extend our concern to the whole human being—his needs and wants, his variety and individuality. As we approach the year 2000, we should move away from a partial view of man toward an appreciation of his wholeness. This calls for a greater realism in politics, one which is not ethically neutral but which seeks to develop measures, such as the use of social indicators, for getting beyond abstract concepts—for example, going beyond an abstract view of equality to a continuing examination of what those practices designed to produce greater equality have, in fact, meant in the lives of real people.

A political philosophy that looks toward a conscious enlargement of the scope of human freedom and potential within the limits of public order suggests new standards for judging governmental processes and mechanisms. We need to ask, for example, whether our present organization of education, health, and welfare services really helps each individual realize his full potential. Can centralized or decentralized management of particular governmental services do better?

The relations between a more holistic view of man and the practicalities of governmental institutions and policies are neither simple nor obvious. Yet they must be mastered if we are to see how American government can contribute meaningfully to the solution of the problems of the future. We need new standards for judging changes in our governmental institutions, processes, and policies.

In a society that aims to provide *full opportunity* for every individual, the right to privacy, for example, would be an obligation, not merely a limitation of the government's wiretapping and dossier collecting. Similarly, the standard for public education would not be *equal* schooling for everyone, but education of a quantity and quality that would permit everyone to go as far as he could. This change would help prevent the kind of human waste characteristic of our society in the past.

The more traditional appeals to limited legal rights and equality of opportunity are early phases in the process of affirming qualitative life improvements. We need to move beyond these concepts, and in fact fulfill them, by replacing minimal and "fair shares" criteria with personal-fulfillment and social-investment criteria, based on a view of the individual and society evolving along broad cultural, social, economic, and political fronts.

Such a society would be concerned not only with the rate of increase of total national production, or the advance of the economy as a whole, but also with the progress of the individual, or at least of each social and income group. Today only the total Gross National Product figure is known and publicized. Even such a basic statistic as annual income distribution by classes is extremely hard to obtain. It is even harder to obtain some notion of the end product of governmental programs aimed at greater equality and human development. The improved approach would put the G.N.P. figure in proper perspective by also publishing data showing the rate of increase in the *lifetime* earning power of different groups, particularly the disadvantaged. Such an index would be directly influenced by the caliber of education received by the various groups, skills acquired, discrimination in getting and holding well-paid jobs, life expectancy, the rate of mental and physical illness, and other items that affect the relative gains and losses in the standing of diverse social groups. The index itself is not of great importance, and better measures will probably be developed, but it is symbolic of the kind of concerns that should take first place.

2. INDIVIDUAL FREEDOM OF ACTION AND SOCIAL ORDER

The question whether we are more or less free now than in the past is moot and not particularly fruitful. In some ways we are more free, in others more restricted. When nearly everyone lived on a farm, almost anybody could throw garbage out of his window, shoot a gun into the air anytime, or keep a pig as a pet. We forfeited these freedoms by moving into the city. On the other hand, the average American of the eighteenth and nineteenth centuries was much more restricted in his social and economic life, and his legal defenses were much more limited than they are today.

In looking ahead to the year 2000, the more cogent question is whether our inherited political and legal patterns provide the maximum possible scope for individual freedom consistent with the contemporary requirements for maintaining a relatively peaceful and orderly society. Or, conversely, do these derived patterns adequately protect the interests of the many, clustered in highly vulnerable agglomerations, against the self-interested activities of the few?

In fact, the mechanisms for reconciling individual freedom of action with public order seem hopelessly out of date. They derive largely from earlier periods when the policing of personal morals was readily accepted and individual freedom was equated with certain civic rights like free speech. There is an enormous difference between the view that freedom is crucial to human development and the view that freedom must be subordinated to the maintenance of a moral climate, measured by a judicial thermometer. By now the old arguments for conformity—to tame a wilderness, to absorb and "Americanize" immigrants, or to achieve efficiency in production —are pointless.

The pressures and limitations introduced by large numbers and high density call for constraints of a different order to achieve different objectives. In the future, the way in which individual and group freedoms deviate from social norms will depend, even more than in the past, on the degree of separation and privacy that is possible, so that one man's freedom is not another man's poison. The separated nudist colony is a sound example of a self-governing subsociety. On a general level, such a principle would permit different ethnic, cultural, religious, or "life-style" groups to maintain their own self-disciplined designs for living within the necessary constraints of social order. This kind of "multi-modal social order" [8] would differ from the attempts to maintain a uni-modal society that encourages a variety of deviations and evasions. The more clearly our national goals are specified, and the more ably administered our regulatory and control activities can be, the more scope can be given to a "multi-modal social order." But along with adequate scope for variety, a diverse society must be concerned with extending the belief in common values pertaining to human rights and dignity.

If we build a sturdy philosophical base for individual freedom and social order, the imagination is free to devise ways of enlarging the scope for freedom of action and thought. A surprising number of groups in the United States today feel discriminated against, from "way-out" religious sects to the socially and sexually deviant groups. Many of these cluster in the worst slums in search of anonymity or self-protection. By the year 2000, we should be learning how to design cities with some self-contained areas; social services that function without snooping; and laws that can accommodate different patterns of living. This, not repression, is the way to maintain loyalty to the society, particularly as the restraints of "earning a living" are loosened and our society becomes even more affluent.

In the crowded society of the future, not only must a regard for human dignity be taken seriously by the courts in arbitrating between individual freedom of action and civic order, but more emphasis must be placed on the improvement of administrative and regulatory mechanisms, particularly the day-to-day quality of the police, education, welfare, health, and other human-resources governmental services—on high-caliber, well-paid, appropriately trained policemen (guardians of the peace), teachers (full-opportunity agents), social workers (caretakers), and other agents of the public.

To have a counterweight to a wider range of freedom and opportunity, we must encourage the concept of social obligations, the idea that certain duties that are a part of the effective operation of democratic society are required of all its members. It is very difficult to be specific about such duties, since they can so easily be interpreted to justify the status quo. However, increased duties are the inevitable counterparts of increased individual and group rights. In this regard, both the internal and governmental obligations established for professional groups—scientists and technologists, as well as doctors, lawyers, and the like—are especially important because such groups actually form "governments" in themselves and have a tremendous impact on society.

All groups, especially variant "life-style" communities, will themselves have to govern the activities of their members, so as to avoid interference with the rights of others, or accept restrictions imposed by outside controlling agencies. And the obligations include money. Americans today widely accept as a duty the payment of all national taxes, but have no qualms about avoiding local taxes. The sense of duty must be extended to support public services at least within the metropolitan area where they work.

The acceptance of certain social obligations by individuals and groups is, of course, at the heart of the problem of reconciling individual freedom with social order. A major question is the extent to which individuals will stick to the democratic rules of the game while pursuing their self-interest—a crucial subject throughout the present volume. Several of the contributors note that, in the language of Norton Long, government is "an ecology of games" and the function of government is to provide a framework for many special-interest, local, subsystem "games," and to settle the conflicts that may occur. Since the primary goal of government is to prolong itself, it can be expected to alter either the framework it provides or the mediations it offers so as to keep a maximum number of persons playing. There can be social order only when there is general acceptance of the framework and the mediations. As Matthew Holden suggests, political stabilization will result when the ratio of "disorderly" to "orderly" actions (in other words, actions within the rules-of-the-game) is kept within the system's tolerance level over prolonged periods.

Many of the contributors stress the importance of a broad base of *participation*—both the reality and the sense of participation—in all aspects of government that affect one's own welfare. The concept of participation should be broadened to encompass those formerly excluded (the poor, the socially disadvantaged, the young, the old), and should extend not only to voting (Kenneth Karst shows how the variable franchise can be employed to this end) and hearings to keep the channels of persuasion open, but also to a continuing constituents-to-Congress dialogue. A much more decentralized administrative structure should be established to bring government closer to the local citizen. Minority groups must be given access to the media in order to convey their needs to relevant portions of the public. And government employees must be allowed greater participation in politics and policy making. As Karst argues, when half or more of the Gross National Product passes through government hands, and a much larger portion of the working population is employed by government, severe restrictions on the political activity of civil servants will no longer be tolerated.

Clearly, the substance of politics, and not just the forms and procedures, is of great moment, and this brings us back to the "framework" issue—the philosophical principles that will dominate American political life in the next three decades. Will equality of personal standing and a concern for qualitative life improvements join equality of opportunity in the lexicon of American political values?

3. THE UNITED STATES IN THE WORLD ORDER

America's inherited political philosophy about the world outside has its main roots in the idea of national sovereignty—inevitable in a nation born of revolution against a colonial power. But consider the extraordinary differences among President Washington's advice that we avoid entangling alliances, the effort of the Monroe Doctrine to keep European powers out of the Western Hemisphere, and the vigorous if not always discreet acceptance of America's responsibility for preventing the extension of Communist influence anywhere in the free world.

The Constitution says little about the national government's role in foreign affairs; it merely assigns certain tasks to the President and the Senate. There was no bill of particulars about international relations until Wilson's Fourteen Points, which raised hopes about the possibility of a new world order, but these hopes were soon punctured by American politics and by nationalism abroad. The possibility of international cooperation for peace seemed dim even after the founding of the United Nations several decades later, and this skepticism was soon justified by the Cold War and by the wars in Korea and Vietnam.

Actually, one can find almost no philosophical basis for determining what the government's role in international relations will be in the year 2000. Indeed, even those concepts we accept in theory are abandoned in actual situations when they prove difficult or possibly embarrassing to our immediate national interests. For example, we do not support United Nations decisions that conflict with national concerns. We claim that we seek political rather than military solutions to the world's problems, yet we lead the world in armaments and have offered few political initiatives. We would like to encourage disarmament, but our disarmament efforts are sporadic and limited in scope. Economic and technical assistance abroad has been reduced to "bargain-basement" proportions. The Peace Corps is an isolated gesture on a vest-pocket scale. Nor can we argue that the upper limits have been reached when our overseas aid declines annually in proportion to the G.N.P. It is now well below 1 percent of the G.N.P.

A new approach to world affairs might conceivably be built on two foundations: human dignity and rights, paralleling a key domestic issue; and the meaning and content given to the idea of international leadership.

Human rights must encompass respect for persons of varying cultures. Our competitive, individualistic attitudes, developed earlier by the vast American challenge, have deformed our view of human worth and achievement, which we tend to associate with productiveness and the color of a man's skin. Since human dignity and human worth cannot be compartmentalized, we will probably extend our concern for human beings overseas as we extend our concern for disadvantaged groups at home, *and the other way around.* It is no accident that radical militants have developed the "third-world" concept as a weapon in their fight for revolutionary social change in the United States. It is to be hoped that within the next generation we shall extend the frontiers of our loyalty and compassion to view foreign aid as a community responsibility rather than as a charitable or purely self-interested gesture. To accept this view is to begin the slow and painful process of building a true world *community.*

A second foundation for a new approach to world affairs would be a determined effort by the United States to influence and accelerate the evolutionary process already under way toward world economic integration, which would inevitably be followed by closer political relations. This is the theme of Lester R. Brown's paper and a subtheme of the paper by George C. Lodge.

Possibly the best thing about America's role in world affairs since World War II has been its active promotion of such regional economic arrangements as the European and Latin American common markets. Countries that are tied together economically are likely to avoid disputes and to develop improved techniques for arriving at consensus. In a world of regional groupings there will still be tension and conflict, but it will nonetheless be on its way toward a more rational order. Two basic forces—advancing technology and the almost universal desire for human betterment (symbolized in the drive for modernization)—are powerful levers for change in the international order; they should be encouraged at every possible turn to become forces for economic, and ultimately for political, integration.

At the end of the 1960's, owing in part to the widespread disillusion with the Vietnam war and the political imperative of American disengagement, one could foresee a strongly supported effort over the ensuing three decades to find new and improved bases for peaceful international relations. There was growing skepticism about the search for military superiority with its almost inevitable offensive-defensive escalations. But the American international posture was still essentially reactive. Could American government in the next three decades hope to achieve

(1) a stronger international outlook in Congress (was there some *practical* way of electing senators who would not be limited by a local constituency?);

(2) genuine civilian control over military strategy and policy (strengthening the security-planning capacity of the President and providing Congress with the means for evaluating military policy and spending); and

(3) greater institutional capacity (a flexible foreign-assistance foundation in place of the present inadequate aid mechanisms) to take the initiative in promoting a richer, more interdependent, more peaceful world?

It all depends on how soon the American people and American political parties and leaders can accept a positive, rather than a purely reactive, view of America's world-leadership role, and how soon the quest for peace will generate widespread enthusiasm.

III The Future Structure of American Government

Is government in the United States equipped to deal with the big problems that lie ahead? What must be done to improve its ability to handle the projected tasks in an efficient, just, and democratic manner?

America's present governmental structure is the accumulated product of past struggles with societal problems and past political and organizational compromises. Most significantly, it reflects the struggles of the past four decades, particularly the problems posed by the Great Depression of the 1930's and the continuing series of wars. The institutions profoundly reflect the underlying structural changes of the period; in Bell's terminology, the development of a national, communal, postindustrial society. As a result, there has been a great expansion of governmental activities in the social, economic, military, and scientific and technologic realms, and a corresponding growth of public agencies.

The institutional forms and processes have evolved as much in reaction to the inadequacies of the inherited structure as they have responded to the inherent requirements of the new problems. The Depression forced government agencies to take on many activities that had formerly been largely in private or voluntary hands. In welfare and in banking, for example, private groups lacked adequate resources, or could not be counted on to function equitably and responsibly. The relative growth of the federal government has been due to the incapacity of state and local governments to cope with the problems of recent decades, as well as to the national character of many of the new problems. Similarly, the expansion of executive power has reflected shortcomings in the legislative system, as well as the demands of a continuing series of internal and external emergencies, and the growth of new constituencies (science, universities, the military) that tend to work principally through executive mechanisms. The courts have had to resolve certain far-reaching human, social, and political issues because the other two governmental branches have been paralyzed by existing constraints.

Most of these developments have been pragmatic, demanding little conscious application of philosophical or organizational principles. How these experiences can be used in planning for the future has been a major concern of the papers in this volume. While there was inevitably disagreement among members of the Working Group about the way government in the United States might best be organized to cope with the major societal problems that have been identified, several broad principles were defined for reorganizing governmental institutions and processes in the future.

First, the *built-in flexibility and adaptability* of governmental institutions should be able to cope with a rapidly changing society and its problems. We cannot fully predict their future since the problems and the politics surrounding them may take unexpected forms. Thus, the basic adaptability of government is especially important in an age when change is accelerating at a dizzying pace. Donald Schon probes this question in his essay. In discussing the sources of innovation and lag in institutions, he suggests how relevance and freshness might be maintained in both governmental and private organizations. And he introduces some new terms that are likely to become part of the language of government, such as "ideas in good currency" and "gardens of competence." Rexford G. Tugwell believes that inherent governmental flexibility and adaptability call for a reorganization of government along entirely new lines, and therefore a new United States Constitution will be required by the year 2000. In the discussion that followed Tugwell's presentation, it became apparent that not many in the group agreed with him. The difficulties he points to in the present system, however, are not easily resolved.

A second important principle of governmental reorganization is the need to separate the governmental assumption of *responsibility* for a given problem and the actual governmental *activities* designed to cope with it. The former is a matter of public choice, the latter a question of convenience and efficiency. The extension of government bureaucracy to match broadening governmental responsibility stems from the depression 1930's and the wartime 1940's, and must now be updated for the future. In some situations, private enterprise and nonprofit groups can provide greater flexibility, innovation, and adaptability than governmental units, and should be allowed to do so.

But if certain activities are to be more decentralized in the future, the government must develop measurable objectives and well-defined policy standards for evaluating performance to retain the necessary degree of control. This is, in fact, the focal point of Robert Nathan's essay. Drawing on his extensive experience in private and public affairs, Nathan explores how relationships between the government and private groups can have maximum flexibility and responsible achievement of public goals by the turn of the century.

The theme of decentralization appears again in the discussion of American federalism. The federal system was created largely to protect the rights of individuals and groups in terms of the underlying political philosophy of the day. Even now, so many years later, one can appreciate the compromises about state sovereignty that had to be made from 1787 to 1789, and the fears that surrounded the idea of an all-powerful national government. Gradually the federal government, with occasional help from the Supreme Court, was able to broaden its economic and developmental activities more or less in line with the needs of the time. Ironically, the very state and local governments whose rights the Constitution supposedly set out to protect have been damaged the most by this outmoded view of the different levels of government. The state governments have scarcely any meaningful role in the scheme of things, while the idea of local self-government has all too often been a covert way of setting up high-income one-race enclaves, leaving the old central cities to cope with the toughest problems.

The concept of states' rights has hampered serious consideration of the state governments' basic ability to meet human needs. The federal government has used them as agents for carrying out national programs, often ignoring the overall allocation of resources within a state and the impact of such decentralized administration on the welfare of different social and racial groups. Vested interests have been able to use the concept of states' rights in retaining built-in social and economic advantages and in obtaining concessions from the national government. Because of this, political groups and administrators concerned with the welfare of the poor have resisted handing over certain socially sensitive programs to the states. The overall result has been a hodgepodge of state activities whose combined logic is hard to grasp and a weakening of the states' capacity to plan and carry out a coherent set of functions.

Similarly, meaningful local self-government has been permitted to deteriorate. Only the Supreme Court has been deeply concerned with governmental forms and structures to meet new and changing situations—for example, the one-man–one-vote decision. Going far beyond congressional civil-rights legislation, the Court has consistently emphasized the implications for human rights in existing governmental forms (in voting, criminal procedures, school districting), providing a logical framework for decisions about such forms and procedures. Concern for human dignity and full opportunity is the appropriate standard for judging the most effective *division of labor* among different levels of government. The choice of who does what should be made not by the courts, but, through the mediation of politics, by the executive and legislative branches of the federal, state, and local governments, in line with the changing needs of our society.

If human dignity and full opportunity are the standards for intergovernmental division of labor, the federal government would need to undertake certain tasks in order to achieve key national goals or values. For example, the national government should accept the responsibility for establishing a floor under all the essential human services—education, health, welfare—so that the Appalachian youngster would not come to Chicago or Detroit as an untutored, uncultured migrant condemned to live at the edges of society for the remainder of his life.[9]

Also, the states are involved when their size or the fact that they stand between the national and local governments gives them certain natural advantages. They are in an advantageous position for promoting economic development where it is closely tied to natural-resources development, large-scale infrastructure (transportation, utilities, large-scale recreational and urban development), and highly selective economic assistance to firms and individual families based on special regional circumstances. In this context, the states are appropriate "building blocks" for regional development and they can best use this advantage by carrying out many of their activities through interstate cooperation. This is particularly the case in developmental problems of a suprastate nature (such as river basin and transportation development) or of assistance to multicounty efforts within the states. Properly equipped state governments can be of great help to smaller, submetropolitan urban communities (say, with a population of under 50,000) whose inhabitants can achieve a physical and cultural environment conducive to full opportunity and human dignity.

Finally, rational division of labor among the various levels of government would allow the larger urban communities to achieve genuine local sef-government, including enough money to create physically, socially, and culturally healthy environments. Under anticipated conditions, this means dealing with the problems posed by racial and income segregation, increasing citizen participation in decision and action programs, particularly by insuring a meaningful political voice for the residents of the inner city, and allocating the costs of upkeep in equitable fashion.

Several of the essays stress the principle that *the relative financial capability of the different levels of government should not necessarily determine either the relative responsibility for a given problem area or the volume of actual operations.* Other criteria must come into play as well. Decentralization, once associated with delivering public services to isolated communities across a vast nation, will have renewed advantages in the future: greater scope for experimentation with different life styles; greater scope for self-government on the part of minority groups; and an improved ability to cope with the special conditions of variable urbanism in the different sections of the country. The federal government is hardly equipped to deal knowledgeably and sensitively with the detailed development and management problems of the different neighborhoods and communities throughout the country.

The problem, it is generally agreed, is not one of complete separation of functions among the various levels of government, but rather a relative distribution of responsibility. Some members of the Working Group place such great value on decentralization that they want to concentrate on how the federal government can effectively channel adequate funds into states and localities. Congressman Henry Reuss, starting from the same basic premises about decentralization, nevertheless stresses the fact that even with adequate funds these cannot be realized unless the states and localities are reorganized and modernized so that they can in fact rise to the challenges of the future. He would use the tool of federal tax-sharing with the states and localities, contingent on national government approval of state reorganization plans.

Participatory democracy, the notion that people should have a voice in the decisions that influence their lives, is another useful principle for reorganizing the governmental structure. But how can this principle be given specific form and content? The Working Group's discussion reflects the uncertainty surrounding this question. We were not able to arrive at criteria for judging the kinds of issues that should be subject to local community decisions. If the principle were strictly observed, community groups would have the right to exclude Negroes and other minorities if they felt this would disrupt the character of the neighborhood, and community groups would have vetoes on road planning and construction even where the regional broad-system context would be crucial. Few guidelines now exist for realizing the best in participatory democracy while minimizing its potentially disruptive and inequitable features. Congressman Brademas treats a neglected aspect of the problem, namely, how political leaders can be exposed to a much wider spectrum of community views on key issues.

A related matter is the old problem of building a sufficiently strong base of general public understanding and participation to support the growing jurisdiction and power of government. One significant trouble with democracy is that its responsibilities and activities tend to be greater than the capacity of the people and their representatives to deal with them intelligently and humanely. Civic education should be greatly improved, but today it is the least understood and most neglected aspect of educational development.[10]

While most members of the Working Group are attracted to greater decentralization of government in order to achieve greater adaptability and popular control, James D. Barber thinks this is an extension of the already established trend toward pluralization in government, in which he sees a host of unfortunate consequences, ranging from a loss of efficiency to a loss of democratic control. Thus, two important issues for the future of government in the United States are joined.

The accretion of presidential power at the expense of Congress is a much-discussed issue of government structure, but most members of the Working Group considered this a misleading way of formulating a basic problem in the organization of the national government. The real issue is the strengthening of *both* the executive and the legislative branches. Each has vast responsibilities that at present it is unable to discharge fully and effectively. Each lacks adequate means of acquiring needed information promptly and in convenient form, and each needs better policy analyses of international, national, and local affairs.

In this volume, William Capron outlines a series of measures for modernizing the executive branch, and Congressman Brademas suggests how Congress can meet its extensive international, national, and local responsibilities. Rexford G. Tugwell proposes far-reaching changes not only for the executive and legislative but for the judicial branch as well, looking toward a future United States where the demands for the *right* to consume may outrun our capacity to produce. All three find our existing governmental organization for the conduct of international affairs particularly weak, if American leadership in the evolving world order is to be more creative.

IV How Much Pessimism or Optimism is Justified?

The intricacies of governmental structure can become an insidious trap. It all begins to seem so orderly and rational: here a problem, there a new unit or a new technique to meet it. We have had to keep reminding ourselves that social problems, social change, and evolving group values all have their own dynamics. Government has no magic formula for "solving" all the thorny problems and helping all of us realize our most cherished values. The United States is made up of many groups and many values and many interests. The struggle for power and advantage is often ruthless, generally unequal. And government is itself one of the instruments in this struggle.

Beyond coping with the great social problems of the present or future, there is another basic task, that of maintaining the processes and mechanisms by which we can keep government fairly representative, decently concerned with the interests of the many rather than the few and the powerful, and relatively sensitive to the variable values of the many groups that make up the nation. Here the great majority of the group is extremely optimistic. Across the entire panorama of problems and issues, the greatest pessimism has to do with race relations. The struggle for equality and human dignity, at home and overseas, calls for the most far-reaching changes in our political philosophy. Government in the year 2000 will be successful, internally and externally, only if the "we" of the great American majority is broadly inclusive.

NOTES

1. Much of the material in this introduction was initially contained in a paper presented to the members of the Working Group on United States Government in the Year 2000 to suggest guidelines for the group discussions.

2. Some advances in technology, however, including the computer, potentially make the protection of privacy easier than before.

3. Questions of human rights are raised specifically in Kenneth L. Karst's essay in this volume.

4. These dangers are discussed by Matthew Holden, Jr., Harold Orlans, and Rexford G. Tugwell.

5. The dilemmas of future urban politics of the future are examined in the essay by Martin and Margy Meyerson and in the discussion comments (from the transcript) by James L. Sundquist, Karl Deutsch, and others.

6. Three essays, those of George C. Lodge, Lester R. Brown, and Herman Kahn, deal with these issues.

7. James A. Maxwell, *Financing State and Local Government,* rev. ed. (Washington, D.C.: The Brookings Institution, 1969), p. 14.

8. Lawrence Frank's term, in a letter to the author.

9. Such a national floor under human service was proposed over twenty-five years ago by Alvin H. Hansen and the author in *State and Local Finance in the National Economy* (New York: W. W. Norton, 1944).

10. I am grateful to H. Field Haviland, Jr., for highlighting this point in his comments on a earlier draft of this essay.

An Introductory Portion of the Transcript:

THE "PUBLIC" AND "PRIVATE" REALMS

PARTICIPANTS

Lester R. Brown
Karl W. Deutsch
John Dixon
Robert R. Nathan
Harvey S. Perloff
James L. Sundquist
John Voss
John G. Wofford

PERLOFF: Public and private roles within our society, and how these roles are likely to change by the year 2000, must be clarified if we are to deal with the future of American government. How specific can we be in suggesting what is appropriately "public"?

NATHAN: There is not only the question of what kinds of problems should be dealt with by government, but how to determine criteria for the *type* of role government will play in certain areas. A choice has to be made between outright government operation, government regulation, or simply the provision of government incentives to action. Such problems as air and water pollution, for example, necessarily involve the government, but we must determine how much and what kind of involvement we want. Should the government exert increasing control that virtually eliminates private action, or does it limit itself pretty much to setting up standards, techniques, devices, and instruments that are almost self-regulatory, so that the private role remains predominant?

SUNDQUIST: There are various degrees of public-private relationships whereby things are quasi-public and quasi-private. Another problem is that of fitting big private institutions into the society in such a way that they can synchronize their public function with the truly public agencies.

DIXON: For purposes of argument let us visualize this little group here as a "board of directors" with real societal responsibility. We would quickly find that merely to distinguish between "public" and "private" is not good enough. If we regard government as a corporate entity similar to General Motors when it was created, the Chevrolet, Buick, and Cadillac divisions are private, and the government is the central overall corporate structure. What is kept centralized? The central General Motors corporation deals with the budget process and fiscal policies. Similarly, the federal government would probably retain regulatory and incentive powers and leave detailed operations to other groups.

NATHAN: It is a good analogy, but I think the government should do more than make regulatory decisions. If the government role is limited to incentive techniques and devices, the impact is weaker than that of government regulation and public ownership and operations.

PERLOFF: Yet there is a very striking difference between an entity whose objectives are fairly clear, such as a profit-making organization, and an entity like government, whose objectives have to be "discovered" and reconciled.

SUNDQUIST: Dixon's superboard of directors sounds as if it is going to run not something simple like General Motors but an entire society. It would have to be designed to operate like the solar system, without any day-to-day management. But we do not have the kind of political structure, either legislative or executive, that can manage what the government is trying to undertake even now. We need a much stronger case for changing the entire system if we hope to revolutionize the governmental structure.

BROWN: The root force here is technology. Changing technology requires both central planning and a much more sophisticated system of government.

SUNDQUIST: It is not a question of necessity but of human capability. Can a government run by laymen make decisions that involve highly technical subjects? There are many indications that the volume, complexity, and magnitude of the decisions to be made have outgrown the capacity of our institutions to make them. Traditionally, we have always assumed that government reorganization might solve this dilemma, but I think we have to worry now about human limitations.

PERLOFF: Surely we want to keep things like art and music in the private realm? There is something valuable about privacy and noncontrol. We do not want to become so management-oriented that the government almost unthinkingly begins to absorb more and more key elements in society simply because it is convenient for the administrator.

VOSS: What other areas would you consider clearly private?

PERLOFF: For our time, I think it would be healthy and appropriate to talk not about areas that are untouchable but rather about broadly held and highly regarded human values and how the government can enhance them, give the individual the greatest possible scope, and at the same time cope with the technological issues.

Changing Nature of Governmental Functions

NATHAN: There is another aspect to this. Government cannot cope with a vast range of problems, and in the last few years government agencies have been farming out functions I had always considered entirely governmental: policy analyses, policy directions, surveys and studies, and evaluations of budgetary problems, as the Budget Bureau now has to do. In this sense government is moving backward. Instead of taking on new functions it is distributing the old functions while retaining for itself the programmatic and the policy evaluation.

WOFFORD: How does this differ from asking an outside task force to cope with a particular problem or policy issue?

NATHAN: I am talking about administration, not just brain-tapping. Now it may be a temporary phenomenon but the initiation and elaboration of this process is not sporadic any more, even though, of course, final decisions continue to be made by government.

SUNDQUIST: Does this mean that the system is failing or that the problems are changing?

NATHAN: It reflects the complexity of managing this dynamic, growing, expanding, pervasive area of interrelationships in our whole society.

DIXON: The significant issue here is that nobody in government is analyzing the implication of this trend toward farming out policy analysis. It is unhealthy. Think how much those of us in the present study learn from it. If it were done by people in the government, it would combat their gray, monotonous outlook.

VOSS: The use of consultants is not simply a way of farming out problem solving; in industry the consultant often educates management in new professional skills, a very healthy kind of educative process. It indicates that the governmental agency knows where to go for new ideas. Consider the function of Rand in the Air Force and Defense Departments.

PERLOFF: Outside assistance also helps to avoid overburdening the government. If the government were to tackle every problem directly, urgent issues like war and peace or human rights would not receive the attention they need. Nor do we adjust quickly enough to increased complexity through fundamental organizational and process changes.

NATHAN: This is really a question of political theory.

BROWN: There is another critical area we should discuss. Congressmen are voting these days on literally hundreds of issues ranging from fiscal policy to weapons systems that only a handful of people in both houses really understand. In this system there are a number of issues—from traffic lights and musical-instrument regulations to the sugar lobby and the missile system—which only a handful of people in the Congress know anything about. And on some of these issues there may not be anyone who is really expert. There is a real risk that special interest groups may begin to exert more and more influence in a manner harmful to society. The purpose of the Congress is to express the will of the people, not of special and narrow interest groups.

NATHAN: Most people feel we are moving toward more governmental participation, but I am not so sure this is really true. In recent years we have been moving away from certain governmental activities, and not by design.

SUNDQUIST: We started out by agreeing that the line between the public and private sectors is going to become more and more blurred, and that the role of the public will expand, while the public/private boundary is moved back. Dixon's General Motors analogy suggests that pieces of the private sector and pieces of the public sector are going to operate as independent orbiting bodies with some kind of central control that ties together the various public and private realms.

Perhaps we should reexamine that premise. Do we really need to shift the public/private balance as much as we thought? Do we really need that much central control? If so, then the adequacy of governmental institutions is an important question. But if it seems best to continue in our present manner, then there would be no increasing burden on the governmental institutions, and the system could operate itself. This is the heart of the public/private question.

PERLOFF: Bob Nathan suggested that the type of activity is very important. If, for example, the government collects garbage while private units determine the quality of our life, is such a division appropriate?

Many government tasks are routine and do not involve high-level policy making. On the other hand, because there are so many such tasks, the few men who are busy administering them have no time for high-level policy. We may soon find that the local and the federal governments are so busy with picayune matters that no one is worrying about freedom, or the quality of life, or perhaps even war and peace.

SUNDQUIST: It does not make much difference who actually runs mass transit or collects the garbage. The burden of the decision-making process will remain public.

PERLOFF: Why do you feel it is necessary for government to exercise more control over the private units?

SUNDQUIST: The government has to exercise more of a board-of-directors' type of loose control over the economy, because the policies of major corporations profoundly influence every facet of our life. They make the investment decisions that determine whether and how fast the economy grows. The location of their plants determines wo gets employed—people in rural areas for instance, or people in ghettos. They determine whether equality of opportunities is going to be a fact, whether or not we have air or water pollution. This will be even more true by the year 2000. We cannot permit private corporations to veto our national purposes.

Governmental Concern for the Whole System

DIXON: In one theory of public/private, the "goods" have both buyers and sellers. The entrepreneurial incentive, the profit motive, the market mechanism all focus on those who want to sell the "goods" that people want. But nobody is concerned with the "bads," and the concern of the government has to be for the "bads." What entrepreneur now wants to touch the public transit except to make a financial ploy? Who cares about the culturally deprived? Here the General Motors model is weak. But let us visualize a society as a living organism—with a heart, spleen, liver, and so forth. In a system of free enterprise, who worries about the balance among the various organs? It is the government that must be concerned about the interrelationships and functions. This is where we get into criteria, incentives, and roles.

PERLOFF: Both analogies are useful. Unlike more totalitarian nations, our social system has a great many self-adjusting mechanisms, and the government has to act at only a few critical points, when things do not work out properly. In other words, the government should be concerned when the social costs and benefits diverge substantially from private costs and benefits—as in the case of air and water pollution, traffic congestion, and the like.

We need the kind of long-range planning and policy making that can give the greatest possible scope to the self-regulating mechanisms, rather than last minute ad-hoc repairs. An example is our futile approach to the problem of housing for the poor—building huge institutional units of so-called public housing. And we persist in this traditional approach. Our use of zoning, subdivision, and other controls to prevent urban sprawl is the most awkward and self-defeating way to attack that problem. Despite the great number of people involved in this kind of activity, no one seems to have time for evaluation and for thinking through more effective ways to achieve the objectives.

Governmental Regulation of Private Corporations

SUNDQUIST: The United States started pushing back the public/private boundary in 1890 with the Sherman Antitrust Act. For the next forty years the federal government did little to interfere with the rights of private corporations. In the 1930's the government began regulating both labor relations and security issuances. It did nothing more until the Employment Act of 1946, which sought to influence investment and employment policies.

In the 1950's and 1960's we passed pollution-control legislation, which put some of the responsibility on industry. Although we do not yet know how to enforce that, it does represent a national decision. We also established civil-rights policies for corporations. This legislation represents a variety of public activities; some are regulation, some are control, and some are influences. Some set the climate in which things will happen.

In the future, public intervention will probably be needed most in determining the location of industry—near the population or vice versa. The Area Redevelopment Act expressed a policy and provided some incentives to industry to locate in areas of surplus population—but this has not had any dramatic effect on the distribution of industry. We are now becoming more and more concerned about the movement of industry away from the people in the ghettos. The country must decide whether it wants to continue concentrating industry in the megalopolis or distribute it in the countryside where people would rather live.

Another problem is the structuring of industry by size. Instead of developing a well-integrated antitrust program, we have been merely correcting obvious deficiencies in a random fashion. But we have no real structural control over the way industry is organized, the size of the units, and competition.

Still another area of decision is the role of the private corporation in a national manpower system. Not only employment service but occupational training could be made responsibilities of industry under public control, rather than remain, as now, largely in public hands. If we want full employment by 2000, we should be thinking in terms of assigning quotas of employable people to potential employers—if not through direct allocation, then through powerful incentive schemes so that each employer would take his share of the hard-to-employ, the hard-to-train, the hard-to-utilize, and use them. And this would be related to the policy of location. In these three areas we may want this public/private boundary pushed back significantly in the next thirty years.

VOSS: The support of science and technology is another instance of the weakening boundary between public and private. At present, two-thirds of all research conducted by private industry is paid for by the federal government. Technological innovations that create new products and opportunities for private industry are made possible by extensive government support for research and development. Was the 747 or the supersonic transport (SST) a private or a public development?

New Technology, New Values, New Roles for Government

PERLOFF: If we are to cope with the problems of the future, we will have to make our governmental institutions more adaptable. Why are so many of our institutions now out of date? Is it due to changing values?

SUNDQUIST: No, it is rather a product of the complexity of society.

In our system, if the President is not exercising positive leadership on behalf of a particular program, nothing happens. And the President of the United States can focus his attention on only one thing at a time. In the same way, though Congress meets throughout the year, it does not have time for all the matters that need its attention.

WOFFORD: Is it true that the President and the Congress can cope with only one thing at a time? Under the committee and subcommittee system, Congress is dealing with hundreds of issues at any one moment, although only a few can be considered in floor debate, and the same is true, I think, of the executive branch.

SUNDQUIST: This is true only of routine decisions. But new approaches and policies need the personal participation of the President. For example, the President's total preoccupation with Vietnam precluded any significant progress on the domestic front although it was economically feasible to do both simultaneously. As for Congress, the sheer work load is becoming too heavy, on the floor and in the committees, to get through all the bottlenecks. By 2000 the problems of society may overwhelm the decision-making centers in a quantitative and qualitative way.

PERLOFF: In addition, we should consider the impact of new conceptions of public responsibility. For example, in the 1930's the American people began to view unemployment as a social rather than an individual problem and held the federal government morally responsible for maintaining full employment. The key factor here was the change in popular view about the appropriate role of the government in this area.

Where Are Innovations Likely to Originate?

PERLOFF: After the industrial revolution, the main innovative role was taken by industry, particularly the corporation. In the post-industrial society of today, with its new problems of the quality of life, education, equity, poverty, and race relations, the profit-oriented corporation may no longer be best for the innovative-creative role. Where can the vitality needed for new kinds of activities be found?

DIXON: The American government is not promoting much innovation. In housing, for example, most government policies retard innovation. Eventually I believe we may have to follow the example of societies like China and India, where the governments bought up the land in order to make basic structural changes in the society and the economy. At some point the federal and state governments may feel compelled to buy up all the sewer systems and junk them in order to introduce new kinds of waste disposal.

PERLOFF: Where do the innovative people want to work—in government, in private enterprise, or in some kind of nonprofit unit?

SUNDQUIST: Over the last twenty years, the government—particularly state and local—has not been getting its share of the best people. To solve this, either put the functions where the good people are or try to get better people into government service. Since our system, unlike the Russians', precludes the assigning of people to functions, we have to offer the proper inducements.

VOSS: We should aim not at recruiting technologists, but at circulating individuals between the private and public sectors. Instead, private industry and the government today aim, wrongly, at giving a scientist life tenure. But the creativeness that is the bulwark of technological innovation in industry comes from moving the innovative people back and forth.

The Learning Process in Politics

DEUTSCH: We can think of politics as that sphere of human behavior where a certain probability of enforcement comes together with a certain probability of compliance. Most automobile drivers stop at a red light voluntarily, but the possibility of receiving a ticket marginally enforces the law-abiding habits of most motorists. But voluntary compliance is nine-tenths of the invisible structure of law. Without it, one does not have law—only a noble experiment, like Prohibition. In the political sphere, both enforcement and compliance are needed. Whenever we strive to influence people in some particular category, then we must make uniform the action we want to become spontaneous. The timing of such action is crucial and is determined by the nature of the government involved. A conservative government, for example, might pass a law at a time when approximately two-thirds of its people had already learned to do the new thing, and the government would use the law to pull the stragglers in line. On the other hand, a dictatorship will sometimes attempt to make the peasants comply with a plan before half the population has learned it. Yet even such a government would not legislate before it had a minimal number of people to enforce what the government wanted to do. A democracy can sometimes do it when about 51 percent of the population agrees.

I am suggesting that you can use the power of government to accelerate social learning. Most people will learn very fast because a law has been passed. Government will not wither away, for this reason: whenever you must make people behave with more coordination, more speed, and more uniformity than they would spontaneously, government is one of the best ways of accomplishing the task.

In the semi-machine or paleotechnic age, we produced machines that were insensitive and destructive; in the reasonably erudite machine age we produce machines that are sensitive and self-correcting. The elevator door is an example. What we can do with machines we can do with bureaucracies. A present-day bureaucracy is typically a machine, made of men, designed to operate according to uniform rules on a small variety of cases. A self-correcting feedback machine adjusts what it does to the information coming back from the results of its actions. It can, therefore, fit a different response to a wide variety of different cases. I would suggest that by the year 2000, bureaucracies may begin to enter an age of responsiveness.

Though we speak a great deal today about "responsiveness" and "sensitivity training," we need many more intake channels of information in the government, better facilities for accurate recognition of different cases and needs. We need a wider range of memories, relevant memories that the government can rapidly reach and bring to bear on the incoming information, and instruments of action that can respond more flexibly and more quickly to whatever is needed. Data banks that now tend to be just a means for bureaucrats to push people around could become a means for adjusting government to make it much more of a servant of freedom than it is now. This involves a substantial investment, which should be made at once in the measurement techniques and data pools to give government the memories, the perception, and the recognition patterns it will need in five and ten years.

Furthermore, a concept of learning capacity should be central to thinking about government. Since learning capacity is proportional to recommittable resources, we should try to make the government—and private management—develop certain bodies of resources that can be recommitted for new task forces. With greater flexibility, the entire learning capacity of society increases.

We may need a new theory of decentralization. How decentralized should a society be? The answer can be calculated properly only if you take into consideration a factor that is usually ignored—the value of a quick response. Unfortunately, in most government work we do not even try to measure the value of a prompt reply. We need techniques for measuring the costs of delay, the costs of error or unresponsiveness, and the value of satisfactions. This would lead to a new collaboration between the administration people and electrical engineers.

The new techniques would enable us to adjust our structures to the loads. About twenty years ago we began to design telephone exchanges that open additional circuits whenever a particular traffic load gets very heavy. Why not experiment with a state system that might decide to hire just as many judges in automobile cases and open as many additional courts as is necessary to process the automobile claims within three months? We would then be adjusting structures to our performance criteria and opening up additional structures whenever necessary. Instead of thinking that we must either submit to the environment or dominate it, we might think of a dialogue with the environment, of getting along with it.

I

RIGHTS AND VALUES

INDIVIDUAL RIGHTS AND DUTIES IN THE YEAR 2000: THE INSTITUTIONAL FRAMEWORK

Kenneth L. Karst

> Democracy, then, thought Melville, is a moment in history, not the end toward which all history runs. "Each age," he remarked, "thinks its own is eternal." Yet every age is new and the problems of good and evil in it are new. Throughout all time Ahab, fate's lieutenant, must pursue Moby Dick, without hope of respite or of victory.
>
> —RALPH H. GABRIEL
> *The Course of American Democratic Thought*[1]

Perhaps Melville was guilty of the very error he sought to expose. The idea of individualism, personified for him in Ahab, was destined for radical revision long before anyone began to think seriously about postindustrial society. In evaluating the nature of individual rights and duties in the technified, affluent, urbanized, "sensate" society of the year 2000, we must ask whether such rights and duties will have meaning for an Ahab on water skis.[2] But first we need to be clear about what the terms mean to us.

To our own generation, "individual rights" are legitimate claims by the individual against the community, claims which may demand participation in a benefit, but which more typically assert an immunity from the demands imposed by organized society. The term, in other words, includes "civil rights" and "civil liberties." The civil-rights movement of the early 1960's confused the two ideas by calling for access to housing, employment, and lunch counters in the name of "freedom"—but we are none the worse for it. "Duties" in this essay are simply obligations to the community that are legitimately enforceable. Thus rights and duties can be considered complementary: one starts where the other leaves off. If the community can legitimately command the performance of a duty, then the individual has no *right* to refuse, and vice versa. Since our task is to make projections about the United States, this essay speaks mostly about rights, but much of the discussion can be applied, by inversion, to the analysis of a citizen's duties.

What are the historical roots of the emphasis on "rights" that has come to have such great influence in our society? The "rights" mentality had its origin in protections of property against the state, and came to flower in the constitutional safeguards of property and economic liberty that were created in Melville's century—a century that began with John Marshall and ended with Andrew Carnegie.[3] In the early 1800's, the Marshall Court protected enterprise principally by a vigorous interpretation of the commerce clause, which, in form, only distributed governmental power. Since major efforts by Congress to regulate the national economy did not begin until late in the nineteenth century, the Supreme Court's denials of state legislative power had the effect of freeing enterprise from regulation. The political capital of the judiciary, and of the Supreme Court in particular, had to be rebuilt after the near-disaster of *Dred Scott,* and the rebuilding took the form of an alliance with industry and enterprise. The ability of the Warren Court to carry off its vital contributions to the current "egalitarian revolution" is directly traceable to the Court's protection of economic liberty at the turn of the century.

The American Constitution protects individual rights by two principal means: indirectly, by distributing power among various agencies and levels of government, and directly, by imposing some general limitations on governmental activity, at whatever level. The latter has recently been extended to include governmental obligations to provide some kinds of benefit, but always, as in the civil-rights movement, in the name of the traditional constitutional "limits" on government. Each of these techniques for protecting individual rights raises distinct questions about the world of 2000.

Dispersal versus Concentration of Power, and the Problem of Political Participation

The centralization of legislative power in the national government has proceeded apace; as a result in which the effective checks on that government are now political, not constitutional. The process that began with the economic-regulation decisions of the 1930's has run its course. Recent decisions upholding congressional power to protect individual rights very nearly give Congress the power to define the extent of its own constitutional authority, as against challenges based on theories of federalism and state sovereignty. War and other overseas commitments reinforce the centralizing influences of transportation and communication, and the failures of state governments to respond to the needs of an urbanized society are linked with increasing federal activity in a causal cycle. And centralization, it is claimed, impedes the protection of individual rights.

But it does not. Just as individual treatment based on computers may benefit as well as harm individual freedom, so the centralization of decision-making power may promote as well as threaten the exercise of individual rights, as two recent examples make clear. The first is the constitutional validation of extended congressional legislative power, as defined in the various civil-rights acts, to punish private invasions of constitutional rights. When a Mississippi gang murders some civil-rights workers, the offenders can now be prosecuted and punished for committing a federal crime. The second example is the application, through a recent series of decisions, of the most important procedural guarantees of the Bill of Rights to state-court proceedings and to local police practices. These decisions have created uniform national standards of fairness in criminal procedure under the supervision of the federal courts and, ultimately, the Supreme Court. In both instances, decision-making power is further centralized in federal institutions, and the result is increased protection of individual rights.

In the year 2000, as now, freedom will be meaningful only within a social order. While the major decisions will surely be made by the national government, their effect can be liberating as well as repressive. Maximum liberty within such a system will depend on effective means of participating in the processes of decision. Two distinct kinds of political participation deserve attention—the right to vote, and the right to a hearing from those who make decisions.

Universal manhood suffrage was the ideal of Jacksonian democracy. A century and a half later, we are on the verge of achieving it—just in time for its obsolescence in many contexts. Freedom of choice is no freedom at all unless the choice is based on some minimal information. To borrow an illustration from Lon Fuller, the man who puts his chips on number 17 in a roulette game is not really making a meaningful choice, however "free" he was to bet on number 23. The prospect of the instant electronic poll in which each citizen stays home and votes on issues is appalling because the sheer quantity of relevant information is unmanageable. Though electronic data processing (EDP) can extend our ability to get information for intelligent voting, I doubt that many voters will be inclined to tune their home consoles to the Library of Congress when they could be watching the 2000 Roller Derby. Consider the vast collection of material on Vietnam easily available today—and the equally vast inclination for most of us to make our judgments without studying it. If it be argued that EDP can condense such material into manageable form, the presifting process will have taken much of the effective decision making away from the public.

Furthermore, a legislative issue placed before the voters in a general ballot cannot easily be presented as anything but an either/or choice, with two divisive results: (a) direct legislation by voters tends to be more extreme, more attuned to one group's legislative position, than legislation emerging from the process of compromise in a representative legislature; (b) similarly, direct legislation puts minority interests at a disadvantage, whereas representative government permits a minority to trade its strength in the legislative body for a larger group's support of the minority's positions. Both the need for specialized decision making and the need to promote social cohesion imply a continuation of representative government, not an electronic "town meeting" of the nation.

But if in 2000 the decisions at high levels of government can profit from the deliberation and compromises that representative government makes possible, they are also likely to seem even more remote from large numbers of the voters than similar decisions do today. Judgments about war and peace and major national economic issues will continue to be made at the highest levels, and popular "participation" in their making will be at least as indirect as it is now.

The increasing remoteness of most individuals from national decision making carries with it a real danger of large-scale alienation. There is a parallel risk that some groups will become more or less permanent minorities, "participating" in the political process mainly through threats of violence. This problem of the left-outs is critical, but increased political participation in local government appears to be an attainable goal. Local governments will continue to have primary control over those features of the environment (especially urban) that make up what we call the quality of life. Precisely in these areas of decision making are the problems of alienation and left-out minorities most severe.

One response to both problems would be a variable franchise for some local and special-service government units. "Maximum feasible participation of the poor," the requirement of the recent antipoverty legislation, points this way. An existing example in local government is the vote taken among residents or property owners in a neighborhood on certain proposed zoning changes. By conferring on the affected individuals real power to control some community affairs, such a variable franchise fosters a genuine sense of community participation and also minimizes the "absentee management" so often resented in government programs.

If increasing diversity in governmental structure is on the way, as Daniel P. Moynihan persuasively predicts, then we shall have the chance to experiment with a variety of electoral patterns as special-function units of local government proliferate.[4] Qualifications for voting in certain elections might relate to occupational status, income status, or taxes or other contributions paid to funds administered for special purposes; even having a child in school might be a qualifying factor.

Shareholders in a private corporation cast votes that are weighted according to their investment; some classes of shareholders may be entitled to vote only on limited issues of corporate policy. In the public sphere, however, we have become accustomed to an electoral system based primarily on residence within a contiguous geographical district. Proposals for "decentralization" or "local control" do not depart from this geographical principle, though some other forms of variable franchise do. The prevailing geographical orientation works well, combined with the one-man–one-vote principle, to maximize equality among individual voters' influences on representative government. But treating unequals equally raises both constitutional problems and problems of justice. For some purposes it may be entirely appropriate to give greater-than-equal voting power to members of a disadvantaged group—for example, permitting only the "poor" to vote for the governing board of a local poverty-relief agency, and denying that vote to others in the same area.

The present geographical-residence system of voter qualification was designed not for our generation but for a society in which a man's place of residence correlated rather highly with his various political interests. In an increasingly urbanized society, however, it becomes clearer every day that a neighborhood is not necessarily a community. Even in the suburbs one seldom knows one's neighbors well. One thing we do have in common with the man across the street is the street itself. But not all public matters should be tied to geography. Schools, for example, have been oriented on a geographical basis—but at great social cost, as we are now learning.

Earlier, we suggested that a variable franchise might help to bring additional people into the process of public decision making. But if our objective be increased political participation, we must remember two major difficulties with experiments in nongeographical voting qualifications: (1) the danger of losing political responsibility as voting units vary, and (2) the danger that a pattern of varying voting qualifications will in fact decrease the political strength of the disadvantaged.

As water districts and housing districts and poverty-program districts flower and germinate, political responsibility in local government may be withering. Who can name the key officials of his Rapid Transit or Air Pollution Control District? Would political responsibility increase if those officials were directly elected? The model of the local school board suggests it would. But suppose the constituencies were different for the various elected boards, some of them defined geographically but others based on qualifications like old age or poverty? The first vital question in each case is whether the members of the proposed franchise unit are likely to have the kind of interest in its elections that will result in widespread participation. The answer to that question ought to be within the reach of today's social-research techniques.

A more serious danger in varying voting qualifications is the possibility that variations will favor the wealthy and politically powerful who already have multiple connections with the political system. This factor probaby influenced the Supreme Court's recent invalidation of special qualifications for voting in certain school-board and utility-bond elections. In the Court's new formulation, limitation of the franchise must be justified by a "compelling state interest." But because there may be rewards in experimentation and because the

Supreme Court left the door open for justified departures from the geographical pattern, we can expect a few such efforts to be made. The task of justification, because it is mainly a task of definition, rests largely with the social scientists who study our cities. Over the next generation one of their most important functions will be the progressive refinement of our understanding the kinds of communities that *are* communities in urban America.

In 2000, we shall still have to find political forms to resolve the tension between fund raising outside disadvantaged areas and the need to give control over spending to persons within those areas. The grant-in-aid is our present device: the state or national government is the taxing unit, and the money is distributed according to need. By 2000, we can expect greater use of grants-in-aid and also some new forms with the same purpose, such as taxes on suburban residents (for example, a city income tax), or percentage allocations of general state revenues to local governments, not tied to specific purposes. (Some uncommitted funds must be included, so that some freedom of the market can be exercised.)

The phrase "maximum feasible participation" in antipoverty legislation can have a variety of meanings. Some of the men who originally coined it thought of the phrase as little more than a pious statement of their good intentions to listen to ghetto residents—or at least to the civil-rights leaders of that time. Others saw the phrase as a legislative command that real decision-making power be given the ghetto residents.[5] I believe that the latter should guide the administration of the poverty program, but it is also important to listen to representatives of the affected group. A voice is often worth as much as a vote. A second kind of political participation we should seek to maintain in the year 2000 is the right to a hearing, the right to a chance at persuading the decision makers.

In a society riddled by alienation, a *sense* of participation will be crucial. With more leisure and early retirement, millions will have the chance to take an active part in community affairs. These people can be productive if we can devise forms of community organization —public or private or a blend of both—to take advantage of their talents.

There are other justifications, beyond the importance of a sense of participation in decision making, for stressing the right to a hearing. In 2000 it will be politically urgent to keep the channels of persuasion open to minority views. Even the interest groups defeated by ultimate decisions must be heard, since the scrutiny of conflicting views helps prevent courses of action that are harsher than they need be. The choices we make today about UHF television channels, cable television, and communications satellites will determine whether minorities will be able to reach relevant portions of the public.

Finally, when half or more of the Gross National Product passes through government hands and much more of the working population is employed by government, can we continue to tolerate severe restrictions on the political activity of government employees? For 2000, the variable franchise is debatable; major surgery on the Hatch Act is not.

Direct Limitations of Governmental Power, the New Equality, and the Role of the Judiciary

One major way in which our Constitution protects the rights of individuals is through setting such general limits as "freedom of speech," "due process of law," and "the equal protection of the laws." But these standards, to Learned Hand's eloquent despair, are only "moral adjurations, the more imperious because inscrutable, but with only that content which each generation must pour into them anew in the light of its own experience." [6] We know what content our generation has added to (and subtracted from) these words. What will they mean to the next generation? The answer requires an examination of the institutional setting in which constitutional abstractions have taken on specific meaning.

Normally, courts create, modify, and discard constitutional rights in the context of ordinary litigation. A court decides whether a statute or the conduct of a policeman accords with the Constitution's commands, because it must make that decision in order to decide the particular case before it. The governmental conduct in question is, therefore, usually examined after it has been applied in a flesh-and-blood situation. Furthermore, the court makes constitutional law in light of the practical operation of the government's conduct, as illumined by the case before it. A judge's decision requires him to balance costs against benefits, as any legislator, any planner, would do. But the court is not simply deciding a case; it is also making law, by references to principles of general application. It is this susceptibility of a dispute to settlement by reference to authoritative principle that makes it suitable for decision by a court.

It will be seen that there are vast numbers of decisions by government officials that are not appropriate for judicial decision. The decision of the Department of Defense to buy one type of aircraft rather than another may have enormous implications for the economic well-being of thousands of individuals in San Diego and Seattle, but it is not a decision that lends itself to principled review. In 2000, this kind of decision seems likely to be even more typical of what government does than it is today. We must ask whether there will be much for courts to do about individual rights in the year 2000. And if we foresee a decreased importance for the judiciary's traditional role, two further questions emerge: Are there new roles to assign to the judiciary? And how shall we institutionalize the protection of individual rights?

In the nineteenth century, the courts sought to protect the individual's power to make free choices in the market. We protected property, Willard Hurst reminds us, not for what it was, but for what it could do; ventures, not holdings, were the courts' favorite objects. Now that we have an impressive industrial base, our private law has become oriented toward security. And in our public law as well, security often takes precedence over the protection of property and enterprise, so much so that the federal courts have virtually abdicated their former role as protectors of economic and property rights against state legislative regulation.

By the year 2000, the *traditional* property protections will be even further diminished, but in their place we can expect an elaborate set of protections of individuals' economic rights against the community, rights that might be called *property* rights if the word were not so burdened with doctrine.

These new rights will have been created in the name of equality, a principle that will go beyond equal opportunity toward the constitutional sanction of claims to compensatory justice in education, employment, welfare, and other areas that have only begun to be identified.[7] In addition to expanding the content of "equal protection," affirmative obligations are being imposed on government to secure equality for its citizens. We may anticipate a progressive extension of the demands of equal protection to many areas; the *potential* list of such interests would cover the full range of human wants.[8] The judiciary will select from that vast catalogue of interests on the basis of its own evaluation of the priorities and of those set by the claimant groups themselves.

The courts are likely to have considerable success in defining new areas where compensatory justice must be carried out. In specifying amounts and degrees, the judiciary probably will be less successful. The experience to date suggests that principled decision making works well when the questions are cast in general, doctrinally manageable terms. It is easy to determine whether the state must provide an indigent criminal defendant with counsel. Difficulties emerge in more specific inquiries. When state-provided counsel makes a serious tactical mistake at the trial, has the state really provided adequate counsel? If a minimum family income is to be decreed by the year 2000, shall it be $3000 a year? $6000?

Difficult or not, definition and articulation of new interests is a function courts can perform very well, even better than legislatures. Those who assert that courts must ultimately fail at these tasks for want of power to levy taxes forget two things. First, the political branches of government, particularly state and local, will not necessarily ignore the courts' pronouncements on the government's responsibilities. Second, there is already ample precedent for judges to order city councils and school boards to levy taxes. The judges of 2000, by putting effective pressure on political decision makers to respond to newly identified interests, can continue to make contributions to the protection of individual rights.

But there are limits to what courts can do in this area. Sometimes the courts' only meaningful remedy is to prevent the state from acting, either by injunction or by permitting an appeal from an administrative order before the order takes effect. In the year 2000, this kind of protection probably will be less available than it is today, because some kinds of automated governmental action will be able to be taken so swiftly. In the economic realm, for example, decisions about credit, government purchasing, taxes, and the like will be made on virtually a daily basis.

In such a context, one way of avoiding judicial problems is to *define* our individual rights, or our rules about litigation, so narrowly that the activity in question cannot be challenged. For example, the Federal Reserve Board can adjust the rediscount rate without giving a principled justification. But not all the issues are so simple. The point to remember is that in the year 2000, "preventive relief" must seek to be truly preventive. It must be built into the relevant processes of decision, so that the regulatory program (and the computer program) will not permit unacceptable harm to the rights we seek to protect.

Built-in controls are of vital importance in a world of "systems" where responsibility is diffuse. If the controls are not part of the initial decision-making process, no one may respond to the claimant who says he has been wronged. Moreover, controls of this sort will be constitutional in a classic sense, operating (as our current constitutional protections normally do not) in advance of the impact of governmental action on individual interests, on the basis of a before-the-fact legislative balance. Such limitations are so severe that we should not build one of them into a program without considerable thought. Built-in protections also sacrifice some of the particularized scrutiny that is the genius of our present system of rights. But perhaps the regulatory controls—and the corresponding safeguards—can be made so sophisticated as to allow for a considerable diversity of application. The result may be not a greater standardization of rights, but a greater adjustment of rights to individual needs. The borderline between "individualized justice" and arbitrariness is indistinct, and all concerned must remember that what comes out of a computer is no better than what goes in.

The degree to which we shall accept these built-in controls depends in part on our ability to develop the social accounting systems that have recently been discussed. When we set out to computerize the "balancing" system, we need agreement on both the weights to be assigned to various values and the degree to which a given fact or action involves one or another of the values. The latter problem is not insoluble; even though there may be a great many variables, interacting in unknown ways, we may be able to predict results, just as economists can predict the result of a tax change. The first problem, though—agreement on the importance of the values—will be complicated in 2000 by an increased social diversity. The solution, no doubt, will be to agree on some minimum quantity of freedom, including such things as the rights that are necessary for the individual's continued participation in the political process.

Another obstacle to judicial protection against arbitrary administrative action is the need for discretion—for action that need not be measured against principled criteria—in much of what government does from day to day. At the level where broad policy is made, the present structure of at least the national government insures careful consideration of a wide variety of interests, with resulting safeguards against arbitrariness. But on the lowest levels of administration, where these broad policies are applied to individual cases, there are many opportunities for arbitrary action. Here, where a scholarship may be denied, admission to a hospital refused, or a federal grant denied to a politically controversial local organization, we need some substitute for judicial review in the administrative world of the year 2000.

Internal administrative controls may take the form of setting agency policies to govern in "discretionary" areas, plus higher-echelon spot checks or their equivalent. (Some say computers will help give management greater control over the public and private bureaucracy; here again we can see that centralized control may in some cases protect rather than inhibit individual rights.) The controls may even be formalized in intra-agency appeals procedures. Either sort of control tends to reduce the area of discretion and produce more specific standards that can be written into statutes or regulations; either one, then, tends to increase the possibility of a principled review, perhaps even by a court. Another way to reduce the danger of arbitrariness is to guarantee the affected parties a hearing, formal or not, on their claims. And finally, publicity is a check; the agency may be required to publish or even explain its decisions, or an ombudsman may investigate charges and publicize cases of administrative unfairness. All of these internal administrative controls exist, in varying stages of development, in America today. It is urgent that they be perfected during the next generation.

The antagonism between principled and discretionary elements in the process of decision is nearly as old as adjudication itself. The guarantees of procedural fairness associated with the adversary system in criminal cases are, in part, an effort to give legitimacy to the discretionary decision of a judge or jury, when the correctness of the decision cannot be tested against principle by any scientific means. If behavioral science has by 2000 radically improved its ability to evaluate human conduct, we may expect a decline in the importance of the protections of procedural due process.[9]

Also, the procedural guarantees are likely to be of less importance when the goal of the process is perceived to be therapeutic rather than punitive. The recent trend of constitutional decisions has been toward bringing many cases of "treatment" under the guarantees of fair procedure. But in the year 2000, new therapeutic techniques (for example, drugs and electronic brain stimulation), plus improved predictive ability, will have altered the present blend of punitive and therapeutic responses to crime in the direction of individualized discretionary therapeutic treatment.[10]

The Importance of Options

The system for protecting individual rights may either help or hinder society's capacity to adapt to new situations. One big advantage of the freedoms of the market is that they permit such adaptations. When the market freedoms diminish, it will be necessary, as we create a new structure of rights, to avoid the dangers of rigidity. Our constitutional history to date represents one way to institutionalize an ability to be flexible: some individual rights can be cast in terms that permit the courts to find new substantive content in the rights as they are measured against new social contexts.

Another approach to the same goal would be to establish specialized planning institutions that would identify and articulate new "rights" as new government programs are planned. The agencies with primary planning responsibility might be required to submit their plans, in broad outline, to the "rights" planners, who might be given either as much as a veto or as little as the right to express their views before the plans are adopted. Such an agency could become expert on the strategy of protecting individual rights in a "systems" world.

If we try to maintain flexibility, we can also show some necessary humility about our generation's right to decide what our children's world will be like. Every action today, of course, has some effect on tomorrow's world, and inaction is often the moral equivalent of action. I concede that the price of excessive modesty in this context may be a failure of responsibility; every generation must try to cure the ills that seem clear to it. I suggest only that when our not-so-humble predictors of the future tell us that values may be changing, we ought to be cautious about making irreversible decisions in the name of protecting individual rights.

The concept of privacy, for example, relates to a cluster of values that have received a lot of attention recently; yet there is reason to believe that many of the privacy-related values that seem important to us will be of marginal interest to those who follow.[11] The point is not that we should fail to protect the values of privacy, but that we ought not to make irrevocable choices. For example: we should probably not destroy records, even juvenile quasi-criminal records, in order to protect reputations, because tomorrow's decision makers, by their standards, may *properly* choose the value of full information over the value of this kind of privacy.

From Status to Contract to . . . What?

The emergence of a "rights" mentality, we have seen, coincided with the establishment and defense of the freedoms of the market. Ideally, the free individual's rational decisions in his own self-interest promoted the good of the community. In the postindustrial world, this image of the society will have been replaced by what some writers have called a new feudalism—a security-oriented society that emphasizes relationships, not transactions. If the year 1900 was the apogee of "contract" individualism, surely we have not yet seen the end of the descent. But it would be a mistake to assume that we are on the verge of returning to the "status" society described by Maine. The disciples of McLuhan to the contrary, the year 2000 will not see us transformed into a neotribal state. Even within a highly administered society, many freedoms associated with the market will remain (even in political markets); increased affluence will permit a social diversity hitherto unknown; there will be rewards, economic and otherwise, for individual talents and efforts—and even a system of "rights," such as pensions, to protect the fruits of labor. The taming of institutional power has long since begun, and will undoubtedly continue.

The concept of individual rights, in other words, will increasingly come to include rights against groups and institutions that are currently considered "private." It is perhaps true in some political-power sense that "the individual . . . is significant only as a member of a group," as Arthur S. Miller has said, echoing Duguit. In our own time, the protections of group-association rights against both public and private attack have expanded rapidly. At the same time, the Supreme Court and other institutions have begun to recognize that many fundamental interests of a constitutional dimension are threatened by private or quasi-public conduct. By the year 2000, the distinction between public law and private law, never strong in the Anglo-American tradition, will have been discarded entirely, as will the notion that the absence of a formal connection with government immunizes a "private" group from responsibility toward constitutionally protected interests. In short, the focus will have shifted from protection *of* the group to protection *against* the group. Clearly a "civil-service" attitude toward all kinds of relationships, including employment, is on its way (and in 2000, nearly everyone gainfully occupied will be an employee).

We are now seeing the beginning of an expansion of "membership" rights in a variety of nongovernmental contexts. Students in public colleges and universities are already entitled to the guarantees of due process in academic disciplinary proceedings; the extension to "private" colleges is imminent. There has been a proliferation of employee grievance procedures. By 2000 we can expect a well-developed system of intragroup procedures to deal with all kinds of claims by individuals against the groups they belong to. The civil-service model will be a natural one.

Another kind of membership right is the right of members to participate in the group's management decisions. "Students' rights," the campus slogan of the 1960's, did not refer to procedural rights in disciplinary cases, but to students' wish for an effective voice in setting university policy. There are already stirrings toward that end. By 2000, many more of our young people will be spending longer periods of their lives as university students. The universities, as society's "gatekeepers" (Daniel Bell's word), already have a critical impact on their students' lives, and in 2000 it will be even greater. The right of this recently recognized "minority" group to "maximum feasible participation" will surely be accepted and written into law by the year 2000.

Employees, too, will have gained rights to participate in decision making. As the bureaucracy becomes more highly trained, its people will not easily take to routine employment; it would also be a waste to neglect their closeness to some of the organization's problems. As a result, we can expect considerable decentralization of some kinds of decisions, and legal protections of the "right" to this sort of decisional power within a hierarchy, as an aspect of "fair labor standards."

Yet some countertrends are already visible. With greater affluence and leisure, many people will turn away from organized expressions of self toward a different kind of individualism, introspective and even withdrawn. Today's hippies are more puritan than they like to think; they are not in the tradition of Samuel Gompers or Susan B. Anthony. We need a wide measure of institutional acceptance for those who do not choose to participate in the new system of community rights and obligations. They, too, will have rights to participate in the new equality, not because they have "earned" anything but because they are members of society.[12]

Indeed, the question of "drop-outs" symbolizes a number of the issues about individual rights in the year 2000. First, we must maintain opportunities for diversity within a workable social order, for this is the heart of freedom. Again, we must preserve flexibility; "individual rights" can also be a battle cry against social change (remember the 1930's and the Liberty League). Between preserving options and establishing "built-in" controls, there is a tension as old as the law's perennial dilemmas about stability and change. Finally, there is the mildly disturbing possibility that, after all, economic development itself has produced effective protection of individual rights. Do we owe our present rights to the rise of a large middle class that demanded regularized, institutionalized protections against arbitrariness? That possibility is disturbing only because it makes much constitutional law seem narrowly professional, even technical. On the other hand, the theory suggests that the move away from a contract-market style of individualism implies not the abandonment of our "rights" mentality but its refinement. For readers of recent anti-utopias, perhaps that is a cheerful note on which to end.

NOTES

1. Ralph H. Gabriel, *The Course of American Democratic Thought* (New York: The Ronald Press, 1940), p. 75.

2. In this essay I have accepted a minimum consensus view of the American economy and society of the year 2000 taken largely from Herman Kahn and Anthony J. Weiner, eds., *The Year 2000* (New York: Macmillan Company, 1967), and from *Dædalus,* Vol. 96, No. 3 (1967). The basic assumption, of course, is that we shall have avoided both nuclear war and ecological catastrophe. If that assumption should prove false, estimates about individual rights will have a low priority. The avoidance of the latter threat itself implies changes in the substance of individual rights. For example, the right of procreation, which the Supreme Court once called "one of the basic civil rights of man," surely will be seriously qualified as the need for population control comes to be widely accepted.

3. The Magna Carta itself, from which we derive much of the symbolism of individual rights, was at first largely for the protection of baronial property interests against the King's interference.

4. Note the discussion of special-purpose units and "neighborhood corporations" in Harvey S. Perloff's paper, "Modernizing Urban Development," *Dædalus,* Vol. 96, No. 3 (1967), pp. 789–800; and in Richard Nathan's essay in this volume.

5. A third interpretation is that the intention was to provide jobs for the poor within the antipoverty program.

6. Learned Hand, *The Spirit of Liberty,* ed. Dilliard (New York: Alfred A. Knopf, 1952), p. 180.

7. An alternative way to say the same thing is this: as planning comes to include progressively more "life-cycle" or "social" factors, our concepts of rights will be correspondingly expanded. See the essay by Harvey S. Perloff in this volume.

8. By 2000, the right to education, partly created by legislation and partly by the courts in the name of equal protection, will likely include higher education at public expense; adult education, perhaps at the employer's expense; special courses for retired persons for their new functions in community activities. More significantly, the schools will be asked to make up for environmental inequalities in the whole social structure of the disadvantaged areas. "Real equality," Karl Deutsch says, "is to give right-handed children the right-handed writing desks, and left-handed children the left-handed writing desks."

9. If a lie detector with 99 percent accuracy were developed, the present rules excluding such evidence would have to be explained on a new basis.

10. Readers of *A Clockwork Orange,* Anthony Burgess's chilling futuristic novel, may feel that the institutional issues raised by a complete reliance on

therapy seem insoluble, viewed against today's levels of understanding in the behavioral sciences. The danger of loss of dignity and individuality in the context of "total therapy" has caused my colleague Herbert Morris to coin the phrase "the right to be punished."

11. The present emphasis on privacy may turn it into a doctrinal catch-all for courts that wish to protect a wide variety of personal interests under the heading of "the right to be let alone," which equates privacy and freedom.

12. Similarly, the use of criminal law to repress moral diversity that does no demonstrable harm to others (for example, the smoking of marijuana, the possession of pornography) will surely be much reduced by the year 2000. The parallel development of the law of welfare, already begun, is the disappearance of such rules as the "man in the house" limitation on aid to children of unmarried women.

II

PROMOTING CIVIC ORDER AND POLITICAL COHESION

THE FRAGMENTATION AND COHESION OF SOCIETY

Harold Orlans

> Short as is our life, and feeble as is our reason, we cannot cmancipate ourselves from the influence of our environment. Even the wildest dreamers reflect in their dreams the contemporary social state: and much more impossible is it to form a conception of a true political system, radically different from that amidst which we live. The highest order of minds cannot discern the characteristics of the coming period. . . .
>
> —AUGUSTE COMTE
> *The Positive Philosophy*

Part I: Vignettes of the Year 2000 *

FRAGMENTATION

The average number of marriages is now 6.3 per lifetime; it is zero for Hollywood stars, being prohibited as unprofessional and a violation of the terms of standard studio contracts.

As many women as men hold responsible executive positions; the Roman style of marriages between older men and younger women is in fashion; polygamy has been legalized in the ghettos to make the husbands go around further; in the suburbs, husbands and wives visit their neighbors' bedrooms as casually as children visit their friends' playrooms. White brothels cater to Negroes, gigolos cater to older women, and male brothels cater to both men and women. In

* It may be useful for the reader at this point to be aware of the author's statement later in the text: "The fanciful episodes I have sketched are not intended to represent alternative futures so much as alternative directions in which the American people may evolve; and since a people can harbor at least as many inconsistencies as a man, we may well evolve in both directions at once." (Editor.)

1990, ravishing playmate Jane Playme (magna cum laude, Radcliffe Law School, whose anthem goes

I am a
Hon-ey of a
Fi-duc-iary
Ju-dic-iary
Bunny)

was installed as the first female Attorney General.

Children are educated at private English-cum-military boarding schools, subsidized by Friedman-Jencks-Dixon [1] type of government grants to their parents, as a result of the Supreme Court decision of 1981, pronouncing compulsory public education a violation of the Eighth Amendment (prohibition of cruel and unusual punishment).

Girls and pot (instead of liquor and cigars) are provided routinely at conferences of the American Academy of Arts and Sciences; boys and LSD IV (a fourth-generation drug, with patented dial-a-dream TV-feely feedback, marketed jointly by A.T.&T. and the Wilhelm Reich Orgone Institute) are served by less puritanical institutions. Only pep pills and 100-proof liquor are furnished by square organizations such as Dupont, the Department of Defense, and the Brookings Institution.

Pornography on TV is being broadcast live from Japan via moon-station relay, under an experimental program of the University of Hawaii's East-West Center, financed by the Ford Foundation and the National Institute of Mental Health. As part of the experiment, a carefully representative panel is able to converse with, and give directions to, the actors. Instructions and performances are, of course, recorded and will be available for restudy by students specially qualified for dispassion.[2]

In 1994, the American Civil Liberties Union defended the right of a couple to couple in public. Its position was upheld by the Supreme Court in a stirring verdict written by newly appointed Associate Justice Playme, closing with Webster's famous peroration, "Liberty and Union, now and forever, one and inseparable."

In the late 1980's, the nation's most influential intellectuals (like the nuclear physicists in the 1940's) voluntarily agreed not to publish their most important findings and policy recommendations. These have been circulated within the guild (admission costs more than a New York hacker's medallion) via coded, cooperatively owned coaxial-cable service managed by a joint committee of the Social Science Research Council and the National Academy of Sciences, and released only to those governmental or private clients who can pay what-the-traffic-will-bear rates.

Through more normal political channels, high-energy physicists have persuaded the government to build an accelerator girdling the moon, which can also direct radioactive death rays at any nation. The President of the National Academy of Sciences has happily announced the remarriage of pure science and the military, which had been disrupted by guilt-ridden utopian scientists during the 1970's.

For a time, the FBI's audacious junior auxiliary, the Super Snoopers (or SS), halved the average period during which the Ten Most Wanted Men remained at large, but the unit was disbanded after three successive directors had been removed for extortion. They were not prosecuted, ostensibly because they were juveniles, but in fact because they had been in possession of an embarrassing photograph of the FBI director, a letter revealing that the Attorney General had received 1000 acres of choice Berkshire woodland for nominating a Harvard law professor to the Supreme Court, and proof that the President had rigged the preelection polls and then the circuitry of the computerized voting machines in marginal states to ensure his reelection.

Silent guns, burglar tools, infrared telescopic cameras, and electronic eavesdropping and recording devices obtained from mail-order houses and Army surplus stores are commonly used by dull youth and bright children alike for fun, profit, and malice.

City water has been polluted and poisoned so often by delinquents and deranged men that purifiers have been installed on household taps, and the well-to-do have returned to the use of well water.

The underworld, grown even more powerful than it was during Prohibition, has been glorified anew by the cinema and the avant-garde of the day. Atom bombs stolen from military stores or assembled from plutonium siphoned from nuclear reactors (which now supply 60 percent of the nation's electric power), with the connivance of bribed or terrorized inspectors, have been increasingly employed for financial and political extortion.

Sit-ins, riots, and assassinations have been largely replaced as modes of political and personal protest by ingenious kinds of desecration and sabotage, which are difficult to control because they have constantly shifting forms and objectives. For example, pacifists have chopped down flagpoles and mutilated statues (particularly of generals); mailed fecal matter to draft boards; released infected lice, roaches, rats, and mosquitoes at Defense installations; and disabled all toilets at induction centers and railway stations. Militants, of course, have gone much further, sabotaging airport control towers, telephone exchanges, fire stations, and hospital operating rooms; releasing the inmates of jails, asylums, homes for the retarded, and zoos; blowing up, in New York City alone, the Lincoln Tunnel and more than thirty subway trains; and (their most outrageous act) napalm-bombing from the surrounding roofs half a million people assembled in Times Square on New Year's Eve. Their rationale has been that most politicians are opportunists not worth killing by principled men; it is the people who are responsible for the crimes of society, and hence it is the people upon whom justice should be pronounced.

Convenient trees having long since been cut down, white men must now be lynched on city lamp posts, and blacks on suburban telephone poles. Racial peace reigns in three Deep South states, from which the last Negroes departed in 1988 in air-conditioned state limousines. However, for reasons that the National Putnam Letters Committee is investigating, the crime rate has continued to rise despite their departure. Committee psychologists believe black blood still flows in white veins, while committee sociologists suspect that slaves corrupted their masters.

As the suburbs were methodically burned out by urban rioters, the middle classes withdrew to moated skyscrapers, commuting to work, window to window, by Defense-issue armored one-man back-pack jets originally developed for overseas duty; the towers are guarded by paralyzing or lethal rays operated by guards with TV monitors in plush underground bunkers.

Every citizen seven years old and over has new, used, or rusty firearms, and bowls of free bullets have been added to those for mints and matches beside restaurant cashiers. Many of the arms are issued for the use of local citizens' militia, and others for a subscription to the illustrated monthly magazine of the amalgamated National Rifle Raffle Association (NRRA) and the American Morticians Association. (Having vindicated the right of adults to defend themselves by a simultaneous muster of their members outside the home of every congressman during the fall recess of 1972, the NRRA extended the privilege to children, appropriately enough, on July 4, 1976.) The few paupers, widows, and mental defectives too poor, timid, or witless to acquire arms have been given them by children in Halloween masks, thought to have been organized by the Super Snoopers, but later exposed as a Chinese Communist agent's front to dispose of surplus Congo munitions.

When citizen militias could no longer maintain the peace, the standing Army of ten million men was progressively withdrawn from overseas commitments and, in 1995, from Hawaii and Alaska as well. By 1996, guerilla warfare had spread from the cities to mountain and rural areas. Private armies directed by Ph.D. criminals, retired generals, Black Powerites, Birchites, Mexican irredentists, and other extremists then controlled the Deep South, Southern California, Las Vegas, Empire Ranch, Morningside Heights, Harlem, Martha's Vineyard, and numerous other enclaves. In 1997, while the Army was occupied suppressing riots, the Navy putting out fires at thirteen major ports, and the Air Force reactivating missiles disabled by pacifist saboteurs (spearheaded by 500 graduate students in electrical engineering and aided by Russian intelligence), Russia occupied Alaska, Japan, the Hawaiian Islands, Ireland, Boston, Mexico, Southwest Texas, and Puerto Rico and Manhattan, without a shot being fired. Vermont, New Hampshire, Maine, Cape Cod, and adjoining islands declared themselves an independent federation under Canadian protection.

Two years ago, suicide pills laced with LSD V (known in the trade as C^2aw, after its Czech synthesizer—"Capek's caper or the absolute at will") were made available on prescription and subsequently as a bonus offer by the Trip of the Month Club upon receipt of a certified heir's social-security number.

With C^2aw catering to the masses, the deposed SS directors established for the elite what has come to be known as SURCEASE,[3] the ultimate inimitable luxurious passage by rocket into the sun. During the five-month journey, every wish is gratified by superlative synchronized manifold-orifice all-point cerebral-sensory equipment manufactured by Albert Des Esseintes (a collateral descendant of both Einstein and Huysmans), serviced around the clock by SURCEASE staff. The versatile equipment enables the passenger to spend every moment exactly as he wishes—reading or listening to anything on earth; sleeping and dreaming alone or with whomever he may fancy; eating, drinking, and smelling whatever he may wish; recapitulating any part of his or any other human experience known or recorded in any form. Upon entering the incandescent zone, there resounds the majestic junkie hymn that captures the heroic spirit of the year 2000, as "Gloomy Sunday" had caught the melancholy mood of an earlier year. In counterpoint to the throbbing chorus, the baritone sings with mounting joy of the final release of the son from the sins of the father until, in a finale surpassing Beethoven's Ninth, the chorus rejoins overpoweringly, "Mother—give me the sun! The Sun!"[4]

COHESION

Many historians have sought to explain the change in the nation's moral climate visible in the 1980's, and many factors doubtless contributed to it: simple satiation; the restoration of much of Freud's original doctrine, which had been overthrown by psychiatrists whose political liberalism had so confounded their professional judgment that they fancied man as a piece of clay molded neither by God, nature, nor history, but by parents and society (with, of course, psychiatrists serving as sculptors); the celebrated campaign of the clergy, which, for once, was so sensible and realistic that they were soon joined by prominent atheists, anarchists, businessmen, and scientists; and the fortuitous eruption of a drug-resistant venereal disease whose virulence was proportionate to the degree of promiscuity (Hollywood, Haight-Ashbury, the Mafia, much of the Eastern intelligentsia, the Jet Set, and Vassar were decimated; surprisingly, many welfare mothers remained healthy as lambs and others as ewes; all told, the disease was a sociologist's delight).

It now appears, however, that the trend was initiated by the same man who had contributed so much to the morality (or immorality) of the 1960's—*Playboy* publisher Hugh Hefner. For reasons honestly stated in his diary (which cannot be disclosed until 2088), during his last years Hefner underwent a conversion similar to Tolstoy's and sought with desperate earnestness, if not entire success, to renounce sex. At a critical moment in his struggle, a drunken and embittered editor substituted the photo of a luscious naked baby for a luscious naked babe on the *Playboy* cover. He was, of course, promptly fired, and most of the issue was successfully recalled; but in the few cities where distribution could not be stopped, the magazine sold out immediately.

The message was not lost on Hefner. The opportunity again arising, as it had in the 1950's, to merge his moral and business instincts, he recast the magazine (retitled *Chivalry*), substituting themes of innocence for those of sophistication, delicacy for grossness, and moral and emotional questionings for sexual fantasies. The formula proved so successful that other publications, and the communication and entertainment media in general, gradually followed suit. Before anyone knew what was happening, the tide of pornography had retreated from Main Street to the docks and from the best-seller list to the small pulp edition; nudity, sadism, violence, and vulgarity were replaced by romantic humanism, and today a genuine classicism is emerging: in music, painting, fiction, and poetry, cacophony has yielded to harmony and "modern" art to real art.

With the economies obtained by the reduction of style changes, industry now maintains a fuller inventory of parts, and stores offer a greater variety of choice at all seasons. As status competition hinges on the longevity and durability of clothes, houses, trees, marriages, and jobs, there has been a notable decline in divorce and in residential mobility, balanced by an increase in vacation travel and the development of several institutionalized forms for conducting affairs with the willing consent of uninjured spouses. (As Kalven predicted, rooms in which privacy can be secured are indeed now rented by the hour in major cities. What he neglected to note is that this has been true for untold centuries.) [5]

As the suburbs aged, government policy encouraged the construction there of housing for the aged and the relatively poor (dire poverty, like smallpox, having long since been eliminated); better work and recreation facilities were provided when traffic jams made it impossible to commute to work in the central cities; and so the once sterile plots of middle-class housing turned into normal communities.

Guns have long been outlawed, and even the police carry only a beam that disables but does not kill; educated, esteemed, and humane, the police force now attracts the kind of youth who once went into hospital work or the Peace Corps. But the main credit for the dramatic reduction in crime belongs to the Tan Man movement (spawned by the Urban Coalition) and its central-city affiliate, the Brown Town, which triumphed over Black Power fanatics by restoring such tranquillity to the city that a mass influx of the middle classes developed, business flourished, and local government could readily furnish the services needed to make city life rewarding and pleasant.

After the doctrine of parental responsibility for child behavior was discarded as psychologically and morally unsound, as well as futile in practice and wrong in fact, it was superseded by the notion that each person—child or adult—was responsible for his own actions. Children's courts were set up in every neighborhood to discipline child vandals and delinquents, often sentencing them to various forms of useful labor and ensuring that their punishment was prompt and commensurate with their offense. The courts have been so successful that some parents (recognizing the consequences of their indulgence, but unable to change their ways) have asked them to arbitrate over serious delinquencies committed within their homes.

Telephones and doorbells have simple on-off switches, and all houses have been encased in a transparent plastic film that prevents electronic eavesdropping, softens outside noises, and reduces the cost of both exterior maintenance and interior heating. Since 1990, offonotomies, performed routinely at birth, enable hearing itself to be turned off or on by a single grating of the teeth. Developed by a surgeon whose childhood had been spent next to the Third Avenue El and adopted initially by pneumatic-drill operators, jazz musicians, and soldiers in the tank and artillery corps, the operation was later recognized by clinical psychologists and marriage counselors as the ultimate defense of sanity in a world gone, if not entirely mad, then very noisy.

After the managing editor got a hernia lifting four copies of the Sunday edition, *The New York Times* adopted the format of the old London *Times,* with small advertisements on the front page and the Sunday issue restricted to sixteen pages. The loss of advertising revenue was made up by savings in production and distribution, and by subsidies from the U.S. Forest Service; the year that the new format was introduced, the *Times* received special commendations from the American Library and the American Historical Associations. Resources for the Future, Inc., calculated that, as a result, at least $301.3 million was saved during the next decade in the construction, enlargement, and equipment of libraries; postal, indexing, messenger, and refuse-removal costs (making full allowance for the reuse of newspaper and its value as insulation and land fill); the cost of erosion control; and the value of water retained by the world's forests —not counting the vast economic value of the time saved at every stage in the process of collecting, writing, publishing, reading, and regurgitating information.

Following the *Times*' lead, the Association of University Professors and the American Council on Education issued a joint resolution condemning all doctoral dissertations over fifty pages long, and the government and the Carnegie Corporation adopted a uniform clause in research grants prohibiting the publication of transcripts or verbal remarks in any form and penalizing grantees for publishing when they had nothing new to say. The rule-of-thumb penalty was $1 per unnecessary word, half of the grant being withheld pending receipt of the final report. A magical reduction in the volume of publication ensued, ending all talk of the "information explosion"; so spare did writing become that wits spoke instead of the "information implosion."

So well educated and intellectually demanding is the populace now (95 percent of adults having college degrees) that only two TV channels remain. One is reserved for news and live sports, and the other for transcriptions of legislative sessions and other political events. Entertainment, instruction, music, drama, and so on are drawn from a virtually limitless tape catalogue housed in the National Library of Movement and Sound that can be searched and displayed by a simple electronic console and panel. So varied is popular taste and so vast the holdings of the Library that rarely do more than 1000 of the nation's 300,000,000 consoles (one is usually available for every member of the family) show the same tape on any day.

To restore space for living in the home and garden, cooperative tool, game, and equipment loan and service centers have sprung up, from which the latest cameras, projectors, lawn mowers, power saws, trampolines, telescopes, skis, and other relatively expensive but little-used articles can be quickly obtained.

The Office of the Congressional Ombudsman, established in 1977 (the successful presidential candidate had made it a plank of his platform the previous year), has, over the years, helped ordinary people feel that the government is not simply a device for taxation, regulation, obfuscation, and self-justification, but can also show some simple human kindness.

To bring government closer to the people, Congress began meeting outside Washington, and federal agencies were dispersed intact to cities throughout the country, leasing their unoccupied Washington offices to private business. It happened that the entire staff of a certain bureau, celebrating the move aboard a cruise ship in the Potomac, drifted out to sea and was never heard from again, nor was their absence noted until two years later, when a political scientist from Syracuse sought to do a case study of the move.

Biologists have replaced physicists as the leaders of government science affairs, since their knowledge of human limitations and their understanding of ecological balance have proved more useful in establishing sensible policies for a large stable population. Victims of their own success at a science whose procedures have become largely routinized and computerized, economists now have a status approximating that of accountants. The "in thing" is a kind of clinical political science, the one true intellectual triumph of the otherwise ill-fated John F. Kennedy School of Government that (for reasons too painful to narrate) unfairly affiliated with the Massachusetts Institute of Technology in 1980 as the Fairlie School of Politics (which was, in fact, a successful cover for policy research openly contracted for by the CIA, with funds covertly supplied by the Office of Economic Opportunity and the Department of Agriculture).

In 1992, a Negro ex-colonel in military intelligence (who, as a volunteer, had rallied the Tibetans to overthrow Chinese rule and who served as head of the Joint Chiefs of Staff from 1988 to 1992) was elected President as a middle-of-the-road Republican after his supporters had (against his wishes) publicized the fact that his Jewish Democrat opponent had been a socialist in high school.

In the year 2000, the body of Martin Luther King, Jr., was re-interred [6] beneath a simple stone fronting the Lincoln Memorial, carrying the single inscription written by an unknown schoolchild: He Helped Us All Regain Our Self-Respect.

Part II

It is hard to imagine, let alone cite convincing examples of, an utterly anarchic society—one in which families and individuals fend solely for themselves without governance from, or concord with, others. The kind of examples that come to mind—the retreat from Caporetto; Hiroshima the moment after doom descended; Washington aflame in 1814 or 1968; London during the Black Death; or Russia in Zhivago's time, torn between Red and White armies—have an unnatural, eerie character, as if the normal social processes were set aside during an interregnum in which terrible events are commonplace and unrecorded; the old order has gone but no new order has emerged, and ungovernable, savage forces are at large. For (though he can live for periods, as he dies, alone) man is, as Aristotle observed, basically a social animal. Society gives him a language, a historical time and a social place, a sense of purpose and direction, and the political issues and cultural forms, if not the full substance, of his life.

Anarchy may afford a vision of utopia as well as one of chaos. However, most past anarchistic utopias have been set in simple surroundings, for if each man is to do as he pleases, he must control the means of his own subsistence; and in our hyperindustrial, urbanized world, anarchy is more apt to signify chaos. In any setting, anarchy suits healthy youth decidedly better than it does infants, pregnant women, the aged, or invalid. And the indulgences that the idle youth or the idle rich enjoy can turn readily enough into exactions and impositions.

The anarchistic spirit has been extolled by American businessmen and economists as well as by Goodwin and Kropotkin. Clement Attlee once called the Tories "anarchists in pin-striped trousers"; it is plain that the spirit of anarchy, whether derived from our rural forebears or our robber barons, runs deep in American life. It is a spirit of lawlessness, distrust, and disrespect toward government, and of reliance upon free—that is, unrestrained—individual and corporate enterprise. It is also a spirit of violence, which, as one Black Power militant notes, "is as American as cherry pie."

In the year 2000, things will probably not be so different from the year 1969 as we on this Commission are inclined either to believe or to hope. Doubtless the Statue of Liberty will still stand in Upper New York Bay, though her hem may be somewhat scorched and her bosom bared; in all its contradictory impulses of abandon and propriety, cruelty and compassion, lewdness and modesty, avarice and charity, the American character will remain recognizably American.

The fanciful episodes I have sketched are not intended to represent alternative futures so much as alternative directions in which the American people may evolve; and since a people can harbor at least as many inconsistencies as a man, we may well evolve in both directions at once.

Though a convincing portrait of the mottled American character can hardly be painted in one color, skeptics and optimists alike have daubed even its blackest and bloodiest features with rose. Thus, H. L. Mencken suggested that "sheer high spirits" precipitated the typical southern lynching[7]—and he may even be right; but the victim was no less dead though the mob was cheerful. "Despite our lynchings, gang wars, race riots, and casual military undertakings," Richard Rovere does "not think our people are particularly given to violence. . . . [If] our popular culture is so hung up on violence and sadism . . . [this] may have less to do with the need for violence than with the third-rateness of the culture and with the kind of talent that turns out all this awful stuff." Rovere adds, "Ours is a culture largely manufactured for export [a new conception of culture that eluded Franz Boas and T. S. Eliot] and the very worst of it is a smash hit all over the world."[8] Ergo: our own people have no special need for violence but the rest of the world's peoples do! Many of my good Brookings colleagues were not inclined to see in the murder of a second Kennedy and the yearly murder of thousands of other men grounds for the indictment of American society leveled by many psychologists, sociologists, and Europeans, and entertained by President Johnson in establishing the National Commission on the Causes and Prevention of Violence.[9] And many of my good colleagues in the Academy working party felt that the cloud that now hangs over our cities will lift after the flood of southern migrants peaks—and perhaps it will; we pray it will, but the flames that have burned have charred our land black, the blood that has flowed has stained it red, not rose, and the rains cannot bleach color thus engrained.

My colleagues are perceptive, but at so tragic and uncertain a time, why are they so optimistic?

In part, I imagine, because most Americans are congenital optimists. Optimism is the reigning national spirit, a kind of Couéism infecting intellectuals as well as businessmen—the idea that every day, in almost every way, we are getting better.

In part, because the suggestion that the power of darkness may subdue the power of light is professionally offensive. It is not the function of an intellectual to yield the spirit of reason that goeth upward to the spirit of the beast that goeth downward; unsporting death triumphs in real life, but not in the life of the mind.

In part, perhaps, because emotional though they may sometimes become in their argumentation, intellectuals are usually more sheltered from violence and bloodshed than ghetto residents, police and military men, farmers, longshoremen, truck drivers, bartenders, butchers, and countless other Americans. And, being spared the frequent sight of blood and brute force (observing crime mainly in newspapers and meat in cellophane parcels), they simply underestimate the extent to which violence abounds.

And in part, because liberals do not want to give ammunition to the forces of repression. There is, indeed, a real danger that violence may breed repression, which may breed new violence in mindless procession. That is dangerous and unpleasant, but it is neither good democratic politics nor good social science to disregard dangerous and unpleasant facts.

The political rise of the intellectual does not, to my mind, afford as much ground for optimism as some intellectuals have immodestly suggested. If, as Daniel Bell argues, the coming era will be dominated by intellectual institutions, as earlier eras were dominated by the institutions and interests of business or agriculture, woe betide us. For reason can cut the bonds holding us together as readily as those holding us in thrall, and the application by each special interest of more knowledge and more reason honed to each special purpose will hardly render our politics less bloody (though, when the scalpel is sharp enough, it may take longer to feel the pain).

Beyond politics lie other socially destructive uses of intellect. "To be always examining and never deciding," observed Comte, "would be regarded as something like madness in private conduct."[10] Yet what is the intellectual, especially the social scientist and most especially the contemporary American sociologist, but a mind always examining, always questioning the necessity of prevailing forms and customs, always seeking to replace the arbitrary inheritance of the past by a more rational order—as if society can be remodeled every year like a department store? A society is sustained by its unexamined principles as a body is sustained by its autonomic functions; too much overcritical reflection unravels first the fabric of our assumptions and then the remaining thread of action. A government of intellectuals acting like intellectuals would quickly bring the affairs of any nation to a halt; it is probably just as well that so many remain cloistered on campuses and in "think tanks," where they can daily shake the nation's foundation without disturbing its routine.

Of course, we must expect intellectuals to be at least as vigorous as any other group in advancing their own interests; and, as their tools are subtle and their standard of living high, their public exactions will be substantial.

The nation stands today at a dangerous juncture, beset by an excess of reasonable as well as unreasonable protest, by an excess of murder and hatred, an excess of instant self-gratification; there is a dearth of moderation, a dearth of clear, meaningful political alternatives, and a dearth of great and noble men in and out of public life. Great men cannot be manufactured at will, and their number will not grow if they are murdered at will. We have suffered terribly from the fact that a small man can grow large enough to enter history by bringing a greater man down. "You shoot at yourself, America," exclaimed Yevtushenko upon the murder of Robert Kennedy; indeed, our national situation at times resembles that of the French Navy, whose ships turned their guns upon each other and sank themselves at Toulon in 1942. For the murder of Martin Luther King, Jr., and the two Kennedy brothers there is no solution and no atonement. But there is a number of issues important to the nation's internal stability about which something can be done. Among these are: first, the issue of the Negro; second, the issue of the Negro; and third, the issue of the Negro.

"The news of King's death has stunned us. What can happen now? . . . I can imagine no greater disaster for America," my wife wrote from London, and surely a great many shared that reaction. Racism, the instinctive feeling that a Negro man is first a Negro, and not a man like other men, has been the primal American sin. When and how will it be expiated? When will children of color be given back the native charter of humanity that white men take from them at birth? When and how this question is answered will determine the nature of American society in the year 2000, and if there will then be a society that we would want to acknowledge as recognizably American. For if the summer of 1967 and the spring of 1968 have taught us anything at all (and the seeming inability of many students to learn is evidently shared by many congressmen and their constituents) it is that, blinded and in chains like Samson, the Negro can bring down the American temple.

The question of the Negro can no longer be delegated to police and welfare departments, for it is a central question for all government; it can no longer be delegated to social workers and sociologists, for it is a question central to all who wish to understand our society and to preserve the large part of it that is worth preserving. It is even possible that the solution that will once again bind up the nation's wounds will come not from any accurate analysis of a problem that has too many irrational features to yield simply to reason, but from paying enough attention to the problem. As Willy Loman's wife says in *Death of a Salesman,* "Attention must be paid." And if some of the attention that the nation paid to Martin Luther King, Jr., upon his death is given to his cause while we live, it may just happen that one day we will all be truly free at last.

Another issue warranting attention is the larger significance of standards of public deportment and public amenities, the quality of the nation's facade—the refuse and filth on the sidewalks and in public toilets, the slag heaps and car dumps by the roadside, the soot in the air and offal in the streams, the vandalism in cemeteries and the glass in the streets. Is there a relation between the character of public amenities and public decorum? Between raucous commercialism and raucous behavior? Between the consumption of alcohol, dope, and pornography and the degree of confidence and self-confidence in our moral standards? Between license and violence in art and in life?

A bad facade does not necessarily go with a bad character or a good facade with a good one (Dorian Gray was handsome and dissolute; in Scandinavia cleanliness and madness seem as closely allied as are dirt and madness in the United States). Moreover, people will disagree on what good and bad amenities and conduct are. But the appearance of too many public places is offensive; far too little money and effort are spent on maintaining them; and by the year 2000 the vast gulf between the comforts of suburban homes and the discomforts of most central cities must be bridged if the social cleavages they betoken are also to be bridged. We cannot be sure; the destructive forces in the higher as well as the lower reaches of this society are so strong that excessive optimism is a form of folly; but it is just possible that if our cities are humanized they will not be burned down.

Then there is the neglected issue of voluntary self-restraint and of legal restraints on those who are unrestrained in public. Where and when is freedom of conduct and expression desirable and permissible, and when is it not? When does it contribute to individual health and social stability, and when to individual and social degeneracy and destructiveness? The standard liberal doctrine that restraint is dangerous both politically and psychologically, while uninhibited freedom of expression is beneficial, is too simple to be convincing or to meet the practical exigencies of ordering peacefully the affairs of a tumultuous and increasingly mobile and crowded people. Mobility implies a lack of knowledge about or responsibility for communities encountered en route, while crowding means that privacy and quiet will become increasingly difficult and expensive to come by and, correspondingly, that the conduct of an individual or firm can impinge on more and more persons in public places (and also, of course, in the home via truly national communication media).

In this situation, existing community standards and laws will require continuing adaptation to ensure that they perpetuate not a noble ideology of British lords, French philosophers, American colonists, or Viennese psychoanalysts, but the equally noble ideology that will be needed to sustain a huge, motley democratic society in the year 2000. Opinion will differ about what these community standards should be. In my opinion, more and not less restraint will be called for in public situations to which the entire community may normally be exposed; public defecation, pornography, sadism, and loud and obtrusive displays that assault the mind should then be proscribed as physical assault is today.

Plainly, this type of restraint is best achieved by voluntary compliance, which is, in fact, the only way in which it can be effective, since the law is best enforced when it is least invoked. Some of the most exacting restraints upon private property and personal conduct are those that are freely assumed in buying certain homes or joining certain clubs. The purpose of public restraint is not to impose middle-class standards upon the poor or puritanism upon hedonists, but to enable all members of an aggressively self-serving society to walk together in peace. To protect the values of individual groups from enforced conformity to the larger consensus, a diversified moral ecology should be encouraged. Restraint is required in the central city if a man is not to be deafened, a woman molested, a child corrupted, and the general image of society debased to its loudest and most vulgar denominators. But elsewhere in the metropolis and nation, in defined zones entered freely and inhabited by those who know what they will encounter, inversion and perversion could flourish; dope could be smoked; nudists, polygamists, and bums could disport themselves.

We might thus also tolerate a larger degree of economic and political diversity. If the Tennessee Valley Authority can function and cooperative stores can coexist with capitalist ones now, why, in the year 2000, could there not be socialism in Wisconsin, Black Power in Mississippi and the District of Columbia (with the federal government enjoying extraterritorial rights, like the United Nations in New York), an Indian-Eskimo coalition governing Alaska, and Ronald Reagan, Jr., governing California?

The last issue that may be posed involves the character of our political and economic institutions as well as of our personal lives—the lives of the poor as well as the well-to-do, of intellectuals as well as illiterates. The question is: how can we achieve a better balance between the special and the general interest?

The unions in contempt of court and of their fellow men; the businessmen whose wares, warranties, and prices are misrepresented; the civil servants who prefer security to raising awkward questions; the comfortable who would rather buy another car than subsidize their maid's public transportation; the biologists who oppose the licensing of animal experimentation and the riflemen who oppose the licensing of firearms—these and a thousand comparable groups persistently put their special interests before the general good, or are so blind to the interests of others that they think them the same as their own.

Can the basic fault lie to any degree with the American philosophy of boundless individual opportunity, which can lead, in due course, to boundless expectations and demands? Is a philosophy of endless frontiers and resources suited to a world whose boundaries and resources are defined? Is it really essential to human happiness that the individual's right to acquire and bequeath wealth remain unlimited? (Would, for example, a $100,000 or $500,000 limit on annual income and a $1 million or $5 million limit on individual wealth really shatter the shell of the commonwealth?) When parkland and coastland are limited, should vast stretches remain private in perpetuity? When the nation's minerals are limited, should there be no limit to the individual's right to exhaust them?

Sooner or later—if not by the year 2000, then by 2100 or 3000—such questions will have to be answered differently from the way they are today. One can hope that Americans (who then will all have the same beautiful tan complexion) will have come to live in fuller harmony with themselves and with nature; death will be acknowledged more openly and inflicted less often; technology will be more subdued and humanity more exalted. That unimaginable new America will reflect sadly on the epitaph of the old America:

> In the nation that is not
> Nothing stands that stood before;
> There revenges are forgot,
> And the hater hates no more.

NOTES

1. Milton Friedman of the University of Chicago; Christopher Jencks of the Institute for Policy Studies; and John Dixon of the Xerox Corporation and the Working Party on Government of the Commission on the Year 2000.

2. In other words, castrates.

3. From the telephonist's "CEASE, Sir" (for the Celestial Euthanasia and Suicide Eidola, with murder a lucrative sideline), later adapted in the firm's gold-embossed childskin brochure to *Supremely Uplifting Rocket to Cosmic Elysium and Sunshine Evermore* (Copyright © 2000 by SS).

4. Osvald's line in Ibsen's *Ghosts.* Could either the SS or the junkie composer have been inspired by Schiller's "Ode to Joy," so strangely prophetic of their passage to the sun?

> Freude, schöner Götterfunken,
> Tochter aus Elysium,
> Wir betreten feuer-trunken,
> Himmlische, dein Heiligtum!
> . . .

Froh, wie seine Sonnen fliegen
  Durch des Himmels prächt'gen Plan,
  Laufet, Brüder, eure Bahn,
Freudig, wie ein Held zum Siegen.

. . .

  Brüder! über'm Sternenzelt
Muss ein lieber Vater wohnen. . . .
  Such' ihn über'm Sternenzelt!
Über Sternen muss er wohnen.

5. "It may be a final ironic commentary on how bad things have become by 2000 when someone will make a fortune merely by providing, on a monthly, weekly, daily, or even hourly basis, a room of one's own." (Harry Kalven, Jr., "The Problems of Privacy in the Year 2000," *Dædalus,* Vol. 96, No. 3 [1967], p. 882). The mercenary landlords of certain city houses now refuse to rent rooms for *more* than an hour.

6. The first draft of this essay, written in November 1967 before the murder of Martin Luther King, Jr., read "interred."

7. As cited by Samuel Eliot Morison (who concurs with Mencken) in *The Oxford History of the American People* (New York: Oxford University Press, 1965), p. 794.

8. See Richard Rovere, "Reflections: Half Out of Our Tree," *New Yorker,* October 28, 1967; reprinted in the *Congressional Record,* daily ed., November 2, 1967, p. S15721.

9. In such questions as the following, which the President put to the Commission:

"Is there something in the environment of American society or the structure of American institutions that causes contempt for the rights of others, and incidents of violence? If there is, how can we correct it?

"Has permissiveness toward extreme behavior in our society encouraged an increase in violence . . . ?

"Are the seeds of violence nurtured through the public's airwaves, the screens of neighborhood theaters, the news media, and other forms of communication from our leaders that reach the family and reach our young?" (*Congressional Record,* daily ed., June 11, 1968, p. E5246.)

10. Auguste Comte, *The Positive Philosophy,* trans. Harriet Martineau (London: George Bell & Sons, 1896), II, 153. Note his additional remarks: ". . . social order must ever be incompatible with a perpetual discussion of the foundations of society. Systematic toleration can exist only with regard to opinions which are considered indifferent or doubtful. . . ." And ". . . political good sense has adopted, to express the first requisite of all organization, that fine axiom of the Catholic Church; *in necessary things, unity: in doubtful things, liberty: in all things, charity* . . ." (p. 154, Comte's italics).

ACHIEVING ORDER AND STABILITY: THE FUTURE OF BLACK-WHITE RELATIONS

Matthew Holden, Jr.

Introduction

This essay is based on the critical assumption that conflict within human groupings is inescapable, and order is therefore always problematic. Conflict is simply the natural consequence of differences among human beings, whether they are friendly, hostile, or neutral toward each other. The problem of order is not to eliminate conflict, but to give it structure, so that it may be kept within the boundaries and forms that most participants will regard as legitimate and acceptable. In sum, the problem of "order" is to establish a "constitution" (rules-of-the-game) for the polity. Orderly action is action that takes place within those rules. But there is also an inevitable tendency for some claimants to take action beyond those rules, a process determined by the energy of claimants who would otherwise lose, by their attitudes toward the claimants who would win if the rules were followed, or by the costs that they think orderly action would impose upon them, of which the most extreme is that they will be out of the game permanently if they lose on the one occasion. Political stabilization requires keeping the ratio of "disorderly" to "orderly" actions within the tolerance levels of the system over prolonged periods. If any forecast may be made comfortably, it is that the politics of order and stabilization in the year 2000 will be at least as severe and complex as anything experienced in the 1960's, although by then Americans may have learned to cope more effectively with the problematic character of order.

There are several rather obvious potential sources of disorder.

(1) The general cultural problem of violence, or the political meaning of murder. Government may, as a normative proposition, have a "legitimate" monopoly on the right to kill,[1] but it is neither complete nor effective. The homicide rate is the measure of its effectiveness, and one future source of stress is the growth of a mistaken belief that people ought to be secure, and a corresponding belief that people are less secure than they were in the past.[2] This dual development leads to increasing political support, by the politically salient middle and upper classes, for the ordinary agencies of public coercion (and for the practices of official illegality, which are as much "disorderly," in other words, "unconstitutional," as any private practices).[3]

(2) The problem of pervasive disaffection and disorder among groups that have highly transitory membership and no well-defined common interest. Such groups can become the foci of disorder, as the current student activities show, yet the conditions under which they may become regular parts of a pattern of disorder (as in Indian student politics) are not very clear.

(3) More apparent and troublesome, the conflicts and necessities of specific groups, where there is an identifiable common interest or an identifiable and stable membership. In American politics, one might inquire into the elements of disorder that might be associated with status degradation for particular professions; for example, what would happen if the police were "handcuffed" too much for their comfort, or if the military were faced with a situation in which the present expectation of international violence were noticeably diminished. There are potential problems of disorder if the values and feelings of the Radical Right cannot be reconciled with the values and feelings of other Americans and with the normalities of the political process. Or, there might be a source of disorder in the white poor—a quiescent element now, but far more "alienated" than the black[4]—in the event there were a sustained and visible rise in black status but none in their own.

All of these problems have a certain relevance, but for present purposes we shall discuss (at least directly) only one aspect of the third focus: intergroup politics and the special problems of black-white politics. It provides a contemporary test of such importance that its resolution (or nonresolution) will have decisive consequences for the politics of order in the year 2000.

Forms of American Order and Residual Problems

Constitutions, as expressions of the preferred form of order, may—when they relate to the simultaneous existence of two or more groups in the same polity—create "empires," "markets," or "communities." As an actual working social arrangement, a constitution lays down rules about five key matters: (a) what sorts of persons shall count as full members of the system (entitled to any and all of its prerogatives and benefits), what sorts shall count as qualified or limited members (either as children who have not yet attained the rights of adults, or as adults who have some rights—but not the rights of all adults), and what sorts shall be "outside" people (aliens, slaves, and so on), entitled to nothing except that which members are willing to give them; (b) who shall be eligible for recruitment into what decision-making roles, by what criteria, and through what selection and elimination procedures; (c) who shall speak and act with deference, consideration, contempt, and so forth toward whom in the course of making public decisions; (d) what substantive outputs (policies) shall be mandatory, permissible, or proscribed (as private property defense is, within limits, mandatory under the American "constitution"); and (e) by what procedures shall changes in the constitution be proposed and accepted or rejected.[5]

If members of one group are understood to be permanently unequal to members of some other group, within this structure of rules, then we may say that the polity has an "imperial" order or constitution. In such a case, the dominant group exercises rule over an internal "colony" of "dependent" people. If the constitution somehow includes more than one group as technically eligible for membership, but the relations between the participants are defined primarily in terms of log-rolling, mutual coercion, and so on (as in Irish-Yankee politics in nineteenth-century Boston), then we may call the system a "political market." If there is actually a high degree of shared moral appreciation so that members regard each other as *fellow* participants whose presence is inherently valuable—not merely a matter of convenience—then one has the elements of an "integrated political community."

It is possible, and indeed probable, that any political system will simultaneously embody elements of empire, market, and community. It is also probable that within a political system there will be changes over time that show the predominance of "imperial," "market," or "communal" elements, and the evolution of that system from one form to another. We may call the evolution from empire to community an *integrative* process, and the change from community to empire *disintegrative*. Both processes have operated in the history of the United States. In the minds of most American citizens, the United States is probably appropriately symbolized by the Pledge of Allegiance—"one nation . . . indivisible." But it is useful to recall how recent this apparently solid political community is. For just about half the life of the Republic, American politics was some mix of "community" (chiefly when defined as an Anglo-Protestant entity), "market" (in North-South terms), and "empire" (in the relation of Protestant to Catholic and of white to black, Indian, or Oriental).

The absence of political community before 1877 is suggested in nine important crises between the Federal Convention of 1787 and the settlement of the Hayes-Tilden election. Three of these involved the ultimate challenge to a government's authority, a threat to its territorial integrity. Four represented challenges to the authority of the government, but not to territorial integrity, and had they been effective, would have altered the system for some time to come. Two were factional and regional confrontations; the authority of the central government was not challenged, but special negotiations, instead of normal political processes, were necessary to determine the distribution of power (see table).

TABLE I

Nine Major Crises

TERRITORIAL	CENTRAL AUTHORITY	NEGOTIATIONS ABOUT POWER DISTRIBUTION
The Burr-Wilkinson Conspiracy	Virginia-Kentucky Resolutions	Missouri Compromise
The Hartford Convention	Whiskey Rebellion	Hayes-Tilden Settlement
	South Carolina Nullification	
The Civil War	Compromise of 1850—Dred Scott	

In the emergence of the trade unions between 1877 and 1935, the class war involved a severe political battle to alter the imperial relations of capital and labor, but there was never a serious threat to the authority or future of the American governmental system. As a political market, the United States became virtually unshakable and was increasingly transformed into a political community at the national level. Much more than national politics, local politics has given evidence of being "imperial" in character. The business systems, the political parties, the bureaucracies, and the church systems in the metropolitan areas tend to have rather rigid stratifications, particularly ethnic ones, through which the subordinates have broken only by long and bitter struggle.

But in both national and local politics one aspect of the imperial order has been most clearly defined and effectively maintained: racial politics. "The two nations" are not purely metaphorical.[6] Just as legal frontiers, however initiated, create frameworks for behavior that in turn result in new cultures,[7] so do the invisible but real frontiers within a single power system.

Since the foundation of the Republic, black men have been defined as "nonmembers" in the South and as extremely limited partial members in the North.[8] At best, the position of northern blacks was extremely ambiguous until the Civil War amendments, which admitted them legally to the ranks of citizenship. After the war, the Reconstruction amounted to a brief attempt at "development," much as that word is now used in new nations to mean increased political participation, educational advances, and economic development among the liberated black peasantry. It failed because it required a more sophisticated and prolonged pacification policy than the government found possible, given the priorities of forming a wider community among white southerners and northerners and of transcontinental economic development. In short, part of the price for consolidating the national political "market" and for moving toward political "community" was northern nonintervention in the undeclared black-white civil war that continued for twenty-five years after the Hayes-Tilden Settlement.

The formation of a post-Civil War political "community" was, in short, purchased at the price of an "imperialism" between white and black. This "imperialism" is (or was) reflected in the precedence of white over black in every element of the "constitution." The country settled down to a mixed regime of quasi-apartheid, official in the South, unofficial in the North, actively supported by the Wilson administration and opposed by no other until the New Deal. The Roosevelt administration dealt with the matter obliquely, and not until the Truman administration was a calculated attempt to reduce the presumption of white dominance even theoretically contemplated as executive and congressional policy.

This is an important perspective to bring to a forward view of racial politics. An ordinary college graduate of the class of 1969, born in 1948, would have seen the 1968 debates on open occupancy. Not until the year of his own birth had the Supreme Court found that racial restrictive covenants could not be enforced by law. A younger brother born, say, about 1953 would have been the first member of the family not to remember segregation in public accommodations in downtown Washington. A tenth-grader in this same family who was taking a civics course that described the Executive Office of the President might learn that the year of his birth (1955) was the first time any black man was given a senior appointment on the President's staff.[9]

In discussions of the progress of black Americans, the changes of the past fifteen years are often cited. They refer to the relief of active public privations and to active public constraint upon private limitations. If one thinks of the social behavior involved, one begins to have some insight into the importance of racial politics as an element of future instability. The Kerner Report, in evoking the possibilities of two "separate and unequal" societies, both clarified and obscured the social realities. It referred to a future reality of grave political trouble, but it failed to perceive the extent to which the "imperial" structure of racial politics has *already* created the two social entities—the "two nations."

How will the present confrontation of these two social worlds affect the achievement of a political design based on the requirements of the Perloff Doctrine?[10] In general, it is easier to estimate the future of racial politics if we treat it as a problem in which the "integrative" capabilities of American society are increasing, but in which "disintegrative" loads upon American society are multiplying as well. It is, in Deutsch's phrase, a "race between capabilities and loads."[11] The capabilities lie in (a) the extent to which reciprocity between white and black values is possible, (b) economic conditions that allow favorable adjustments in the racial structure, and (c) organizational resources for combining cultural and economic resources in some viable form. Racial politics is thus a residual problem in the creation of a form of American order expressive of political community.

The Problem of Cultural and Value Capability

The relatively limited scope of values and attitudes favorable to community has been sharply accentuated by the sudden vogue of the term "white racism." This phrase is misleading if it ignores the varieties of fact to which it actually refers and their implications for social change.

The most common meaning of "racism" is the simple belief in the natural superiority of whites and a preference for active policies in support of white dominance. The desire to maintain a particular style of life and a particular social distance necessarily entails defense of the racial status quo. In this sense, defense of a property system in which any X has unlimited right to sell (or refuse to sell) to any Y contributes to the existent racial structure if there are widespread socio-economic sanctions that inhibit Y's becoming a purchaser if Y is black. A change in the racial status quo must come through an alteration of socio-economic patterns whereby black persons do become like their white counterparts, except in color and ancestry.

The active defense for policies of white dominance remains relatively trivial in politics outside the South, but support for social change is nonetheless rather limited. This reflects what sociologists call "attitude salience"—people's reluctance to support specific changes when they realize what change will cost. For example: a political party in a northern state nominates a black man for statewide office only when he is a special candidate or one among many whose nomination is part of a systematic power-sharing device. "Black consciousness" raises more complicated issues. Few whites would have been comfortable with the idea of elevating Malcolm X into the national pantheon, although they would have been much more responsive to Martin Luther King.

But "white racism" is not the only obstacle to cultural exchange. Black politics increasingly overlaps with collective psychiatry and collective drama, and black politics is not unique in this.[12] Politics has always been a symbolic means of relieving the tedium and pain of brutal daily experience.[13] We see this in the gladiatorial combat of Imperial Rome no less than in the Afro hairdo and the singing of "We Shall Overcome." The important fact about black politics now is its intensity, a response to the subordination and insult that black men feel they experience in American culture, and in the need to find means of acting out their resentment of that experience.

Collective psychiatry in politics is an essential element of the power struggle between black militants and black moderates, and it is more important than the actual differences of strategy. The militants' strategy of calculated action is actually remarkably conservative, for it seeks urban political control on the model of the American Irish in the nineteenth century.[14] But collective psychiatry is expressed in the *rhetoric* of black politics, a language of defiance, menace, and rejection that has been growing in currency over the past sixty years.

It is perhaps even more critical that the newer recruits to the black middle class—which has always provided the catalytic element in black organization—are increasingly drawn from the now-urbanized black peasantry and share the essential cultural values of that peasantry, especially blancophobia. The emergence of "black consciousness" thus reflects the transformation of the essential black peasant tradition into a new and educated form of cultural nationalism. This simultaneously enhances collective self-respect and creates new cultural distance from whites.

For this reason, it is misleading to formulate the racial crisis simply in economic terms—and to develop policy responses in similar terms. If economic questions were in themselves so critical, one could not explain the remarkable similarity in the responses of low-income, lower-middle, upper-middle, and upper-income black respondents to questions about black leadership, violence, the future, and the like. Yet when the Harris poll asked black respondents to evaluate what Stokely Carmichael (among others) has done, the responses were very similar.[15] Moreover, it is no surprise that the black political movement has become most volatile when the black population is better off economically, in absolute ways, than it has ever been before. (It is *not* better off *relative to whites*, but it is better off in the sense that a larger proportion of blacks have more economic goods than ever before.)[16] The historic push in civil rights did come from the black bourgeoisie,[17] and thus the growth of that bourgeoisie is of course followed by the growth of more overt and defiant black politics. Black politics, both rhetorical and physical, is an effort to *enforce* upon whites both atonement for past psychic injuries and a demonstration of present respect.

Black politics as collective psychiatry forces its adherents constantly to escalate their demands, to formulate them in the most diffuse terms, and, thus, to define whatever "concessions" are made by the whites as "irrelevant" after they have been made. This also undermines any incentives the opposite party might have for finding common ground, since the whites can never be confident that common ground will be common enough to be worth the search.

The Problem of Economics

To emphasize the element of value exchange and the problems associated with collective psychiatry is not to deny the relevance of economics. For a subordinate population, economic growth is a necessary part of the integrative process if people are to develop the competences that confer power opportunities in the society. It is no accident that the socially dominant, the best educated, and the most affluent tend to be the same people. Economic rewards in American society are indicators of the social value placed upon one's worth and usefulness. This is the practical significance of the idea of "equitable pay," or of the pressures in industry for occupational groups, such as skilled tradesmen in the auto industry, not merely to be well-paid but to define "well-paid" relative to the pay of those over whom they have always taken precedence. The same problems arise from the fact that black college graduates on the whole earn less than white high-school graduates.

However, economic well-being among American blacks has not been faced seriously. For instance, it is essential to most proposals for change that the economic positions of blacks improve at rapid rates. Yet this leads to invidious comparisons by the existing white middle class, whose affluence is based not on capital but on income and credit, and who arrived at that state from a relatively impoverished recent past. In this sense, the politics of inflation becomes critically relevant to the future politics of racial adjustment. A domestic Marshall Plan is at war with attempts to control inflation, yet the control of inflation is likely to be both economically and politically essential if the white middle class has received no appreciable benefits (in real income) from pay raises in the past two years.

The Problem of Organization and Leadership

Cultural values and economic opportunities are seldom so clearly arranged that decision making becomes automatic. The problem of organization and leadership is one of creating strategies and interpretations of reality that will be widely accepted by many sectors of society. This is particularly important when the necessary decisions involve a qualitative change in the political system, such as bringing an excluded population and a formerly dominant population into some new and common relationship and status. Some factors at work in American society and in the politics of the modern world suggest that the capacity of organization and leadership for this purpose may actually diminish.

The problem lies first in the nature of the Integral State: the emergent American political system in which decision making is highly centralized (in other words, no important American issues can now be entirely resolved privately or without the intervention of public decision makers at the highest levels). Every major private institutional system—from higher education to the Catholic Church to the *Fortune* "500"—is now critically affected, day by day, by decisions made in the federal government. But if decision making is so centralized that the "public-private" distinction loses much of its former relevance, this does not mean that power is similarly centralized.

The distribution of power is much more complex. In some respects, power is distributed among many centers at the national level: the private systems that are constituencies of governmental agencies and that impose constraints on those agencies; that participate in governmental decision making at the level of program preparation; that administer governmental programs, and so on. But power is also affected by the "technocratic" bias reflected in the attitudes of the scientific-technological intellectuals who have made "systems analysis" a byword in sophisticated political conversation. These intellectuals and their administrative colleagues seek a withering away of politics and the making of public decisions according to their criteria of rationality.[18]

The scale of government, the multicentric relationships between public and private institutions, and the emergence of technocratic decision making are virtually inevitable in the modern world. But they create an important political problem in the form of an empathy gap between major decision makers and the diverse populations found throughout the country. This gap reduces the power of leadership to offer strategies and interpretations that large numbers of people will find both comprehensible and persuasive, and thus reduces the capacity of decision makers to provide effective leadership on such pervasive issues as the change in the racial structure of the national government. It is in this context that "participatory democracy" acquires its emotional appeal. The concept has no precise meaning, but it does clearly imply that the usual representative processes (election, decision making, feedback, new election) do not provide individuals and groups with adequate freedom to influence the course of public policy. It also implies the right of the dissatisfied not merely to participate more intensively but to be guaranteed that the results they prefer will be served in fact. And this in turn has been interpreted to mean much wider latitude for direct action by a claimant against any target, if the favorable decisions do not come or do not come fast enough.

Under such circumstances, leadership both in governmental and nongovernmental institutions has some extremely complex problems, made still more complex by the fact that national leadership tends to be of higher social rank than its followers and that it tends to take a much more flexible view of racial change. For example, a major international union whose leadership is strongly committed to racial equality found that its white members resisted even the symbolic deference of putting the flag at half mast on the day of Martin Luther King's funeral.

In the same way, the Urban Coalitions across the nation represent the activities of big businessmen, church leaders, and (to some degree) urban political leaders, who must run against the grain in trying to develop pertinent programs. The proposals of the leadership inflict the most hardship on the followers themselves and relatively little on the leadership. Similar problems arise in black politics. Once activated, the black population at large is most likely to support the most visibly militant leaders, which means there will be a continuing instability in black politics until the internal controversies are resolved. However, given the separate institutional development of black life, the tendencies in black politics do not easily meet the working requirements of the Integral State or the necessities of the white follower-audience.

Five Possible Directions

In effect, we suggest that the possibilities for convergent values, economic interests, or organizational processes are—on present assumptions and knowledge—rather limited, while the problem of racial conflict is extremely urgent. Assuming this is so, we can then define a little more clearly the possibilities for racial development in the next three decades. In essence, there are five.

(1) By a dynamics of mutual alarm, in which white and black frighten each other into successively more drastic escalations, one could foresee the actual disruption of the political system as it exists and the reassertion of a more rigid structure of "empire" than has been contemplated in recent years. (a) This could involve the South African model, with para-military controls for white supremacy. (b) A more drastic step would be some variation of territorial separatism of the sort recently advocated by some black nationalists. (c) The most drastic step would, of course, be an actual adaptation of the Nazi model of physical extermination.

(2) At a lower level of coercion one could conceive of the systematic national development of a plural-society model, in which two populations would coexist, but in which the main tasks of defining

black-white relationships and insuring the new form of order would rest in the hands of agencies of coercion.

(3) At a still lower level of coercion is the continuation of the "disguised" plural society that now exists. The conventional image of group mobility in American life is that the several groups advance through an increase in opportunities for their most energetic and talented members, in other words, those members most capable of adopting the cultural patina of the dominant group. One can envisage a future in which the black Americans of the year 2000 occupy a position comparable to that of the Polish- or Italo-Americans in the year 1969. The symbolism and the existence of the present economy makes life at least reasonably prosperous for the Italo-American working class and lower-middle class in such a way that the relative rigidity of the walls between Italo-American and non-Italo-American channels is disguised. If all our conventional expectations about American society were to hold, the "integrationist" position would produce something like the same results for black Americans.

(4) A still different outcome would be the plural society—"peaceful" edition—with two novel features. First, a strong element of reciprocal agreement that cultural coexistence is desirable. Second, the development of new institutional forms that would provide some formal structure for bargaining between the two populations.

(5) Finally, if the "integrationist" position were carried out to the practical conclusion dictated by its rhetoric—rather than the probable conclusion dictated by reality—there might emerge a common order in which the element of "community" would be predominant. Racial diversity would not cease to exist, but relatively few important institutional judgments—public or private—would be predicated on racial distinctions.

Elements of a Forecast

(1) A LOW PROBABILITY FOR THE ESTABLISHMENT OF POLITICAL COMMUNITY

A complete political community in which race plays no part seems inconceivable because it requires too many alterations of life as we know it.

The blacks' demand for social transformation at a very rapid rate, partly because of the long delay in any significant transformation,[19] now leads to a rhetoric in which the changes so recently defined as essential are now defined as trivial. This is the core of the argument that the problem requires "time." Integrative processes require different sets of people to learn new habits of trust and of action. The growth of urban violence (which expresses, among other things, the black distrust of whites and the need to defy whites) is interpreted as an "unreasonable," a "threatening," and an "insulting" position.

Concretely, this has led to some extremely important policy and institutional developments that are adverse to the requirements of the Perloff Docrine, because they point toward the reassertion of a white-black "empire" rather than a white-black political "community."

Three years ago it was taken for granted that any person had the right to move about freely in the streets of the American city. But now the curfew, which presumes that anyone on the streets is ipso facto suspicious, has become a standard measure of control, imposed at least once a year in New York, Chicago, Detroit, and several dozen smaller cities, not to mention the nation's capital.

Urban police departments have undertaken to improve their armament, their police intelligence systems, and their tactical units on the expectation of further street violence. The National Guard has now had to learn how to deal with urban disruption, and a situation has arisen in which the Guard in any state with a large black population may reasonably predict that it will be called into action during a calendar year. Similarly, the Department of Defense has found it obligatory to create a special unit for civil violence control with a task important enough to merit the command of a three-star general. In short, the military role in the maintenance of domestic order has become more important than it has been at any time since the labor disputes between 1877 and the 1890's.

The most important development, however, has been the rise of private tensions and fears. In 1968, in at least one city, more than two and one half times as many hand guns were being purchased legally as in 1966.[20] There are other related elements in this picture:

housewives' gun clinics sponsored by some suburban police departments, private "home-guard" units in white areas, and a few such units in black areas.

Each of these events is contrary to the requirements of a political community. Yet our present concern with such developments may be alarmist. After all, this sort of thing is not new. The Detroit civil crisis in 1967 was not "the worst riot in American history." Fights between Catholic Irishmen and Protestant Irishmen in Philadelphia in the 1840's killed one person per 15,000 of the population. In the New York "Orange Riots" of 1871, the ratio was one to 27,000. A little reflection on the nineteenth-century riots with which we are familiar shows that the Detroit uprising was noticeably smaller in scale than many earlier disturbances. Urban violence was bigger and deeper in the nineteenth century than it is in the twentieth. If the United States could safely come through those experiences, it will probably survive the present tumults. If we are aware of the fact that American history has not been all sweetness, light, and warm good will—that the Republic has survived and improved through times of trouble—we can be particularly sensitive to the more optimistic views of such a critic as James Sundquist.[21]

(2) WHY AMERICAN APARTHEID IS LESS IMPROBABLE THAN POLITICAL COMMUNITY

The grim horror of an American apartheid would of course violate all the criteria of the Perloff Doctrine. Yet it seems less improbable than a genuine biracial political community, because of the self-evident fact that "loads" have already begun to outstrip "capabilities." Let me indicate more explicitly why I take this position in contrast to Sundquist's optimism.

Sundquist and those of his persuasion give two reasons for believing that capabilities will increasingly outstrip loads (the reverse of my estimate): one, the probable rise of black men to political power in the cities, providing new opportunities and self-confidence, and reducing the sense of alienation;[22] two, the fact that racial faction is primarily confined to the northern metropolitan areas (which is correct), but that not everybody lives in such an area. Those who are outside the immediate field of conflict will (in the interests of their own stake in national peace) throw their weight on the side of relevant social reform.

These arguments may be correct, but they are not persuasive. The first seems deficient from the viewpoint of time and the scale of required social adjustments. In the parallel immigrant experience, the various nationalities began to have effective control of local governments about forty to fifty years after they attained significant proportions of the urban population.[23] The election of Hatcher in Gary, Indiana, and Stokes in Cleveland, Ohio, indicates that the black electoral accession is following about the same scale (taking the World War I migrations as the nuclei of the first quantitatively significant movements into the cities). But the immigrant nationalities spent another forty years consolidating their power in state and local politics before national leaders were forced to admit their importance in the party system. In the interim, the kind of power they had in local government was less relevant to the social welfare or symbolic integration of the immigrant population than it was to the self-interest of the electoral leaders. Moreover, the demands on local governments were relatively limited.

If this pattern were to hold for the blacks, their politicians would achieve in the years 2000–2010 the sort of political power available to the Irish Democrats in 1920–1928. Between now and then, their political control would be grossly "irrelevant" to the emergent demands of urban black populations. Even if they wanted a more significant modernizing role, the place of local government in the Integral State is too trivial to make their power significant for such roles. The black electoral politicians would find themselves undercut by black agitator politicians who would find a ready audience in a black population, not measurably better off, which felt grossly disillusioned.

If black electoral politicians were accused of "selling out" simply because they could not "deliver," a politics of terror and assassination could easily develop. One would envisage not mass uprising, but relatively small clusters of people prepared to adopt Irish Republican Army (or Irgun) methods.

Terrorist politics would almost certainly produce an ever stronger white reaction (and some black reaction) so that civil order by force would be the prime condition for any political change.[24] The interplay of these two forces could lead to a South African type of solution. As the scale of natural interplay between administrative agencies and the terrorist underground increased, the coercive agencies would acquire a vested interest in their social role as the prime managers of racial conflict, displacing the agencies oriented toward noncoercive social reform, and an American equivalent of the concentration camp would, without planning, come into existence. The middle group, which in Sundquist's opinion would seek social peace by social reform, could not long stand the pressures of increasing physical danger and would in time concede that order in the sheer physical sense would have to precede reform.

This "scenario" is not to be dismissed out of hand. On the other hand, it is probably not the most likely of our five possibilities. The impediments to it lie in the pervasive ambiguities about race and American culture. "Racism" is not a sufficient explanation of American practice. If it were, we would be closer to the South African solution than we are. It is surprising that so few black people have been hurt in white areas in the present climate, and several factors are pertinent to this: If there is a profound unwillingness to change personal habits of discrimination, there is also a recognition that discrimination is "wrong" and that some forms of modification are legitimate. This helps explain some experiences that the racism hypothesis does not cover.

Item: The white upper-middle class responded very quickly, at the symbolic level, to the assassination of Dr. King. The significance lies in the desire to find common ground for black-white reconciliation, while there remains a reluctance to suffer the psychological or pragmatic pains of large-scale social adjustment. There is a vague and yet not trivial recognition of the costs of permitting a complete deterioration, and this will probably grow as the politics of racial change involves people who are skilled at counting these costs.

Item: No one has yet publicly calculated the economic cost of the 1967 uprisings. But the potential costs of future disorders would be even greater. How would the automobile industry function if it were unable to move loads of new cars easily? Since the expressways (for motor carriers) and the railroads (for flat cars) in every major metropolitan area run through the black ghettos, goods could be moved only with the protection of guards and troops.

Item: No one has yet calculated the institutional changes for effective suppressive control over black areas, which would mean rigid controls over all whites as well.

(3) A "PLURAL" SOCIETY WITH COEXISTENCE IS MOST PROBABLE

We exclude the fifth choice because we can find no grounds for imagining so broad a change of behaviors and attitudes within a short time. The first choice is possible, but not the most probable. This leaves us with some choice of a "plural" society, with the more or less indefinite continuity of two populations.

If we assume a significant increase in the machinery of coercive control but relatively small changes in the economic or cultural features of American society, then the problem of order is likely to be met by a kind of garrisoned plural society. Under present circumstances, the continued economic and educational growth of a black bourgeoisie is inevitable. If new economic policies of the sort presently being discussed (guaranteed annual incomes or black entrepreneurial development) become actual policy, that growth would probably increase somewhat, and so would the black working class (as against the so-called "underclass"). These two elements of the black population would thus continue to improve their status, but a large proportion of the very poor would remain no better off than they are now. Under such conditions, the material for much disorder would remain, but would never develop into large explosions of the sort leading to American apartheid.

The fourth possibility is an actual projection of the present state of affairs, with no significant change in either social policies or control policies. The "plural society in disguise" would continue out of the present mix of limited but increasing opportunities for the better-educated or the more skillful, and of relatively few escape holes for the relatively poor. Such a society would depend upon two important developments: the opportunities for the better-educated or the more skillful would have to seem numerous enough so that the symbolism of widening opportunity would inspire those for whom it would in fact be largely illusory. And the displays of force against the more rebellious would have to be effective enough to prove that such behavior had no significant payoffs.

The third alternative is primarily "imperial" with a modest element of the market, and the fourth primarily "market" with a modest element of empire. But neither seems likely. The dynamics of black politics permits and requires a great deal of internal conflict, but it does not permit a calculated separation of the black bourgeoisie from the black poor. Despite relative prosperity, the black bourgeoisie live a precarious life, and they are literally incapable of the explicit harshness and self-interestedness that the third and fourth options would impose. In the end they would probably opt for an uncomfortable racial alliance.

If this line of reasoning is correct, then the most probable alternative would seem to be a calculated strategy of "coexistence" or "co-determination." Such a strategy would give blacks a sense of movement strong enough to reduce the tension and disorganization of black politics and at the same time provide assurance of an ordered life for white Americans. No such patterns have been devised thus far, but one set of policy and institutional modifications may seem appropriate: a federalism based on "division of labor" would have to be abandoned, for this implies coherent national objectives concrete enough to allocate the different parts to different levels of government without reciprocal interference. The advantage of imprecise allocations of authority lies precisely in the fact that different groups will have unequal measures of influence and power at different levels. If groups are not to be frozen out altogether, they must be able to use the levels at which they operate in order to influence the levels at which they do not operate.

What institutional arrangements would provide a significant opportunity for the exercise of social power by black populations? Since capital accumulates slowly, private channels, based necessarily upon money, will develop slowly. Public channels are probably much more promising, but to gain access to public channels may require some drastic action. One possible solution is the development of new forms of statehood. Essentially, this would mean devising amendments to the formal Constitution of the United States so that those cities likely to have black administrations by 1976 could be converted into states. Such a design would have several advantages:

(a) Unlike the same territories, organized as cities, the new state governments would be able to make economic policy decisions, not just fiscal decisions. Their governments would thus have a vested interest in making decisions to entice industry into the urban locations. In light of the industrial interest in social peace, corporations would probably cooperate, except when clear economc or technological reasons forbade it.

(b) Such a series of states would provide a senatorial bloc with a high vested interest in federal expenditures in urban areas, just as Arizona senators have a vested interest in federal water investments or Washington senators in defense contracts. The usual logrolling process would operate.

(c) Given the facts of congressional life, the delegations would have every incentive to go through the usual routines of building up their own power, but this would produce far more symbolic value for black populations than any series of mayors, and the same would be true for the governors of the states. The joint roles of such governors and such members of Congress would create a far more responsive and imaginative attention to racial issues than any federal departments or regulatory agencies now provide.

(d) This scheme would eliminate the inevitable confrontations between suburban legislative delegations (almost exclusively representing white constituencies) and central city delegations over the resources of the existing states.

(e) Since the city-states would to some degree be dependent on federal channels for certain revenues, black politicians would be forced not merely to articulate the feelings and grievances of their constituencies but to carry out responsible governmental programs to serve them.

As for black participation in the national bureaucracy, it must be remembered that political leadership at the center is simply overburdened. The American presidency can no longer work well with all major pressures convergent on one human being. Several vice-presidents should be added whose collective agreement would be necessary for authoritative decisions. At least one of the vice-presidents should be a black man, and the normal political processes would feed him the concerns of the black populations.

If the racial crisis is in fact as serious as we believe, then every federal agency should be obliged to consider whether its programs and activities enhance or diminish racial peace. This question should be asked as often as those about the balance of payments, the stability of the dollar, or the relative military strength of the Soviet Union and the United States.

In moving from the most complex to the least complex proposals, there is a single policy proposal that is the sine qua non for any program of racial peace: domestic disarmament. It would provide both white and black with the assurance that neither could assault the other en masse. Some such step would help to contain politics and political conflict within nonlethal channels—an essential prelude to the measures discussed above.

Such political, organizational, and tactical measures would open the way to social policies designed step-by-step to enhance the creation of a communal order, so that by the year 2000 our grimmer fantasies will not only seem improbable, but will turn out to have been decisively wrong.

NOTES

1. The customary statement of government's legitimate monopoly on "violence" (instead of only "killing") is obviously wrong. Kenneth Waltz has pointed out, for instance, that the customary formulation would preclude parental whipping of children.

2. Study of nineteenth-century urban history makes it clear that twentieth-century urban Americans are generally more secure than their predecessors were.

3. See Matthew Holden, Jr., "Politics, Public Order, and Pluralism," in *The Allocation of Justice,* ed. James R. Klonoski and Robert I. Mendelsohn (Boston: Little, Brown & Co., forthcoming).

4. William Brink and Louis Harris, *Black and White* (New York: Simon and Schuster, 1966).

5. This last point raises more than the mere technicalities of processing amendments through Congress, into state legislatures, and the like. For example, how legitimate or illegitimate shall a Poor People's March and a Resurrection City be?

6. Matthew Holden, Jr., *The Republican Crisis* (San Francisco: Chandler, 1969), particularly Chapter 2.

7. See Pieter Geyl, *History of the Low Countries* (New York: Macmillan, 1964), Chapter 1, particularly pp. 15–16.

8. See Leon F. Litwack, *North of Slavery* (Chicago: University of Chicago Press, 1965).

9. He would also learn of that black man's humiliations, including the inability to get what every senior executive needs, a secretary, until one girl volunteered out of her sense of Christian duty. E. Frederic Morrow, *Black Man in the White House* (New York: Macfadden Books, 1963), pp. 11–13.

10. Harvey S. Perloff, in "Adapting Our Political Philosophy to the Needs of 2000 A.D.," suggests the following criteria: (a) a philosophical "base" emphasizing legal rights, "full" opportunity, and increased scope for individual and group freedom; (b) a sophisticated interweave of public and private organizations in decision making; and (c) a "new" federalism based upon a governmental "division of labor."

11. Karl W. Deutsch *et al., Political Community for the North Atlantic Area* (Princeton: Princeton University Press, 1957).

12. In some respects, black politics is similar to the politics of the Goldwater purists (as against the "regular" Republicans) in 1964.

13. Murray Edelman, *The Symbolic Uses of Politics* (Urbana: University of Illinois Press, 1964).

14. Stokely Carmichael and Charles V. Hamilton, *Black Power* (New York: Random House, 1967).

15. William Brink and Louis Harris, *Black and White, op. cit.*, Appendix D.

16. However, the rhetoric of black-and-white politics should not lead us into confusing the two issues.

17. This is discussed in my forthcoming book, *The Republic in Crisis*, particularly Chapter 5.

18. The social-indicators "movement" is a symptom of what I mean here.

19. This is perhaps the most significant and historically the most accurate use of "racism" in the Kerner Report: the historical insistence on white supremacy, which has created the existent structure.

20. Please note that this does not take account of illegal purchases of firearms or purchases of rifles and heavier weapons for which no legal requirements exist. This information was supplied in confidence by the office of the mayor of that city. The information may be made available to legitimately interested scholars by special arrangement with the author of this essay.

21. James L. Sundquist, "Politics in the Year 2000," in this volume.

22. *Ibid.*

23. Some of the material is developed in detail in my book *Ethnicity in the Urban Political Order* (in preparation).

24. See Walter Lippmann in *Newsweek*, August 19, 1968.

RETAINING ALIENATED MINORITIES IN THE POLITICAL MAINSTREAM

John G. Wofford

The following is divided into three sections:

A "working paper," essentially unchanged, presented to a meeting of the Working Group on United States Government on May 17, 1968; edited excerpts from the discussion that followed the presentation of the paper; and a few concluding thoughts. This format is, I think, more useful than a formal exposition of various points of view.

I

The American two-party system has endured a long time. Will it endure into the year 2000? And will it accommodate itself to the needs of four minorities—blacks, upper-middle-class youth, lower-middle-class whites, the anti-Communist right—now largely alienated from the system?

Traditional analysis credits at least three factors for the enduring character of the two-party system: first, the initial yes-or-no clarity of issues, such as revolution and the Constitution; second, an electoral arrangement that encourages coalitions designed to achieve a majority (a single chief executive and single-member congressional districts); and third, a popular consensus on fundamental political premises that always places each major party near the center mark.[1]

Let us assume that the historical tradition and electoral system remain the same. The issue, then, is whether the widespread consensus about the proper bounds of the political game is disintegrating in a way that threatens the two-party system as we now know it —a loose coalition of state and local organizations and alliances that come together every four years to try to elect a President, but with each coalition representing a spectrum of political views.

Sundquist has brilliantly depicted several alternative scenarios for the two parties. Let me, for the moment, reverse the process and try to sketch some scenarios from the point of view of the particular minorities with which we are concerned here.

There are at least four ways in which such minorities can influence the two-party system:

First, the minority can simply fall into the system as we know it.

Second, it can be influential in effecting a major realignment of the two parties.

Third, it can form a third party, probably in concert with other minorities. V. O. Key tells us the circumstances that are likely to produce a third party: [2]

> The occurrence of great episodes of third-party activity depends on *the rise of movements or bursts of sentiment which cannot work themselves out through a major party*. Whether the day of the third party is done depends on whether such circumstances will again develop.

And fourth, it can remain outside the party structure completely, either as an activist revolutionary movement seeking radically to end the existing order; or as a passive and depressed spectator of a political game considered irrelevant but not subject to change either from within or without.

I should point out that when I speak of "retaining" alienated minorities within the two-party system, I do not necessarily imply that the group as a whole must be wildly active. The vast bulk of our population is not politically activist, doing little more than coming out to vote in elections. Approximately three-fourths of every age group in a recent Gallup poll said they were interested in politics either "a fair amount" or "only a little." [3] Not more than 5 to 10 percent of the electorate can be considered politically active, and a much, much smaller percentage influences the inner workings of any local party apparatus. Thus I assume that to "retain" minorities within the two-party system does not necessarily mean large-scale active participation, but, rather, at least passive acquiescence. The norm is acquiescence, not participation; those who participate—and they are important—are leaders.

Here are a few thoughts on each of the minorities.

1. BLACKS

It is hard to estimate how large a segment of the black community is presently alienated or will become alienated from the two-party system. Among the leaders, the "old-timers" (Whitney Young, Roy Wilkins, A. Philip Randolph, Bayard Rustin, and so on) are for the most part uncommitted to either major party or capable of maintaining an independent bargaining position with the ultimate threat of supporting a presidential candidate from the other party. Each of these men has his own independent power base from which he maneuvers and bargains.

Black mayors, such as those in Washington, D.C., Cleveland, Ohio, and Gary, Indiana, based as they are on a particular, local constituency, can be expected to take a less independent stance. All of them happen to be Democrats, and they can be expected to support the Democratic presidential candidate in virtually every case except the extreme (Wallace or Maddox). Like John Lindsay and Charles Percy on the Republican side, these men are ambitious not only locally but nationally, and their ambitions are most likely to keep them within a major party, even if the party is not wholly receptive to their particular needs or views. National ambition is a powerful force in maintaining the two-party system—so long as the party ranks remain open to local winners. With strong local bases of power, local officials—including many black mayors of central cities—are likely to have strong bargaining positions within the party apparatus.

What of the new "militants," like Dick Gregory, Stokely Carmichael, Rap Brown, Eldridge Cleaver, and others? Their future is not easy to predict. First, it is not clear what their constituency is. To the extent that they represent a call to revolution, their following is probably quite small. Most blacks are as concerned as whites about a decline in public order.[4] Recent studies indicate that about one quarter of the blacks have reached a middle-class income level, and most of the others probably want to move into the middle class. A Boston survey of black attitudes indicates that most would like to live in integrated housing.[5] Of course, once riots or revolutions are under way, they may attract unexpected support, but we should not assume that the "underclass" will automatically follow the advocates of separatist revolution.

By "separatist revolution," I do not mean to assume that the objectives of the new militants are clear. Indeed, their objectives are even less clear-cut than their constituency. In *Black Power,* Carmichael and Hamilton declare that the old political order must be swept aside, but its successor is left ambiguous.

Revolutionary rhetoric is full of ambiguous objectives, but ambiguity in the American racial context is understandable. Central city blacks have the power to create chaos, but it is hard to picture a truly separatist future beyond that. Even if ten or fifteen central cities become largely black, they will be dealing with white society at almost every turn—metropolitan areas, state legislatures, Congress. Black enclaves will have to negotiate and accommodate and bargain just as cities do now.

Other futures are possible for the black community. One, not altogether improbable, is to be ruthlessly repressed in a backlash in which American ghettos will compare with Warsaw in death and destruction. This may be what some of the militants hope to precipitate, although it is enormously risky.

Two other futures are possible: gradual and effective integration into suburban society, or gradual dispersal into the suburbs without effective integration. In the latter case, mini-ghettos would develop in suburbs as far as twenty to thirty miles from the central city, with unchanging poverty, greater isolation, and less political power to effect change.

Despite the militants' vagueness, their rhetoric has already had an enormous impact upon the American political process. "Blacks," "black power," "community control," "white racism" are now accepted phrases. But paradoxically, as the rhetoric of the militants becomes more widely accepted, it has deprived them of one of their special strengths—a language with peculiar persuasiveness in the ghetto. The language of militancy is now used by nonmilitants for much more pragmatic evolutionary ends.

Thus "community control" and cries for more black teachers, cops, and businesses are not only no longer shocking, but are in fact viewed by many moderates as one of the great hopes for the ghetto. If ghetto residents can be given substantial control over their environment, they are more likely to act responsibly and with a feeling of having a stake in American society. Even more important will be the ghetto leaders who will emerge in a process of increasing community control. They will be forced into the game of politics as they jostle with teachers' associations and legislatures and boards of education and mayors and city councils. Indeed, ghetto leaders will be increasingly elected as councilmen and mayors. Nothing could be better for the health of the American body politic in general, and for the two-party system in particular.

The risk, of course, is that these new leaders will lose contact with the communities that produced and selected them. But if their power base remains the ghetto, they will be forced to keep in touch. It is difficult but not impossible.

The challenge of ghetto leadership points to the larger challenge the ghetto poses for the two-party system. Even if this system does rise to that challenge, we still have a large alienated underclass living in misery and with a great potential for disruption of life in our cities and in the larger body politic.

My prediction, admittedly optimistic, is that out of this misery and disruption the black community will move into the mainstream of American political, economic, and social life. In the process, our two major parties will open their ranks to accept new leadership coming up from the ghettos.

2. UPPER-MIDDLE-CLASS YOUTH

A portion of college and postcollege youth, most of them from the upper-middle class, makes a point of being alienated from the moral, social, sexual, and political traditions of middle-class America. And the two-party system is included in their scorn.

What are their charges against American society? Chiefly the hypocrisy they find in the society around them. They are preached at about their own sexual behavior, but feel that adults are more promiscuous without admitting it. In the palliatives thrown to the poor, they see little to justify the grandiose rhetoric about a war against poverty. They believed the rhetoric of the 1964 presidential campaign—for many, it was an introduction to political awareness—but felt stunned and cheated when the candidate of peace escalated the Vietnam war.

As in the case of the black militants, it is hard to estimate the constituency of the student radicals, since the radical rhetoric (antiwar, in this case) has been taken over by the moderates. On the Columbia University campus during the crisis in 1968, there were far more people outside Low Library than the radicals inside; not until the police attacked the onlookers did the radicals gain majority support. But the supporters were not all of one mind. A politically radical position, I suspect, has only a small constituency.

This is not to suggest that students are not responding to the cry for "participation" in university affairs. Demonstrations are breaking out on many campuses even though most students are not prepared to try the techniques of disruption advocated by the radicals, many of whom are rightly perceived by the moderates as aiming more at anarchistic destruction than at reform and rebuilding. But disruptions aside, there is a widespread student desire to participate in the governance of the university—on curriculum committees, on faculty appointment committees, on disciplinary committees. As one professor at a major law school has said, students on these committees probably would not be particularly helpful and they would not be particularly harmful, but the students themselves are likely to get a great educational experience.

As in the black-power movement, where the desire for community control is a healthy development, so in the student movement the desire to participate actively in university decisions is healthy: it appeals to some of our basic American ideological traditions—from the town meeting to representative democracy—and it suggests a deep faith on the part of some students that, even if the rest of society is hopeless, the university still has a potential for morality and vitality.

With the right leadership, this concern with participation in the university processes can be transformed into a concern with participation in the political process. There were signs of such a transformation in the Eugene McCarthy campaign, as *The New York Times* noted on March 14, 1968:

> Eugene McCarthy has done vastly more than mobilize an army of young Americans for doorbell ringing and envelope stuffing. He has demonstrated to the men who wield political power in America and to some who would like to wield it that it is still possible to close the generation gap and to counter the alienation of America's young people from the American system.

Some of this commitment is already being transferred from the national to the local level. In Minnesota, for instance, students engineered what the press described as "a major upheaval" in the Democratic-Farmer-Labor Party (D-F-L) in taking substantial control of the party apparatus in Minneapolis and its suburbs. As one of the leaders of the upheaval, a twenty-five-year-old law student said; "We now take our rightful place in this party. The youth of Minnesota have taken over the machinery. They have beaten the system . . . we are going to remake the D-F-L." [6] This suggests that students are willing to undertake the kind of sustained organizational effort at the local level that is needed in order to have an impact on state and national party candidates and positions.

With an end to the Vietnam war, government and politics will be viewed with less hostility. Most students will probably end up joining the ranks of "the establishment" and in the process will refresh, reinvigorate, and to some extent redirect it toward a realistic concern with the problems of race and poverty. Some disenchantment with politics will occur from time to time, but I think commitment will win out over disillusionment. The qualities of leadership, power, ambition, and responsibility do exist in the present student population—and our two parties are likely to benefit greatly from them.

3. LOWER-MIDDLE-CLASS WHITES

I am less sanguine about the prospects for retaining lower-middle-class whites within the two-party system. The appeal of a George Wallace or a Lester Maddox is great among large segments of this group, for interesting reasons.

Wallace and Maddox are part of the populist antigovernment tradition. Maddox, we are told, likes nothing better than dealing with complaints of individual citizens against the government—and he does not think of himself as responsible for his own executive agencies' actions. The people who support him are equally alienated from government, particularly from the liberal-conservative consensus that believes the government should solve the social problems of the time.

Policemen and taxi drivers, civil servants and labor-union members, these people, for the most part, want to be left alone—and as far from blacks as possible. Although Wallace has failed to build his third-party apparatus on a firm foundation, under the leadership of someone competent at party organization the movement could, in the long run, pose a real threat to the two-party system.

What is more likely, however, is that both major parties will attempt to state their policies in a way that can appeal to these alienated voters. How they can do that and at the same time appeal to blacks and students is a major dilemma for both parties.

4. THE ANTI-COMMUNIST RIGHT

The anti-Communist right came into its own when Barry Goldwater was nominated in 1964. Through meticulous attention to the details of state nominating procedures, the anti-Communist rightists had enough votes to win by the time the convention took place. They are likely to bide their time during the Nixon regime and await the opportunities of 1972 or 1976.

In short, they seem prepared to work within the existing party structure. They are for the most part people who have arrived—solid middle or upper-middle class. They have an economic stake in the status quo and are not likely to be revolutionary unless the consensus moves substantially left, leaving the right threatened and isolated. I do not think this will happen. Instead, the anti-Communist right will set its sights on right-wing candidates handsome enough and popular enough to pull votes from the center.

There is yet another part to the anti-Communist right—the lunatic fringe, concerned more with personal and national purity than with personal or national power. The people of this fringe vote against fluoridation [7] and oppose contacts with foreign countries. My guess is that they are more likely to take their toll locally—in opposing school-bond issues and open housing—than nationally, and that they have been seriously eclipsed in the right-wing movement by the big operators, who do want to play the power game and are willing to sacrifice some personal purity in the process.

How radical the anti-Communist right might become in the event of more Vietnams (and more negotiated settlements that end in a stalemate) is one of the important unknowns. Whether a new Joseph McCarthyism would arise or whether America in the future will adjust rationally and constructively to a more limited role in world affairs are important questions.

CONCLUSION

My essential prognosis is that because the leaders in these four groups are ambitious, and the two parties are flexible enough in structure to absorb these ambitions, the two parties will remain basically as we know them. There undoubtedly will be challenges from third and even fourth parties, but the two major parties will be numerically and strategically strong enough to retain most political power, at least at the state and national levels.

This prediction about the future of the two-party system is optimistic—not because I am so sure I am right, but because perhaps by overstating the positive, we can highlight some of the negative factors omitted from the above discussion.

II

At Harvey Perloff's suggestion, most of the discussion of this essay has centered on why the four minority groups were alienated from the political process in the first place. "If we could understand what causes this kind of trouble," Perloff said, "we might be able to think of ways of avoiding it in the future."

Some basic causes for alienation from the two-party system were suggested:

1. Discontent—psychological and social—with the rate of change, some groups finding it too fast, other not fast enough.

2. Anger at being poor at a time when expectations of economic position have risen—the "revolution of rising expectations" so familiar in underdeveloped countries.

3. Anxiety about the absence of "ideology," of a clear set of political and social objectives based on a sound philosophical explanation of the world and man's place in it.

4. Frustration because society is not living up to its ideals and its potential; and impatience at the lag between thought and action in rational solutions to social problems.

5. A decreasing sense of national purpose, combined with an increased sense of the importance of the purposes and problems of one's own subgroup, often defined through one's relation to a particular bureaucracy, whether it be corporate (the "corporation-

man" mentality) or governmental (the teachers, the postal workers, and so on).

Excerpts from the discussion follow (Participants: James David Barber, Lester R. Brown, John Dixon, George C. Lodge, Harold Orlans, Harvey S. Perloff, John Voss, John G. Wofford):

BARBER: Historically, Wofford's optimism is sound, and that is what makes it so difficult for those of us who want to be apocalyptic and say the world is going to hell. In the past so many apparently alienated groups have somehow been included in the party system. One of the most intriguing things in the paper, it seems to me, is how small the alienated segments of these groups are, and yet how much attention the society pays to them. Maybe it is because they are setting new expectations about rates of change, what one has a right to expect and demand from his social environment.

PERLOFF: The feeling about rates of change seems to be critically important. There have been some excellent articles recently on the kinds of people who make up the extreme right, for example. These people are quite troubled by the rapid rate of social change. And it may increase in the future. Thus, more and more people may be pushed into this category unless something is done about minimizing the sense of fear and threat. Probably a good bit can be done through the educational system and the political system to help people cope more effectively with rapid change.

BARBER: Other groups are reacting to a different estimate of what the rate of change ought to be. Some blacks, for example, think the rate of change should be faster. But the totally alienated section of the group is small. It is an intriguing long-range, historical, and sociological problem to explain why we worry about Stokely Carmichael, whose following, Whitney Young says, is Carmichael himself and twenty others.

ORLANS: Politically he certainly represents an insignificant minority, but emotionally he is speaking for the majority. His complaint that the Negroes are not being treated with dignity is, of course, shared by the entire Negro community, and that is his constituency. The others are not going to go out on the street as Carmichael does, but they will not object to what he says, to the emotional content, to his standing for black dignity.

WOFFORD: Yes, it is essentially his description of their situation that appeals to them. He states it well. But the options from that are ambivalent. The people who respond to that description do not necessarily want a separatist society as a solution to their problem.

BARBER: If you are thinking about these groups as possibly being incorporated into one party or the other—and we should remember that other interest groups with diverse, sometimes extreme and often vague goals have been incorporated in the past—then the question of the nature of the constituency, whether emotional or programmatic, is not so important; it is a matter of who is going to show up at the national convention and vote for the platform and the candidates.

ORLANS: I think your conception of our political system is too narrow. We may well have, beyond the two parties, a politics of pointless emotional violence that is not rational. It is part of the American social and political structure—we are a violent nation. Why should we not expect to have that kind of continuing exhibition in the political arena that cannot be dealt with rationally? It is one of the trends of the century, the pointless protest, like the Nazis', of bringing down the building on top of them.

WOFFORD: Where does that lead you?

ORLANS: Gangsterism, looting, burning, unorganized forays. I think it highly unlikely that we would ever have successful guerrilla warfare leading to a revolution, as some Black Power people imagine. But even if it is going to fail, it can still contain you and occupy your attention. It may be simply an undercurrent in our political life, though an annoying one. We have had enough signs of this in the past; it is easy to project this sort of thing continuing at least at the level we now have. It breaks out, let us say, in a five-year period in the cities, then for five years on campus, then another five years when the garbage men and police go on strike. By the way, I do not think we have enough minorities. One reason the students feel they have the license to behave as they do is that a lot of other interest groups are also indulging themselves.

VOSS: I have a little difficulty with the concept of "alienation," which is a new kind of concept. We did not talk of "alienation" in the 1930's when we had similar kinds of social trouble. We put it in a rather different context. I think that what we mean by "alienation" is the protests of people who are often inarticulate or unclear about their antagonism toward the system, which is rational and orderly and well-planned according to the needs of the people who run the system. I would suggest that we are talking beyond the present—not about a number of identifiable alienated minorities, but probably about the protests of a rather wide range of subgroups in American society against the orderly planning and rational control that will increasingly dominate our technological society. If one were to take a different cut at the so-called mainstream of American society, there actually is less cohesion in values, greater opportunity for diversity of thought and life style and minority opinion. The more of these we have, the more opportunities there are for people to set themselves against what they consider "the system," or rational planning, or orderly exercises of power. Beyond our present difficulties we may see a lot more fragmentation, a lot more of this often pointless protest. The last thing in the world that the Columbia University protesters wanted was to run Columbia. The curious thing about the goals of many of the people now representing alienated minorities is that they have no very clear idea what they would do with society if they were in control of it. This contrasts sharply with protesters in the 1930's, who had a kind of political ideology; they knew precisely what they would do and how they would do it.

What we are going through now can point toward many different kinds of trouble to come, perhaps less dramatic, less well-organized, less cohesive, but with broad-ranging effects on our society. I can see, for example, instead of one cohesive black minority in our society, many different black minorities, white minorities, semi-integrated minorities—all of them unable to communicate with what used to be the mainstream of American society. In other words, I am suggesting an increase at one level of social anomie, although you can turn the thing around and say this is an increase in diversity, in pluralism, in opportunities for social experimentation.

WOFFORD: I would never describe the mainstream of American political life as rationally planned and ordered, or even as committed to rational planning. I do not think that alienation of the kind we have been talking about can be explained as a reaction against rational planning.

VOSS: What I am suggesting is that in an increasingly technological society you require more forms of rational management and control, and there is a major source of conflict between the interest of the subgroup and the interest of the whole community. There is probably no rational way of deciding these conflicts, and this will lead to kinds of protests in which the issues cannot be clearly articulated.

LODGE: Could I try another approach? I am thinking about the conflict between what is fundamentally pragmatic and what is ideological. American politics, perhaps more than any other political system in the world, has been strong and viable because of its pragmatism and the consensus nature of the two parties and the ingenious way it has responded to crises and so on. But while this has been true, increasingly I sense anxiety about the purposes of the system and the purposes of the community. In other words, I feel a sense of anxiety about the absence of ideology, of vision. The need for ideology is probably anti-American. But, for example, in considering the Goldwater movement and why he got as far as he did, I think he quenched an ideological thirst, however misguided; he provided a doctrine. A good deal of the student unrest is explained in the same way. While students profess suspicion of ideology and commitment to pragmatism, what I think really gnaws at them is a question of purpose, of vision: by what criteria do we judge a successful community, or a good community? This is exacerbated by the failure of religion to offer new answers, and particularly by the failure of American religion. That is to say, if you look at Catholicism in Europe or Latin America, it provides much more food for thought about what the community ought to be than does American religion, because of the separation of the church and state and our peculiar sensitivities on this score. The spiritual and political worlds have lost the ability to order the material world, to provide meaning and purpose for technological achievement. It is dangerous if the political world cannot order the technical world. I would say, for example, that one of the principal reasons Kennedy beat Nixon was that Kennedy seemed to have an awareness of ideological need. He was the least ideological of people, but he gave that impression. Someone said recently that Eugene McCarthy is the American version of a Christian Democrat. Think of the support he got by giving the impression that he had a vision. What this means in terms of Republicans and Democrats I do not know, but I do think that

Johnson's fall from grace was due more to his pragmatism and lack of sensitivity to this ideological problem than it was to the Vietnam war.

BARBER: Ideology is profoundly important. Take upper-middle-class youth, which in the future will make demands on the political system in a different way than we have had before. Eisenhower assessed political change by stating that we made more cars this year than last. Kennedy tried to impose a different standard for society; namely, the performance of the system in relation to its resources, considered in the light of its needs. With millions of college-educated people produced at increasing rates, there will be a strong thrust toward intellectualization of politics, and intellectuals tend to demand ideology and immediate performance. Pragmatism is anathema to a certain kind of intellectual development, and most intellectuals think of Congress as the house of pragmatism. If that kind of social expectation is applied to a system that has, historically, performed very well indeed on a pragmatic basis, what will be the outcome, particularly for the political system?

WOFFORD: Why do you project that demand for ideology from our supposedly pragmatic educational system? Demand for immediate performance is one thing, but demand for ideology is quite another.

BARBER: Projecting into the year 2000, when everybody will have a Ph.D., I do not think our higher education system will have a pragmatic thrust. On the contrary, it will demand rationality and to some extent ideology.

ORLANS: Most congressmen are college-educated. In this regard, Barber has left something out of the consequences of higher education.

VOSS: But our education has still another kind of goal. The ideology that students are seeking today does not involve a theory of history in which certain objective goals are realized at the end of a given period of time. The students' goals have to do with autonomy, self-realization, participation. When we apply this in terms of doctrines of management and organizing firms effectively, we see that this has a pervasive influence in our society and creates some tensions and problems of semi-alienation or isolation that we will have to deal with politically in the year 2000.

LODGE: I disagree with that, along the lines of what Barber was saying. The students today, even more than those of five years ago, are heavily preoccupied with the kind of community we are trying to make, rather than with individual fulfillment. The old criteria for success are no longer clear or accepted, and the student wants political leadership with vision. I think that a future third party will be an ideological party, dedicated to aims much like those of Latin American Christian Democracy.

VOSS: The student concerned about what kind of society we live in is concerned about intangible things that can be measured only by personal values such as participation, individual autonomy, the capacity for self-realization, opportunities for education. And these are goals of process rather than of programmatic objectives.

ORLANS: I think the social scientist, the gifted one, is going to provide this ideology of the future. He provides it now. Of all the men in public life today, the one who has spoken most convincingly and forcefully about our problems is John Gardner, and he has some background in the social sciences. This ideology will not be analytic; it will have a religious component, an element of faith.

BARBER: The implication of this is a rising level of expectation within the political order and new demands on the political order to be ideological, to perform, to produce. Can the parties of inclusiveness that Wofford describes satisfy those needs?

BROWN: I wonder who will be the minority groups in five, ten, thirty years. Those we now have are rather clearly defined, and one can think of all kinds of possibilities. But in terms of the system, what matters is how many there may be and whether the number of alienated groups is increasing. If rapid technological change does not mesh with the political world, I can envisage a situation in which the number of minority groups just keeps increasing until we turn into a society of minority groups—teachers, postal workers, Negroes, and so forth. What impact will this have on the structure of the society, the political system, and the problems of government at various levels?

WOFFORD: Why do you think that is not what we have had in the past?

BROWN: I think it may be an accurate description of what has been happening. It seems to me that the number of minority groups eager to express themselves as minority groups seems to be increasing. If that is the case, and if it continues, then what does this imply for our society and our political system?

VOSS: But look at America a hundred years ago, at the kinds of conformity, the uniformity of values, and the sense of people belonging to certain class groups and structures that were rather pervasive throughout the country. We have witnessed the gradual decline of this uniformity and sense of general values. It seems to me that if you project a trend from a hundred years ago to thirty years in the future, you see a rising amount of autonomy, of isolation, of separation of groups, and the emergence of many more subcultures, with opportunities to pursue their own goals to some extent in isolation from one another. This has two parts; on the positive side there is greater autonomy and pluralism, and on the negative side much more destructiveness to certain existing and traditional kinds of social order. The question is whether this can be merged into our traditional two-party system, and how.

WOFFORD: How do the intense feelings of immigrant groups between the Civil War and World War I fit into that historical analysis?

VOSS: They wanted to be part of the society and to achieve some kind of traditional American identity in a typical middle-class sense. One can see this coming to a peak in the 1930's and 1940's, and then a gradual decline. I think there are many indicators of a growing autonomy, of distinct groups. One can see a decline in the circulation and influence of mass magazines like *Life* and *Look*. And the television networks are looking for new kinds of technological means to adapt TV programs to isolated audiences.

BARBER: Do you find that encouraging?

VOSS: To the extent that it emphasizes the values of autonomy and individual self-realization, of process rather than of end, I find this very encouraging. But it is also unsettling because it pulls away the protection of many different kinds of authority, and particularly the protection of ideological authority.

BARBER: But our problem here is the political party mechanism. Suppose you have all these groups developing this way, and each of them discovers the strike mechanism—teachers, students at Columbia, Negroes on the Mall—one after another?

VOSS: As automation makes opportunities for decentralized control, for pulling things away from the center, effective political power may not rest as much in Washington and in the major debates of political parties as it does in the semipolitical sectors of American society. There may be a decentralization of many effective kinds of decision making away from Washington, thus changing the role of the political parties. Although there may be much more centralization of some kinds of decision making in Washington, there will be a new balance between decentralization and centralization that will change the role of the political parties.

WOFFORD: Right now the two-party system is not working at the local level in the big cities, but I do not think this has always been true. A Lindsay on a fusion ticket, and a Hatcher who has to buck the party structure, and a Kevin White coming up through a multigroup system, do support what you were saying. On the other hand, on the national level we are always going to elect a President.

LODGE: If pluralistic self-fulfillment continues, then the two-party structure is made for that kind of setup, in which ideologies are not terribly important. But I do not think it will continue. Look, for example, at all the talk about cooperative forms of both economic and political structures. The real threat to the parties is their pragmatism, their nonideological character.

WOFFORD: As I understand it, by "ideology" you do not mean a program, you mean a sense of purpose.

LODGE: It is useful to remember the Italian Socialists' definition of ideology—a dynamic vision of the problems of a community in its being and its becoming.

PERLOFF: Is that not basically European? If we assume that the young people today are not reaching for ideology—and I feel they are not—we can see them as functioning in an established American tradition. They are pragmatic, and what they want is a minimum level of national decency. The feelings and sources of trouble today are basically similar to those of the 1930's, when young people were saying unemployment is wrong, the system is evil. That does not mean that then or now they were reaching for any special kind of ideology.

VOSS: But they are reaching for a sense of participation in the community of their fellow students or fellow citizens.

PERLOFF: But this minimum sense of rightness is hundreds of years old and basic to politics, basic to everything. At certain points people just get angry. The younger ones are more idealistic and not as ready to accept existing conditions. If this is the case, then we should not expect any strange unlikely developments in reaching out for ideology.

LODGE: But I think it goes way beyond Vietnam and poor people, into a fundamental suspicion of the purposes of the United States in the world, of the Agency for International Development (AID), of the military, and the like.

ORLANS: Do you not find it odd that you are searching for ideology here, yet all along you have said that the strength of the American political system, of American society, has been its practicalness, its not being ideological? You are raising a fundamental question.

LODGE: Our greatest strength has become our greatest weakness in the minds of thinking young people.

DIXON: We keep moving between the mechanics of the governing process and its purposes, but I am not sure they can be separated. There has to be some informing value system even higher than participation: in thinking of government, the concept of justice, for example, is central.

PERLOFF: Is the belief in democracy an ideology?

DIXON: There is no end of ideology. It is ideology or its manifestations that have hit Columbia and Harvard.

LODGE: Rather, the frustrating search for an ideology.

VOSS: Exactly. This is Perloff's student reaching out for a kind of moral community of shared values, but it is not an ideology. An ideology, I think, is an attempt to define certain kinds of political or social pressures in terms of some universal standards of value, often involving a philosophy of history, a theory of how a particular problem is related to the entire structure of the universe. Ideology attempts to be universal, although often such a claim is a rationalization of the interests of some special group or the explanation of a specific kind of problem. In that sense, Goldwaterism was an ideology because it was an articulated set of ideas. An ideology is a secular substitute for religion, but merely aspiring to ideas is not an ideology.

PERLOFF: Our young people do not want ideology in this sense.

They are disturbed by the breakdown of what they were told is "The American Way," but they do not have an articulated set of ideas for the future.

DIXON: Let us forget about ideology and instead say "moral values." The concept of governing is based on ideas of justice. According to Isaiah, where there is justice, there is order; where there is injustice, there is disorder. Let us call it a search for moral relevance. Governments, clothing, and institutions change, but the informing hopes and aspirations last through time.

PERLOFF: This is exactly what I think is involved here. You do not have order if you do not have a sense of justice. The students today are seeking not ideology but a sense of justice.

WOFFORD: Or decency.

BARBER: One thing we can predict about the year 2000 is that many more people are going to be much more highly educated. Justice is an idea, ideas are the province of the university, and universities are the province of the educated. In a bourgeois society, unlike a peasant society, justice is an important idea. If it comes about too slowly, serious tension will arise in the political order. People in the future will not accept halfway measures. It may not be a more civilized age, but it will be more ideological and impatient.

ORLANS: Not necessarily. Justice might simply become a topic for conversation. Take this working group: we are involved in a kind of group therapy. What makes us function is what makes A.T.&T. function—talk. There is absolutely no limit to the capacity of people to talk. But it does not follow that ideas can so readily be carried out.

PERLOFF: And this, of course, is where the political parties come into play.

III

The discussion, I think, supports my forecast that the two-party system can remain strong enough to survive into the twenty-first century. None of the basic causes for political alienation must necessarily result in a fundamental splintering of the party structures—if both parties keep themselves open to new minorities as they appear.

Just because one group is dissatisfied with the rate of change does not mean that the two major parties are indifferent. For those who feel change has been too rapid, the Republican Party provides a conserving attitude and tends to bring along those groups whose values lag behind the changes that have occurred. An Eisenhower is important every generation or so, because he can render past social change acceptable. And for those who find the rate of change too slow, the Democratic Party offers a more activist response to problems and issues. If the two parties continue in their traditional patterns, most blacks and students might find their way into the Democratic fold; and parts of the lower-middle-class whites and the anti-Communist right into the Republican.

Similarly, for those who are impatient with the lag between thinking about and solving social problems, the two existing parties offer as much as any party can. Most social problems do not have simple solutions, and complexity tends to lead more to evolution than to revolution. As people and movements grow older, they become more patient. Both Democrats and Republicans must demonstrate that the American party structure is capable of moving effectively where problems have been identified and reasonable solutions proposed. Both parties have faced this challenge in the past, and there is no reason why they cannot do so in the future.

Those seeking an "ideology" can find it within our two-party system, for at its root is a set of beliefs and assumptions about man, the universe, and the proper role of government. When individualism is linked to "decency" and "justice," we have a viable basis for a community, with limits on individual self-interest but with limits, also, on the powers of government and, indeed, on the powers of parties. None of this is far from what the "new left" is seeking. Perhaps I am wrong, but to the extent that both major parties accept and reflect this basic ideology, there is nothing missing that an effective party conscience cannot provide. Vision is needed, not a new "ism."

The economically disadvantaged will be more likely to fold into the two-party system if they share in society's affluence. Sharing in affluence means that in an affluent society there is an "acceptable minimum" below which society simply will not permit people to fall. But such a principle will be difficult to apply to particular cases because in an increasingly affluent society the acceptable minimum will continually be rising. We can expect constant friction and irritation, because widespread affluence will not make all groups automatically content. The parties can survive this friction by pushing hard for economic advancement and by making sure that the society remains open to individual upward mobility. Serious danger will arise only if a group, as a group, feels stuck at the bottom.

In a pluralistic society, the existence of groups whose members believe their own values are more important than so-called "national" values is not a new phenomenon. National purpose is not constant for most people, but it emerges mainly during periods of war or other national crises. A balance between interests of subgroups and those of the nation is not a new challenge to our two parties; it has existed since the early days of the Republic.

If the two parties maintain a sense of vision about the future, the party system as we have known it will survive. This will depend, of course, upon individuals in each party—but leadership of the kind has always been essential to party, and national, survival.

NOTES

1. See V. O. Key, Jr., *Politics, Parties, and Pressure Groups* (New York: Thomas Y. Crowell, 5th ed., 1964), pp. 207–210.
2. *Ibid.*, p. 281.
3. Gallup Poll, reported in *The New York Times*, April 7, 1968, p. 49.
4. James Q. Wilson, "The Urban Unease," *The Public Interest*, No. 12, Summer 1968.
5. Jeffrey Jowell, "Law and Bureaucracy in the City: Welfare Anti-Discrimination Laws, and Urban Renewal in Boston—A Study of the Limits of Legal Action." (Unpublished dissertation, Harvard University Law School, Cambridge, Mass., 1970).
6. *The Boston Globe*, March 7, 1968, p. 1.
7. See Jay Marmor, V. W. Bernard, and P. Ottenberg, "Psychodynamics of Group Opposition to Health Programs," *American Journal of Orthopsychiatry*, 330 (1960); and Richard Schmuck and Mark Chesler, "Superpatriot Opposition to Community Mental Health Programs," *Community Mental Health Journal*, 382 (1967).

POLITICS IN THE YEAR 2000

James L. Sundquist

The presidential election of 1968 took place in an atmosphere of turmoil in which many forces clearly were at work. It was a time of alienation of the black and the young from the traditional American political system. It was a time of direct action and violence, climaxed in the confrontation of Chicago. It was a time of struggle between old and new ideas, within both major parties and without. By the common consent of thoughtful men, it was a time of crisis when the capacity of the American system to cope with domestic and external challenge, or even to survive, was in question. It was a time when John W. Gardner could deliver an address entitled "How Twentieth-Century Civilization Collapsed." [1]

But history is full of crises. Sometimes civilizations do collapse, but more often they somehow survive. I remember a Senate debate some years ago that reached its climax in the ringing words of one participant: "Mr. President, this is no ordinary crisis!" What is it this time, another ordinary crisis or the real thing? Even Mr. Gardner, after describing from the perspective of the twenty-third century how men three hundred years before had "brought everything tumbling down," closed his address by admitting that he was not sure it really had happened. But then again it could.

A generation ago there was another time of crisis. Men saw in the collapse of American capitalism the end of its political and governmental system too, and bright minds were busy designing the new system that would replace the old. But they erred by projecting as irreversible trends the events of their day that proved to be only transitory. The Depression was eventually cured—by war rather than wisdom, but nonetheless cured—and when it was over the country still had the same political system. It was still a two-party democracy, with Democrats and Republicans vying peacefully at each election and alternating in the seats of power, both of them wiser for the shattering experiences of the 1930's.

Not just that decade but the whole long history of American democracy gives reassurance. Stability and resiliency have been the hallmarks of our system. American two-party politics had its beginnings in colonial days, became the dominant pattern by 1800, and has been with us in its present form for more than a century. During that time the system has survived not only the Depression but a Civil War and the dissension surrounding two world wars and several lesser conflicts. It has taken in stride vast social change—the end of slavery, the industrial revolution, the urban revolution, the rise of the labor movement, millions of immigrants, the secularization of society. Charismatic figures have arisen from time to time to attack the fundamentals of the free political system—Father Coughlin, Huey Long, Joseph McCarthy—but they have gone and have left no lasting mark. Violence and direct action have taken many forms—draft rioters, embattled farmers, Molly Maguires, sit-down strikers, massive resistance, the Ku Klux Klan. Yet through all the change and turmoil the country's political institutions have, if anything, grown stronger. Political competition is probably keener than it ever has been, genuine political participation more widespread, entry into party activity easier, elections fairer and freer, legislative bodies more representative and more competent. Only a few years ago, when the Johnson landslide set free the imprisoned legislative labor of a decade, the country reveled in how well its political system could perform.

So by the year 2000 the apocalyptic visions of today may appear as dated as those of a generation ago do now. But then again they may not. One can also err—and this kind of error may be more disastrous—by dismissing as transitory what are the beginnings of long-term, irreversible trends. If the American system is to come tumbling down, the collapse will begin with little cracks in the structure that widen into bigger ones. The question, then, is whether some of the new debilitating factors so visible in 1968—or some less visible—will by the year 2000 alter the basic characteristics of the political system.

Let us consider the future of American politics in several stages. First, assuming that the two-party system survives its current challenges, what will it look like? Here the technique of Kahn and Wiener is useful: Let us attempt a "surprise-free" projection of the two-party system as it is now evolving, followed by alternative scenarios based on the introduction of surprise factors. Then let us try to appraise the strength and permanence of those trends that now appear to be undermining the traditional political system itself.

A "Surprise-Free" Political Projection

A projection of present political trends is anything but static, for the American political system is going through a period of change that can truly be called revolutionary. By the year 2000 the realignment of parties that has been under way with gathering speed for a generation will have reached its climax, and the effects of that realignment upon our governmental institutions will be profound.

THE DEMISE OF THE "SOLID SOUTH"

The current realignment is finally erasing the regional pattern of American politics that was established by the Civil War and solidified by the McKinley-Bryan contest of 1896—the pattern of a Democratic "solid South" and an almost equally solid Republican North, with each party spanning the conservative-liberal spectrum in its region. Regional parties in a national society are basically unnatural, and they were bound to give way eventually to a pattern of national parties based upon economic interests and political principles rather than geography. But party loyalties seared into a people's consciousness by civil war do not quickly fade.

The dissolution of the Republican North can be dated from 1932, when the Depression discredited the Republican Party and gave the Democrats respectability. Within a generation after that date, two-party competition had been established on a continuing basis in every northern state. Adjusted for a lag of twenty years, the experience of the North is now being repeated in the South almost as a mirror image.

The South turned the corner toward two-party politics in 1952, when the issues of communism and corruption and the patriotic appeal of General Eisenhower made Republicans respectable. As in the North, once the ancient bonds were broken, the development of two-party competition came rapidly. Table I shows the thirteen-fold growth since 1950 of Republican representation in Congress from the eleven states of the Confederacy. In 1964, while Lyndon Johnson the southerner swept the North, five of the six states carried by Barry Goldwater were in the deepest South. In 1966 Republican governors were elected in Florida and Arkansas for the first time in history, and Republican senators in South Carolina and Tennessee for the first time since Reconstruction, and Florida followed with a Republican senator in 1968. Of the states of the once-solid South, only five—Alabama, Georgia, Louisiana, Mississippi, and Virginia—had yet to elect a Republican to statewide office. But Georgia came very close to choosing a Republican governor in 1966; and Alabama, Georgia, and Virginia have all sent Republicans to Congress from districts that were reliably Democratic a decade or two ago. Youthful southern Republican leaders of the 1960's—such men as Kirk in Florida, Baker in Tennessee, and Tower in Texas—appear as the mirror images of the dynamic Democratic generation of twenty years ago, which broke through the Republican

TABLE I

Growth in Number of Republicans Elected to the House of Representatives from the South

	1950	1952	1954	1956	1958	1960	1962	1964	1966	1968
Alabama	—	—	—	—	—	—	—	5	3	3
Arkansas	—	—	—	—	—	—	—	—	1	1
Florida	—	—	1	1	1	1	2	2	3	3
Georgia	—	—	—	—	—	—	—	1	2	2
Louisiana	—	—	—	—	—	—	—	—	—	—
Mississippi	—	—	—	—	—	—	—	1	—	—
North Carolina	—	1	1	1	1	1	2	2	3	4
South Carolina	—	—	—	—	—	—	—	—	1	1
Tennessee	2	2	2	2	2	2	3	3	4	4
Texas	—	—	1	1	1	1	2	—	2	3
Virginia	—	3	2	2	2	2	2	2	4	5
Total	2	6	7	7	7	7	11	16	23	26
Total Representatives	105	106	106	106	106	106	106	106	106	106
Percentage Republicans	2	6	7	7	7	7	10	15	22	25

hegemony and established two-party competition on a permanent basis in Illinois, Minnesota, Michigan, and other northern states. If the twenty-year lag between the regions continues to hold true, then the last southern state to elect a Republican governor will turn its statehouse over to the GOP around 1982, two decades after Vermont, the last state of the solid Republican North, succumbed to two-party politics.

By the time southern politics has been realigned on the national two-party pattern—with state Republican parties to the right of center and Democratic parties to the left—the effect on both national parties will be profound. The conservative wing of the Democratic Party, which no longer has any base at all in the North, will be declining rapidly in numbers and influence in the South as well. A few conservative Democrats will change parties, as did Strom Thurmond and Albert Watson in South Carolina, but in the main the change will be a generational one. Young southern conservatives will seek their political careers as Republicans (or as Wallaceites), while the growing number of Negro voters will, as in the North, look to the Democratic Party as their road to power. As the elder Democratic conservatives retire or are toppled, the men who take their places in positions of party leadership will be men aligned with the national Democratic Party. And that party will thus become, for the first time in modern history, a cohesive body united on a national scale by a common philosophy and program.

The effects of southern realignment upon the Republican Party are less clear, dependent upon whether the influx of southern conservatives into the national Republican Party means also an influx of die-hard segregationists who will be allowed to set the tone of the national party. Barry Goldwater in 1964 permitted that to happen; adopting the so-called "Southern strategy," he opened the party's doors to all southern conservatives, intransigents and moderates alike, and for the first time in history a Republican presidential candidate ran far stronger in the South than in the rest of the country. In 1968, Richard Nixon tempered the blatancy of Goldwater's southern strategy, but that strategy was still visible: Nixon gave the arch-segregationists a veto over his vice-presidential running mate, he promised the South that he would relax enforcement of school-desegregation guidelines, he adopted a campaign theme of "law and order" calculated to appeal to anti-Negro sentiment, and he made little effort to win the northern Negro vote. When the election returns came he had lost the big cities, and it was his southern strength that saved him.

In the early months of his administration, Nixon appeared to be trying, as Eisenhower had tried and as the Democrats had tried a generation ago, to straddle the strategic issue; and he succeeded in holding the support of both the Strom Thurmonds and the Jacob Javitses of his party. But the issues are too sharp and irrepressible to permit him to straddle long. Before he faces the electorate again, he will have made his choice. He must define the party's strategy for the long term—either the southern strategy or the alternative "big-city" strategy advocated by the northern liberal and moderate Republicans, which calls for the party to embrace unequivocally the cause of civil rights and Negro progress, and seeks to make the Republican Party the majority party by winning the adherence of Negroes and their urban allies, rather than of southern segregationists.

Nixon's entire record—both before and since his inauguration—suggests that when the time for choosing comes, his sympathies will be with the liberals and moderates of his party. But if he were guided only by the most crass political considerations, he would go in that direction anyway. If the object of a party's leader is only, in Goldwater's deathless phrase, to "go shooting where the ducks are," the ducks are no longer on southern ponds. George Wallace is in politics to stay, and he has now safely bagged the birds that Goldwater found so available and enticing six years ago.

The prospect then—in our surprise-free projection—is for the Republican Party under Nixon to abandon the southern strategy and go hunting for the northern ducks instead. (The prospects, if the party makes the other choice, are considered below under the heading "Surprises.") But the southern segregationists and their northern fellow thinkers are not going to vanish. As they are denied a home in the Republican Party upon being driven out by the Democrats, they will maintain the Wallace third party as their political instrument, and it may dominate most of the Deep South for the next couple of decades and perhaps longer, until the issues of civil rights and integration fade into history. It will make no substantial progress outside the Deep South, however, and in the rest of the country the Republican and Democratic parties will compete on reasonably equal terms, divided as at present along activist-conservative (or liberal-conservative) lines.

The significance for American government of the disappearance of the solid South can hardly be overestimated. In their gloomy tracts on "the deadlock of democracy,"[2] scholars and pundits have referred to the frustration by the Congress of the mandate given the President and his party. But the deadlock—in times when the mandate has been decisive—has been due entirely to a single cause, the existence of the solid South. It is not northern and western Democrats who frustrate Democratic presidents, but the southern legislators of Republican principles who call themselves Democrats and are therefore allowed to hold positions of power as Democrats under the congressional seniority system. Republican presidents in their turn are frustrated because the Democrats, again due to the existence of the solid South, are able to retain congressional majorities and thus organize both houses of Congress in the face of a conservative mandate from the people—as they did after the Eisenhower landslide of 1956 as well as after the narrower Nixon victory of 1968. The realignment of the party system into two cohesive and reasonably homogeneous groupings will transform the legislative process and executive legislative relations as we have known them. Deadlock between the President and the Congress will be the exception rather than the rule; they will work most of the time in a relationship of reasonable harmony that has been achieved heretofore only during fleeting intervals, like 1933–1936 and 1964–1965, and then lost again for decades.

SHIFTING ISSUES AND COALITIONS

While the "surprise-free" projection shows continuing stability of the two-party system, this is not to say that the two parties in 2000 will be composed of the same coalitions of social and economic groups, separated by the same issues, as in 1968. But the same pattern of party confrontation will prevail—a predominantly activist, or liberal, Democratic Party competing with a predominantly conservative Republican Party, as has been the pattern since the realignment of the New Deal period.

The reason for this constancy is that the primary organizing principle of the party system (apart from regionalism, discussed above) is not interest groups or particular issues as such, but *attitudes*. At any given time, one group of political participants responds to the social and economic problems of the day with proposals for governmental action. Another group then responds to the demand for action with a warning against the dangers of adverse side-effects—debt, inflation, interference with free enterprise, centralization of government, bureaucratic incompetence—and says, "Go slow." The former group has not had a fixed program deduced from ideology like those the socialist parties of Europe have presented, but a pragmatic approach like those the socialist parties are developing. For that reason, I prefer the word "activist," which suggests that the distinguishing feature is one of attitude or even temperament, rather than the word "liberal," which to some persons carries overtones of doctrinal rigidity.

Traditionally, of course, activism as an attitude has centered in the "have-not" social and economic groups, because governmental action can be a quick means to the redistribution of wealth and income. Organized labor and the less affluent farmers have sought governmental action to strengthen their position vis-à-vis employers and industry. Immigrant groups, who were "have-not" upon arrival, found their natural home in the activist party. During the Depression, it was natural that a coalition of farmers, labor, and minority groups would take form to back a program of government intervention in economic matters.

The Roosevelt coalition has been crumbling for some time, as affluence transformed "have-nots" into "haves." The typical voter in 1932 was a farmer or a blue-collar worker struggling for a livelihood. Now the farm vote is rapidly becoming negligible, and the typical voter is a relatively well-paid urban or suburban white-collar worker. By 2000, he will be a highly skilled or subprofessional worker with an income (in today's dollars) in the $12,000–$20,000 range. The Roosevelt coalition will have all but disappeared. What will happen to the Democratic Party that was based on it?

Again let us attempt the "surprise-free" projection. Looking back over the last thirty years, we see changes as dramatic in the Democratic program as in the composition of the party. In the 1930's, the party appeal was couched in terms of the class struggle—"have-nots" against "haves"—and its program was largely redistributional: price supports and cheap electricity for the farmers, the right to organize and a minimum wage for workers, jobs for the unemployed, social security for those who could not work. By the 1960's, the major elements of the Democratic program were not of this character, except for Medicare. There is a redistributional element, to be sure, in civil-rights measures and the war on poverty and programs for urban housing, but if the Democratic Party had to rely for its support upon a coalition of the beneficiaries of these programs, it would get nowhere—the poor did not initiate and lobby through Congress the war on poverty; they were hardly involved at all. The core of the Democratic Party's support now lies among the relatively affluent who gain nothing from the redistributional aspects of these measures—indeed, they lose through higher taxes. The new, affluent Democratic Party is activist because the current condition of American society is, in various aspects, incompatible with the party members' conception of what that society should be like.

By the year 2000, the typical Democrat will have even less direct interest in redistributional measures of the type that were the central strands of the party's program not so many years ago. But he will still be concerned about a host of public problems, some of them exacerbated by his very affluence. The economically secure suburban voter will be concerned about congestion; about traffic; about the pollution of water, air, and soil; about the taming of technology; about amenity in urban living; about preservation and improvement of the natural outdoor environment; about parklands and recreation; about racial conflict; about opportunity for America's underclass; about crime and morals and mental health; about education and child development and the plight of the aged; about poverty in the Southern Hemisphere and rapprochement with the communist world. It is significant that between the 1930's and the 1960's, while the program and the composition of the Democratic Party changed radically, the appeal of the party, as measured in elections and in polls, was about as great in the latter decade as in the former. The same will hold true in the year 2000. The activist party, composed of those who advance innovative solutions to the problems of the day, will retain an advantage over the conservative party that, while also moving, remains a step behind and throws up warning flags. But the Democrats will lose whenever their tempo of reform—and their levels of taxation—exceed the toleration of the electorate, and the pattern of politics will remain essentially one of a cyclical alternation in power of two strong parties.

Some Possible Surprises

A political party alignment along an activist-conservative axis presupposes cohesion among the activists. They were bound together, in the past, by their common economic interests and their temperamental kinship. If their interests diverged on particular issues, they sublimated their disagreements in log-rolling: labor supported farm price supports, and Democratic farmers supported the National Labor Relations Act.

But in the 1960's it became apparent that two issues might be powerful enough to sunder the activist coalition and disrupt the smooth course of party realignment. One issue is race, and the other is foreign policy, as symbolized by Vietnam.

A RACIAL REALIGNMENT

A scenario of racial politics in the next three decades, as written from a year-2000 perspective, might run like this: The election of Carl Stokes as mayor of Cleveland, Ohio, and that of Richard Hatcher as mayor of Gary, Indiana, in 1967, were the first of a series of harsh and bitter contests in which Negroes rose to power in American cities. Through sheer numbers they captured control of the Democratic Party in city after city, and the party retained enough strength among traditionally Democratic white voters to elect its Negro candidate. By the year 2000, some three-fourths of the country's largest cities had Negro mayors.

But by 1978, and particularly in the 1980's, the Negro political leaders coming to power were of a different stamp from Stokes and Hatcher and Walter Washington, the appointive mayor of Washington, D.C. They were of the generation who came of voting age after the era of Negro militancy began, and they entered politics after the riots of the early 1970's had resulted in semipermanent curfews enforced by the National Guard in the Negro sections of most major cities. The more militantly these leaders behaved, the more rapid the political climb. Martin Luther King, Jr., was forgotten, and NAACP and Urban League leaders no longer were welcome in the ghettos; they spent their time delivering speeches on tolerance to suburban church groups. Eldridge Cleaver and Stokely Carmichael and a rising generation of kindred spirits were the heroes of the black urban masses. After Cleaver and Carmichael went into voluntary exile, even more outspoken white-haters came to command such large followings that no aspiring Negro politician dared voice any other sentiment.

In those cities where the Negroes made up a majority of the voting population, the new generation of black mayors made no pretense of running integrated city administrations. They had promised "black power" and they delivered it; long-time white civil servants fought a rearguard action in the courts and the state legislatures, but eventually they were driven out, just as they had been when black regimes came to power in the African republics. Their successors ranged from incompetents to rascals, and after the black militants took over the city school systems and built black-studies programs with strong antiwhite overtones, the white exodus to the suburbs turned into a stampede. Moreover, many moderate Negro leaders joined the flight to the suburbs, assisted by the federal fair-housing legislation enacted in 1968.

The cities' fiscal plight was serious enough even before the Negroes achieved power, but subsequent events brought downright fiscal chaos. As public services deteriorated, the mayors could only appeal for federal aid, but Congress did not rush to bail out the "black-power" politicians. The exodus of the whites was followed by the closing of downtown stores, many of which were boycotted by the Negroes anyway; lawyers, doctors, and other professional men moved their offices to the suburbs, and major corporations found it timely to construct new headquarters buildings at convenient sites near airports outside the city limits. The drop in employment in central business districts had its impact especially on Negroes, who could not follow their jobs to the new suburban commercial and industrial centers because public transportation systems had never linked the ghettos to those centers.

Pleas by the newspapers and civic leaders for rescue of the cities were frustrated by the political division between the cities and their suburbs. Only in Atlanta, Richmond, and a half dozen smaller southern centers did the white population stave off disaster by combining cities with surrounding counties to preserve or reestablish white majorities; all of these consolidations were under challenge in the courts, however, and in the first such case to reach the Supreme Court the consolidation was overturned on the ground that it was an arbitrary act to deprive Negroes of their political rights. Every proposal for financial relief through state aid or commuter taxes was defeated in state legislatures through the political power of the suburban-rural alliance against the cities.

As the Democratic Party in urban centers was taken over by Negro majorities, Democratic organizations in white working-class neighborhoods went over en masse to the Republicans or to George Wallace's American Independent Party. In the North, the move was usually to the Republican Party, because in most localities the suburban-based leadership of that party had extended a welcome in the form of a strong commitment to the repeal of open-housing legislation and the strengthening of "law-and-order" measures. It was also committed to resisting all schemes to tax the suburbs for the support of city services. Some Republican leaders like Jacob Javits and Clifford Case fought gallantly against the increasing bigotry of the Republican Party, but it was a lost cause, and when Javits and Case finally switched allegiance to the Democrats, few other Republicans followed. GOP theorist Kevin Phillips was named chairman of the Republican National Committee in 1977, as the man in the best position to negotiate a merger of the Republican Party with George Wallace's powerful American Independent Party. When the merger was completed, the Republican Party became the majority party in the United States for the first time since 1929, and Wallace was the inevitable vice-presidential candidate on the 1980 Spiro Agnew ticket against the Democratic team of Edward Kennedy and Carl Stokes. The election was, for all practical purposes, decided at the time of the Republican convention, when Negroes who had threatened to take their case to the streets if Wallace were put on the ticket did so in city after city. In particular, the brutal attack by a band of Negroes upon the wives of three Republican delegates outside the convention hall inflamed public opinion, and the slogan

"A Vote for Kennedy Is a Vote for Black Power" brought so overwhelming a landslide that the Democratic Party appeared dead for a generation.

A FOREIGN-POLICY REALIGNMENT

An equally dreary scenario can be written around the consequences of a long period of international confrontation and conflict—indeed, one version has already been written by Raymond Gastil.[3] But whereas his scenario leads to the ultimate merger of the Republican and Democratic parties in a totalitarian state, mine ends in a realignment of the parties on the basis of conflict between the American world view as it has developed since World War II and a rising neo-isolationism.

The scenario begins with the McCarthy campaign of 1968, which mustered into politics thousands of young activists who mobilized the larger universities and canvassed the voters and delegates of fifty states on behalf of peace. To them the defeat of McCarthy by Hubert Humphrey at the Democratic convention was a shattering experience. As they saw it, only a political system that was wholly corrupt could nominate for president the very symbol of the Vietnam policy and the "old politics" that had been repudiated in every single one of the party's primaries. Some wrote off party politics as hopeless and turned to direct action as their road to influence. But others responded by joining in an angry four-year crusade to capture control of the Democratic Party by 1972. In that objective they failed, but they did succeed in so dividing the party that by 1972 the reelection of President Nixon was inevitable.

Under the pressure of that year's campaign, however, Nixon had promised to end the war, and he was therefore compelled by 1973 to bring the last of the American troops home from Vietnam, where they had been shoring up the democratic elements of the coalition government installed in Saigon by the Paris agreement ending Vietnam hostilities. Two weeks after the last Marines embarked, the communists seized full control of South Vietnam, executed Generals Thieu and Ky, and began the massacre of uncounted tens of thousands of their supporters. Laos fell to the communists three weeks later, and the Cambodian rulers fled into exile, leaving that land in chaos. Early in 1974 the government of Thailand appealed for American aid to protect it against the danger of invasion from across the border. The President responded by blaming the collapse of Southeast Asia upon the Democrats—specifically, upon assurances by Senators Mansfield and Fulbright in a Senate "great debate" that the United States would never again intervene in a land war on the Asian mainland—and by drawing a new defense perimeter for the United States along Thailand's eastern border. After an incident off the Thai coast, in January 1975, the President asked Congress for a Gulf of Siam resolution giving him a free hand to fulfill American commitments to that country under the Southeast Asia treaty. Mansfield and Fulbright, still smarting from the President's allegation that they had "lost Vietnam," declared they would "sign no more blank checks." The resolution, they contended, would mean "another Vietnam" that this time would embroil the whole of Southeast Asia, and they launched a filibuster to block the resolution. A majority of the Senate clearly favored the resolution, but the filibusterers needed only thirty-four votes to block cloture, and they could count on thirty-five Democrats and five Republicans. After ten weeks of acrimony in which the filibusterers challenged the wisdom of the President and he in turn impugned their patriotism, the filibustering senators rallied their forty votes against a series of cloture motions and the resolution was shelved. But the controversy raged on inside and outside Congress throughout 1975 and 1976, while rebels seized one provincial capital after another in rural Thailand, and revolts also broke out in Burma, East Pakistan, and the Philippines as the United States stood by.

The South as a whole rallied solidly behind the President, and so did the small cities and towns of the Midwest. The *Chicago Tribune,* the *New York Daily News,* the Hearst newspapers, and other faithful GOP organs thundered against "the little band of willful men" who had betrayed the entire tradition of the Democratic Party from Woodrow Wilson to Lyndon Johnson, and they were backed by diocesan papers sounding the alarm against world communism. In the Irish wards of the big cities, and in some of the Italian wards, the Democratic Party became "the party of betrayal," and the Republicans for the first time in half a century began to outnumber the Democrats in party registration in the big cities. The young intellectuals who had marched and demonstrated throughout the land in support of the Senate filibuster won control of the Democratic Party in many northern cities where it had been abandoned by its former stalwarts, but they could not prevent a Republican landslide in 1976 almost as decisive as the Democratic landslide of 1964. Senator Mansfield and seven other anti-Thailand filibusterers went down in the Democratic debacle, and that was the end of Senate opposition to intervention in Southeast Asia.

The Gulf of Siam resolution was passed even before the new President was inaugurated, and Marines were on their way to Thailand before the end of January. Troops were dispatched also to Burma and East Pakistan, and military missions were in the Philippines and Indonesia training and equipping the armies of those countries. But the nation's campuses—outside the South—were no more reconciled to intervention than they had been during the losing 1976 campaign. The crisis came in 1978, when the President extended the draft to college students; for the first time since the Civil War, America had draft riots, and there was serious concern about defections to the enemy if some American units were tested in combat. But now the students and the "peaceniks" suddenly found themselves with allies—the President had been forced to ask for an increase in corporate and individual income taxes to balance the expanded military budget and for price and wage controls, and the converts to neo-isolationism were being counted in the millions. In a strange twist of history the Republicans had become the war party and the Democrats were offering a return to normalcy; the Republicans were the party of high spending and inflation, and the Democrats were invoking the puritan ethic. But not all was changed: the Republican-controlled House of Representatives set investigators looking for the Soviet and Red Chinese agents who had organized the draft riots, while a Democratic-controlled Senate committee launched a counterinvestigation of the relations between the Republican administration and the military-industrial complex. For the next two decades the parties were polarized on the issue of foreign involvement, while each party spanned the activist-conservative spectrum on the domestic issues that had been the basis of the party contest for eight decades before "the realignment of 1976," as it became known.

THE UNLIKELIHOOD OF EITHER

I have called these two scenarios "surprises" not because (or not merely because) they are distasteful. Party realignment in the United States just does not come about easily—as all the new third parties formed in recent times of crisis have discovered. There is a large body of party adherents, particularly in the older age groups, to whom changing parties would be like changing churches; such a voter may cross the line occasionally, as a worshiper may visit an alien church, but conversion and rebaptism would be an experience approaching trauma. Thus millions of Eisenhower Democrats in 1952 and 1956 and millions of Johnson Republicans in 1964 were, like the Roosevelt Republicans of a generation earlier, just visitors. They went home again, and their excursions left no mark upon the basic party system.

A party realignment has preconditions: the political tensions giving rise to the new alignment must be so powerful and all-consuming that they override and displace the attachment to existing parties based upon habit, emotional identification, patronage, political ambition, and the entire range of public issues that underlie the existing alignment. But a prolonged internal strain of such intensity on the race issue would be intolerable—it would tend to be self-correcting through revulsion against tension itself. True, in the period of the Civil War, tensions on racial questions were sustained and engrossing enough to shift the party system on its axis. But open housing and school integration in our time hardly compare as emotional issues with slavery and secession in their time, and in the mid-nineteenth century, moreover, parties were newer and the two-party system less deeply embedded in tradition.

Before the scenario of racial politics had done more than begin its course, then, a revulsion would be inevitable. Not everybody, after all, would be living in or near a city where Negroes had become politically dominant, and those not directly affected would not align with either side—not, at least, with the degree of passion that the realignment script supposes. Their energies, rather, would be directed toward dampening the conflict before it not only disrupted the party system but consumed the nation. On a national scale, this means that the senators and congressmen from the mountains and the plains and the rural North and West—from all the states and districts where there are few Negroes—would provide leadership and a mediating influence (as did Congressman McCulloch of Piqua, Ohio, in the passage of the civil rights legislation of the 1960's, and Senator Harris of Oklahoma in the deliberations of the Kerner Commission on Civil Disorders), as well as the decisive votes for enactment of the necessary measures. They would come to the rescue of the black cities rather than bear the responsibility for sacrificing the moderates to the militants on both sides and precipitating civil war.

Even in the suburbs, moreover, the Republican Party is not likely to be taken over by any influx of anti-Negro whites. A few county and suburban town committees may succumb, but the leadership of those areas will be isolated within state party organizations—certainly within the national organization. The temptation, after all, has been dangling before the Republican Party for some time. Its congressional leaders have flirted with the white backlash now and then, but they have always stopped short of embracing it. A consistent GOP effort toward rapprochement with the Negroes and their allies, as projected in the opening section of this paper, is a more credible possibility. The prospect is that civil rights and the problems of the ghettos will remain what they are now—part of the agenda that separates the activist party and the conservative party. The Democrats, as a national party, will be willing to move somewhat faster and spend somewhat more; the Republicans will be a little slower. But the differences will be those of degree; and there will be enough consensus on the basic measures essential to domestic tranquility to enact them and carry them out.

An analogous argument applies to the foreign-policy scenario. One can visualize a short period during which hawks and doves are at each other's throats, but it is difficult to foresee a sustained period of that kind. If Vietnam has proved anything, it has demonstrated again that national unity is a prerequisite for the conduct of a foreign war. So when the doves become numerous, as at present, a miiltant foreign policy simply becomes impossible, and the hawks perforce give way. A new succession of crises could, of course, give the hawks the upper hand. But in any case a period of basic conflict over foreign policy is bound to be self-terminating, because if the division in the country and in Congress is anywhere near being equal, there cannot even be a foreign policy. In such times the country finds a leader who has, or seems to have, a formula for consensus —like Eisenhower in 1953. The formula may be as ill-defined as Eisenhower's was, but it serves to subdue the emotional elements of the internal conflict before they lead to anything as drastic as a realignment of the party system.

Party Attachment and Alienation

The discussion so far has been based upon the assumption that in the year 2000 political issues will still be fought out through the traditional party system of American democracy, with either the present alignment of parties or a new one. But will it? Or will the alienation that now characterizes so much of American society continue to grow and spread until the essential political struggle is between those who seek solutions through the party process and those who seek them through other means—withdrawal, direct action, violence —with opposing alienated groups provoking each other to extreme and forceful measures? Such conflict could lead, as in Gastil's scenario, to the suspension of free elections and the adoption, almost on schedule, of many of the trappings of Orwell's *1984*.

If the art of predicting is to distinguish, among those trends that have brought us where we are, the ephemeral from the permanent, the cyclical from the secular, then what are the trends that produce the current gloomy forecasts, and into which categories do they fall?

The alienation that arises from two clearly identifiable causes can be considered first. One cause is Vietnam, the other is the many-faceted misery of the ghettos. The two compound each other, as the war in Vietnam prevents the release of the nation's resources and energies to attack the problems of the cities. And so alienation pervades two groups primarily—the young and the Negroes.

The American system has in the past responded to alienation of this kind, and the responsiveness of the system is the key to its stability. Democratic parties, in their nature, seek to broaden their support; to win the allegiance of disaffected groups, they modify their policies. Or, to put the proposition in reciprocal form, those who have grievances find that the political party is not their enemy but their instrument. American parties are not, like the traditional

European parties, built on fixed ideological positions enforced from the top by coteries of old men. They are decentralized, federal structures, with many centers of power, open to influence at many points, as groups pressing particular issues capture control of precinct, ward, county, and state organizations and elect their adherents to local office, state legislatures, and Congress. The threat of third-party organizations brings concessions; if it does not, then the actuality of new parties can do so. We have already seen how the young opposed to the Vietnam war found in Eugene McCarthy their instrument to force the retirement of a President and ultimately to bring about a reversal in the nation's policy toward the Vietnam war.

The Negroes are also finding avenues to power within the system, and they will find more—just as farmers, laborers, and immigrant groups before them did, and by the same means: the organization and assertion of numerical strength, at the voting booth and elsewhere. Through the normal channels of politics, their numbers have been reflected in a growing share of elective and appointive public offices and in a widening influence on public policy and administration. Beginning in 1964, the federal government took decisive steps to accelerate the rise of Negro power and influence. Civil-rights legislation extended the right to vote, and the community-action program established mechanisms for self-determination in the Negro neighborhoods of cities. When Congress amended the Economic Opportunity Act in 1967 to make it possible for the power structure in each community to take control of the community-action program, it was too late. The revolution in urban politics had gone too far in most communities to be reversible, and the power structure declined the invitation to assert control. Meanwhile, the principle of participation by the poor has been further institutionalized in the model-cities program, as well as in local actions in some cities to decentralize school administration and other services of government. As the urban Negro achieves real political power and overcomes his helplessness, his alienation from the political system will be mitigated.

If, at that point, the lower-income whites in their turn are offended by a political system that seems to give too much to their competitors, the same line of reasoning applies to them. The political process is open, and responsive, to them too. They will use it, in one form or another, and the struggle for position and influence between groups will still be within the system, in the traditional pattern of American politics. A permanent withdrawal of any group from political competition is hard to visualize.

Those who contend that the alienation of the young these days is something different and special, peculiar to the late twentieth century and therefore not subject to comparison with previous eras, have yet to produce, I believe, the evidence that will sustain their point. It may be that almost the entire phenomenon of alienated youth can be traced to a single cause—Vietnam. To the country as a whole, that far-off conflict has been almost incidental: for the first three years after 1965, it did not affect prices, or taxes, or the availability of consumer goods in a way that caused hardship or even any substantial inconvenience. Indeed, as is the way with wars, it brought a boom economy. Even after the surtax of 1968, the impact of the war on Americans above draft age is still not severe. But in contrast, during all this time, Vietnam has been a very personal thing, and quite absorbing, for the generation that has to do the fighting. And the fighting generation, this time, has not had the benefit of a Pearl Harbor to erase its doubts; indeed, it hears respected leaders call the war "immoral." The alienation of the young should surprise nobody—the wonder would be if they were docile. When Vietnam passes into history it may leave some residue of the professionally alienated, like the Depression-bred communists who remained outside the system after the Depression had been cured, but that is all. The others will return. It was only a half-dozen years ago, after all, that we marveled at how deeply engaged the young could be in such purely altruistic causes as the Peace Corps and the civil-rights struggle.

Alienation is present to some degree in all countries and at all times, but it waxes when institutions are rigid and it wanes when they respond. The characteristic of the American party system—in contrast, perhaps, to some of our other institutions—is its extraordinary flexibility. If we live now at a moment when our political institutions seem slow to respond to particular groups and grievances, we are looking at a circumstance that our whole political history suggests is transitory. As the pressure increases, the system does respond, because the people who are aggrieved possess the means, simply through participation, to see to it that it does.

One caveat must be entered: we have been talking here primarily about the *political* side of the political-governmental system as a whole. The *governmental* side can sometimes be perilously slow to respond, even when the political mandate from the people is clear. From the eighteenth century we have inherited a legacy of checks and balances, and to these our own century has added—or acquiesced in—self-imposed barriers to action, like the Senate filibuster and the congressional seniority system. When the pressures become great enough, of course, these barriers give way—as the Supreme Court gave way to the other two branches in the 1930's, and as the filibuster yielded to public opinion in the civil-rights acts of the 1960's. But meanwhile the dangers are obvious: The aspirations of aggrieved groups may outrun their patience, and they may turn against democratic institutions themselves. So the institutional barriers to responsive government must be the particular target of attack of those who prize American democracy. Some of those barriers are party rules and practices in many states that discourage wide public participation in party affairs, such as in the choice of delegates to national conventions. Some are in congressional traditions and practices—mainly the filibuster, which can prevent majority rule in the Senate, and the arbitrary powers of committee chairmen chosen by seniority, which can be used to thwart the will of both houses. Much of the congressional problem will disappear, as I noted earlier, when the solid South finally vanishes from the political map, and parties become homogeneous on the basis of program and principle rather than geography. By the year 2000, in all probability, all of these barriers to responsive government will have been dismantled.[4]

There remains the question of competence: The government may fail to solve the problems that give rise to grievance, not for lack of will but for lack of wisdom or administrative capability. But so far the competence of the American government appears to have advanced about as rapidly as the problems that it must cope with have grown in complexity, and I see no reason why this relationship should change. Moreover, it is still unresponsiveness, rather than ineffectiveness, that is the more likely cause of alienation. Citizens will tolerate a reasonable amount of error from a government that tries—as long as they look upon the government as genuinely theirs.

Now what of the secular phenomena? Several trends can be identified that seem to reinforce the tendency toward alienation, or at least toward a slackening of the ties between the citizen and his party that have contributed to the stability of our party system.

One is the waning of political ideology, which is so striking in the socialist and even the communist parties of Europe and is also apparent here. Earlier, I compared party affiliation to religious affiliation; especially during and after the Civil War, American parties were identified with the moral issues over which the war had been fought, and a citizen joined his party as he joined a church. In later years, new verities developed: the Republicans accepted "the gospel of free enterprise," and the Democrats saw salvation in trade unionism. But now the verities are waning. Today the new economics attacks head-on the "puritan ethic" of the balanced budget—and wins. Republicans and Democrats alike now run for office as pragmatists and "problem solvers"; the basic reason that Barry Goldwater seemed an anachronism to the American people was not that his principles were outdated but that they were fixed.

As the domain of scientific knowledge pushes forward, the realm of ideology retreats.[5] The engineers, the biologists, the physicists, the economists, and other purveyors of hard data—by the year 2000, let it be hoped, also the sociologists, psychologists, and political scientists—find public policy in their computers, and it does not matter which party is in power: the same solutions flow automatically from the same data analyzed in the same way and are accepted by consensus. So some programs and policies once derived from philosophy, dogma, and principle stem now from the evaluated experimentation of political pragmatists. But the voter cannot form an emotional attachment to an equation or an engineering firm. To the extent that both parties abandon ideology for pragmatism, the citizen's attachment to his party will slacken, and he will assign greater weight in his voting decisions to other factors—especially, we may assume, the personality of candidates.

But if ideology is the essential cement that binds the citizen to his party, then as ideology declines will not the parties themselves disintegrate? John Voss, for one, suggests that the major parties will fade in significance when they no longer carry clashing ideological positions into battle: in the end, they may find themselves combined in a common defense against messianic political groups outside the system that are attacking rationality itself, feeding upon the anxieties that are the fallout of a highly competitive society. The antirational campaigns against fluoridation and against integration become the prototypes of the future politics. But what is secular and what is cyclical? Antirational movements, too, have waxed and waned throughout our history—we need look back no further than the rise and fall of Joseph McCarthy. The rational elements of both parties combined against McCarthyism finally, but that did not lessen their competition on other issues.

Despite the advance of analysis, moreover, it will never cover all the crucial questions that politics must decide. For one thing, the boundaries of governmental concern advance, too; as old questions become subject to consensus settlement based on data and analysis, new questions arise outside the boundaries of settled scientific method. Furthermore, analysis does not necessarily produce consensus. For example, it may with some precision compute the benefits to be gained through a given expenditure of public funds, but it will not settle the value question of whether the result is worth the money. Do the people who get the benefits deserve them? Are the costs being charged to the right people? How much redistribution of wealth and income through taxing and spending is the right amount? What should be the tempo of government reform? What value should be placed upon the amenities of life—clean water, clean air, natural and urban beauty, nonvocational education, public recreation? What is it worth to the white suburbanite to rescue the black city in which he works? These are the kinds of questions that divide parties now, and there is no convincing reason to believe that they are being, or will be, less sharply drawn. The elections of the 1960's turned on differences in party programs, attitudes, and philosophies that may have been less sharp, say, than those of the 1930's but sharper than those of the 1920's. This, too, seems cyclical: parties are pulled toward the center by the attraction of the votes clustered there, but they are pulled back again by the dynamics of their internal composition. Though conservatism and activism may become matters less of ideology than before, people are still distributed along an activist-conservative spectrum according to their temperaments, their attitudes, and their value judgments. The two parties are necessarily anchored on either side of the midpoint of the spectrum, because they reflect—they do not determine—the views of their followers. Even though the parties may be increasingly pragmatic and flexible in determining their positions, this does not mean—not by the year 2000, at any rate—that party competition or the parties themselves will be obsolescent.

A second permanent—and growing—influence upon the attachment of the citizen to his party is television. We may be just entering the television age of politics, and the ultimate consequences of its marketing techniques, when perfected, may be profound indeed. Where voters once relied upon the party label as a proxy for candidates they could not get to know, now they can develop the illusion of personal acquaintance with the candidates through a one-way conversation in the living room, and they feel qualified to make judgments of character and competence on what they see and hear. A high premium is put upon personality in a candidate—specifically, upon those attributes that make the "TV personality." The influence of all organizations—not just parties—is weakened, and political behavior becomes more atomistic than before. Telegenic candidates—if they have money—can appeal over the heads of party and bloc leaders directly to the voting public, and through the polls and the primaries compel the attention of party leaders. Televised politics arouses interest and stimulates participation among hosts of political amateurs, who can be assembled into impromptu organizations to challenge the established party structures. One beneficial result is that party politics is taken out of the back room; leaders must appeal in the open to the party rank-and-file, because if they do not they can be sure their opponents will, and they must be prepared to respond to popular movements as these may be whipped up through television. For the first time, a prominent—or even an obscure—senator can challenge an incumbent President of his own party with at least a chance of overthrowing him. Similarly, a minority-party candidate like John Lindsay in New York can more readily break the hold of one-party politics in a city or a state.

On the other side, the prospect that a candidate can be marketed with ditties—while his stand on the issues is predetermined by polling and behavioral research—is chilling. Alarmists can point to the elections of George Murphy and Ronald Reagan in California—presumably impossible before the advent of the late, late show—and perhaps even to John Kennedy's triumph over Richard Nixon in 1960. Yet when all is said, the changes wrought so far by twenty years of television are less than fundamental. The picture tube may have brought younger and handsomer—and wealthier—candidates, but it has not basically altered the structure of the two-party system. The fears expressed so widely two decades ago that television would usher in a new age of the demagogue have not been realized. If anything, the instrument has worked the other way: television has enabled the voters to see through the shallowness of demagogues. And even the outcome of the Kennedy-Nixon debates cannot be interpreted as a contest of television personalities. One need only ask whether Kennedy would have won the debates if he had been cast in the role of defending the record of a tired Eisenhower administration while Nixon had been free to advocate a New Frontier. The impact was a combination of each man's personality with the image of his party and with what he had to say. In that sense, television helped the voters to analyze the candidate and their programs on their merits—helped to lead, not to mislead.

Vietnam, race, alienation—all these loom large today. But from the perspective of the year 2000 they will appear as perhaps not even among the most serious of the crises that the American political system, in the preceding century and a third, had met and surmounted.

NOTES

1. John W. Gardner, "How Twentieth-Century Civilization Collapsed," commencement address at Cornell University, Ithaca, N.Y., June 1, 1968.

2. The phrase is from James MacGregor Burns's book of that title (Englewood Cliffs, N.J.: Prentice-Hall, 1963).

3. Raymond D. Gastil, "The Road Through 'Victory' to Totalitarianism," one of a "pair of related, pessimistic scenarios," in *The Year 2000: A Framework for Speculation on the Next Thirty-Three Years,* ed. Herman Kahn and Anthony J. Wiener (New York: Macmillan, 1967), pp. 229–306.

4. For a fuller discussion of these points, see James L. Sundquist, *Politics and Policy: The Eisenhower, Kennedy, and Johnson Years* (Washington, D.C.: Brookings Institution, 1968), especially Chapter 12.

5. This thesis is developed by Robert E. Lane in "The Decline of Politics and Ideology in a Knowledgeable Society," *American Sociological Review,* 31, No. 5 (October 1966).

COMMENT ON "POLITICS IN THE YEAR 2000"

John Voss

James Sundquist is right in arguing that we should expect continuity and stability in our political system in the next thirty years, at least in the sense that radical or sudden changes in direction are unlikely. However, it is open to question whether our traditional party structure and our mechanisms for making political and social decisions will survive without substantial change.

In comparison with any previous period in American history, our political institutions are now stronger, more powerful, and indeed more able to cope with crises, in the sense of being able to mobilize resources to deal with them. In part, this strength is due to the fact that government agencies at all levels have assumed so many critical functions. And it can be argued that our political institutions are stable: although we are beset with problems of race and poverty, and with challenges to any number of our traditional policies, there are very few who question the ability of our formal political structure to survive or who present any viable, or even consistent, alternative to that structure. If we compare our present difficulties with those of the 1930's, it is clear that there is far more agreement now among the major parties on programs for the solution of our problems and far less division about basic political philosophy.

One result of this relative stability in the political structure is the gradual weakening of organized political parties, insofar as they represent alternative theories about the role of government or the nature of economics or social institutions. At the level of local government, national political parties are largely anachronistic or at best are local coalitions of interest groups bearing little relationship to national party principles. Only at the extremes—Governor Reagan of California is a good example—is there a clear difference between

Democrats and Republicans at the level of state politics. And in national politics, the campaign of Barry Goldwater was a convincing demonstration of the political folly of presenting the voters with even the appearance of a choice between well-defined alternatives.

If our own political party structure is clearly less ideological and divisive than it was even a generation ago, America is not in a unique position. This decline in the ideological base of political divisiveness is characteristic of all advanced industrial countries. The differences between major political parties in democratic countries represent only the echo of former ideological strife or ethnic and religious conflict. What is it that divides the Labor and Conservative parties in England or the Reds and Blacks in Austria? What ideological gulf separates the Liberals from the Progressive Conservatives in Canada?

It is not difficult to explain the decline of traditional political ideology and the weakening of party structures. In America, at any rate, parties have been based on regional politics (which, as Sundquist points out, is hardly viable in a centralized society), on ethnic affiliation, and most importantly, on economic interests and class conflict. As long as most Americans (the blacks, of course, are partial exceptions) consider themselves to some extent participants in the economic system, or, to put it another way, as long as there are no major or strident demands for the redistribution of wealth, the old class division can hardly provide a viable base for political contests.

Much of the rhetoric that moved activists and liberals even a generation ago is irrelevant today. There is no coherent or systematic conception of national goals to replace those relatively simple economic and related social goals of the New Deal. The problem is not that we have no goals, but that current issues—conservation, educational policy, race, poverty, crime, the use of leisure, and so on—have not been refined into a coherent and articulated set of political ideas. Assuming that can be done, to what political power base is the achievement of those ideas tied? To the educated middle classes Sundquist suggests that as class and socio-economic antagonisms decline, political differences will essentially be ones of mood and temper, activist versus conservative, between members of the middle classes.

My argument is that the old alliances and alignments in American politics that created division between Democrats and Republicans (however loose these divisions may have been) have probably been broken beyond repair. In the more complex societal situation of the future, it is difficult to see the sources of party divisions as the sources of party vitality.

It is quite clear that the old liberal belief in progress—a generalized faith that man and his institutions are perfectible through reason or some historical agent operating automatically—has given way to a more somber view of history. We solve some problems only to create new and frequently less tractable ones; if technology and science have conquered nature and made possible unprecedented abundance, some consequences of technological advances, both primary and secondary, are ominous and frightening. If we project goals into the future in many different areas (for example, in education, health, national income), we find it difficult to articulate these discrete goals into any comprehensive view of the nature of society or the good life. Our social and political goals have become much more diffuse in the last generation: we now talk about autonomy and integrity, privacy, the full development of capacity, equality of opportunity, education, conservation, and the like. I think that without a comprehensive view of the nature of society or a systematic statement of goals and how one should achieve them, Sundquist's activists can hardly form the base of a national party. Some people will be activist about some issues, and conservative or even reactionary about others. Even scientists, who have regarded themselves as major agents of change, and who have had an almost implicit faith in scientific innovation as being unambiguously desirable, may emerge as one of the more conservative forces in society—the guardians who will place locks on the laboratory door because they are aware of the price we pay for technological progress in the form of unintended and undesirable secondary consequences.

Abundance and leisure, not to mention the increasing toleration for deviance, have contributed to the growth of a large number of special forms of cultural and social identification that have diminished the sense of sharing in the loose constellation of middle-class values that was uniquely American. It is easy to measure this erosion of common values in the gradual decline of a mass audience for the established media—newspapers, magazines, and television. As individuals are able to find their primary identification with subgroups or special-interest groups, the political parties in our society will have to become more, and not less, responsive to special interests. And the coalitions that they represent will become less permanent, because the new special-interest groups will not have permanent or stable memberships, there will be more of them, and they will be changing constantly as some disappear and new ones emerge to take their place.

In addition to the effect of diversity on common values, not a threatening prospect in itself, there are more ominous indications of the basis for reactive emotional, and indeed authoritarian, political movements. A society that relies increasingly on rational, orderly planning by highly educated people in many different sectors, and particularly planning for suboptimal goals (in other words, less than romantic or utopian goals), will generate reactions from those who find themselves with no voice or power in the planning process, or who at least think that they are without such a voice. Insofar as there is a sense of the loss of institutional stability in traditional and personal social ties in a mobile, personally competitive society, it will be relatively easy to mount attacks against at least some aspects of national planning by the meritocracy. It seems unlikely that there will be any revolt against the technocratic meritocracy as such, since it is highly unlikely that its members will form a coherent class; their ranks shade off into the partly educated, who are as likely as the uneducated—perhaps even more likely, because they are articulate—to express their personal and social insecurities in reactive forms.

It can be argued that the attitude of both liberals and conservatives in politics has become less moralistic—and this at a time when it is clear that our national sensitivity to moral issues has become much more acute. Race and poverty, the primary moral issues of our time, are national rather than partisan issues. Code words like white racism, the establishment, or the military-industrial complex have manifest and latent moral connotations in the old sense, but they operate outside the party structure—they are conscious accusations of the minority against the politics of the majority. To the liberal Democrat, a Nixon or a Rockefeller may be wrong or misguided or have unfortunate qualities or personality, but neither one is simply evil or exploitative in the sense that conservatives in the past were supposed to sacrifice human needs for economic gain or for abstract principle. Whether or not this decline in the moralistic tone of our politics is a sign of maturity and stability, it is likely that the impulse to moralism will remain constant and that it will seek expression on the fringes of our political system. Much of the present discontent among students and minorities, both black and white, is a reflection of the inability of the party system to accommodate or to mobilize moralistic impulses, genuine or self-serving, which seem to concern so many Americans. In an increasingly fragmented society with far more personal freedom, it is difficult to see how it will be possible to maintain even the appearance of common, widely shared values as the base of a set of political ideas around which a party can mobilize.

Our political and institutional structure is characterized by a pervasive and elusive sense of powerlessness. One can observe this feature most clearly in international affairs: if advanced industrial countries have unprecedented military power, they are unable to use this power effectively against even their weakest antagonists without disastrous political consequences. Their capacity to use their immense political or economic power in the underdeveloped world is similarly but less dramatically inhibited. In domestic politics our awareness of problems has become more acute and sensitive, and the potential resources for their solution have increased. But we *appear* to be unable to solve them (I think that we do much better than we appear to do) or to develop effective programs to deal with them. What political party or pressure group has a convincing solution for poverty or racial conflict? Who knows how to solve the urgent political tensions facing New York, not to mention Newark?

A half century ago it was possible to believe in civic reform (although at the same time one was cynical about whether those who advocated it believed what they were saying) and it was possible to believe that the election of the Progressive Party or Wilson's Democratic Party would result in significant changes in the direction and structure of our society. Now our difficulties are in large part due to our sense of powerlessness. No decision can be made—in technology, social policy, international affairs—without taking account of its secondary and often highly undesirable consequences. In an institution, an executive cannot change policy without promoting simultaneous decisions in many parts of the organization, and in many of these subsequent areas he has no real power. In short, the systems or ecological models that describe our conception of social processes may not be congruent with our traditional ideas of direct action through representative institutions and simple political alternatives that can be decided through rational debate and orderly choice.

Part of the difficulty is certainly that our expectations have outstripped our capacity for change, and part of it is that we are much more sophisticated in understanding the inherent limits of change and the realities of social and political processes. Our problems are not more intractable than they were, but we are at once more sensitive to their complexity and more critical of our goals.

Thus it is possible that we shall see in the next generation a gradual withering of the traditional political-party structure. Without suggesting that we are facing a period of radical or apocalyptic change in the structure of our political system or our mechanisms for arriving at political and social decisions, it is not a bad guess to say that we may be at one of those turning points in history (we have had others before) in which our values, our faith in historical progress, our vision of the future will reflect the new realities and disjunctions of a postindustrial society. Many of these changes are central to the political process and our mechanisms for making social choices. Although we will probably still use the labels Democratic and Republican in the year 2000, we may also have other equally important political labels. In any case, the substance that the old labels represent will have very little relationship to those issues that have traditionally occupied the major parties.

III

UNITED STATES WORLD RESPONSIBILITIES

From the Transcript

DOMESTIC IMPLICATIONS OF OUR INTERNATIONAL RESPONSIBILITIES AND THE ROLE OF THE MILITARY

PARTICIPANTS

Lester R. Brown
Matthew Holden, Jr.
Herman Kahn
Robert R. Nathan
Harold Orlans
Harvey S. Perloff
James L. Sundquist
Rexford G. Tugwell
John G. Wofford

PERLOFF: A whole set of problems about the future emerges from our international responsibilities and our responses to them. For example, our country seems to have little interest in strengthening the United Nations. Why?

WOFFORD: Perhaps because the UN hasn't done too much, and is able to function only when a local authority is willing to have it function, unless the big powers step in and decide to operate under the guise of the UN.

BROWN: The nature of future relationships between countries will be influenced by the future of the nation-state as a political entity. The basic forces at work—technology combined with rising aspirations around the world—are beginning to weave the various nation-states together. In agriculture, for example, all the nations except the United States and Russia must import at least some of the basic raw materials needed to sustain a modern fertilizer industry. This degree of interdependence did not exist when traditional agriculture predominated throughout most of the world.

Industrial economies are being developed that increasingly exceed the nation-state in size. Our own national economy can no longer sustain IBM as a company: its size has spread it around the world. There is a proliferation of binational or multinational cooperative development efforts. Consider the Indus River project of India and Pakistan, where even at the height of the Kashmir conflict the locks that controlled the interchange of water across the border functioned right on schedule. Electrical power grids in Western European countries are now intertwined. Rising levels of international trade and the growing exchange of technology also create more interdependence. The interesting thing is that these international relationships are reducing the traditional independence of the nation-state. The big exception to this trend is the small have-not states, which exist only on a subsistence level.

PERLOFF: What kind of problems for government will arise by 2000 as a result of changes under way?

NATHAN: By 2000 there will almost inevitably be an increase in regionalism and some transfer of responsibility and authority to an international institution. Our whole perspective is going to be challenged by this development, since our own country will witness the growth of an internationally oriented set of individuals in both public and private sectors who move into these institutions.

We shall have to reexamine our basic attitude in dealing with individuals in their respective roles as American citizens and as international civil servants. There are implications for our ideas on civil liberties. It will demand a reorientation of loyalties and responsibilities. This will be a very real problem for the American government.

PERLOFF: Vis-à-vis the whole world, what would be an appropriate philosophy or approach for a nation like ours in the next thirty years? Our political theory is a national one and has no place for international affairs.

NATHAN: In a meaningful sense, the realities of the next thirty years will be international. There will be forty or fifty nuclear powers, and this implies the need for an international police force. Moreover, we shall have the problem of an international poverty program with as many political considerations as the domestic one has today. These developments require new political conceptions and new responses, which are difficult to formulate.

PERLOFF: Can we respond decisively to international problems when both houses of Congress are locally rather than internationally oriented? Perhaps we should start thinking very seriously about electing one-third of the Senate "at large." I'm assuming that senators would be more internationally oriented since they would be elected by the whole country, somewhat like the President.

NATHAN: The alternative may be regional and world assemblies and legislative bodies with "at-large" delegates elected by the people —rather like the relationship of the state to the federal and the federal to the international.

PERLOFF: This would be an international reaction to world events. But I'm thinking of our own reaction to our role in the world.

NATHAN: One of our basic problems—and an exceedingly complex one—is the reconciliation or coordination of diverse ideological economic institutions in this closer international coordination. What do you do with tariffs, with trade arrangements, with investment flows, given these international differences in ideologies? How do we adapt and orient our own economic life to these new conditions? How would resources allocation, for instance, be influenced by freer trade and a movement toward the one-world approach? This is facing us today in agriculture. Another grave problem is our agricultural production in relation to world food demands and to our own internal economic problems. We must consider raw materials, conservation, and manpower utilization. How will we mobilize, use, and organize our own economic resources in a world of ideological diversity when our own evolving needs may cause serious eruptions in our internal economic relationships?

SUNDQUIST: Here is an area of substantive problems that our political institutions have to deal with. And they are not so different in kind from other decisions we make. In dealing with national problems, the President moves from one set of problems to another, but the decision-making process is essentially the same. It's a matter of getting information and analyzing problems and dealing with the agencies of departments concerned. An international problem may tend to involve more departments, but otherwise it's not different in kind. These issues will not require a unique series of political and governmental structural solutions.

KAHN: I think the highly developed parts of the world will be very cosmopolitan in the year 2000, and then we will have waves of nationalism, with nationalism becoming a kind of religion. A very large part of the world will be both highly industrialized and highly chauvinistic, with simply no international interest.

TUGWELL: Will these nations have nuclear bombs?

KAHN: By 2000, thirty or forty nations will have them. My scenario for nuclear diffusion is about as follows: in the mid-1970's it will be the Japanese; three or four years later the Germans and/or the Indians; soon after that the Italians; then the Swedes and the Swiss because they are no longer invulnerable and will want more modern weapons. But I don't think the bomb will affect matters as much as one might think. Looking ahead to the year 2000, I doubt if there will be any sense of sentimentality or guilt feelings toward the underdeveloped nations. In fact, you will probably have a new racism in the world. The people who are doing well will, on the whole, feel smug and superior. In such a situation we will have two alternatives. The first is the classic method of intervention of the nineteenth century, to protect the travelers, the merchants, and so on. The second is staying clear of all such situations and complacently watching other people kill each other. This is a completely new way to look at the problem and is probably the new American attitude toward such problems as Cyprus or the Congo.

TUGWELL: This has never been our attitude in the past. What makes you think we are going to change?

KAHN: From 1945 until about 1960 the Americans thought it was their job to see that nobody killed anybody, to be world policemen, in other words, and on the whole we did a good job. But in recent years it has become a thankless job, with poor results, and has created more problems than solutions. What will be the role of the military in such an international situation? I assume the strategic forces will be relatively trivial, with between one and one and one-half million. People will be hired from the open market for this technical, skilled work. In addition, there will be a force for intervention purposes, probably used mostly for narrow national interests. And to the extent that you have an international intervention, it is very likely to be the Swedes, the Swiss, and the Canadians who will intervene, as Sweden does now under UN auspices. But this is a professional force that intervenes without American commitment. We will continue to have a major investment at least in the missile defense area, simply because the Russians are not going to want China to be able to attack them, for example, and we don't want China to be able to attack us. It will not be difficult for us to keep ahead of France and China for the next ten to twenty years.

ORLANS: I don't understand what it means to "keep ahead" or to "keep up with" China.

KAHN: As long as the Chinese are not clever enough to think of a method of attack that we haven't thought about, or do not think of a bizarre attack, we can, on paper, have 100-percent defense against Chinese attacks.

PERLOFF: What factors will determine the role of the military in American social and political life?

KAHN: There will be two kinds of military—one a kind of mercenary force that literally goes out there and gets shot at and killed, and America just watches it without any emotional commitment.

PERLOFF: What about the top level?

KAHN: People going into the military forces will be more curiously anti-American than their counterparts were in 1910 and 1920. Roughly speaking, from 1912–1918 to 1939 the average American military officer was a very strange person. He couldn't get a job anywhere else.

ORLANS: And economically this mercenary force will be a stabilizing factor in the American economy, like the social-security system?

KAHN: It will be small, about 4 percent. One assumes that the world will be having a tremendous amount of turmoil in the underdeveloped areas. This force would be used for defense against every country except the Soviet Union.

HOLDEN: Will this mercenary force see itself as performing a critical function for the United States, the way the current military do? And will the rest of the population agree?

KAHN: I'm assuming the ideological conflict has pretty much watered itself down to nothing, so that we look upon every battle not as a battle between two ideologies, but simply as a local battle. Now, I do think this mercenary force will see itself as a world police force, upholding law and order. But somehow most people won't accept that.

BROWN: You predict quite a bit of violence in the year 2000. Will it take the form of inner-directed frustration within governments, like the Calcutta situation, or an external crisis, like Kashmir?

KAHN: Both. But there will be no big drama in the world, no Cold War to make everything important. Every nation in the world except Burma wants to industrialize, and many of them will do so by the end of the century. You'll have internal divisions of a different sort.

PERLOFF: Is it conceivable that organizational ability and research development capacity would put the military in a position to carry out new and unique functions? Not the military as we usually think of it, but the military performing quite different functions all around the world. In Israel, for example, the Army plays an educational and integrating role. If we assume the possibility of change, what would be the American version of this?

KAHN: Possibly three or four functions. You can train military and engineering forces for other countries and use the engineering forces to build roads and things like that. It's been a tradition in the United States that every time you send a division overseas you send an extra Marine Corps unit to plan buildings, and the like.

PERLOFF: This discussion has raised a number of issues that deserve more detailed attention. I hope that several of you will be willing to expand your comments into formal essays. It also seems clear that we should enlarge our group in order to cover additional international problems of importance for the future of the American government.

*THOUGHTS ON GOVERNMENT IN INTERNATIONAL AFFAIRS**

George C. Lodge

My predictions about government in international affairs in the year 2000 rest on two presumptions:

1. By 2000 the human race, by adapting sufficiently to the nuclear environment, will have escaped suicide. Having successfully crossed the evolutionary threshold on which it is now so dangerously poised, it will move toward integration and synthesis in all areas and conditions of life; races, nations, peoples; politics, economies, cultures, and technologies.

2. At the same time, human survival will be recognized in 2000 more clearly than it is today as being the one overriding priority objective of people and their governments. It will be clear that the principal threats to survival are big war and famine. The chief stimulus to war will lie in the conflicts that will inevitably attend the integration and synthesis predicted above. Famine, on the other hand, will be caused chiefly by the failure to achieve this integration and synthesis, or in the continuing disparity between population growth and food production, distribution, and consumption.

Merging these two ideas, I predict that the policies, programs, and structure with which the American government will face the world in 2000 will be shaped to a primary survival objective: *To eliminate the causes of big war and increase the production of food through a process of integration and synthesis, regionally and globally, of political, social, economic, and technological systems.*

While the three components of this objective are harmonious, they are potentially discordant. Although essential to survival, they contain the ingredients of conflict. The integration of nations into regional groups, leading to a more perfect political world order and

* This essay was written in 1968. The reader is asked to take this into account.

eventually to some form of world government, seems sensible and essential. Such integration, for example, is prerequisite to the establishment and acceptance of a world police force capable of controlling aggressors. It is also necessary for the better organization of land, markets, distribution systems, credit, technology, and people —necessary for the support and encouragement of a radical increase in food production and effective control of famine. In the present design of nations, it is quite possible that within ten years the food-rich United States will have to decide which nations are going to "live" and which must "die" because of their impossible food/people ratio and potential. This is hardly a peaceable outlook.

Essential as international integration is, it will bring substantial conflict and threat of war. Integration requires the diminution of sovereignty, the lessening of nationalism, and the reallocation of many forms of political and economic power, all of which can make for extraordinary tension. Some questions come to mind: What are the meaningful purposes of survival? What are the objectives of integration and synthesis? What criteria and priorities will guide the shifts of power? Will the many countries of Latin America, Africa, and Asia have to become true nations before they can enter into regional combinations, or can they skip the troublesome nationalizing-centralizing processes of the more developed world?

The resolution of these questions requires a variety of changes in the philosophy and structure of American government. By 2000 the United States will have grouped its interests more precisely and will have become used to its great power. Comfortable with power, we will have gained the wisdom and the confidence to use it more perceptively and humbly, more subtly and with clearer purpose, than we do today. We will have learned its limitations. We will know which elements of power can with greater effect be relinquished to international authority, and which cannot.

By 2000 we will understand considerably more about the nature of "development" and its vital connection with peace, survival, and world order. Development is change, and useful change must be carefully aimed and directed. Since direction and aim are functions of socio-political institutions and leaders, development is primarily social and political, and secondarily economic. We will wonder at our foolishness in consigning it to the economists for so long. For its mysteries are more essentially related to the synergistic art of the political scientist, the sociologist, the psychologist, the anthropologist, and the theologian. If "change" is to be "development," it must have direction and be organized for permanence, continuity, and protection from the forces of the status quo. We will realize that these conditions can be provided by certain institutions—the "engines of change." They are the only useful concerns of the economist and the technician, because these institutions convert economic fuel into purposeful and directed power for development. By 2000 we will clearly perceive how mid-century economic and technical-aid programs failed to reflect an understanding of the radical socio-political prerequisites for change and development. A backward glance at the programs of the 1960's in South Vietnam and Latin America will reveal that we sustained long beyond their time ineffective and doomed social and political structures which themselves were the principal obstacle to the change and development we thought we were encouraging.

It will be clear that the construction and mobilization of effective engines of change in Latin America and South Vietnam are an essentially revolutionary process, carrying with it profound and radical alterations in the structure of basic economic, political, and social systems. We will no longer be comfortable in the sublime conviction that "development" means only a relatively smooth transfer of matter from the rich to the poor. We will ask ourslves with increased poignancy and respect: Why change? Who shall we change? How fast? Why?

To change rigid, traditional, and oligarchical environments is not only exceedingly difficult, but is also fraught with violence and the threat of war. The environmental constraints obstructing change and sustaining the status quo will prove to be sturdy, but they must be undone if there is to be increased production of food and the fulfillment of the circle of requirements which such an increase depends upon: a degree of hope, confidence, and power over the environment, leading to increased motivation, a willingness on the part of the poor but popular majority to trust one another and organize. Their organizations will themselves become engines of change to continue the process, altering the forces that control land, markets, credit, politics, justice, and economics.

As we come to realize the awesome task of change in the pursuit of our objective and commit ourselves to the inevitable revolutionary process, we will come to see with increasing clarity how limited is the capacity of government in causing change, for government finds it hard to alter the power on which it rests. Governments, at one level or another, naturally resist the agitation required to reallocate power. It will be clear by 2000 that many parts of the world, particularly in Latin America, which we call democratic nations, are neither democratic nor nations. We will not hold this against them; we will understand that given their histories and experiences it could not have been otherwise.

Due to the limitations of government in administering change, particularly among that portion of the population that is isolated from its control or representation, we will understand that government "foreign aid," given to unmotivated and unorganized areas, is not only wasteful but potentially harmful. Bitter experience will have sharpened our realization:

1. Matter is of no value without purpose and a sense of direction. Structural change and growth require vision and a doctrine.

2. The enrichment of an administrative bureaucracy without local roots is apt to thwart change and bring corruption. When administrators cannot perform the tasks they are paid to do, they become dishonest.

3. When matter and technique come from "the outside," unrelated to local initiatives, the people are only further convinced of how little they control their own destinies and are discouraged from organizing to help themselves.

Effective engines of change, effective means of motivation and organization, effective integrators will come in different molds and models: There will be communal-cooperative organization, such as the Israeli kibbutz, the Brazilian Peasant League, the Venezuelan campesino federations, and so forth. They are characterized by strong spiritual and inspirational elements, a means through which religion will have substantial political effect, contributing ideological direction to an unsatisfactorily barren pragmatism.

The traditional bargaining labor unions will continue to have primary political importance in the developing world, often as the machines of political parties.

Perhaps most important will be new versions of the large, integrated business enterprise. With different combinations of public-private management, these will be the world's most efficient integrators and most effective engines of change. The corporation of 2000 will, for example, have the basic managerial competence for undoing the knots that currently hinder the food production, processing, distribution, and marketing process. The integrating capacity of the multinational corporation of 2000 will be particularly remarkable, for its functions and authority will be not only political, social, economic, cultural, and technical, but also psychological, motivational, and organizational. In 2000 the world will be laced by the branches and subsidiaries of several thousand multibillion-dollar corporations. Their direction will emanate largely from the United States, also from the Soviet Union, Europe, and Japan, but their ownership will be spread throughout the world in a vast complexity of public and private combinations. Their managers, true citizens of the world, will be from every land. New international law and organization will supervise and regulate their activity. This organization, at first commercial, financial, and economic, will tend to force a world political order that by 2000 will be on its way to becoming truly a world government.

Although limited in ability to initiate or cause radical change, those governments so inclined will, as always, play a crucial role in providing the climate for its introduction. In northern Brazil, for example, the direct efforts of government have begun to bring effective change; the government allows the peasant organizations sponsored by the radical Church to exist and it also encourages new entrepreneurial business corporations through tax and other incentives.

What structure of American government will be formed to cope with this world of 2000? Primarily, of course, the structure must rest on our purpose, which itself depends on how we perceive our interests. The overriding interest will be survival and peace, and peace will depend upon two factors:

1. The protection of our vital political, economic, and commercial interests. These will be sharply redefined in the early 1970's to reflect the realities of world power, particularly as it is held by the United States, the Soviet Union, China, Western Europe, and Japan.

2. The control of conflict. New distinctions will be made between Conflict A, which may be necessary to bring about the measure of change essential for long-term stability (that is, peace), and Conflict B, which is wasteful, damaging, and unnecessary to peace.

Hitler's armies exemplify the latter, Mexican development the former. Mexico's admirable stage of development today would not have been reached without the violence, bloodshed, and conflict of its Revolution. It seems unlikely that even by 2000 the requirement for violent conflict will have been eliminated, any more than will the need of people for heroes and legends around which to organize themselves. To be sure, international devices for the assessment and control of conflict will have been created, but the United States will undoubtedly continue to have interests and obligations not fully cared for by these devices.

As we have noted, the American government by 2000 will see quite clearly that its interests require the introduction of change, and consequently of a degree of conflict, into many areas of the world, particularly Latin America, Asia, and Africa. Understanding the process of change better than it does today, the American government will use different means of pursuing it.

Even today we are aware that in this sense the structures of government are unsatisfactory. Donald Schon calls the Department of Agriculture a "memorial to nineteenth-century productivity problems." Clearly it has neither the competence nor the experience to handle important responsibilities for American initiatives in the world food crisis. If the problems of the world food crisis are consigned to this department, they will not receive the integrated attention they must have. The crisis is at once political, social, and economic, and its solution involves many factors of paramount interest to the State, Defense, Commerce, and Justice Departments. Increased food production in Brazil, for example, requires the radical political reorganization of the Northeast; great capital resources will have to be mobilized into combinations of power that will control the market, reducing competition in order to organize the most efficient and practical pricing, distribution, and marketing system. These may be "combinations in restraint of trade," but they will be critical to the establishment of political stability and civic order.

Two small examples from the 1960's—W. R. Grace in Colombia, and Development and Resources, Inc., in Iran—illustrate how American corporations can act as integrating engines of multiple change within a context of increased food production. Grace, in cooperation with the Colombian land reform institute, has arranged to buy tomatoes from newly settled campesinos, process them into paste and ketchup, and market them through their world-wide system. In one stroke, Grace has provided the means by which land reform can raise agricultural productivity, not lower it, by providing poor farmers with markets and technology. Development and Resources, under contract with the government of Iran, has provided the integrated capacity to convert the arid south into an Imperial Valley, opening the markets of the world to its produce. By 2000 it will be apparent that these were prototypes of change more profoundly political and social than agricultural in their effect.

Although bureaucracies have enormous endurance—especially big and political ones—by 2000 the reorganization of Washington governmental structures to conform more conveniently to the integrating challenges of the world will be well on its way.

The big departments will remain (some merged, such as Commerce with Labor), and several new ones will be added to handle space, undersea, and other matters. Most significant, however, will be the increase in size and importance of the Office of Management and Budget and related offices of the White House, emerging first as coordinated task forces to deal with specific problems and growing into Schon's "gardens of competence." The task-force approach will have increasing appeal because of its ability to mobilize rapidly high interdisciplinary talent to deal with a particular challenge in a rational and programmed fashion, cutting across traditional bureaucratic lines when necessary. Its effectiveness will depend upon the weight and priority assigned to its work by political leadership, particularly the President and his appointees.

As the elimination of big war becomes increasingly accepted as a primary objective, the function of the military will change. While it will function principally as a deterrent and an international police force, the Department of Defense will probably continue expanding into such jurisdictions as "civic action." With its superior administrative form and discipline and its access to funds, it may improve the work of weaker and more confused organizations such as the Agency for International Development.

The attempts of the military to wield both sword and plowshare will be hotly challenged by other Washington power groups, and I cannot even guess what the outcome will be. Indeed, I find the role of the military in 2000 a major and a troubling enigma.

Because many foreign governments are weak at effecting change in their own jurisdictions and it is difficult for the American government to force them to do so, there will be some basic shifts in the organization of foreign aid. The bulk of American nonmilitary contributions to political, economic, and social development, which will total about $70 billion a year (5 percent of the G.N.P.), will be made through international institutions: development banks, United Nations agencies, and international organizations of labor and cooperatives. More direct contributions will be made through American profit and, more especially, nonprofit corporations and groups. These will have close liaison with government for planning, but will operate independently, and they will form a highly varied complex of national and multinational components.

These new structures, which will be more on the fringes of our government than in its midst, will reflect two phenomena that became clear in the late 1960's. One is the debilitating tension between those American interests that want to introduce change into change-resistant environments, and those interests that require orderly and official military, economic, and diplomatic relationships with the regimes in power in the countries concerned. It is untenable to have these conflicting interests represented in the same department or even in the same government. Only if they are separate and distinct can they have the necessary fluidity, flexibility, and mystery. Thus the new structures for international action in 2000 will reflect the troublesome differences between the purposes of today's change-oriented government agencies, such as AID, the Peace Corps, and to some extent the CIA, and the purposes of the State and Defense Departments, whose assignment is more traditional and necessarily tied to the regime in power.

The second is that these new structures will also be designed to avert the obvious difficulties inherent in any American—or other—government attempting to bring about change in another state. By 2000 we will clearly see the necessity of doing just this—that is, pragmatically realizing declarations like that of the Alliance for Progress—but by then we will have become more proficient at it. We will not only understand that revolutionary change is inevitable, and essential for peace, but we will have become better at promoting it.

American government funding for some of these more strategic activities will be handled through a government-financed foundation, whose trustees will represent Congress, the Executive Branch, and the public. This foundation will be particularly important in financing the research and teaching activities of American universities in Latin America, Asia, and Africa. It also will play a substantial role in financing and piecing together elaborate developmental schemes of which the W. R. Grace and Development and Resources examples are forerunners. The foundation might take the lead in establishing corporations that would draw on the entrepreneurial and managerial skills of American and European industry, include federations of workers and farmers in Latin America or Asia as partners, call for capital from international investment centers, and arrange complex international marketing and trading patterns throughout the world. Peace Corps volunteers and trade-union representatives from the United States, Canada, Europe, and the less-developed world would coordinate their activities with these giant enterprises. Their substantial profits would be returned not to the stockholders of one country but to the multinational partners. As these corporations matured they would be passed on to an international organization for continuing surveillance.

The present functions of AID will be greatly altered, with the bulk transferred to international agencies of one sort or another, and the more strategic, innovative, and experimental handled through our foundation or one of its satellites. Embassies may continue to have small development advisory staffs, and the State Department will keep track of the numerous independent operations, but State and its embassies will nevertheless be substantially removed from these operations.

We may well be prepared to assign a major directing role for world economic and social development to a half-dozen small nations such as Yugoslavia, Israel, Tunisia, Thailand, Burma, and Costa Rica. Representatives of such nations might form the governing board of the United Nations and other regional and international development organizations. We will in fact be grateful to diminish our power and control in this way, if other major powers are similarly prepared to diminish theirs. But such mutual diminution can take place only if we define our interests with increased precision, weighing priorities, so that we can arrive at satisfactory criteria for the abdication of power.

The decline of traditional nationalism in the developed and less-developed regions of the world involves pain and violence. The great powers, especially the United States, the Soviet Union, Europe, and Japan, will have to keep the violence minimal and under international control. A central question of 2000 will be how to develop international, regional organizations before the nationalizing process is completed. It must be hastened through a variety of nongovernmental engines of change, and at the same time a practical and acceptable system of world-conflict arbitration must be created. Soviet, European, American, Japanese, and Chinese scientists and academicians will start working on the formula for this machinery in the 1970's. By 2000 a model should be in operation. Since the governmental bureaucracies of the developed countries are naturally conservative, they will impede this process.

The United States and the world will be particularly perplexed in 2000 by questions of ideology and philosophy, and semantics will still pose a major obstacle to communication and understanding. Words like capitalism, socialism, and communism will have become meaningless. Religions will become increasingly secular and, in the broadest sense of the word, political, concerned with justice, ethics, and morality rather than with mystery, faith, and the spirit. This bothersome ideological gap will present the greatest single obstacle to integration and synthesis because without the dynamic vision of an ideology, it will be difficult to agree on goals, interests, priorities, and criteria for conflict arbitration. The demands on philosophers to derive new theories of virtue, government, perception, and reality will be enormous because scientific knowledge will be so abundant. Since survival itself depends upon some universal convictions about the purpose of survival, the greatest challenge for 2000 will be to give order and meaning to this scientific knowledge. But it is doubtful whether government can do more in this ideological realm than see the problem clearly and acknowledge its importance.

Political leaders will be particularly hard-pressed to formulate new purposes, to set new priorities, and to form and reflect upon the values of new generations, and they may thus turn increasingly to the secular thought of theologians such as Maritain and de Chardin.

Clearly, development means change, but what is its purpose? What right does one nation have to seek to change another? For what purpose, what goal? Charity is only a partial answer; the matter of interest must also be faced. The Marshall Plan may well be the last instance of foreign assistance falling within a people's own determined structure. Can assistance be legitimate if a people has not determined a structure? If so, what are the standards of legitimacy? By 2000 the economic notions of Adam Smith and the Protestant ethic will be of little help in defining purpose. Government can help most in this area by responding hospitably to such institutions as universities that are equipped to carry on investigations of this metaphysical kind.

In a sense, the challenge will be no different from the one we face today. What Henry Kissinger has written about the nations of the Atlantic community also applies to the nations of the world as a whole: The problem is "to find a way of dreaming together about the kind of world they want to bring about, rather than about the circumstances in which they might wish to blow it up." [1]

NOTE

1. Statement delivered before the Senate Foreign Relations Committee, June 27, 1966, reprinted in *The Reporter*, July 14, 1966.

THE NATION-STATE, THE MULTINATIONAL CORPORATION, AND THE CHANGING WORLD ORDER

Lester R. Brown

At this point in history it is clear that the existing international order is changing, moving slowly toward one world. Two basic forces, advancing technology and the almost universal desire for human betterment, are the principal sources of change. This movement toward one world, a result of the forces inherent in modernization, is spontaneous and independent of the United Nations and any planned attempts at political unification; and it poses new and unique problems for the nation-states as they attempt to adjust to the changing order.

The need for a new political theory, much discussed by the Commission on the Year 2000, is most apparent at the supranational level. The nation-state as we have known it over the past few centuries is, largely for economic reasons, diminishing in importance as a distinct and independent political unit. More and more decisions made within it are influenced by what goes on outside its boundaries. Many functions of government, once the sole province of the nation-state, are gravitating toward various supranational institutions and multinational or global corporations.

From an economist's point of view, the changing world order is fundamentally a process of technological and economic change. If this effort by an economist to interpret the political implications of economic processes seems a bit brash, consider a statement made recently by P. M. S. Blackett, President of the Royal Society in London: "If we only discussed those things about which we are knowledgeable, a deathly silence would descend upon the earth."

I. Economic Interdependence among Nation-States

The growing economic interdependence among nation-states is due to several factors. The increasingly large economies of scale—that is, the substantial gains from production and marketing on a mass basis—associated with the use of modern industrial technology force countries to depend more on each other. Except for the United States, most of the technology any given country needs to progress economically must be imported from another country. No individual country other than the United States is likely to account for more than, say, one-tenth of the new technology being developed. As economies develop, the widespread advantages of freer trade between countries in both raw materials and products becomes more obvious. The development of a shared resource or the construction of interlocking power grids or petroleum pipelines illustrates instances where binational and multinational cooperation can be exceedingly beneficial to all involved.

Economic integration through reduction of trade barriers between countries, in process throughout the postwar period, has taken place within the framework of the General Agreement on Tariffs and Trade (GATT). For many countries, however, the worldwide pace and scope of tariff reduction and trade expansion has not progressed at a sufficiently rapid rate to fit plans for economic growth, and these countries have formed regional economic groupings. Their feelings are reflected in the following comments by George Ball:

> In these twenty postwar years, we have come to recognize in action, though not always in words, that the political boundaries of nation-states are too narrow and constricted to define the scope and activities of modern business. This recognition has found some reflection, though not enough, in political action. Six countries of Western Europe have frontally attacked the stifling restrictions imposed on trade by shedding the ancient concept of nation-states. They have created a common market. In the summer of 1968 goods will move with full freedom throughout Western Europe to serve the needs of nearly two hundred million people.[1]

The reasons for regional economic groupings often vary. The European Economic Community (EEC) wanted to provide for the member countries large markets comparable in size to those in the United States. This would permit national firms to use economies of scale for further growth.

A more recent and much smaller economic group is the five-nation Central American Common Market (CACM). The Central American countries had severely limited possibilities for attracting foreign private investment along with accompanying technology and management and marketing know-how on an individual basis. As a common market, however, they represent a much more attractive investment prospect as the recent step-up in foreign private investment in Central America indicates.

Another instance of mutually beneficial economic integration is that of the United States and Canada. Although not yet functioning as a common market, the two countries are rather thoroughly integrated in several important aspects. Other established regional economic groupings are the seven-member European Free Trade Association and the East African Common Market, consisting of Kenya, Tanzania, and Uganda.[2]

One of the most compelling reasons for economic integration, within either regional or worldwide groupings of countries, is the economy of scale associated with the use of modern manufacturing and research technology, which has occasionally assumed immense proportions.

One of the best examples is the supersonic transport (SST). The United States and the Soviet Union individually, and Great Britain and France cooperatively, have been developing an SST. Only the United States and the Soviet Union have the economic and technical resources to pursue this venture alone; Britain and France found it necessary to combine their resources and expertise. Given the usual demands on national resources, neither alone could hope to compete. The United States will spend more than a billion dollars—$15 per taxpayer—just to build a single prototype. The retail cost of each plane will be an estimated $40 million.

Consider the computer industry. International Business Machines, the dominant computer firm in the world, has in many ways outgrown the American economy. It could not fund its vast research and development program if it did not have access to the world market for computers.

Or consider space exploration. There are a number of cooperative efforts under way to launch satellites, principally instrumented satellites assembled by other countries, using United States launchers and boosters to put them into orbit. We may in time see much more cooperation in this area.

The postwar period has been characterized by an unusually large number of binational and multinational efforts to develop resources. The Indus River system, shared by India and Pakistan, has involved close cooperation between the two countries, even when they have been at war. The St. Lawrence Seaway, a joint United States-Canadian project, has contributed to the development of both countries. Oil pipelines, transporting large quantities of crude petroleum between the Soviet Union and Western Europe, and among the Middle Eastern countries, are another example of cooperative efforts to develop raw materials.

Electric power grids tying Western European countries together reduce the overall generating capacity needed to meet the sum of their individual needs. Electrical-power generating facilities, now nearly completed in Paraguay, will be used to provide electric power not only for Paraguay but also for neighboring Brazil and Argentina. It is entirely possible that we will someday see a worldwide electrical power grid, permitting the system to balance high daytime requirements in one area of the globe with low nighttime requirements in a distant area, thus permitting vast savings.

The extent to which governing responsibilities, once the exclusive domain of the nation-state, are being shared by various supranational organizations is not widely known. This is particularly true of such institutions as the GATT and the EEC. One of the principal reasons that the Kennedy Round of GATT negotiations took five years was the realization that negotiating a meaningful trade liberalization in agriculture required negotiating domestic farm policies in the GATT member countries. Internal price-support levels, marketing quotas, and acreage controls were involved.

Another area in which a supranational body—the International Monetary Fund—is influencing the formulation of domestic policies is monetary and fiscal policy. Even the United States, economically the Fund's most powerful member, must heed the warnings and consider the advice given by the Fund's leadership, which greatly influences the economic policies of the developing countries, as does the International Bank for Reconstruction and Development (World Bank). Much of their influence derives from their multinational character. Stringent reforms imposed upon developing countries in exchange for resources that the Fund and the Bank can make available are accepted much more readily than they would be if the conditions were imposed by a particular country.

An extensive listing could be made of international bodies that have assumed various responsibilities of government, such as communications, transportation, fishing rights, patents, and ocean exploration. The cumulative number of treaties and conventions regulating various activities in member countries is becoming quite impressive.

Most of the more important supranational institutions have come into existence since World War II. As countries become interested in participating in the world economy in a meaningful way, they must face the prospect of losing some of their sovereignty. This is occurring to an extent not always fully realized, because it is a gradual and not always visible process.

II. The Multinational Corporation

The world today can be viewed in a simplified sense as a matrix of interacting political institutions, principally nation-states, on the one hand, and economic institutions, principally multinational corporations, on the other. The emergence of the corporation as an influential institution is rather recent, occurring largely, though not entirely, in this century. The multinational corporation, contrasted with the traditionally more common national corporation, has achieved much of its prominence since World War II. As most of the large corporations become multinational, the interaction between governments and the multinational firms increases.

Of all the institutions in existence today the corporation is one of the most modern. It is both flexible and efficient, and its ability to survive and flourish is seldom matched.[3] Today's multinational or global corporations are also very large, and the largest have an annual product greater than that of all but a handful of countries. Relative size of corporations and nation-states is indicated in Table I, where countries and corporations are ranked according to their Gross National Product and gross annual sales receipts. The seventeen largest economic entities are countries, but General Motors, the world's largest corporation, ranks eighteenth. It is larger than Argentina, Czechoslovakia, and Pakistan and in the same league as

TABLE I.

Ranking of Countries and Corporations According to Size of Annual Product or Sales 1968[a]

RANK	ECONOMIC ENTITY	ANNUAL PRODUCT * (billion dollars)
1	United States	880.77
2	U.S.S.R.	228.45[a]
3	Japan	141.81
4	Germany, West	132.48
5	France	126.23
6	United Kingdom	102.67
7	Italy	74.98
8	China, Mainland	68.80[a]
9	Canada	62.44
10	India	44.32
11	Brazil	32.90
12	Mexico	26.74
13	Sweden	25.57
14	Netherlands	25.23
15	Spain	25.20
16	Poland	24.90[a]
17	Australia	23.14
18	*General Motors*	22.76
19	Germany, East	22.21[a]
20	Belgium	20.75
21	Switzerland	17.16
22	Argentina	16.28
23	Czechoslovakia	15.88[a]
24	Pakistan	14.55
25	*Standard Oil (N.J.)*	14.09
26	*Ford Motor*	14.08
27	South Africa	14.02
28	Rumania	13.89[a]
29	Denmark	12.39
30	Turkey	11.60
31	Austria	11.40
32	Yugoslavia	10.57[a]
33	Indonesia	9.60[a]
[b]34	*Royal Dutch/Shell Group (N-B)*	9.22
35	Hungary	9.20[a]
36	Venezuela	9.11
37	Norway	9.02
38	*General Electric*	8.38
39	Iran	8.28
40	Greece	7.55
41	*Chrysler*	7.45
42	Philippines	7.21
43	*I.B.M.*	6.89
44	*Mobil Oil*	6.22
45	Colombia	6.10
46	Chile	5.82
47	Korea, South	5.82
48	Bulgaria	5.73[a]
49	U.A.R.	5.69[a]
50	Thailand	5.56
[b]51	*Unilever (B-N)*	5.53
52	*Texaco*	5.46
53	Nigeria	5.34
54	Portugal	5.01
55	New Zealand	4.86
56	Israel	4.67
57	*Gulf Oil*	4.56
58	*U.S. Steel*	4.54
59	Peru	4.22
60	Taiwan	4.16
61	*I.T.T.*	4.07
62	*Western Electric*	4.03
63	*Standard Oil (Calif.)*	3.63
64	*McDonnell-Douglas*	3.61
65	*DuPont*	3.48
66	Malaysia	3.34
67	*Shell Oil*	3.32
68	*Westinghouse*	3.30
69	*Boeing*	3.27
[b]70	*British Petroleum (B)*	3.26
71	*Standard Oil (Ind.)*	3.21
72	*R.C.A.*	3.11
73	Algeria	3.00
74	Morocco	3.00

Continued on p. 178

Continued from p. 177

RANK	ECONOMIC ENTITY	ANNUAL PRODUCT * (billion dollars)
75	Ireland	2.98
76	Vietnam, South	2.98
[b]77	*Imperial Chem. Industries (B)*	2.97
78	*Gen. Tel. & Electronics*	2.93
79	*Goodyear Tire & Rubber*	2.93
[b]80	*Volkswagenwerk (G)*	2.93
81	*Bethlehem Steel*	2.86
82	*Swift*	2.83
83	Korea, North	2.82[a]
84	*Ling-Temco-Vought*	2.77
85	*Union Carbide*	2.69
[b]86	*Philips' Gloeilampenfabrieken (N)*	2.69
87	*General Dynamics*	2.66
88	Cuba	2.65[a]
89	*Eastman Kodak*	2.64
90	*N. American Rockwell*	2.64
[b]91	*British Steel (B)*	2.62
92	Hong Kong	2.57
93	*Proctor & Gamble*	2.54
94	*International Harvester*	2.54
95	*National Dairy Products*	2.43
96	*United Aircraft*	2.41
[b]97	*Montecatini Edison (I)*	2.32
[b]98	*National Coal Board (B)*	2.30
[b]99	*Hitachi (J)*	2.28
100	*Continental Oil*	2.25

* The indicators used are the gross national product for countries and gross annual sales for corporations. Though not strictly comparable (a value added figure would have been more appropriate for industry), they are sufficiently close for illustrative purposes.

[a] 1967, most recent data available.

[b] Foreign firm.

(B) Great Britain; (G) Germany; (I) Italy; (J) Japan; (N) the Netherlands.

Poland, Australia, and East Germany. Standard Oil of New Jersey, which ranks twenty-fifth, heads an economic empire more productive than either the Republic of South Africa or Rumania.

Of the fifty largest economic entities, forty-two are countries and eight are corporations; of the top one hundred, forty-four are corporations. A decade hence the number of corporations in the top fifty may well be much greater, since the larger ones are growing much faster than the average country. During the 1960's, the ten largest multinational corporations expanded at some 8 percent per year, nearly double the growth rate for nation-states.

The larger or global corporations for the most part have their headquarters within the United States. Of the top ten firms, eight are American, the remaining two European. Of the top forty multinational corporations, thirty-three are based in the United States.

Some of the functions once considered to be the sole province of the nation-state are shifting to the global corporation, as corporations now formulate economic policies at both the national level and on a global scale. There is clearly overlap and sometimes conflict between the objectives and the policies of corporations on the one hand and nation-states on the other. Governments wishing to plan independently are often frustrated by decisions made by the management of a global corporation, perhaps headquartered on the opposite side of the world.[4] In many instances the corporation may command more production resources than the nation-state. In a random bilateral confrontation between any developing country and one of the fifty largest multinational corporations, the odds are that the corporation will be the larger of the two in economic terms.

Corporations accumulate capital and therefore influence the rate of savings and investment. They influence the pattern of investment both in geographic terms and by area of activity. They conduct research and develop most of the new technologies. They employ people and they provide income for investors; literally millions of people, either stockholders or employees, may depend upon a single corporation for part or all of their livelihood.

The state-corporation conflict will be further aggravated if the United States, home base of many of the multinational firms, tries to use overseas corporate subsidiaries as instruments of its foreign policy, particularly in such areas as East-West trade. But conflicts between corporations and states are offset by the indispensability of the global corporation in the development process. More and more of the world's advanced technology is developed by, and is the property of, private firms.

If individual countries are to gain access to this technology, they must attract investment, which brings technology with it; import technology in the form of finished goods (such as jet aircraft, computers, or hybrid seed); or purchase the licensing rights from the firms that possess the technology. Less advanced countries may be forced to import the finished products, though many are increasingly trying to attract foreign investment. More advanced countries may be interested primarily in licensing arrangements. American firms now earn a staggering \$1.4 billion per year on their licensing and royalties arrangements abroad.[5]

The global corporations are the great disseminators of technology today, dispensing not only technology on a grand scale but also management and marketing know-how—skills they have in abundance. Indeed, one of the prized assets of a global corporation, from a host country's point of view, is its worldwide network of export outlets.[6]

Investment by American firms overseas has expanded very rapidly during the period since the Korean War. If the rate of growth prevailing from 1950 to 1966 were to continue for another sixteen years, the aggregate investment would expand from $86 billion to nearly *$400 billion sixteen years hence*. Thus, aggregate American overseas investments would be far larger than the total product of any other country, and in fact as large as the current economies of the Soviet Union, West Germany, and Japan combined. But various constraints, including a lack of profitable investment opportunities, balance-of-payments deficits, and resistance to American investments, will undoubtedly reduce the future rate below that of the recent past. Nonetheless, in Raymond Vernon's words, ". . . it would be astonishing if they did not grow very rapidly in the years just ahead."[7]

European and Japanese firms seem to hold their positions rather well in such older industries as chemistry, engineering, metallurgy, rubber, and textiles, and overseas investments by American firms in these areas are relatively modest. In the new technologically based industries, however, centered on electronics, optics, solid-state physics, high-energy physics, instrumentation, and plastics, American firms are rapidly expanding, and they dominate in several countries. As new-technology industries become more important, American technological dominance will probably be even greater.[8]

III. American Economic Dominance

In this century, no single nation-state has so dominated the world economy as does the United States today. Its G.N.P., totaling $1,000 billion annually, is as large as those of the next six ranking countries combined. The annual increment in its G.N.P. is as large as the total G.N.P. of all but a handful of the world's countries.

Several factors have contributed to this vast lead of the American economy—its generous endowment of rich agricultural land and mineral resources, a stable political system, a set of values and an economic system that emphasize and reward hard work, its avoidance of international warfare within its own boundaries, and its unprecedented social mobility. Some new factors also are emerging.

Historically Americans have tended to acknowledge that their educational system was somehow inferior to that of Europe. In the immediate post-Sputnik era—the late fifties and early sixties—widespread efforts were made to improve the educational system, particularly in the physical sciences.

Today the United States is educating its population to an unparalleled degree. Of its 20–24 age group, 43 percent are in college, contrasting with 16 percent in France, 8 percent in West Germany, and 5 percent in the United Kingdom. Despite some continuing weaknesses at the primary and secondary levels, the American educational system is beginning to demonstrate its strength in many ways, for it seems better suited to the modern world than many of the more traditional European and Asian systems.

The availability of trained management personnel in the United States is in marked contrast to that of the rest of the world. Some, such as Diebold, see this as the principal explanation for the varying rates of progress in the United States and the rest of the world,[9] and there is growing foreign agreement on this point. It has been described with particular eloquence by Jean-Jacques Servan-Schreiber in *The American Challenge*.[10]

The United States will continue to be the land of opportunity and therefore will attract the skilled, the educated, and the talented from throughout the world like a giant geographic magnet, making it even more potent technologically and economically.

This "brain drain" draws from both developed and less-developed regions. During the period from 1962 to 1966, more than 60,000 professionals and technical workers came to the United States from Europe.[11] Even more serious is the loss of skilled manpower from non-European countries. Efforts to reduce emigration, particularly from poorer countries, may become more effective, but the United States will probably continue, though unintentionally, to be a net importer of skilled manpower through the remainder of this century.

Worldwide investment in research and development has increased several-fold over the past thirty years, much of it within the United States, where annual research-and-development expenditures now total $27 billion, in contrast to $9 billion in Western Europe.

Several indicators show the magnitude of the American technological lead over the rest of the world. One is the volume of exports —more specifically, the net export balance of products of advanced-technology industries such as jet aircraft or electronic computers. Another is the ratio between the annual sale of licensing rights, patents, and royalties abroad by American firms for various industrial processes. At present American firms receive more than $1.4 billion annually from foreign firms, as against outlays that are only a fraction of this sum.

American expenditures on research and development have increased much more rapidly than the Gross National Product. If the economy continues to expand rapidly and if the proportion of G.N.P. used for research and development continues to edge upward, as seems likely, American investment in this activity may well double within the next ten to fifteen years.

IV. American Government and the Changing World Order

My basic proposition is that the existing world order is changing, moving slowly toward one world. Economic, political, and cultural ties are increasing, and the sovereignty of the nation-state is decreasing. Geographic boundaries that originated in a time of limited human mobility are now becoming increasingly blurred.

A unified world economy would, in many important respects, be highly desirable. As economic ties between countries in the form of trade, corporate investment, aid, finance, tourism, and binational or multinational resource-development efforts increase and strengthen, political interdependence also increases, and the prospect of armed conflict between nation-states diminishes.

Many elements of American foreign policy since World War II have supported the overall objective of worldwide economic integration. A series of negotiations within the framework of the General Agreement on Tariffs and Trade over the past twenty years has resulted in a broad liberalization of international trade. Negotiated reductions in trade barriers resulting from the Kennedy Round of these negotiations will contribute further to this objective.

In addition, the United States has strongly supported the establishment of such supranational organizations as the International Monetary Fund and the International Bank for Reconstruction and Development, which are making a substantial, though inadequately appreciated, contribution to the movement toward one world. Regional development banks, first in Latin America and later in Africa and Asia, have received American encouragement and financial support.

The United States has also given strong support to such regional economic groupings as the European Economic Community, the Central American Common Market, and the European Free Trade Association. On its own, the United States has worked for closer economic ties in both trade and investment with Canada, and has actively encouraged the formation of a Latin American Common Market.

Because of its dominant role in the world economy, the United States is in a unique position to further the movement toward one world. Policies for the future must deal with the obstacles to further integration of the world economy. Past policies which have facilitated international economic integration should be continued. Others, such as continuing cold-war policies inhibiting trade between the United States and the communist economies, should be abandoned.

We must also formulate policies and use our resources to reduce the more persistent economic gaps between north and south, and bring literally hundreds of millions of subsistence families into the marketplace. Only as this occurs can the countries in which these people reside become fully integrated into the world economy.

As American technological and economic leadership continues, conscious efforts must be made to ameliorate the adverse effects of the "American presence." This problem is aggravated by a growing tendency for those living outside the United States to confuse modernization with Americanization. We can set an example by reorienting our own thinking away from a national society toward a more global one. Expanded cultural exchanges will help.

Through education we can share some of our advances with other countries. American universities should begin establishing campuses in other countries with the primary purpose of serving students within those countries. If American resources are used to assist in establishing campuses abroad, the educational gap could be narrowed and the brain drain perhaps arrested. In recent years, efforts toward worldwide economic integration have focused on the freer movement of goods. Parallel efforts should be made to liberalize the movement of capital and, on a short-term basis, of people.

The large corporation is being forced to become multinational in order to remain competitive, because it must have access to the lowest-cost raw materials, the most efficient labor forces, and the most lucrative markets. The global corporation will become even more prominent as economies become more advanced and technology relatively more important. The key problem will be how to minimize the conflict between the nation-state and the global corporation.

Specific actions can be taken to denationalize, or disperse more widely, the ownership, management, labor force, production, purchases, and sales of global firms. Shares can be marketed on a growing number of security exchanges around the world.

The concept of one world is not new, but the dream has traditionally been that of the political scientist, and often of a rather utopian world government. Instead, we are now moving toward one world along a very different path—that of economic integration followed by closer political relationships. This is an exciting prospect, as is the prospect that we as a country can profoundly influence and accelerate this evolutionary process. To do so, we must have a clear vision of the kind of integrated world we want. We must also identify the basic forces that are shaping the world of the future and harness them, rather than dissipate our energies in conflict with them.

NOTES

1. George W. Ball, "Cosmocorp: The Importance of Being Stateless," *Columbia Journal of World Business,* November–December 1967, p. 25.

2. Anthony Astrachan, "New East African Trading Group is Launched," *The Washington Post,* December 3, 1967.

3. Raymond Vernon, "Multinational Enterprise and National Sovereignty," *Harvard Business Review,* March–April 1967, p. 157.

4. For further discussion of this point, see Ball, "Cosmocorp: The Importance of Being Stateless," *op. cit.,* pp. 28–30; and Vernon, "Multinational Enterprise and National Sovereignty," *op. cit.,* pp. 159–160, 166–168.

5. Department of Commerce.

6. Vernon, "Multinational Enterprise and National Sovereignty," *op. cit.,* p. 160.

7. *Ibid.,* p. 157.

8. "The Technological Gap," *The Economist,* March 16, 1968, p. 72.

9. John Diebold, "Is the Gap Technological?", *Foreign Affairs,* January 1968, p. 283.

10. (Paris: Denöel, 1967). (New York: Atheneum, 1969).

11. Diebold, "Is the Gap Technological?", *op. cit.,* p. 278.

THE MILITARY

Herman Kahn

I wish to describe in this essay some possible interactions at the end of this century between the defense establishment and the federal and state institutions. This may be more conjectural than the other essays in this volume, not because nonmilitary American life will not change enormously, but because many of the nonmilitary changes will come mainly out of an internal dynamic. In most domestic issues one can presumably make intelligent guesses about how current trends will develop. In military affairs, international trends and contexts will probably be more important than domestic trends. But a major point of this essay will be that domestic issues and attitudes may prove more important as constraints and determinants of many aspects of the "military future" than has been the case in the last two decades.

The Basic Common Context

This essay will examine four basic if oversimplified international contexts in order to cover a range of possibilities. In all four cases I will assume (unless explicitly modified) that the world has developed according to the following socio-economic-political scenario.

We start with the current international system of 150 more or less independent and sovereign nations. Except for the rather modest evolutions noted below, most of the system's current characteristics will probably continue. Each of these nations considers itself best able to judge how it will attempt to advance its perceived national interests, and how, if at all, it will participate in promoting the common welfare—reserving for its own decision what military preparations it will make and under what conditions they will be used. There are, of course, many constraints on the independent action of the units in this nation-state system, but some current limitations, such as a tendency toward bipolar discipline and authority in the world, and much "great power authority and prestige," have been eroding and seem likely to erode even further by 2000.

During the next thirty years, we will undoubtedly see both international competition and cooperation; balancing, integrating, and disruptive processes; peacemaking as well as violence. But to a degree that would have surprised many in the past there will also be a great deal of self-restraint and self-deterrence—particularly in the use or threat of violence by large nations. What many consider a "war system" may seem increasingly able to maintain peace while at the same time remaining on the edge of crisis and increasingly capable of horrendous levels of violence. In other words, we are more likely to have anxiety and apocalyptic rhetoric rather than violence. Yet, for the reasons listed below, military force and logic will in general, by the year 2000, seem less central in the conduct of day-to-day international relations—*except perhaps in important parts of Afro-Asia*—than they are today. One of the surprises of the 1960's has been their relative irrelevance.

With the possible exception of China and some Afro-Asian countries, the following seems likely:

1. Even if there is a growth of various kinds of neo-isolationist sentiments in different nations, the world will still be regarded as one human community. No group will, for ethnic or national reasons, be regarded as *Untermenschen,* and everyone will be conceded some degree of human rights. There will also be many pluralistic security communities (a political and moral relationship between certain states which makes war or even the use of force "unthinkable" in most situations) as well as a larger unified worldwide economy and market place.

2. Internal economic and technological development will probably continue to be the technique for achieving most national objectives—including a base for power and influence as well as wealth itself.

3. Modern technology and other developments will continue to lessen the historic strategic value of many geographical areas (even today, there are no American "lifelines" such as the Suez Canal was in the past for Great Britain).

4. These trends are apparent at the present time. Nations, by and large, no longer try to use force to gain plunder, slaves, foreign territory, commercial advantage, and the like.

5. Compared to many past eras, even ideological (and religious) motives for force seem on the wane. Despite the continuing "search for meaning and purpose," this erosion of ideological pressures in war and international politics seems likely to continue well through the 1970's.

In addition to these basic reasons for a declining use of military power and military calculations, the following superficial trends will probably exist and strengthen the general trend:

1. The United States, the UN, the OAS, and others will frequently act as policemen, but they will also be prepared to limit or reverse the ultimate success of acts of aggression, thus making them appear unprofitable from the beginning.

2. All-out war (and, therefore, to some degree, any war) will continue to seem psychologically and morally "unthinkable" or "impossible" to many nations, especially large ones.

3. With some exceptions, little serious irredentism will exist in Europe, North and South America, and Japan.

4. Current relatively high standards of international behavior among the developed and powerful nations seem likely to continue.

5. As a result, the 1970's, while not without tumult, are likely to see a general, even if uncertain, peace based as much on satisfaction and acceptance as on deterrence and weakness. This "peace" will of course be marred by many localized outbreaks of violence. But both the violence itself and its consequences are likely to be limited by various mechanisms, such as internal weakness, outside or regional intervention, and so forth.

6. There will be much wishful thinking about the likelihood of keeping certain areas of the world free of national wars for the rest of this century. While such a peaceful state can be easily maintained among the ten large powers and within the Western Hemisphere and Western Europe, it will not exclude all serious crises or intense pressures within the "secure areas" of the world, to say nothing of the less secure (Afro-Asia). Therefore many proxy or geographically limited confrontations among the great powers, as well as the localized conflicts already mentioned, are quite possible, and these

can always escalate, even if there was no initial intention to have such escalation. Memories of past dangers and fears of future escalations are likely to be present even if the "general peace" is actually preserved.

The Distribution of Economic and Military Power in the Basic Common Context

Discussions of the future tend to overemphasize such economic factors as the Gross National Product and advanced technology. As a result, the less quantifiable variables of a society are neglected. The reverse is also common, but, while noneconomic and nontechnological variables more often than not dominate particular crises, the economic and technological variables still set the basic structure and framework of power.[1]

For our immediate purposes, I will tentatively assume that the Gross National Product and the technological level are ordinarily the most important indicators of potential power, influence, and general performance. In actual practice, of course, the combination of G.N.P. and technology with such other variables as population, morale, military and political capability, internal discipline, prestige, authority, and various qualities of the planning, analysis, and decision-making processes, must be considered in any specific situation. Poor and backward, but tough, countries have demonstrated to more advanced but complacent nations that the G.N.P. and technology are not always the crucial yardsticks. But under usual modern conditions, the two variables most likely to make a country influential are the total heft and technological quality of its economy.

Consider now the following context in Table I for worldwide economic and technological development in the year 2000. (The numbers given are forecasts of the country's population in millions; the world's total population is estimated at 6.3 billion.)

Without being too rigid about it, I would think of the following average per-capita incomes (in 1965 dollars) as being roughly (and somewhat arbitrarily) associated with each of the categories in Table I.

1. Visibly Postindustrial	$10,000
2. Early Postindustrial	$5000–$10,000
3. Mass Consumption	$2000–$5000
4. Mature Industrial	$500–$2000
5. Partially Industrial	$200–$500
6. Preindustrial	$50–$200

TABLE I.

Population, Income, and Technology in 2000*

	Population (in millions)		
1. *Visibly Postindustrial* ($10,000 per-capita income)		4. *Mature Industrial*	
United States	320	Union of South Africa	50
Japan	120	Mexico, Uruguay, Chile, Cuba, Colombia, Peru, Panama, Jamaica, etc.	250
Canada	35	North and South Vietnam, Thailand, Philippines, etc.	250
Scandinavia, Switzerland	30	Turkey	75
France, West Germany, Benelux	160	Lebanon, Iraq, Iran, etc.	75
	665		700
2. *Early Postindustrial*		5. *Large and Partially Industrialized*	
United Kingdom	55	Brazil	210
Soviet Union	350	Pakistan	250
Australia, New Zealand	25	China	1,300
Italy, Austria	70	India	950
East Germany, Czechoslovakia	35	Indonesia	240
Israel	5	U.A.R.	70
	540	Nigeria	160
			3,180
3. *Mass Consumption and Largely Modern*		6. *Preindustrial or Small and Partially Industrialized*	
Spain, Portugal, Poland, Yugoslavia, Cyprus, Greece, Bulgaria, Hungary, Ireland	180	Rest of Africa	350
Argentina, Venezuela	60	Rest of Arab World	100
Taiwan, North and South Korea, Hong Kong, Malaysia, Singapore	160	Rest of Asia	300
	400	Rest of Latin America	100
			850

* Population (in millions) within various national categories.

By the year 2000 at least one hundred of these nations will have access to the military technologies of the 1970's and 1980's—in other words, more advanced than the United States and Russia today—and most will have access, in the year 2000, to the even more modern technologies of the 1990's.

Let me give two prosaic but important examples of change. Today the United States faces two major difficulties when intervening in foreign countries—logistics and communications—and other nations find the difficulties of intervening in most areas of the world almost insurmountable. But by 2000 most ordinary logistics and communications problems of an army, no matter where it is used, are likely to be quite trivial, so long as the enemy makes no serious attempts to interfere. My colleague, Donald G. Brennan, thinks that worldwide communications with individual soldiers will become as simple as providing them with accurate wristwatches.

The logistics problem will not be so easily solved, but we will by then have a relatively inexpensive and widely available multimillion-pound plane, a very high-speed, shallow-draft, self-contained boat (for loading and unloading), and the superefficient submarine and submarine "tow train." Since such equipment will be available on the commercial market, this again means that almost any of our one hundred nations could provide itself with an impressive worldwide logistic capability. From the viewpoint of intervention, it will indeed be a small world. But the occasions for such intervention are likely to be few, and the political conditions quite restrictive, at least in some contexts. All these countries will be aware of the weapons potentially available and of the ability of even small nations like Israel to project their power—at least in the absence of effective countermeasures.

Similarly, most of the seven large partially industrialized nations (which together will have about half the population of the world) will include highly industrialized and technical enclaves (just as China today, with a preindustrial standard of living, is still able to make nuclear weapons).

Another major assumption I make in most of what follows is that there will have been neither any large nuclear wars nor much progress in comprehensive arms control or international or multinational security arrangements. But this will not mean that most nations will feel insecure. Much of the world in the year 2000 may live in what we call a "security community," a group of sovereign nations whose relationship renders war virtually unthinkable. Today almost no one in Western Europe worries about a Franco-German war. Few Frenchmen would spend money to acquire a nuclear capability specifically directed against Germany, and even fewer would lose much sleep if France lacked such a capability. Latin America today comes close to being a pluralistic security community, particularly when one takes into account the influence of the United States and the OAS. Africa and Asia, of course, contain few if any security communities, and this may persist to the year 2000. But we can assume that neither the Soviet Union nor Japan will have any interest in expanding territorially into Asia.

Context One: An Integrated and Peaceful World

We will describe this first alternative context in greater detail than the others, since the others can be largely described in their differences from Context One. In this world, the growth of nuclear capability among various nations might even increase the sense of security of many nations. Today, many Western Europeans feel that those parts of the world possessing nuclear weapons or closely allied to nuclear powers are, in effect, free of real threats—in other words, nuclear deterrence works. By the year 2000, particularly in this context, but in most or all of the others as well, no nuclear weapons may have been exploded in war except for the two used against Japan in 1945. The world would have experienced fifty-five years of nonuse of nuclear weapons. By this point, no matter how large the number of nuclear powers and their supply, and no matter how threatening the rhetoric of some of the political leaders, most people would feel little or no actual sense of threat from nuclear war, even if there had been a number of "ostensible" nuclear crises. (As the man in a magazine cartoon published during the Cuban missile crisis says, "Isn't it awful—we'll all be dead by tomorrow. Here, have another drink.")

I should add that this issue of "not being serious" is important but often misunderstood. Many Europeans have told me that during the Cuban missile crisis they momentarily expected nuclear weapons to drop on their heads, but they made no preparations to save their families because "there is nothing one can do." Since they had all seen fallout maps, they must have known that much of Europe and almost all of Africa and Latin America could expect to survive a Soviet-American war. These people generally acknowledged that if they had been as frightened as they claimed, these ideas would have occurred to them. But increasingly most people will view crises as basically unreal and perhaps confuse their surprising lack of immediate concern with fatalism, rather than see it as a basic belief that the crisis is more sound and fury, more illusion and rhetoric, than fact.

However, even within these security communities most nations will undoubtedly have national defense establishments. Moreover, despite the current nonproliferation treaty and the assumption of an integrated and peaceful context, some diffusion of nuclear weapons by the year 2000 seems very possible—at least under current programs and attitudes.[2]

In the early 1960's the Hudson Institute argued that the Japanese would very likely get nuclear weapons by the mid-1970's, and this does not contradict current attitudes as much as people assume. There are Japanese who feel a deep and genuine nuclear pacifism, but they are fewer than is usually believed. This provoked a reaction among many Japanese who thought it an attempt to promote Japanese nuclear rearmament. Many Japanese feel they are a second-class nation today, in part because they do not have nuclear weapons, and they trace their nonnuclear status to defeat in World War II.

In fact this analysis is not as controversial as it may sound. Many West Germans say that they would be willing to have their country give up its claim to nuclear weapons for the rest of history, but when I ask if they would be willing to sign an immediate treaty renouncing the weapons for twenty years, they often reply, "That's a long time!" Then they are surprised at their own reaction. In similar conversations with Japanese, I asked if they realized how Japanese attitudes have changed between 1962 and 1969.

In 1962 the self-defense forces were still quite controversial, but by 1963 this controversy had pretty much died down. By 1965 the "experts" and scholars had begun discussing defense issues in public and nuclear defense issues in private. By 1966 it was possible to discuss nuclear defense issues in public. In 1967 the nuclear nonproliferation treaty aroused the gravest concern in many Japanese circles, with an intense antagonism that cannot be explained in terms of the usual argument that the treaty requires invidious limitations on peaceful uses of the atom. By 1968 there were study groups in Japan, on both the left and the right, examining questions of nuclear strategy and nuclear politics. And finally, in 1969, the question of Japanese acquisition of nuclear weapons began to be discussed more or less freely on popular Japanese TV programs. When I ask a Japanese interviewer to extrapolate the above tendencies and suggest a year in which nuclear armament will be politically possible in Japan, he invariably suggests some time in the early 1970's. But, remarkably, the interviewer is often shocked by his own analysis.

If Japan acquired nuclear weapons, it would be hard to prevent West Germany from following the Japanese example.[3] Then, very likely the Swiss or the Swedes or some other medium-sized power would follow, and three or four states in the category "Large and Partially Industrialized Nations" would seek nuclear weapons to confirm their great-power status.

In such a world it seems clear that both the United States and the Soviet Union (and perhaps Japan) would feel some need for competent active and passive defenses, and possibly an even more competent offense than we have today. But the procurement of active and passive defenses by the United States and the Soviet Union can be used to support strategies that are more likely to dampen the arms race than exacerbate it. Defensive capabilities are likely to use expensive advanced technologies, which can be used as an effective political, moral, technological, strategic, and diplomatic basis for arms control.[4]

The New Political Milieu and Some Important Forces for Change

In discussing some general characteristics of the current and future political milieu, I will emphasize those most likely to have consequences of a sort especially interesting to this group.

1. *Continuation of an eight- or nine-century secular trend* in the

West toward a culture that is cosmopolitan, humanistic, antimilitaristic, nationalistic, intellectual, relativistic, scientific, rationalistic, manipulative, secular, and hedonistic, leading to the postindustrial culture. This trend will be especially important in the "secure areas" of the West.

2. *Revival* in the West of the *post-World War I reaction* against nationalism and its symbols and agencies, and of the similar but weaker post-World War II reaction against the past in much of continental Europe.

3. *Continuation or increase in the current reaction* (exemplified in the New Left, but substantially more widespread) *against modern science and technology, economic and administrative efficiency, and private and governmental bureaucracies.*

4. *Continuing crisis of liberalism* characterized, among other things, by a reaction against individualism and rationalism, and against domination by groups oriented to economic and material efficiency and growth, national security, and/or the values of various governmental, business, and other private-interest groups.

5. *Increasing role of the intellectual,* who challenges all "irrational" and restricting myths; and the questioning of all traditional claims, facts, assumptions, and loyalties.

6. Continuing and perhaps increasing *reaction,* both domestic and foreign, *against the United States (and perhaps the Soviet) government,* which is currently a result of the declining superpower status of the United States, sharply exacerbated by the Bay of Pigs, various revelations about the CIA, a general reaction against "Americanization" in all forms, and above all against the Vietnam war and the nuclear "arms race." Even in Context One much may occur to deepen the current almost worldwide hostility against the American government, at least among younger academics and upper-middle-class progressives.

7. *Continued, even stimulated, rising expectations* (internally in the United States among the lower-income groups and externally within the less-developed countries) and a *lower tolerance* by intellectuals and upper classes generally of "irrational," "indefensible," and "unjust" inequities.

8. *A surprisingly intense generation gap.*

9. In the United States *a spotlight on*—and start of the resolution of—such *"societal failures"* as racial injustices, persistent

poverty, pollution, urban difficulties, tending to cause overemphasis on these issues, *unrealistic expectations,* and a subsequent frustration, disillusionment, and alienation.

10. *Alienation of many upper and upper-middle-class youth*—in part stimulated by the seeming apathy and callousness of the older generation toward various unresolved issues, in part an anarchist-like reaction against bureaucracy and the system, in part a more or less normal cutting of adult apron strings.

11. Finally there are the various *effects of current news media* on the reporting of governmental violence—both internal and external. The influence can be exaggerated—in many cases it seems to be as much the ineptitude of the authorities as the nature of the reporting and of the medium that causes the problem. Since the authorities are not likely to change drastically, this may be a continuing or increasing problem for much of the next thirty years.

By the late 1960's, such things as (1) the general deemphasis on the role and value of force, (2) the growing horror of nuclear weapons and the seeming senselessness of the Vietnam war, (3) the renewed vitality of the neo-Marxist and other intellectual critiques of the system, and (4) the spotlight on societal failures, have all acted to restore the intensity and faith of the cosmopolitan, pacifistic, relativistic, and reformist positions.

Other important forces and trends today are likely to grow in the next thirty years by affecting "the national character," the general political context, or a given American military institution and American civil/military relations:

1. The continuing and increasing challenge to—and erosion of—the ten traditional constraints on individuals and societies, and a consequent search for "meaning and purpose."

2. The rise of a "humanist left."

3. Current protest movements causing "revolutionary" responses to various societal failures.

4. Increasingly "revisionist" communism and capitalism in Europe and the Western Hemisphere.

5. Lower-class populist and other "conservative" reactions and revolts against the above.

6. A general decrease in almost all current forms and agencies of authority.

7. A corresponding worldwide—internal and external—"law-and-order" problem.

8. Better understanding of and new techniques for economic development in some of the less-developed countries.

9. The coming "1985 technological crisis"[5] described years ago by John von Neumann. It must occur, he said, because "the environment in which technological progress must occur has become both undersized and underorganized. . . ."

The Four Alternate World Contexts

The above is our "surprise-free prediction" for the world of 2000. Many of the things mentioned could cause enormous changes in my projection, and indeed the most surprising thing that could happen would be no surprises.

What does all this imply for the American military establishment? Its future size, and its role in domestic affairs and government are best examined within one or more assumed national and world contexts:

1. *The Integrated and Peaceful Context.* This has been discussed in detail above. It should be emphasized, for immediate purposes, that here no serious political or emotional chasm exists between the American people and their military establishment, but many of the intellectuals and the upper-middle-class progressive Americans are more or less passively alienated from the military establishment.

2. *Inward-Looking, Neo-Isolationist Context.* A relatively neo-isolationist and inward-looking America exists in a world that may be as peaceful and prosperous as above, though there will be little arms control or general coordination. We can assume relatively greater internal disunity and hostility than in Context One, and as a result even more apathy and negativism toward many aspects of the American "Establishment"—and toward the Department of Defense in particular. There may be an important degree of active hostility sparked by various minorities and movements of intellectuals generally.

3. *Disarray World.* In this context there is a fair degree of inter-

national hostility, perhaps approaching that of the mid- and late-1950's. Defense budgets might easily be 50 to 100 percent larger than in the previous two contexts, and there would be many pressures for major American interventions of various sorts—for example, when the government feels important national or ideological interests are threatened. It would be possible, but by no means certain, that the New Political Milieu and other such trends would be reversed—much as occurred during World War II and the Cold War—particularly if there had been a lower-middle-class "populist revolt" that had given American politics a permanent change in direction.

4. *A Hostile and Uncontrolled Arms Race World.* Finally, I would like to consider a world in which there is still a great deal of international tension, fear, and hostility. This context might arise directly out of the American withdrawal from the world, implicit in the second context above. The United States leaves it to other nations to make their own security arrangements. In many cases this could produce serious tensions and great turmoil; the political or military events could be ominously similar to those that produced World War I.

This world might easily develop out of Context Three, the Disarray World, in which excessive intervention by the United States or the Soviet Union—or perhaps Japan—creates countervailing powers and hostilities such that the requirements on United States military forces mount higher and higher.

Some Possible Military Consequences

What domestic military consequences might arise in almost any variation of each of these basic contexts?

This range of contexts could produce defense budgets in the United States from as low as $100 billion to as high as five or ten times that figure (assuming that the United States has a population of about 320 million and a per-capita income around $10,000. Therefore the Gross National Product should be about $3 trillion). In the peaceful context one would assume a military budget of about 5 percent of the G.N.P. or less.

In a neo-isolationist, inward-looking world the defense expenditures would possibly drop even more. Yet there may still be some occasion for military intervention and aid abroad. More important, in a neo-isolationist world the arms race is less controlled. I would therefore assume that in Context Two the military budget goes up to about $200 billion a year or more.

In the Disarray World the percentage of budget allocations to military preparations might approach that of the Korean War and its immediate aftermath—some $400 billion a year for defense. Finally, in the Hostile World Context, if the sense of threat justifies more than 20 percent of G.N.P. devoted to defense, a major fraction of a trillion dollars a year might be allocated to national defense.

Let me now consider each of the four contexts in greater detail.

More on the Integrated and Peaceful Context

The terms "integrated" and "peaceful" do not imply an idyllic international situation but are relative to what might easily be the world context. In particular, I would like to assume that in domestic attitudes and values many current trends have persisted, mainly some of the divisive ones. I assume that the United States will move increasingly toward a mosaic society, with a great deal of plurality and, it is hoped, creative diversity in styles of dress, talk, ways of life, in attitudes toward work, the government, the Establishment, and so on. Yet, despite permissiveness, alienation and cynicism seem likely to continue, especially among the young, and there will be continuing concern about this among the majority of Americans.

The hostility of the New Political Milieu toward many of the established values and practices of American society is usually attributed to the Vietnam war, but it may prove to be one of the main continuing trends in this country. As I pointed out earlier, as society and culture become increasingly sensate and cosmopolitan, the nation-state as the nexus of society's loyalties and values will seem less and less satisfactory, particularly to intellectuals.

One can assume, in the Relatively Integrated and Mostly Peaceful Context, that for most of the next thirty years there will be few international pressures enforcing the average intellectual's loyalty to his government. Thus, criticism and dissent against "computer civilization" will surface, but in this context should remain a tolerable part of the national scene. While many Americans will continue to "opt out," this will no longer be seen as a novel act deserving much public concern—so long as nothing drastic occurs to accelerate such alienation. (I think it particularly important that the requirements of military service do not accelerate these trends.) Many Americans, especially the older ones, will have a general feeling of anxiety and pessimism. Instead of the traditional optimism, theories of "decline and fall" will become popular in both serious and popular literature, and there will be a strong current of national self-hatred or doubt.

The military establishment will be respected and valued by political leaders but not by large segments of the public. Yet much of the population will regard "adequate" military preparations and military careers as acceptable.

For simplicity, let me divide our assumed $150 billion defense budget into three equal categories: central war forces, general and special purpose forces, and a proposed "national service system." It should be possible to man the entire military establishment with substantially less than 1 percent of the population—in contrast with the 1.5 percent or more currently in military service in America. Thus I assume there will be sufficient volunteers to man the military establishment—though some kind of national service or other device may be used to encourage enlistments.

As for the $50 billion allocated to the various "national service" functions, at about $10,000 per year per individual, the government could enroll some five million people, which seems a reasonable number, roughly equivalent to the number of "available" people in the twenty-year-old age group, male and female.[6]

Some Arguments for a Volunteer Army and a System of National Service

In this fairly peaceful world, the American military establishment would probably be dominated by considerations of domestic policy and domestic political reactions, not only in the way it fights but also in its recruitment, training, and operating procedures. Just as domestic issues were a primary issue in Vietnam, they may in the future heavily influence the operation of the entire defense establishment. Given the hostility of many upper-middle-class intellectuals, a draft would not be a good way to obtain military manpower. Instead, there could be a national-service program with easy deferments for educational or personal reasons. In addition, the individual in national service could have a choice of the kind of service he is to do.

There might also be special and elite military programs and groups appealing to certain tastes and attitudes and performing important but limited or specialized functions. Army Special Forces might be expanded into a well-trained, highly educated, highly motivated group for worldwide use, in most cases to advise and help indigenous governments but also prepared to fight. Other kinds of paramilitary or semimilitary groups might exist for domestic service or for various kinds of scientific, exploratory, or development activities (a year's tour of duty on the moon, in an undersea installation, in Antarctica, or the Amazon basin). This kind of national service might become quite popular, winning the support of young people who like freedom of choice and of the older people who believe that the young should make some public-service contribution between their permissive youth and their comfortable adulthood.[7]

The Inward-Looking, Neo-Isolationist World

In this projection much the same kind of military establishment as indicated above could exist, but it would probably arouse more domestic protest and animosity. Some will support the military establishment because it protects a "Fortress America," but most people will not feel that the country is seriously threatened. (Yet threats could even be stimulated by a neo-isolationist American policy.) One result of neo-isolationism would be profound political and social fissures in American policy. A "technocratic-center" party might lead the country, but it would be attacked from both the political right, seeking ideological renewal in American society, and the "humanist left" [8]—or, less charitably, the "radical" or "anarchic" left. These leftist critics would support a program similar to that of the American New Left today, though perhaps not so anarchist, self-righteous, and infatuated with violence.

In the Inward-Looking, Neo-Isolationist World, I assume there is little or nothing in the international context to provide special justification for the role and functions of the Establishment and its military preparations, but I may be wrong. Where could the social cement be found? As Henry Owen put it in a recent article,

> Thus traditional notions of the power and authority of national governments no longer command—in the developed world at least—the allegiance that they did in times past. Symbols and slogans which derive from these notions are losing their force. Peoples grope for new concepts which will respond more directly to the needs of our day. The failure to find them as yet accounts for some of the unease and questioning which characterizes this transitional period.[9]

Disarray World

Here international hostility and competition are substantially greater than in the first two worlds. As a result the defense budget could rise to between 10 and 15 percent of the G.N.P., or roughly $400 billion a year, part of it spent on extensive military-aid programs for foreign countries.

If we have the same alienated society postulated in the last context, there might be some use of foreign legions or special elite volunteers who make it unnecessary for the average American to participate in foreign ventures. If nuclear weapons have been used at some point before the year 2000, the international context could be vastly altered. If two small nations wage nuclear war and wipe each other out, then existing sanctions against nuclear weapons would be reinforced. But if one side wins there could be considerable international apprehension. In the Disarray World there is a good chance that the successful nuclear power would not be punished for its nuclear attack and that a nuclear power would "successfully" use its weapons against a nonnuclear power. Or a concept of the tit-for-tat exchange of nuclear weapons could become deeply ingrained everywhere. There would be great interest in protecting the United States from such attacks, and such protection might be relatively easy to achieve.

Whether nuclear weapons had been used or not, military issues would intrude into the national debate more than in the other two worlds. Some might find the military establishment more acceptable, but others would argue that the insanity of such a situation would be totally clear by that time.

In the Disarray World there might be attempts to smuggle nuclear weapons into the United States, and one can easily imagine the government instituting rigid and comprehensive control over entry points and even over internal movements in many areas of the country. "Political police" and clandestine surveillance could increase enormously. Today we find films such as *Seven Days in May* purely fanciful,[10] but in the future they might seem more credible.

The Uncontrolled Arms Race World

This is a context of great crisis and risk. There may be a rather large war raging in Europe or Asia. Nuclear weapons may have been used. One can easily imagine 50 percent of the American G.N.P. in military preparations, some one and one-half trillion dollars a year.

But consider a budget of half that amount. The United States would have to move rapidly for this budget to be meaningful. For example, one can imagine a ballistic missile defense system in space that attacks enemy missiles in their launch phase when they are most vulnerable. Such a system would be expensive to deploy and operate, but might effectively be able not only to have something close to a 100 percent defense but also be able to prevent the other side from deploying such a system. In other words, the first side to seize outer space in this way might in fact control outer space indefinitely.

There would also be extensive passive defense. Indeed, one can imagine everyone in the United States with good access to a reasonably deep shelter. Many people and much industry might also be evacuated from cities because one could build more effective shelter systems in less densely populated areas. With one or two years of advance notice it would be possible to have many of these shelter spaces deep underground, where they would survive even direct hits of multimegaton bombs. For only a fraction of $750 billion a year, one could also place a good deal of the productive capacity of the United States deep underground.

What I am suggesting is simply that with a profound threat to the country, like that posed in the past by Hitler, or even Stalin or Tojo, there might be a reaction in the United States leading to a garrison state. Both the physical and political calculations are going to be uncertain, but I am nevertheless suggesting that this possibility of all-out mobilization in a crisis or "phony-war" period is still meaningful despite the usual assumptions about easily achieved nuclear overkill.

As far as expenditures are concerned, we have already had examples of comparable budget expansions during World War II and the Korean War. The authorization to increase the defense budget enormously in June 1950 completely changed the technological picture. Without it, people would have been saying throughout the 1950's that such weapons systems as the B-52 and Minuteman were "technologically infeasible." So they are if the budget is $15 billion a year. But they are by no means technologically infeasible if the budget is increased by a factor of five. In the conditions of the year 2000 things may be no different. A budget increase by a factor of five makes a great many things technologically feasible. And it is not beyond the bounds of possibility that a Hitler may rise again, saying, "One of us has to be reasonable, and it isn't going to be me."

Conclusion

Many important topics have had to be neglected in this essay. I have ignored the possibility of a radical change in the international situation, confining myself to those cases that were taken most seriously by the other working groups of the commission on international systems. Thus I have assumed that the nation-state system continues and that the major issues of defense and security devolve on the nation-state unless there is a major war, or unless such nations as the United States, the Soviet Union, Japan, China, or a European power should take upon themselves regional or world hegemony.

I have not looked carefully at cases in which the "humanist left" acquires great influence and "changes the rules." For example, one might imagine a situation in which the concept of conscientious objection is so broadened that no one is forced to fight in a war he thinks unjust. Given the concept of national service, which would act as a spur for many people to enlist, this is a perfectly reasonable rule, and it might work out quite well in a large range of situations. Nor have I discussed the possibility that military service becomes so onerous and unpleasant that large inducements must be provided. But such topics would have led us astray from considering major and relatively likely themes.

NOTES

1. Herman Kahn and Anthony J. Wiener, *The Year 2000: A Framework for Speculation on the Next Thirty-Three Years* (New York: Macmillan Co., 1967), Chapters 2 and 3.

2. There are serious possibilities for arms control, but most current thinking and programs are so unrealistic and wishful that the prospects in the next decade or two—and therefore by the year 2000—are rather dim, at least as far as nuclear proliferation is concerned.

3. Many readers will be surprised by this stress on Japan. But the rise of Japan may be as important to the world in the next thirty years as the rise of Germany was in the late nineteenth and early twentieth centuries. In the 1950's Japan grew economically by a factor of three, thus changing from a small power to a medium power. In the 1960's it grew by another factor of three, thus becoming a large power—that is, passing Western Germany and France to become the third largest economy in the world. We expect that in the 1970's it will grow even more rapidly, by more than a factor of three, and thus grow into a gigantic power. The first two leaps were easily absorbed by the international community but how easily will this third one be absorbed? A gigantic power will require more *Lebensraum* and more rearrangements than either of the first two expansions.

4. See arguments in J. J. Holst and William Schneider, Jr., eds., *Why ABM? Policy Issues in the Missile Defense Controversy* (New York: Pergamon Press, 1969), particularly in the articles by D. G. Brennan, Johan Holst, and Herman Kahn.

5. All of these points, as well as the New Political Milieu, are described in a forthcoming book tentatively titled *A First Look at the Seventies*, by Herman Kahn, to be published by Macmillan in 1971.

6. In an egalitarian society there is no reason to differentiate between the sexes except for actual combat. We may also find, as the Israelis have, that if national service becomes a way of life for all young people, it is resented much less and may even be looked forward to as marking the boundary between childhood and adulthood. If it is useful for young people to make some kind of physically or otherwise difficult public-service contribution, the argument would hold for girls as well as boys.

7. As for a volunteer versus a draft army, one can now argue that it would be almost unthinkable for the government to try to fight another large war such as Vietnam or Korea with draftees, if the war was unpopular.

8. The terms "technocratic center" and "humanist left" describe what I think will be the basic confrontation in the United States of 2000. "Humanist left" is a conglomerate term for those who emphasize individual rights almost to the point of anarchy, who are both anti-institutional and anti-establishment, and who want an almost revolutionary reform of society. They are more coherent and serious than today's radicals, and probably more conservative. "Technocratic center" covers simple technicians who keep things running, "stoics" who feel a personal responsibility for public service and the public good, and "epicurean" types who would prefer private life but nonetheless contribute significantly to the operation and stability of society. Many of the "technocratic center" are more accurately a part of a "humanistic center," since they share many values of the left but are too pragmatic or cautious to accept its programs. Both humanist groups focus attention on the kinds of human beings society should be creating.

9. "Foreign Policy Premises for Next Administration," *Foreign Affairs*, 96, No. 4 (July 1968), p. 701.

10. A difference between many countries of continental Europe and the United States, England, and Scandinavia is worth noting here. The latter are basically civilian, and one cannot conceive their enlisted men following the orders of an officer who was explicitly rebelling against the government. This is not necessarily true in such countries as France. Many Frenchmen, Italians, Austrians, Germans, and others believed that there was a real possibility of a coup when General MacArthur came back from Korea and addressed Congress. Yet the thought hardly occurred to Americans, and in fact President Truman did not move a single squad of soldiers or any police unit in anticipation of such a possibility.

IV

SOCIAL CHANGE AND ADAPTABILITY OF GOVERNMENTAL INSTITUTIONS

MAINTAINING AN ADAPTIVE NATIONAL GOVERNMENT

Donald A. Schon

My concern in this essay is with the overriding problem of the federal government of the United States: *How is this massive organization to cope with new problems, and discard the structures and mechanisms that have come into being around old ones?*

The problem is not merely to cope with a particular set of new problems that appear to be critical for the nation at the present time, or to discard the organizational vestiges of a particular form of governmental activity that happens at present to be particularly cumbersome. It is to design and bring into being institutional processes flexible enough so that new problems can continually be confronted and old structures continually discarded.

The problem is both urgent and familiar in every sector of society. Business and industrial firms ask, what business are we really in? In what directions do we wish to grow? How are we to organize in order to meet our corporate goals? How do we manage the process of growth and change?

Within the labor movement, the questions center on similar issues: If labor has succeeded in achieving the goals that gave it vitality in the early years of its development, what new missions can give it continuing vitality? How does it perceive the issues and interests which are labor's as against those of other institutions? How can it plan and carry out the programs and policies appropriate to its new mission? How can it retain its members, reorganize, and develop new leaders and workers appropriate to its new mission? Every major religious group is currently raising parallel questions.

An inventory of our institutions would reveal similar concerns in all areas. No established organization perceives itself as adequate to the challenges it faces. Each senses not only that it must change now to meet current challenges—and that it must discard or modify old organizational forms in order to do so—but that it must seek to do so on a continuing basis. There has been a loss of faith in the stable state.

In this essay, I will not try to explain the emergence of this ubiquitous concern, since ready answers are unsatisfying. There are indeed "unmet needs" and "crises" in every societal domain. But it is not clear, on closer inspection, that any needs are more urgent or unmet now than they have been at any time in the last thirty years. There are references to an accelerating rate of change in technology, as well as in institutions, but, as De Solla Price has shown, it is difficult to make a case for it.[1] What is clear is that over the last decade there has been a lowering of our threshold of tolerance for unmet needs, for social and economic inequities, for obsolescent or inneffective organizations. And it has been accompanied by growing interest in new approaches to organization and management aimed at the design of systems that will be responsive to new problems in a continuing way.

In the federal government, for example, there are signs of growing awareness of the following problems:

- The activity of the task force on reorganization of the federal government.
- The recent study by Congress of its own organization.
- The efforts of the Civil Service Commission to create new categories of federal employees with ties to the federal government rather than to individual agencies.
- The attempt to introduce broadly across government the system of Program Planning and Budgeting first developed in the Department of Defense.
- An acceleration during the last two presidential administrations in the rate of creating new agencies, and of new interagency committees, commissions, and planning groups; and within major agencies, a continuing, if fragmented, process of reorganization.

In reality, however, these are symptoms of awareness of the problem, not serious efforts at solution.

We can approach the basic issues in quite different ways, depending on our view of the federal government. I propose to look at it as an *informational process,* as a *manipulator of policies,* and as a *complex of societies.*

As an informational process the federal government must somehow detect the issues and problems around which to organize its efforts. It must sense the consequences of what it does. It must organize and transfer within its own system the data and the directives on which policies and programs are based. It must undertake the bookkeeping tasks that go with taxation, regulation, and monitoring the state of the systems that are seen to be the legitimate business of government. Moreover, it must recognize this internal and external information system throughout shifts in its environment and in its central problems. These functions fall under what Karl Deutsch has described as the cybernetic model of government.

As a manipulator of policies, the federal government can be seen as a kind of manipulator of control systems. The "levers" available to it are within the keyboard of policies derived from acts of Congress and agency practices. These are constantly changing, as Congress passes new laws, amends old ones, allocates funds, and as officials of the executive branch construct, carry out, and modify policies governing administrative practice. Policies cluster around particular functions and around particular administrative branches of government. Tax policy, for example, centers on the revenue-producing function and on the Department of the Treasury. But policies interact in complex ways. Any goal or function of federal activity turns out to involve a multiplicity of policies, whose interactions form a complex and shifting web. Manipulation of this web or keyboard of policies for particular ends becomes a delicate game. And it is a game in which one can never make a move with consequences that are only the intended ones.

But the federal government is also a set of organizations, related to policies and programs as instruments of action, related to one another as organizational neighbors; competitors, or collaborators, and related to the people in them as societies in which working (and much of nonworking) lives are lived.

Each way of looking at the federal government reveals a different aspect of the central problem of adapting to new problems: From the point of view of government as an informational system, how do new problems come to attention and ideas about them acquire potency for action? This is the process by which ideas come into good currency. From the point of view of government as manipulator of policies, how are we to understand and operate on the interconnecting policies affecting the new goals related to the perception of new problems? From the point of view of government as a complex of societies, how are we to design and carry out strategies by which resources can be organized to attack new problems and to discard obsolete or inhibitive structures and mechanisms?

I. Ideas in Good Currency

The phrase "emergence of ideas in good currency" is a way of talking about the process by which new problems come to the attention of the public and of the federal government and acquire potency for action. This process is one facet of the government-as-information process. In terms of the cybernetic model, it is the process by which government senses the problems it should be responding to.

For all of its importance, this process is surprisingly little understood. We seem to be selectively inattentive to it, taking the ideas in good currency at any one time as givens for the public business. Yet it is clear that ideas in good currency change. They are, in effect, the intellectual fashions that are potent in mobilizing action and resources—for example, in seeking funds from Congress. Seen in this way, some of the ideas in good currency in the middle 1950's were "competition with the Russians", "the missile gap", "basic science", and "the shortage of technical manpower".

By the early 1960's these concepts had begun to move out of good currency, or at least they began to be far less actively used within the executive branch and by members of the executive branch with Congress. Other ideas began to acquire potency for action: the crisis of the cities, the problem of poverty, and citizen participation. It is not, of course, that these ideas were unknown in the 1950's; they were known but not potent, and therefore were not in good currency at that time.

Like other fashions, ideas in good currency obey a law of

limited numbers: only a certain number can function at any given time. New ones tend to displace old ones. Their limitation appears to be due to the fact that they compete for national attention.

What distinguishes ideas in good currency from other fashions—even from other intellectual fashions—is their importance to the process of government. In a sense, the effectiveness of government depends upon the degree of correspondence of ideas in good currency with the state of affairs confronting the nation. Or, if we see ideas in good currency as ways of structuring our national perceptions in order to lead us to act effectively or ineffectively, then effective government depends upon the workability or the pragmatic utility of ideas in good currency.

It is in this sense that we can speak of city governments as failing to find ideas in good currency adequate to the situation presented by black center-city residents. Or that the "government" of major universities may be said to lack ideas in good currency adequate to the state of mind and behavior of students.

In any case, it is apparent that the emergence of ideas in good currency need not be appropriate to the changing situation confronting the nation. A curious fact emerges if we examine the situation of the early 1960's with respect to ideas in good currency representing issues for the federal government in the area of science and technology. Scarcely any of the issues taken to be confronting the nation—issues often described as "crises" by government commissions—have survived to the present time as ideas in good currency.

A brief survey will help to make the point. Among the issues considered critical in the early 1960's were the problems of so-called sick industries; automation and its dislocations; the scientific and technical manpower shortage; and the consequences of disarmament.

In 1963, the Kennedy administration presented to Congress a program known as the Civilian Industrial Technology (CIT) program. It was based largely on the view that those American industries that contributed most to the Gross National Product—building, textiles, primary metals, for example—received the least investment in research and development, whereas those industries that contributed least to the Gross National Product—specifically, industries closely associated with national defense—received the largest part of the nation's research and development budget. To redress the balance, it was proposed to establish a program of federal support for the creation of industrial research institutes aimed at applied research, information dissemination, and technical training, somewhat on the model of the British Department of Scientific and Industrial Research.

The program had grown out of President Kennedy's fourteen-point program for the American textile industry, which had felt itself so threatened by imports that it lobbied for higher quotas and tariffs. To extract certain concessions from the industry, Kennedy offered a program of benefits, among which was federal support of textile-industry research, and the CIT program took off from that point.

Over a three-year period the CIT program was killed—in a maneuver that in itself reveals a great deal about the operation of governmental-industrial systems—but in that same period the textile industry underwent a change. Overall demand for textiles increased, owing partly to the increasing requirements of the Vietnam war and partly to an overall increase in demand stemming from economic prosperity. It was a common joke in the industry that the textile business was like sex: when it was good it was marvelous, and when it was bad it was very nice. The concept of the textile industry as a "sick industry" disappeared from the scene, and with it the public sense of need for federal research support.

In the early 1960's, the Automation Commission came into being to deal with a series of concerns drawn from congressional committees and expressed in a variety of bills. Its title—the Commission on Automation, Economic Progress, and Technological Change—reflects some of this diversity of origin. The Commission was formed on the Noah's Ark principle—two Negroes, two labor leaders, two industrialists, two women, and so on—and began its deliberations at a time when the national unemployment rate stood at approximately 6 percent. It began in a climate of deep concern about automation (sometimes used by Commission members as a synonym for technological change) and the dislocations caused by it.

During the life of the Commission, two parallel streams of events occurred. The Bureau of Labor Statistics investigated the rate of change of productivity in the United States over the preceding twenty years and revealed that (by its calculations) the rate had remained roughly constant at 2.5 percent. During the same period the unemployment rate had dropped from approximately 6 percent to approximately 4 percent. The Commission produced many volumes of analyses and a wide range of recommendations—including the recently celebrated one for a national effort toward social indicators—but it did not recommend a major national remedy for the dislocations of automation.

In the late 1950's, it was not uncommon in scientific and engineering circles to hear talk of the impending shortage of scientific and technical manpower. The research-and-development budget had been growing (at a rate that, wags said, would cause it to intersect with the G.N.P. by 1970); defense research and development had made enormous demands on the nation's technical manpower supply; critics were already concerned about the needs of university research; and it was feared now that NASA's growing needs would exhaust the nation's remaining supply of scientists and engineers, leaving other significant national requirements unmet.

Under the leadership of Dr. James Killian, the Committee on Scientific and Technical Manpower came into being under the aegis of the National Academy of Sciences. During the life of this committee several concurrent events occurred: minor cutbacks (or, rather, decreases in the rate of growth) in defense spending, releasing some hundreds (or perhaps thousands—the numbers were never clear) of engineers who, it was claimed, were walking the streets of Los Angeles and Long Island. And there was increased enrollment in graduate schools of science and engineering as students apparently were influenced by the sustained public discussion of growing demands for scientists and engineers.

The shortage of scientific and technical manpower did not so much disappear as evaporate. When the report of the Committee was published in the mid-sixties, its qualified conclusions did not give rise to further federal action. On the other hand, the problem of alleged cutbacks in defense spending—with their feared consequences for defense-based industry—became the reason for a new interagency committee, whose conclusions, in turn, faded from view as the Vietnam conflict developed.

These examples indicate that the emergence of ideas in good currency is an important part of the way our society detects its problems, formulates approaches to them, and gets feedback on its actions—but it is subject to a number of difficulties.

First, ideas in good currency emerge *in time* and there is typically a lag in their coming into being. A dramatic, but not entirely inaccurate, statement of the case is this: *By the time ideas have come into good currency, they no longer accurately reflect the state of affairs.* Moreover, there is also a lag in the process by which ideas in good currency fade away. Often the situation they refer to will change during the very process of deliberation.

As a corollary, since money for programs and policies can be obtained only with ideas in good currency, funded programs tend to be inappropriate to the present situation. In response, those charged with carrying out such programs frequently play a double game. They seek funds under one heading and spend them under another—as when mental health workers ask for service money under the heading of "research," or as in the 1950's when scientists and engineers asked for research money under the heading of "defense."

It is a task of some urgency to determine whether these lags between the appearance and the disappearance of ideas in good currency can be reduced or whether they are inherent in the process. Is it possible, in short, to make ideas in good currency more appropriate to the time?

These ideas often refer to a future state, but their emergence depends on a present context (for example, as the deliberations over the future consequences of automation were influenced by the then current unemployment rate). Uncertainty about the future inevitably results in many conflicting predictions and leaves the process of deliberation open to shifts in the present context that reflect present anxieties rather than changes in evidence about the future.

There are two main responses to this sort of difficulty. The first is the development of more flexible public responsiveness to the unanticipated (this is discussed in the final section of this essay). The second is the attempt to reduce uncertainty over the future through the use of methods more nearly adequate to the informational complexity of events, the most important being computer simulation. The two approaches are not mutually exclusive although they tend to appeal to different kinds of people.

The process of public deliberation itself influences behavior, sometimes changing or even eliminating the problem under consideration, as the talk about "scientific manpower shortages" affected student selection of graduate programs. The "programs" resulting from these deliberations may be irrelevant or inappropriate precisely because of the unanticipated effects of the deliberations themselves.

What is perhaps most surprising is that the process by which ideas in good currency emerge is so little understood. At a rather general level we can identify some features of the process:

- The role of individual thinkers and writers who introduce, coin, and promulgate ideas.
- The role of "idea brokers" who serve as intermediaries or carriers.
- The role of prestigious institutions that make ideas respectable and bring them to the attention of powerful circles.
- The key "diffusion" function of the mass media.
- The informal networks of individuals—invisible colleges—that introduce and elaborate ideas in good currency.
- The importance of champions of ideas; the role of influential leaders.
- The political significance of ideas in good currency; the important leverage they must have in responding to multiple needs.
- The role of key images or metaphors (such as Roosevelt's "lending your neighbor a garden hose when his house is on fire" as a way of describing lend-lease).
- The process of repeated emergence of ideas—the launching of many trial balloons—resulting gradually in acceptance (as in the case of the idea of "industrial extension," whose trial period lasted nearly a hundred years).
- The role of struggles for intellectual territory, as well as for power over programs and resources. Ideas in good currency trigger the release of resources and weapons in struggles for power.

But these are only hints at the nature of the process. We still lack a practical or useful theory that would enable us to influence the process itself.

II. The Policy Keyboard

Within the federal government, fragmentation of responsibility for design and administration of policies parallels fragmentation in the way congressional committees and agencies of the executive branch operate. Fiscal policy is the province of select congressional committees along with the Council of Economic Advisors, the Bureau of the Budget, and the Treasury. Responsibility for manpower policy spreads across many congressional committees and many agencies of government in addition to the Department of Labor.

The policies active at any given time, and the organizational structure related to their design and implementation, spring from an evolutionary process. The grouping and naming of policies reflect many views of problems and of traditional channels of responsibility. One of the principal features of this grouping and of these channels is compartmentalization—the organization into separate units of design and administration with relatively little interaction among the parts. Compartmentalization is as characteristic of federal programs as it is of federal policies.

Any new problem, however, brings with it requirements for the regrouping of policies and for the rearrangement of their interaction. Each new problem of significance touches many strands in the policy web. Conversely, any integrated attack on a new problem confronting government requires manipulation of a complex keyboard of policies.[2]

Let us consider, as an example, the federal government's explicit interest in the stimulation of technological innovation. Virtually all areas of federal policy affect technological innovation. One can see from the following partial list of such policies how they can critically affect technological innovation:

a) *Antitrust Policy:* It has been sharply debated whether American antitrust policy encourages or inhibits technological innovation. On the one hand, economists like Galbraith have argued that with the transition from the dominant role of the independent inventor in the development of new technology to the current industrial situation, in which such development requires large-scale research and development laboratories, there is a premium on large corporate size. It is maintained that the antitrust policy as currently administered tends to inhibit the formation of large capital-concentrated firms and thereby stands in the way of increased technological change essential to economic growth, and therefore, that there should be a relaxation of antitrust policies.

In a recent paper for the Antitrust Subcommittee of the United States Senate, I argued that technological innovation and invention still tend to be significantly the province of independent inventors and new small firms (particularly, technology-based firms derived from industrial research laboratories and from university departments of science and engineering), while the diffusion of new technology depends heavily upon the marketing and distribution resources characteristic of large firms. As a result, processes of technological change tend to involve a cycle in which firms of different capital size play roles of different importance at the several stages of the process.

b) *Regulatory Policy:* The American pharmaceutical industry, following changes in Food and Drug Administration (FDA) policy in the early 1960's, claimed that government regulation tended actively to discourage investment in research and development by requiring such a costly proof of both the effectiveness and the innocuousness of new drugs as to make it unprofitable to conduct research. Similarly, the railroads argue that federal regulations governing railroad-car design have tended to freeze technology and to prevent significant design change.

c) *Import-Export Policy:* It has been argued that the use of tariffs and quotas as means of protecting domestic industry from foreign competition either protects vulnerable industries during periods in which development can be undertaken and consolidated, or tends to lull such industries into a sense of smug security that reduces their incentive to invent and innovate,

d) *Standards and Codes:* Standards relating to old technology may be used covertly or openly as a means of "freezing" the old technology and impeding the introduction of the new. The current battle over standards between manufacturers of cast iron and plastic building pipe is a case in point.

Codes incorporating multiple standards may be used, again, either to foster or to inhibit the introduction of new technology. The problem of building codes in the United States has been referred to again and again, because its alleged influence on the fragmentation of markets tends to inhibit entry into new building markets on the part of firms not previously established in those markets.

e) *The Use of Federal Purchasing Power:* The assembling of massive purchasing power, based on performance specifications that provide market incentives for invention while leaving open the route of technological solution if performance criteria are met, has been significantly demonstrated in the United States through military weapons systems and, more recently, space programs. Its application to shipping has been started, though not completed, in the Fast Deployment Logistic ship program. Throughout the last seven years, efforts have been made to apply federal purchasing power based on performance standards to spur innovation in the building field (for example, through the Defense Department's purchasing of building and construction), though so far without notable success.

f) *Patent Policy:* The actual effect of patent policy on the introduction of new technology has been the subject of continuing debate almost since its inception. One major argument has concerned the question whether patent policy favors established corporations with large financial resources at the expense of small firms and independent inventors, or the reverse. Thus its supposed effect on technological innovation varies with opinions concerning the relative importance of inventors and small firms as contributors to technological development.

g) *Manpower and Mobility Policy:* I have argued at length elsewhere (see "Innovation by Invasion," *International Science and Technology)* that technological development in established industries, such as textiles, machine tools, and building, tends to occur through invasion of those industries by science-based firms from other fields. This frequently has the effect of dislocating firms, workers, and in some cases whole regional economies. The promotion of technological innovation in these instances would seem to hinge on federal policy about such dislocations. Protectivist response supports threatened industries (as American policy has tended to support coal industries) and serves to raise the price of entry for invading firms, whereas policies that stimulate mobility and facilitate the movement of workers and companies into more promising regions and industrial fields, it may be argued, grease the skids under technological change.

The list is far from complete. Equal attention might be given to fiscal and monetary policy, loan policy, and information policy. The items mentioned serve only to suggest the great complexity of the policy keyboard affecting technological innovation and diffusion, as well as the uncertainty in almost every instance of the particular kind of effect produced. But it is clear that there is a great range of policies through which the United States now influences technological innovation, all short of the policy of directly supporting research and development or investment in new technology.

We are only beginning to understand the significance of this policy keyboard and to think about the development of the techniques required for its systematic use to encourage technological innovation. We do not, for example, use patent, antitrust, regulatory, loan, and manpower policies, the way we have become accustomed to using fiscal and monetary policies, as means of affecting the development of aggregate demand in the national economy. Some of the measures needed for the systematic use of such a policy matrix or keyboard to encourage technological development would be the following:

(1) Development of the sorts of data that would provide more rapid and credible indications of the effect on new technology of the specific measures adopted (for example, the effect of FDA policies on research and innovation in the drug field).

(2) The development of simulation, modeling, or simply more sophisticated analytic techniques that will allow us to understand the complicated interactions of policy moves in diverse areas. For example, we may well be unwittingly producing conflicting rather than reinforcing effects in our current antitrust, patent, and fiscal policies.

(3) The creation of institutions, or connections between institutions, in the federal government that would generate policy–

decision processes recognizing the interconnection of policies from diverse areas (for example, the provision of means to enable congressional committees separately concerned with antitrust, tax, labor, subsidy, and tariff policies to understand the resultant effects of their actions on particular industries, such as textiles).

It has become traditional in the United States to associate only a small number of policies with technological innovation: for example, direct support of research and development, dissemination of scientific information, patent policy, purchasing policy, agency patent and information policy, tax policy. Moreover, we have tended to see these as discrete tools. We have generally not been willing to consider seriously national measures to support technological innovation in civilian industry. But when we have attempted to do so, we have found our understanding of the relationship between federal policies and technological innovation inadequate.

It is safe to say that the same is true of the relationship between federal policies and other problems—particularly, any newly discovered problem—of national concern. One instance of a relatively good grasp of the interaction of policies in relation to a national problem is in the interaction of fiscal and monetary policies in relation to indices of national economic vitality. This may serve as a model—or at least an inspiration—in confronting the problem of understanding and manipulating the policy keyboard to other ends.

III. Change in Government as Society

To put it negatively but by no means altogether inaccurately, government agencies are memorials to old problems. From this point of view the Department of Agriculture is an organizational edifice constructed around the problems of agricultural productivity as they appeared in the United States in the latter part of the nineteenth century. The fundamental solution of these problems, to the point of creaing new problems of agricultural surplus, did not lead to the passing away of the Department of Agriculture but to its expansion; there are still 70,000 agricultural extension agents operating in the United States.

The Department of Labor came into being around the problems of unemployment and labor conflict as they arose in the 1930's. The solution to many of these problems, or at least the development of independent institutions dedicated to their solution, has not led to the disappearance of the Department of Labor but again to its extension. The Department can be seen as an accretion of new organizational structures upon old ones. Such organizations grow organically, and the result of that growth resembles the stratified layers of shells. The Small Business Administration is a monument to congressional nostalgia for the "little man who made it," whose entrepreneurial role in American industry, at least as it was once understood, no longer matters.

The general rule is that agencies come into being and take their particular form in response to rather specific situations of national problem and crisis. When these disappear or change drastically in nature, the old organizational structure designed to cope with them persists. From this point of view, the actual physical structure of Washington, with its layers of buildings in varying architectural styles, is a symbol of this organizational process. In government, as in most established institutional areas, the organizational equivalent of biological death—with its constructive vital functions related to adaptation—is lacking.

To speak of "inertia" or "bureaucratic stagnation" or "resistance to change" is not particularly helpful in explaining this process. It is more suggestive to think of federal agencies as societies. From the point of view of its members, the agency provides a basis for security —not only job security, but a necessary feeling of place and belonging, a focus for loyalty, a definition of role, a sense of identity, an upward path through which progress and promotion are defined, and a set of values for looking at the world.

The concept of the agency as society, with its functional autonomy and its responsiveness to the most deeply felt needs of its members, helps explain the vital persistence of agency structure and organization quite independent of shifts in the character of the situation that brought the agency into being. Even the language used in government, and from agency to agency, makes this clear. I have always been struck by the number of different agencies in which "the bureau" has only one meaning or "the director" refers to only one man.

Units of organization differ, of course, in the extent to which they are deeply rooted in the social functions referred to above. In the Department of Commerce, for example, the Bureau of Standards and the Bureau of the Census are particularly notable in this regard. So are the Coast and Geodetic Survey and the Weather Bureau. Membership in these organizations carries with it connection to a tradition that provides values for the outside world (for example, the critical importance of measurement, precision, detachment, objectivity, scientific method, and fairness) and a sense of self. Rules of government pertaining to personnel, such as those associated with the civil-service system, do not create the loyalty characterizing individual response to organization or the persistence of the organization itself, but merely provide the legal and institutional counterpart of the social function.

Because government agencies are societies, they do not simply display inertia, but rather what might be called dynamic conservatism. They strive actively to remain the same. The particular means by which they do this reflects some of the peculiarities of government organization. One need only consider the feelings of an agency bureaucrat who has lived in government long enough to feel committed to it as a career and to regard retirement benefits associated with government service as his principal form of financial security. If he has lived in the agency for a period of ten years or more, he is likely to have seen at least five changes of chiefs at the political-appointee level. How do you respond when you are a member of an organization whose head keeps being chopped off at regular intervals? An entire array of strategies and life styles associated with survival at minimum cost and in some instances with determined persistence at productive work has grown up to cope with this issue.

The strategies cover probing and exploration of the character, intent, and sophistication of the new incumbent; means of currying favor in, or becoming associated with, a new program; approaches to internal sales; recasting of activities to which one has been committed in new program areas; searches for the tall grass in which to remain unnoticed; ways of giving the boss what he wants with a minimum of effort and derailment of ongoing activity. In a number of government agencies there are individuals of high intelligence and great dedication whose only means of continuing work on problems they judge to be of national importance as well as personal interest is a kind of guerrilla underground activity through which this work is bootlegged, hidden, or recast continually to meet the perceived requirements of new, temporary chiefs.

In addition, the relationship among agencies is often that of a conflict of rival baronies, each jealously guarding its own territory and seeking to expand at the expense of other agencies. A new program entering the federal government does not enter a neutral space but a field of force built out of the territorial vectors of the agencies. These persist from administration to administration, have a longer life cycle than that of any given administration, and lead more or less a life of their own. As a result, it sometimes appears to an outside observer that the federal government contains many extremely intelligent, highly dedicated, experienced individuals who work long hours over long periods of time canceling out one another.

Given these characteristics, what happens when a new national problem emerges—that is to say, when an old national problem comes into good currency and presents itself, through processes that are by no means clear, as a fit subject for federal action?

Some examples of such problems within the last two federal administrations are the following: the decay of the city; pollution of land, sea, and air; relations between universities and their surrounding communities; regional economic development; the problems of industrial work generally grouped under the heading of "automation"; the handling of scientific and technical information; the problems of assessing national requirements for manpower and of developing manpower adequate to these needs.[3]

Typically, as one explores such a problem one finds a highly fragmented picture in which every major agency has a piece of the problem. I remember a conversation about water resources between Luther Hodges, then Secretary of Commerce, and a number of his aides. One of them said, "We have been looking into the matter, and there seem to be about twenty agencies involved in water-resource development." Another said, "That's strange, we have been concerned with pollution control, and there are about twenty agencies involved in that." Hodges suggested that this was perhaps because, after all, there were about twenty major agencies.

The problem of the cities belongs in the Department of Housing and Urban Development (HUD) because of its special concern with urban housing; in the Department of Commerce because of the cities' role in economic development; in the Department of Health, Education, and Welfare (HEW) because the city is a focus for these services; in the Department of Agriculture because the city is a locus for the consumption of agricultural products; in the Department of the Interior because the city is a center for the consumption, distribution, and use of natural resources. Moreover, every major agency turns out to be undertaking programs that relate in some direct or indirect fashion to urban problems. The same is true of every major problem listed above.

As a new federal problem is identified, such fragmentation comes to light. At the same time there is apt to be a seeking of information about the character of fragmented programs related to the problem, and the beginnings of infighting over territory. At this point, several alternative strategies are available to an administration hoping to launch a major attack on the problem:

1. Establishment of an interagency committee whose function is to coordinate and jointly manage the various agency activities relating to the problem area. Such a committee may have a weak role such as "monitoring" activities, or it may have a strong role relating, for example, to the development of standards of interagency activity. I have participated in about six interagency committees that lasted for one year or more; whenever the opportunity came up, I asked other individuals who had also participated in them whether any such committee was effective in carrying out its assigned functions. No one ever said it had been. The committee may make a show of performance during the early stages of its operation, particularly if it is subject to some strong external threat (as the interagency committee on scientific information was during the early 1960's). But usually within a matter of months the principal forces at work seem to be individual agency baronies and territorial demands. The actual, as opposed to the official, agenda comes under the protection of the territorial interests of each agency, prohibiting a cooperative attack on the concrete problems. Nor is this at all surprising.

2. Another strategy is the consolidating reorganization—for example, the establishment of the Department of Housing and Urban Development, and the recent establishment within HEW of the Social Rehabilitation Agency, bringing together such independent groups

as Vocational Rehabilitation, Welfare, the Children's Bureau, and the like. In a smaller way, within the Department of Commerce in the early 1960's, the Environmental Science Survey agency was set up, and the Bureau of Standards reorganized. The success of such reorganizations is greatly dependent on a large-scale infusion of new funding. Without this, they are apt to be a mere coalition of operating units with a thin layer of coordinating administration and a new rhetoric of function that often greatly exceeds the agency's actual ability to perform. It is tempting to continue performing the old functions in the old way under new headings. Active administration will try to impose new activities and to revitalize old structures, and it must engage in a complicated bargaining process with the operating heads of subunits.

3. Still another strategy is the creation of new organizations dedicated to work on the new problem, such as the Peace Corps and the Office of Economic Opportunity. The new organization can represent new vitality, new faces, and enthusiasm for new programs. The organization may be loose and informal and the morale high, but at a fairly predictable point in its life cycle, it will be faced with the problems of bureaucratic aging. After five years, these problems are now what the Peace Corps seems to be principally concerned with, despite the invention of the "five-year flush" as a way of preserving vitality. On a long-term basis the current problems of the Tennessee Valley Authority (TVA) represent a similar dilemma.

In a characteristic pattern, an administration will take a new problem and a new agency under its wing, giving it special attention, appointing a boss of character and energy, and permitting it unusual freedoms within the bureaucratic system, thereby establishing a climate of high morale and creativity. Over time, bureaucratic restrictions will once again encroach upon the agency's territory, internal organizational divisions will become more rigid, the original boss will leave, and a new, more restricted chief will take over.

What one would like to achieve within the government and within every large-scale organizational structure in our society is a more satisfactory way of adapting to the emergence of new problems, discarding old structures as they become inappropriate, and changing the approach, use of personnel, and allocation of resources to suit new tasks as they arise.

The way to approach this sort of adaptation is either through "self-renewing organizations" (where the shift to work on new problems can be done within the boundaries of an existing organization) or through new forms of interagency organization.

A great deal has been written about how to design self-renewing organizations,[4] but there has been little actual accomplishment along these lines. Nevertheless, some relevant points are broadly applicable to all established organizations, and some are peculiar to the federal government.

A primary concern of organizational renewal relates to the opening up of boundaries, both within agencies and between agencies and the outside world. The older and more static federal agencies are separated into airtight compartments whose functions have in the course of time become unclear or irrelevant. They also tend to be isolated from the outside world of other government agencies and broader communities.

The infusion of new blood tends to threaten not only established organizational patterns but also established ways of seeing the world and established ideologies. Young Turks occupy a critical position. An agency head can revitalize his organization by attracting bright young people and putting them in positions of unusual access to policy and program guidance. Informal organizations of young people that cut across divisional or hierarchical boundaries can strengthen their role. One agency head recently constructed an agency of young people, counterpart to his own, to develop counterpart programs and to formulate and test pilot projects.

Characteristically, there develop among federal agencies informal "underground" networks—groups of individuals attracted to the idea of change in agency policy and practice and committed to the use of the informal system to effect that change. Such undergrounds may represent "guerilla movements" aimed at changing agency policy and sometimes at subverting official policy to other ends. Occasionally, agency heads ally themselves with the underground, in order to force change through layers of official bureaucracy. Again, informal connections may be established across agency lines, resulting in coalition efforts to change particular policies or to take advantage of crises to introduce change.

When new problems arise that cut across agency boundaries, informal networks become the principal means of coordinating actual interagency effort. New views of national problems and of the role of the federal government tend to be identified with individual leaders—who come and go, often before much has been done in the programs they helped to define. These leaders therefore tend to lose credibility among the more permanent bureaucrats who will finally take responsibility for carrying out the programs.[5]

Further, the introduction of new program ideas by a new administration brings on political pressures for performance *now*, which often paralyzes or demoralizes the middle levels of the agency. The credibility of leaders has a great deal to do with their ability to protect those below from shifting destructive pressures for immediate (and often contradictory) response—as Franklin Delano Roosevelt protected the TVA and Kennedy the Peace Corps.

But however much an agency may be "loosened up" so as to enable it to face new problems creatively, the resulting renewal may be a one-shot effort, lasting no longer than the tenure of a particular leader or administration. These measures do not of themselves permit a continuing capability for renewal. The problem is sometimes expressed as the need for "institutionalization." From one point of view, the Planning, Programming, and Budgeting Systems (PPBS), fostered by the Bureau of the Budget and based on techniques introduced by Secretary McNamara into the Department of Defense, constitute an attempt to institutionalize the ability for continuing renewal. It seeks to force agencies to define programs functionally, which permits alternative designs for accomplishing functions; to develop ways of measuring agency intent with actual accomplishment; and to budget by function. But it has become clear that PPBS by itself cannot serve this end, since it may either force reconsideration of agency policies and programs or simply repackage old programs without functional or organizational change.

Attempts to institutionalize the informal systems of agencies seem to embody a contradiction: their very vitality depends on their invisibility. Agencies tend to seek new states of stability, forming around the modified programs, structures, and ideologies that resulted from the last wave of innovation.

When the new problem does not lie easily within the boundaries of an established agency, flexible adaptation demands a response different from the ones listed earlier. If the question is one of continuing adaptation rather than a one-shot response, one must think of a structure in which "pools of competence" and task-oriented groups interact. Such an organization has the following characteristics.

Pools of competence are organized around disciplines or around skills of content (such as statistics, computer programming, economics) or of process (planning, program management, coordination). These skills must be relevant to the demands of federal programs and policies and to the duration of specific tasks that draw on them.

The managers of these pools are in a sense gardeners, responsible for adequate use of people, training and retraining, continuity of professional development, management of entry into task-groups and reentry into competence pools, and, most important, providing a basis for professional security throughout a period of changing tasks. Ideally, as John Macey has proposed, such an organization would aim at developing a sense of identity and loyalty to itself and to the objectives of the federal government, rather than to specific agencies or bureaus.

On the other hand, a series of task groups, with a shorter life cycle, would be responsible for specific projects. Members of competence pools would move in and out of task groups in the manner of project management systems in industrial firms. Such a system would organize projects into coherent, connected wholes.

Clearly, such an approach is inappropriate to the management of routine government functions—yet even these have life cycles, as we know from the current crisis in postal operations.

It is appropriate to the management of new government functions that are nonroutine and have relatively short, if unpredictable, life cycles. In this respect, the model outlined above—a kind of federal "project system"—represents in the area of program management what has already become familiar and effective in areas of deliberation, evaluation, and planning. Federal task forces and planning groups are a commonplace for the study of cities, crime, children, privacy. These federal groups are called into being by the President or by heads of offices and agencies, and have limited lives. Their members are drawn from other worlds, and they return to them when the specific tasks are done. The "project-system" model would carry over to program management an approach now broadly applied to analyses of problems and evaluations of programs and crises.

In sum, the federal government's ability to innovate around new problems depends on the development of new techniques and approaches (1) to understand and manage better the process by which new ideas come into good currency—that is, the way new problems are identified and new solutions can be realized; (2) to manipulate the policy keyboard when problems cut across multiple policy areas; and (3) to explore systems permitting the forming of temporary organizations aimed at finite tasks responsive to new problems.

In effect, all of this becomes a new technology of government.

NOTES

1. Derek J. De Solla Price, *Little Science, Big Science* (New York: Columbia University Press, 1963).

2. Similarly, it requires manipulation of a complex keyboard of programs. Concern with poverty as a public issue, for example, has forced us to recognize the multiple conditions of poverty—and the many different programs that must be "coordinated" to attach the problem. The same is true of our interest in problems of housing, health, welfare, and education. These problems have been much discussed recently, and the present discussion of interaction of policies in the wake of new problems is in effect a companion piece to these recent discussions.

3. Some emergent concerns already visible but not yet equally prominent are the problems of the aged and of disabilities associated with aging; management of the processes by which the decentralization of government to regional, state, city, and neighborhood levels can be effected; and problems and opportunities opened up by biomedical technology.

4. See especially the writings of Warren Bennis, Douglas McGregor, and Chrys Argyris.

5. The problem is made more severe by the prevalent myth that invention stops with the first formulation of program. In fact, invention continues throughout the process of implementation.

THE YEAR 2000: RELATIONS OF THE PUBLIC AND PRIVATE SECTORS

Robert R. Nathan

Environment

It is the end of the twentieth century, and relations between government and business in the United States differ considerably from those of thirty years ago. Dramatic changes have occurred within the American economy and in the relationships between people and government. The business cycle has virtually been tamed, and a marked and sustained rate of economic growth is assured. Depressions are obsolete and a slowdown in the rate of growth is now called a recession.

America's affluence is increasingly impressive. The Gross National Product in the year 2000 exceeds $3,000 billion (in 1967 prices), reflecting a quadrupling of total production in real terms during the last third of the twentieth century. Prices have continued to rise an average of 2 percent per year, and therefore the G.N.P. in the current prices of the year 2000 is about $6,000 billion.

The average disposable income per man, woman, and child in the United States is now approximately $6500 at 1967 prices and $13,000 in the current prices of the year 2000. Average family income is $50,000 in the current prices of the new century.

Those who had once worried that the American people might become so inundated with goods and services that they would never be able to use effectively all that could be produced have been proved totally wrong. The greater the productive capacity, the greater has been the growth in demands and wants of the American people. Strong interest in the growth and vigor of the private sector continues, along with the need to determine priorities both in the private sphere and in the public area. There is unabated conflict about the role and size of public spending and public command over resources.

The changes that have taken place in relationships between the public and the private spheres can best be understood in this context of tremendous production and excess demand over supply. A generation ago most Americans would have predicted that these levels of production would mean a considerable degree of relaxation in competitive pressures and priorities for the products of the American economy. They would have expected unsatisfied wants to decline so sharply that the struggle between different groups in the society for higher relative shares would be considerably diminished.

Sharing the Product

Quite the contrary. If anything, there is increased competition for the benefits of the goods and services made available through growth. Workers still want to increase their share in total income distribution, and investors still try to increase absolute profits and their share of the G.N.P. Such sectors as agriculture, trade, and the professions are attempting to expand their share of total income through price and profit channels. Competition is vigorous within broad groups, especially between skilled and unskilled labor. There are continuing pressures from families at the lower income levels, not just those below the $15,000 poverty margin.

It has long been agreed in the United States that the government, supported by business and social institutions, is responsible for setting flexible minimum standards below which no one shall be permitted to go. No consensus has yet been achieved, however, about the techniques for achieving this objective or about the levels for minimum standards.

Suspicious attitudes toward business persist despite the relative abundance of the American economy, owing in part to the large gaps in living standards still evident among different groups, geographical sectors, and occupational categories, which are still causing serious social and economic conflict.

Hunger is no longer a burning issue. The current struggle for higher living standards has to do with elements considered luxuries a generation or two ago and now demanded as essential components of daily living.

Complex Economy

The general pattern of affluence and the way in which it is shared form the background for interpreting what has happened to the relationship between government and business. But we can also observe a significant increase not only in the complexity of the economy and its operation but also in the difficulties government confronts in its efforts to operate efficiently. Similarly, within the business sphere, new technologies, procedures, and arrangements have introduced complexities involving significant changes.

Society has been computerized far beyond what was expected a generation ago. In most industries, automation is the norm, and companies operate vast combinations of machinery and produce a wide range of products with limited manpower. In formerly large-scale clerical operations such as banking and insurance, the computer has virtually taken over.

This does not mean that full employment has become difficult to achieve. On the contrary, as technology has expanded, the rise in production has been substantial, with a tremendous increase in the demand for workers, especially in the fast-growing service areas and in government.

The problem of adapting economic life to a computerized environment is twofold: to match the demand for workers with job supply, and to evolve new arrangements between government and business that move the society toward its enlarging social objectives and at the same time continue to yield the benefits of private enterprise.

Research and Development

One specific area that illuminates this complexity is research and development. At one time, the government had conducted research on a wide scale within public facilities or in association with public-related activities such as military procurement. Then came heavy emphasis on research-and-development contracts with academic and nonprofit institutions. Entering the twenty-first century, we find huge outlays and varied activities in research and development funded by public, business, and foundation sources so vast and intermingled that trends and clear lines of demarcation are hard to define. It is difficult to work through the maze of funding, personnel, activities, and application to identify the respective roles of the public and private sectors. The possible effects of this blending process on other fields and functions is being seriously studied.

Government-Labor-Management

While labor still pursues a fair share of the product of the American economy, the share of total labor income as a component of the national income has remained rather stable over a long period. There has been a relative decline in monetary wages and a relative increase in fringe benefits (vacations, pensions, educational allowances, recreational facilities), but the huge level of aggregate profits continues to be a source of friction in the bargaining process and in general economic policy decisions.

There have been experiments in profit sharing over the past third of the century, but in general neither business nor labor is very keen about it. The government has encouraged innovation in labor-management relations, owing to more consumer pressure for price stability. Strikes are more successfully avoided through sophisticated public relations in labor and management, rather than through specific government regulations and policies.

The government has not neglected labor-management relations; instead, sometimes it supports one side and sometimes the other in an effort at noninflationary policies. The government has sought, quite successfully, to make prices a factor in labor-management negotiations.

Labor leaders recognize that in wage-price races labor tends to be the loser, for industry, in a full-employment economy, is generally able to pass on higher costs by raising prices. The labor movement has also become much more unified in its wage policies, so that unions tend to engage in fewer competitive races and focus instead on real wage increases.

Labor and government, reflecting a serious general concern about inflation, have gradually managed to bring business management around to the position where prices are genuinely discussed and weighed in the process of labor-management bargaining. Originally this effort was left to mediators in government, but recurrent inflation made it clear that overall monetary and fiscal policies had to be supplemented by other measures if antiinflationary measures were to succeed. Consumers alternated between quiescence and protest, but the latter became more frequent, intense, and politically potent.

The government has pursued progressively stronger tactics to force management and labor to discuss prices. For a long time business resisted vigorously, but gradually views on prices expressed in labor negotiations became public knowledge. The resulting favorable public response encouraged the government and all concerned parties to pursue this pattern more seriously.

In general, the government role in labor-management relations has been to persuade rather than to regulate. The government does still concern itself with many labor-management problems, such as setting higher minimum-income standards; exploring ways to raise income-maintainance standards; dealing with on-the-job training, job security, and varied specific fringe benefits; and making sure that bargaining is democratic.

There is more industry-wide bargaining, and this has had a stabilizing influence. Government has been alert to labor and management practices that inhibit productivity and growth.

Government and Regulations

Not only have the nature and structure of the business community changed during the past third of the century, but popular and government attitudes toward business have changed as well. There is less concern with monopoly and the private concentration of power, and more with maximum production and the public interest.

The general policy of government toward business tends toward shaping and focusing private incentives to achieve broad public objectives rather than imposing direct controls and regulations. The results have on the whole been meritorious.

The problem of regulating mass transit illustrates the developments and challenges in other areas of public-utility regulation, although the nature and severity of the problems vary greatly. In general, public ownership of mass transit has not been entirely satisfactory. Both public and private ownership have been subsidized, but resistance to higher fares has been more effective where there is public ownership.

The Federal Government has now established institutions for coordinating the policies and programs of the Interstate Commerce Commission, the Federal Power Commission, the Federal Maritime Commission, and some of the regulatory responsibilities of the Departments of Transportation, Agriculture, and the Treasury. When it became clear that the Federal Government could not effectively regulate all the utilities, since a high degree of local and regional regulatory authority was essential, the Federal Government retained only broad policy functions.

This approach to centralized policies and decentralized regulation has been quite successful. But there are still problems of coordination and differences of opinion about what requires detailed and protective regulation. The public-utility regulators gradually came to accept the idea that regulation should try to simulate the market place, and this realization called for new concepts of regulation embodying incentives for improved efficiency, research and development, innovation, and economizing in the production and distribution of public utilities.

Another interesting aspect of public-utility regulation developed in the final quarter of the twentieth century with the introduction of new principles in rate differentials among various users and for various kinds of products. Given the kind of data now available through the use of computers, the Federal Government has been able to establish general principles affecting conservation and efficiency in the use of scarce resources. Similarly, concern over poverty and income differentials between centers of cities and suburbs has led to relatively higher utility rates in the suburbs than in the center cities.

After considerable controversy, consumer interests are now more effectively represented in the regulation of public utilities by competent individuals whose experience, training, and lack of any vested interest can best serve the public needs. Back in the 1970's, as divisions between rich and poor, black and white, urban and rural intensified, it became clear that new forms of representation were needed.

The main pressures have come from people within the cities who represent the less privileged and minority groups. Special efforts must be made to assure that the interests of the less privileged are meaningfully reflected in policy making and in regulatory activities. Despite bitter divisions over what is truly effective and adequate representation, workable arrangements have evolved.

Opportunities Act

In the late 1960's and the early 1970's there was long and serious consideration of the Opportunities Act. It was enacted in 1976, establishing broad principles for national, social, and welfare objectives, as well as minimum standards.

The purpose of the Opportunities Act was to make the federal government responsible for minimum social and welfare standards. It did not try to spell out quantitative levels or detailed programs any more specifically than the Employment Act of 1946 had done. But the mere statement of goals and objectives served to clarify responsibility and to guide the policies of government, labor, business, farmers, and consumers as they related to the essential needs and wants of the people and the productive capabilities of the economy.

Once the Opportunities Act had become a law of the land, there was a gradual narrowing of policy differences within the country. In time even the most conservative forces came to recognize the responsibility of the total society for those who were less advantaged and less privileged, and an increasing number of projects and programs were designed to alleviate and overcome these difficulties.

As had been the case with the minimum-wage and social-security laws of the 1930's, and with the earlier child-labor laws, employers gradually accepted as reasonable the standards set forth in the Opportunities Act. Thereafter, management was checked by investors; labor leaders by union members; and both by government. Consumers became more observant and vocal. All in all there were fewer controls and regulation, but more checks and balances within the private sector.

The Use of Taxes

In the late 1960's and throughout the 1970's a long and sometimes bitter debate raged over incentives that could induce the private business sector to fulfill the social and welfare objectives set forth by the government, which at the same time would not destroy the progressive and responsive character of the Federal system. The business community favored tax incentives; it did not want a wide variety of subsidies that could become political footballs and sources of corruption and of public condemnation.

One reason for the success of the Employment Act of 1946 was the progressive and responsive nature of the Federal tax system, which served as an important automatic stabilizer. In the 1970's the total tax structure tended once again to become more progressive and responsive, and the government became less opposed to using tax incentives for encouraging business to perform socially desirable functions, such as special employment efforts for the deprived and on-the-job training for the hard-core unemployed.

Self-Regulation

Probably most significant in the relations between government and business was the development of clearer distinctions between policies and concepts on the one hand, and detailed regulations and operations on the other. As political science, economics, and management have come to be better understood, government has been able to form relationships with business, labor, consumers, and farmers that have ensured improved recognition and acceptance of those fundamental policy areas that are the government's responsibility. The details of management and operation, however, are left in the hands of private groups faithful to the fundamental objectives of economic growth, social justice, and the protection of the public.

As in so many fields of activity in the year 2000, the increased data, knowledge, and experience flowing from the use of computers now permit the maintenance of performance standards that in themselves provide considerable self-regulation, self-policing, and self-adjustment.

In the recent past there has been much experimentation with such incentives as taxation and direct subsidies. Tax incentives have seemed simpler, requiring less administrative control. But they have generally proved very costly, and the government gradually has begun to use them more selectively.

Light Hands or Heavy Hands

In the United States in the year 2000 the tremendous increase in total production and the marked rise in living standards for everyone have all served to bring about a modest degree of cooperation both between government and business and government and labor.

The government has devised increasingly objective means for setting and reviewing standards. In such fields as pollution, safety, and consumer protection, the government farms out many more studies, analyses, and reports than it did twenty-five or fifty years ago. Nonprofit and commercial organizations as well as universities are given contracts to analyze the qualities and performance of goods and services, and all the information is made public. This exposes many aspects of private operations to more careful scrutiny, but it has not dampened competitive vigor or innovation.

New organizations resembling those of the 1930's have been established to protect individuals against bank failures, fraudulent stock transactions, mortgage insurance, employer abuses, and discrimination, through insurance and other devices. Here again new regulations tend to be more in the nature of general policy and broad standard setting rather than detailed controls.

Government organizations have broadened their personnel recruitment to include psychologists, motivation analysts, anthropologists, mathematicians, and a whole new range of behavioral scientists. The government tries to determine just what kinds of devices and techniques can be helpful in achieving self-regulation and self-policing, and in evaluating these self-regulatory agencies.

In the year 2000, welfare and social purposes will on the whole have been reconciled with the benefits to be gained from the vigor of private enterprise. From the point of view of production as well as equity, the system seems to work. The principal problems have been those of maneuvering and manipulating incentives and standards to encourage the private sector, but also to sustain the kind of self-policing consistent with a relatively free society. Above all, the government's role has been kept within manageable limits, and the private sector has continued to be the principal vehicle for economic and welfare activities.

SOME CONSEQUENCES OF PLURALIZATION IN GOVERNMENT *

James David Barber

What are the likely consequences for policy making in the future of the fact that governments are "fragmented," "pluralistic," "multicentered," and becoming more so? At all levels of American government, in all major public and private institutions, we see the proliferation of new organizational units at a faster rate than old ones disappear. If this trend continues—to 1984, to the year 2000, to 2068—what will be the main dimensions of a political system originally designed for discord and subsequently patched together by a series of ad-hoc adaptations? Answers for the long run depend in part on a close look at the immediate effects of small-scale increments in pluralization. What happens today and tomorrow as new units are added? The empirical propositions below, none of which is proved, are steps toward formulating bigger pictures of the years beyond the now emerging future, pictures we might be able to improve upon if we could perceive their shapes.

By pluralization I mean the creation of new, distinct but interdependent organizational units. This approach focuses attention on marginal transitions from a system with fewer distinct units to one with more such units. It contrasts with categorical approaches in which a system characterized as pluralistic in some overall sense is

* For helpful comments on drafts of this essay, I am glad to thank Hayward Alker, Gabriel Almond, Chris Argyris, Lewis Coser, Robert Dahl, Karl Deutsch, James Fesler, William Frankena, Fred Greenstein, Albert Hirschman, Henry Kariel, Herbert Kaufman, Richard Lowenthal, Michael Maccoby, Jules Masserman, Richard Merritt, Michael Montias, Daniel P. Moynihan, Paul Mussen, Nelson Polsby, David Riesman, Bruce Russett, Harry Scoble, Charles Tilly, Meredith Wilson, Frank Young, and the members of the Working Group on American Government.

compared with a generally hierarchical or generally anarchistic system. Is Congress pluralistic or hierarchical? I shall not try to answer that. But the creation of a new congressional committee is clearly a step in the pluralistic direction. Similarly the devolution of important responsibilities to field offices in administration or to lower courts in the judiciary constitute pluralistc moves. The proliferation of task forces, coordinating committees, new boards, councils, departments, and offices at any level of government increases the number of separated but functionally interdependent centers of decision. For simplicity's sake I refer to all such bodies as *units* and to the process of their creation as *pluralization.*[1]

1. *Pluralization is self-reinforcing.* That is, the process tends to acquire a momentum of its own, stimulating the creation of separate but interdependent decision centers at an increasing *rate.* In the first place, pluralization becomes a precedent: the establishment of a new unit serves as an example for all others in the system, especially for those operating in the same general problem area. Pluralization enters the list of political strategies as a legitimate gambit for pursuing the stakes of government. (For example, creating a new unit helps focus attention on a new problem.) Arguments against using this strategy are weakened every time a new example appears. Put another way, pluralization progressively becomes the norm, both in the sense of something expected to happen and something reasonable to do.[2]

Second, creation of a single new unit sets in motion interactions with numerous other units. Each such event thus multiplies the number of relationships which must be coordinated to produce action. In time the "load" on coordination channels tends to increase and to reach a point at which it becomes useful to regularize them. Committees or individuals are assigned to pull together the efforts of several units on specific tasks. Participants come to expect interunit relations to be handled by certain formally or informally designated persons. In time, these persons tend to acquire the status of functional specialists in coordination and to gain more and more control over the content of decisions. The opportunities for the proliferation of coordination units increase in an exponential way as the number of new substantive units increases.

A third factor reinforcing pluralist trends is the tendency for old units to react to the challenge of new units by seeking to expand

and/or intensify their own activities. The appearance of a new unit in a task area threatens the prerogatives of all old units in that area.[3] Fears of being replaced or reduced in significance stimulate the old unit to demonstrate its vitality and importance by undertaking new functions. In many cases, it will demand additional functions as the price of its consent to the creation of a new unit. Thus new relationships and activities are multiplied, spreading out in waves from the splash made by any single act of pluralization.

Finally, processes of proliferation are reinforced by new divisions of labor, especially at the lowest levels of decision making. As social change produces new configurations of problems for government, strains appear in the existing organizational fabric. New units are created to fit current conditions more closely. The result is a more detailed and interdependent set of relationships, a finer tuning, between governmental organization and pressing contemporary problems. But the more elaborately an organization is articulated and tied in with the present, the more rapidly it is outdated by the march of events. Specialization thus has built into it a tendency to speed up the frequency of demands for further and/or new specializations, as social change renders existing arrangements obsolete. Meanwhile, institutional loyalties, habits, and interests militate against the elimination of old units as new ones are instituted.[4]

2. *Pluralization increases the incidence of conflicts in the system.*
3. *Pluralization decreases the intensity of conflicts in the system.*

By proliferating new relationships among separate but interdependent decision centers, pluralization provides an increasing number of occasions for conflict. There are at least two reasons for this, one interpersonal and one jurisdictional. Each new pluralistic relationship involves communication at a distance, enhancing opportunities for misreading messages. Inter-unit disparities in timing and emphasis, special languages, and different definitions of the problem increase the probability that mistakes will be made in attributing motives, expectations, plans, and resources to one another. Erroneous interpretations are more difficult to correct quickly by communications in writing or through third parties than in the give-and-take of face-to-face communication. Thus pluralization increases the likelihood of "misunderstandings" developing among decision makers, even if they are determined to cooperate.[5] In addition, however, the disjunction involved in pluralization depersonalizes and thus legitimizes conflict. In the more intimate intra-unit environment, aggressions are repressed and mollified. (If not, intra-unit bickering produces its own paralysis.) It is difficult and risky to express (perhaps even to feel) hostility toward those with whom one is in daily personal contact. Aggressions are more readily channeled toward the new external targets—other units.

Conflict incidence is also increased by the inevitable overlapping of jurisdictions, which accompanies unit proliferation. The event of formalizing a new unit obscures the fact that transfers of function occur gradually. Typically an old unit has been performing at least some of the tasks allotted to the new one: in practice these responsibilities are not suddenly torn away from the old and handed to the new, but are defined and redefined as particular issues arise. Thus jurisdictional conflicts are strung out over the early history of the new unit. Furthermore, new formal jurisdictional boundaries are elaborated, representing new ways of analyzing artificially problems which are in fact highly integrated. In the course of attacking "its" problem, the new unit finds itself more and more involved with connected problems, finds it more and more difficult to avoid trespassing on the jurisdictions of others. Thus the gradual and artificial character of jurisdictional innovations furnishes additional chances for inter-unit combat.[6]

However, the proliferation of decision centers also tends to reduce the intensity of conflicts. This is in part due to the need for economizing energies: involved in a growing number of conflicts, a unit can spend only so much time and trouble on each. To concentrate on any one conflict is to neglect others and risk defeat. The more units active in a field, the more any one of them will be concerned to ward off threats from many directions.

Viewed in the aggregate, the system as it pluralizes is less apt to polarize. That is, the situation in which two large, internally united and persistent alliances face one another in conflict become less likely. As issues change, organizational fragments will cluster differently. The kind of conflict escalation which takes place when two powers of approximately equal strength confront each other is unlikely to go far in a system engaged in dispersing power pluralistically.

4. *Pluralization channels energies into problems of inter-unit relations and away from problems of substantive program evaluation.*

The more units there are involved in a policy process, the more necessary and difficult it is to predict and manipulate their reactions to proposals. Questions are thus increasingly posed in the form "How will units X, Y, and Z receive this proposal?" and "How can we best insure a favorable response?" rather than "What would this program do if put into operation in the field?" These questions are not entirely distinct—one evaluates in part by getting opinions from others. But a new relationship of interdependence means that, to some degree, consent as well as advice must be sought. Therefore increasing attention is devoted to exchanges of information on the current status, predilections, and intentions of other units—in short, on "inside dope" about "what will go" with them. In cybernetic terms, feedback from within the system itself tends to overload the communications network, reducing its capacity to handle feedback from outside the system.[7]

5. *Pluralization increases the number of proposals initiated.*[8]

6. *Pluralization reduces the number of proposals adopted.*

The newly created unit is in a sense an experiment. It is expected to prove the necessity for its very existence within a limited time period, unlike old units whose continuance is assumed. At first its substantive purposes are much clearer than its internal organization and procedures. And external restraints on action are not yet clearly defined. Members of the new unit, all selected at the same time, share attitudes of commitment to the program for which they are responsible; shared attitudes in old units are more likely to center on commitment to the organization as a going concern.[9] The political resources mobilized to bring the new unit into existence are available to support initial proposals for action. The fluidity of the situation both within and without the unit stimulates individuals and the agency as a whole to capture attention by suggesting innovations. For all these reasons, a flow of proposals is likely to spring from newborn units.

Old units of government are apt to respond to these initiatives with a mixture of skepticism and jealousy. In order to maintain and advance their bargaining positions (and to demonstrate that they can be active too), old units are motivated to produce counterproposals. Thus the number of suggestions fed into the machinery of government from existing units increases as pluralization proceeds.

But as units proliferate, the number of proposals adopted—that is, actually put into operation—declines, due to changes in the aggregate character of the system. Initially there is an increase in communication, not only between new and old units but also among old units about what the new one is doing. Gradually these communications lines are transformed into "clearance" channels: officials learn to or are compelled to gather reactions to their proposals from other units. In time, clearance procedures tend to develop into approval-disapproval procedures. That is, pieces of paper are in effect annotated "OK" or "No" in addition to conveying technical or advisory comments. Especially because pluralization exacerbates jurisdictional conflicts, more and more units are motivated to demand veto power over proposals originating in other units. As a matter of course, the "defensive advantage" [10] is strengthened and the probability that any proposal will survive declines. Organizational majority rule—that is, that the *balance* of positive and negative reactions will determine outcomes—gives way to an organizational minorities veto rule—that is, that a minority with intense objections anywhere in the system can stop action. What began as a kind of simultaneous voting system is transformed into a sequential voting system. The number of actual adoptions comes more and more to depend, not on the number of proposals advanced, but on the number of approvals required from separated, differentiated, and interdependent units.[11]

7. *Pluralization raises the probability that proposals will be adopted, when they are adopted, in bunches.* By increasing the opportunities for vetoing and delaying broad government action, pluralization tends to allow social problems to build up to crisis proportions. A point is reached at which failure to act threatens to bring about relatively marked social or political upheavals, demands for redistributing power in the system, agitation for changing the rules of the game. Frustrated in their programmatic efforts, interests turn on the structural characteristics of the system, thus challenging established habits and prerogatives. At this point, many units may suddenly suppress their differences and agree to cooperate.

Once started, cooperation may spread rapidly, in a variety of bandwagon phenomena. First, the more severe any social problem is allowed to become, the more closely it is linked with other social problems. For example, mild and localized juvenile delinquency may be defined as a "youth recreation" problem; chronic and widespread delinquency may be defined as involving unemployment, education, welfare, housing, and health problems. Thus a collection of programs by a wide range of agencies is called for on substantive grounds. Second, in a crisis atmosphere, normal restraints on innovation are temporarily weakened or suspended. Exceptions allowed for particular purposes sap the forcefulness of generalized rules; the agencies may take this opportunity to press for other innovations related only indirectly (or not at all) to the current crisis. The "time is ripe" for "something to be done."

A third reason for the bunching of adoptions in crisis periods is that the price of rapid action is compromise, which may take the form of a "package deal" [12]—lumping together a rather miscellaneous collection of proposals in order to gain consent to the crisis-oriented ones. The more urgent the pressure for action in a hurry, the less stringently criteria of relevance and consistency will be applied.

As the process of pluralization continues, this bunching tendency will result in longer time periods between spurts of increasingly intense and variegated government action.

8. *In the short run, pluralization increases the radicalness of proposals initiated.*

9. *In the long run, pluralization increases the conservatism of proposals initiated and adopted.* The same factors operate here as in the case of the number of proposals initiated and adopted (see above, numbers 5 and 6). But additional cognitive and strategic elements contribute to these trends. Pluralization, by generating specialized units, simultaneously brings some units into more intimate contact with substantive social problems and removes these problems from the immediate concern of other units. The widening of this intimacy-remoteness gap makes it more and more likely that innovative proposals on any particular topic will spring mainly from the specialized unit most immediately concerned. Compared with all other units in the system, the initiator is apt to be the one most aware, knowledgeable, certain, and confident of its judgment about the special difficulties with which it must deal. Its focus of attention is on the needs and wants of its clientele; its orientation is toward solutions of problems. In the initial formulations of proposals, therefore, the new specialized unit asks "What should the government do to take care of this situation?" The odds are that proposals conceived in the midst of a hot struggle with stubborn

social realities will stress the necessity for more action on more fronts as soon as possible.[13]

With ideas of what needs to be done, the new unit turns to strategic considerations: "How can we get consent for an adequate program from the other units in the system?" Looking ahead to the obstacle course that a proposal will have to run, the initiator is tempted to inflate his estimates, on the surmise that other units will discount them. The more approvals required, the greater the temptation. The tendency, then, is for pluralization to stimulate relatively radical proposals from new units. But over time, feedback processes work to modify this tendency. Reviewing units learn that their discounting practices have been anticipated, and come to distrust the sincerity of radical innovators. Initiators learn that inflated requests are hard to defend and that such exaggerations detract from a reputation for integrity. Thus, as organizational units mature, proposals become more and more conservative, representing only marginal departures from the last set of adopted proposals.[14]

The conservative tendencies of reviewing and evaluating units stem in part from their cognitive orientation. Their focus of attention is on proposals, not problems. At least one step removed from the needs and demands of the social situation, they concentrate instead on the information at hand—namely, the new proposal considered in the light of the last one advanced and adopted on this subject. By focusing on departures from precedent, they conserve their intellectual energies and simplify their decision process. The magnitude of each departure looms large in their minds partly because it is the one item of information about which they are sure. The burden of proof is placed on those who want, in effect, to repudiate or at least amend the last decision made. Successive reviews of proposals tend to whittle them down closer and closer to the standing decision left over from the past.[15]

The increasing overlap of clearance procedures in a pluralizing system contributes to this conservative tendency. Decision makers are confronted with a growing number of proposals from many different sources. This in itself makes examination of substantive issues more difficult and increases the tendency to stress comparisons with precedent. It also introduces another basis for decision: comparison with the demands of other units. Lacking substantive reasons for preferring one proposal over the others, the reviewing unit may adopt an equality criterion. That is, approximately equal departures from precedent will be allowed for each proposal. If unit X is granted a 10-percent increase, units Y and Z, on ground of "fairness," also deserve a 10-percent raise. The entry of new units into this picture has at least two effects. It may be necessary to reduce the "fair share" increment in order to accommodate a new proposal within the framework of action on other requests (or, in budget terms, to "hold the line" of total resources allocated). Second, the clearing unit is under pressure to treat proposals from new units on the basis of the same rule they have established for old ones. Yet it is the new units which are most likely to propose relatively radical departures, to provide the cutting edge of innovation and progressivism in the system. The larger the overlap in clearance procedures, then, the greater the drag of the old on the new.[16]

10. *Pluralization increases the cost of government.*

The long-run effects of pluralization are conservative with respect to the character and program costs of individual units. But the costs of operating the aggregate system rise radically as pluralization proceeds. Part of this is simply the incremental cost of creating new units without eliminating or curtailing old ones. Another effect tends to become multiplicative, in the following fashion. Functional interdependence among units makes each of them capable of disrupting the system by striking. The strike is the ultimate weapon; milder forms or threats of non-cooperation are also available. Strikes aimed at gaining non-monetary program goals, such as new legislation, or a reorientation of other units, are unlikely to be successful because the system's sequential veto pattern makes approval unlikely, and because the striking unit finds it difficult to maintain mobilization of its forces in a risky enterprise for programmatic ends (unless members are willing to endure severe and continuing deprivations for the cause). But strikes for money succeed because the threat can be met, by emergency increases in the total budget, without wide (parallel) clearance, and because the striking unit is strongly motivated and thus more able to maintain mobilization. No single unit will be able to use the strike (or semi-strike) mechanism often, but increasing numbers of units will try it once in a while, and increasing interdependence among units will increase the effectiveness of strikes in extracting money. This pattern will be imitated; in a pluralizing system there will be even more imitators. Thus, costs escalate.

Finally, pluralization increases the claimants for money anticipated in any new program. Each will be after its "share." Thus the size of each share gets smaller, as do the odds that any individual share will be "adequate" to achieve the program's stated purposes for that unit. The consequence is an expansion of demands for refunding at higher and longer-term levels.[17]

11. *Pluralization increases the number and complexity of formal rules.*

12. *Pluralization increases the incidence of behavioral departures from formal rules.*

There is a built-in tendency for rules to expand in proportion to the distance and the degree of interdependence among agencies. By simultaneously increasing uncertainty (because it is more difficult to predict what the other units will do) and increasing the probability of conflict (for reasons already described), pluralization stimulates a search for certainty and stability. Formal rules are thus likely to be proposed; they are likely to be adopted for a number of reasons. Most generally, it is difficult to find legitimate, publicly arguable reasons for opposing formal recognition of an existing situation. If, in fact, a new relationship has been established between units A and B, why should anyone object to recognizing and writing down rules to govern this new set of interactions? Of course there are many practical reasons; the point is that they are hard to defend to broader publics.

Second, the rules have important power implications. Old units will attempt to tie down the new ones with jurisdictional and other restrictions, perhaps as the price of consent for the creation of the new units. Those currently in an advantageous position will strive to stabilize the situation by pressing for rules, recognizing that the odds are rising that their authority will be challenged. Finally, changes in organizational structures and functions are likely to conflict with old rules. The incidence of "violations" of increasingly complex formal rules will mount, and there will be demands that the old rules be amended or strengthened to handle this problem. But since repeal and relegislation are much more difficult to accomplish than amendment or accretion, the rules will tend to pile up.

However, this process tends to proceed at a slower rate than the proliferation of ad-hoc, informal linkages among units. Only after a new relationship has been established for some time can it be argued that procedures have become regular, standard, normal, and thus amenable to formalization. Those currently disadvantaged will resist freezing the situation. Furthermore, a special problem arises in formalizing the role of coordinators. As long as this role is left indefinite, the coordinator can appear as a servant or equal of the units coordinated. Formalization tends to elevate him to a higher status and authority, and so may be resisted by the other parties. Finally, as the rules become more complex and detailed, relatively minor shifts in issues loosen the fit between rule and problem; officials increasingly find it necessary to bypass the formalities in order to get anything done. Thus, in a paradoxical way, the more rules there are the less revealing they are to the student of political decision making. As new units proliferate—whether vertically (creating new hierarchical relationships) or horizontally (creating new coordinaate relationships)—the rules will grow more numerous, complex, and irrelevant.[18]

13. *Pluralization enhances the relative power of large, permanent, and highly organized interests in the society.*

Weakly organized interests may be almost as potent as strongly organized ones in stopping government action. In a veto system, control over only one unit is necessary. But as pluralization progresses, in order to get significant proposals adopted interests must exert pressure at an increasing number of points. In normal periods, the proliferation of units increases the time lag between initiation and adoption of proposals. Temporary bursts of activity decline in effectiveness. The interest which can sustain its attack over months or years, from the first suggestions to program implementation in the field, has an immense advantage over its momentarily active opponents. In crisis situations, the prizes go to the groups capable of taking vigorous action on many fronts simultaneously. These tendencies are accelerated by pluralization, so that the interests possessing many political resources—members, money, time, skills, and so on—are progressively advantaged.

Government officials are increasingly motivated to seek powerful allies outside the government, as the incidence of conflict in the system increases. And especially in new programs being implemented by new units, there are good reasons for seeking cooperation from powerful interests. The new unit needs some quick proof of success, some striking demonstration that it deserves to survive and expand. If it can find already in existence an organized interest with expert information, lines of access, and other resources which can be added to its own resources (even with certain conditions attached), the chances for showing some positive result rapidly are better. In deciding which problems to attack first, the new unit is under some pressure to take up arms against problems already nearly solved, and to postpone consideration of those which require much groundwork before any result can be anticipated. Thus, for example, policies formulated to help the disadvantaged in the society are very likely to be transformed in execution into policies regarding the advantaged. The history of farm policies in the United States is perhaps a good illustration (as are many other programs in which the progressive's idealism and energy confront the resentment, apathy, and suspicion of the most needful).

Powerful interests are also likely to be rewarded disproportionately in the initial stages of pluralization. Large, permanent, and highly organized interests are best able to gain a voice in the selection of new unit personnel, the definition of purposes, the magnitude and type of resources allocated, and so forth. The new unit is indebted to and to some degree dependent on the interests which gave it its start.

Large, permanent, and highly organized interests are powerful in any political system. The proposition here advanced is that marginal increases in the number of interdependent but distinct units—in the complexity of government organization—decrease the probability that interests lacking any one of these resources can get the government to take action on a significant scale to meet their needs. Again it should be emphasized that the basis for comparison is not hierarchy versus pluralism, but organizational unity versus marginal diversification.[19]

14. *Pluralization increases the multi-functional character of units.*

Tasks may be distributed among governmental units on the basis of geographical area, subject matter (such as agriculture), or function (such as rule making). But functional divisions of labor will be difficult to maintain over the long run in a pluralizing system. Interests in the society are almost always organized either by area or subject matter rather than by function. We have national labor and business organizations, not separate private organizations for legislating, executing, and judging policies in either field. In an increasingly fragmented government, the probability that any organized interest will succeed in gaining access to *some* unit increases. There are many such entry points; what fails with one may succeed with another. If the purpose is simply to obstruct government action, strong access to one or a few units in a clearance system may be sufficient. If the aim is to get comprehensive programs adopted, other strategies, noted in number 13 above, are indicated. But many interests pursue goals falling between vetoing and broad policy innovation; they seek restricted but positive action by government. Such groups will encourage the functional growth of friendly units, will press them to deal with "the problem as a whole." Since the officials themselves are also likely to desire expanded functions, the interest finds allies on the inside.

Thus the "independence" of regulatory agencies gets stressed; a functionally constructed unit like the House Rules Committee undertakes to review the substance of legislation; the Supreme Court takes initiatives in setting national civil-rights policies; and national-party platform committees are involved in candidate-selection maneuvers.[20] The pluralistic bases for these developments lie in (a) the increasing ease of acquiring access somewhere in the system and (b) the increasing difficulty of acquiring access to many separated units performing different functions on interest-salient problems.

15. *Pluralization increases the demand for and rate of circulation of elites.*

As a system pluralizes, more units will find it necessary to devote more time and effort to recruitment of new personnel and to counteracting offers by other units for present personnel. Specialization of the "personnel" function is likely and will handle most of the problem for staff below the upper levels, but staffing at and near the top cannot easily be delegated in this way; the main decision makers in the organization will then have added to their other duties a good deal of work in identifying, selecting, and recruiting new and replacement staff and in finding ways to retain the talent they have.

The basic reasons for this are fairly simple. A new unit needs a top man (perhaps a "big name"); an executive director; a group of top-level generalists capable of participating in organization-wide decisions; and others. The net increment of demand results from the fact that old units are not eliminated as fast as new ones are created. The identification of top leadership potential is difficult; most units will seek to reduce uncertainty by focusing on persons who have already demonstrated leadership ability—that is, on leaders in other units. This competition will lead to more rapid circulation of elites. From the "recruitee's" standpoint, there is an increasing number of plausible alternative opportunities to his present place. The more such opportunities, the greater the probability that one or more of them will be more attractive than his present position. Careers involving many switches are thus more likely.[21]

16. *Pluralization enhances the roles of lawyers and budget makers.* As coordination becomes more difficult, the significance of common elements increases. Two ubiquitous elements in inter-unit coordination are laws and money. Laws, because relationships among units are defined and linked by laws to more inclusive sets of relations. As laws proliferate and gain importance as manipulable elements, successful action comes to depend more and more on the legal technician and on the lawyer as "omnicompetent amateur" (David Riesman's concept). Money, on the other hand, provides the main basis for comparison among activities by substantively different units, with the consequence that the requesting-budgeting-appropriating-accounting institutions are in an extremely and progressively significant strategic position. Yet neither lawyers nor budgeters, once they have been included in the process, can be excluded effectively from any part of it. While these actors may think of their roles as narrowly technical, they in fact make decisions involving the whole range of substantive decisions. The size and status of legal staffs in government agencies and the kinds of questions raised in appropriations committees would seem to confirm this development.[22]

17. *Pluralization increases the demand for, dependence on, and power of those with extraordinary political talents.* The lawyers and the budgeters gain power because they deal with commensurable commodities. The politicians' speciality is making the incommensurable commensurable. Successful negotiation among proliferating organizations is an extremely difficult art. It requires the ability to anticipate a wide and inconstant range of reactions, to manipulate representations of units to one another without sacrificing plausibility, to parlay limited resources which one only partly controls into effective power, and many other things. Such talents

are extraordinarily scarce, yet without them a fragmented government tends to degenerate into unproductive bickering and stalemate. Robert Moses of New York, Mayor Lee of New Haven, and Lyndon B. Johnson as Senate Majority Leader illustrate the significance of political skills in holding a pluralistic system together.[23]

Only the most sketchy account of these tendencies, illustrated with a few examples, is presented above. Let us suppose for the moment that they are all confirmed by appropriate empirical evidence. What broader, longer-range implications do they suggest for a pluralizing system? At least three basically different kinds of outcomes seem possible.

Meliorative politics. Over the long run, it might be argued, pluralization produces an impressive variety of ideas, proposals, plans, and projects. The system in operation is under constant criticism; it tends to correct itself. Marginal improvements remove at least some frictions and dampen the intensity of conflicts. The system is relatively stable and peaceful, pursuing a moderate course by requiring widespread consensus on any basic policy change. The system is an open one in which a great many interests are linked, through their organizations, to their government. (The joys of participation are widely available.) At a minimum, a pluralistic government is unlikely to be a tyrannical one in any positive sense.

Crisis politics. Others would argue that pluralism's tendencies toward stalemate are extremely dangerous to the long-run peace and stability of the system. The widening gap between, on the one hand, rapid social change and increasing rates of proposal innovation, and on the other hand the growing difficulty of producing effective government action breeds disappointment and disillusionment.[24] The longer social problems go unsolved, the more unlikely it becomes that they can be solved by some modest, limited program. Unorganized, isolated, and impoverished segments of the society are progressively disadvantaged in comparison with the rich rewards heaped on the already better-off. There is, in the long run, always the possibility that, with skillful leadership, the disadvantaged, who have grown suspicious of behind-the-scenes government and cynical from continual disappointment, will take the occasion of some crisis to alter the system in a fundamental way. In any case, ill-considered, irrational policies will characterize government by crisis.

Feudal politics. A third possibility is that units will succeed in reducing their dependence on one another. Each may stake off some segment of government as its special, separate bailiwick. Interest groups may establish connections with particular units and manage to convert them into independent domains, each ruling over its clientele with a minimum of interference from without. The practice of delegating great authority to "czars" for various problem areas might continue and grow, resulting in a system not unlike medieval feudalism. Areal decentralization (for example, in the name of "states' rights" or "community control") might proceed in a similar fashion. The result would be a society governed in relatively distinct groups, each governmental unit being responsible for protecting and caring for many of the needs of its special clientele.

Of these three conceivable outcomes, most political scientists probably would prefer meliorative politics to feudal politics, and feudal politics to a politics of crisis. Yet such evaluations are heavily dependent on the often unexpressed premises of one's political philosophy.[25] Pluralization is a technique of governing, a means toward ends which need to be specified more clearly than they have been. Its existence as a common activity in a surviving system demonstrates neither its inevitability nor its desirabilty[26] Careful testing of hypotheses such as those advanced above might contribute to a more useful evaluative scheme than the polemical posing of grand alternatives can offer.

Until that happens, we are guessing. An entirely plausible guess, of an order different from those above, is that government—that is, those institutions we now call governments—will be largely irrelevant to the major social concerns of the year 2000. The continual raising of hopes which cannot be fulfilled, the domestic "wars" which peter out into bickerings, the transfer of attention from exchanges within the society to exchanges within a government community busily ruling, financing, manning, and coordinating itself—may bring on, not revolution, but simply a turning away from government in favor of other mechanisms for social action. We might then view the activities of formal governmental institutions as expensive entertainment, a series of fake but amusing posturings and rituals spiced up with an occasional foreign escapade, taken seriously only for an irreducible set of domestic and international peace-keeping functions. Even if pluralistic trends continue apace, they may take longer—say to the year 2100, to reach this point. One might look to developments in the wanings of Rome and of medieval society for analogues.

An alternative extension of American experience would suggest that pragmatism will forestall pluralism. Negative feedback will stimulate corrective invention. What might some of these correctives look like? At least the following are imaginable at this point:

POPULATION CONTROL

At some time between now and the year 2000, a "war for simplification," much more comprehensive and thoroughgoing than those in the past, might decimate the population of separate but interdependent units. Large numbers of units would be abolished and their functions either destroyed or captured by the remaining units. Such conflagrations would have to be repeated periodically in order to sustain the effect. A less disruptive invention would be the collapsible unit purposefully created with a congenital defect: a pre-set anticipated life-span at the end of which it automatically ceases to exist. Another would be the practice of requiring the elimination of a comparable unit as a precondition for creating each new one, or of allocating funds so as to permit only such proliferation as could be accommodated within a fixed supply of sustenance.

Pledges of abstinence—for example, a President's campaign oath against pluralization—might be attempted. Alternatively, the creation of new agencies might be restricted to a sharply defined period each year or decade, which would facilitate comparative evaluations of such proposals. Difficult, high-level review procedures might be institutionalized to rule on acts of proliferation, perhaps requiring long, drawn-out preparations. Permission would be granted only with reference to individual cases, setting no precedents. Units which added new functions without creating new organizations would be rewarded financially. Permission to form a new unit might be made contingent upon the approval of the old unit most threatened by the proposal.

SHORT-CIRCUITING

Given the strong pressures for pluralization inherent in an ideologically activist society, measures for unit "population control" are going to be difficult to establish and sustain. More probable is a series of indirect techniques for bypassing or short-circuiting stymied subsystems and achieving other policy purposes at the same time. Leap-over policies such as the negative income tax or guaranteed annual wage might, if established, render much less significant the complexities of welfare structure. In an analogous way, PPBS and other social moniting and accounting systems might provide objective grounds for eliminating units or reallocating functions among existing units, steps very difficult to accomplish as long as program evaluation is neglected, methodologically primitive, and propagandistic.

New political alliances between national leaders and deprived populations may develop through the political parties. Instead of virtually disbanding between national elections, the parties might develop and sustain continuing relationships, much more direct than those of the government, between leaderships and citizens. These continuous parties could furnish a base for making comprehensive demands on the government, mobilizing citizens across government-clientele boundaries, and maintaining the pressure beyond policy formation to policy achievement.

COLLEGIATE POLICY MAKING

Within the government, collegial bodies of policy makers might be constructed and/or strengthened. These would be gatherings of equal generalists responsible for decisions across very wide segments of the policy spectrum. No divisions of labor among colleagues would be permitted; rather the members would be served collectively by extensive specialized staffs in command of technical expertise (particularly information processes) and by specialized groups of wise men as advisers. Conflict among both types of experts would be designed into the system. But the body of colleagues would consider issues only as a plenary consortium, never as complementary specialists. Decision making would be simultaneous; that is, all the members would consider an issue at the same time and would decide it by the majority process. Members would hold no officially defined responsibilities other than their collegiate status.

The supply of such generalists would be increased by carefully designed programs of university training, in which the ability to identify and define key issues, pinpoint the critical evidence required, and resolve conflicting advice would be fostered, through combinations of learning and action. The selection of members would be democratically controlled, but continuing special relations with constituencies would be handled by an ombudsman system (a series of officials selected simultaneously and in parallel with the collegial members).

Such collegial or conjugate [27] bodies would manage even their internal business, such as agenda setting, by common action through majority votes, thus forcing a scheduling consistent with widely shared priorities. Action on comprehensive budgets would probably form the core of their activities in normal times; budgets would in all cases be expressed programmatically, and questions of funding would be considered in conjunction with questions of program content. But the body as a whole would be prohibited from delegating responsibility for decisions to any staff or to any subgroup of members.

Not everything can be accomplished by rearranging decision-making structures. But steps as these might contribute, nevertheless, to eliminate stymies and lessen lags, attract appropriate talents, focus conflict, rationalize program packages, and direct attention to major decisions. The number of such collegiate bodies would not be large.[28]

REORGANIZATION OF PERSONS

Organizations are congeries of persons. In most of the propositions above, pluralization derives its dynamic from human responses to organizational situations. Such responses very often have a strong component of defensiveness. Distrust, aggression, over-control, stereotyping, fear, envy, pride, and a disposition to cloud the truth all contribute to the ineffectiveness of institutional arrangements. In many cases pluralization appears to exacerbate this defensiveness, in part by increasing uncertainties but also by channeling energies and ambitions in ways destructive of productive cooperation. Steps might be taken to counteract this defensiveness more directly than is possible through structural simplification.

In a wide variety of settings, techniques for reducing interpersonal defensiveness have been successfully applied. The training group and other methods for exploring, directly and explicitly, how officials in interaction perceive and respond to one another, and for developing interpersonal trust could contribute to this purpose in the political system. Recent applications of such techniques at policy-making levels of the Department of State illustrate their practicality.[29]

Obviously the baseline for these diagnoses and treatments is a value scheme which emphasizes government as an active force for human welfare, a productive government responding effectively to the social needs of a problematic age. Clearly, productiveness is not worth buying at the cost of democracy; an entire range of related questions, regarding especially the system of parties and elections, needs attention if we are to have a political order that is both fruitful and free.

The answers to such questions, suggested by speculation from unsystematic observation, require both the development of theories which will get at the underlying flow of activity in the political system and the careful testing of induced and deduced hypotheses. Far from being esoteric, "academic" exercises, these efforts will speak directly to the state of the political order in the year 2000. But at present we are not far beyond guessing how to guess.

NOTES

1. Many of the following propositions were suggested long ago in Robert A. Dahl's and Charles E. Lindblom's chapter on "Bargaining: Control Among Leaders," in *Politics, Economics and Welfare* (New York: Harper and Row, 1953); they still need testing.

For an enlightening elaboration of the perils and achievements of one "multi-centered" system, see Wallace S. Sayre and Herbert Kaufman, *Governing New York City* (New York: Russell Sage Foundation, 1960), pp. 716–725.

On decentralization aspects, see Irving Kristol, "Decentralization for What?", *The Public Interest,* 1968; Herbert Kaufman, "Administrative Decentralization and Political Power," *Public Administration Review,* XXIX, No. 1 (January/February 1969).

For examples of categorical approaches and their difficulties, see Odd Ramsoy, *Social Groups as System and Subsystem* (New York: The Free Press, 1963), pp. 45–50; Peter M. Blau and W. Richard Scott, *Formal Organizations: A Comparative Approach* (San Francisco: Chandler Publishing Company, 1962), pp. 40ff; Andrew S. McFarland, *Power and Leadership in Pluralist Systems* (Stanford, Calif.: Stanford University Press, 1969), Chapter 4, "Spurious Pluralism." On marginal time considerations in organization analysis, see S. F. Nadel, *The Theory of Social Structure* (New York: The Free Press, 1957), Chapter VI.

On functional interdependence, see Scott Greer, *Social Organization* (New York: Random House, Inc., 1955), pp. 19–21.

2. Cf. James W. Fesler on factors explaining "the multiplication of the bailiff's functionally specialized subordinates and the attenuation of their subordination to him" in fourteenth-century French administration. One factor was "the increase in the volume of work of the bailiffship. The other was the new ease of thinking of differentiated categories of work. Once differentiation had been conceptualized, any category could be subtracted from the bailiff's own omnicompetent role and entrusted to officials better qualified than he for performance of that specialized function." "French Field Administration: The Beginnings," *Comparative Studies in Society and History,* Vol. V (October 1962), p. 103. It is harder for governments to resist pluralization than it is for industrial enterprises to do so, because the political market does not impose the degree of organizational discipline, concentration of purpose, or measurability of results found in the economic marketplace.

3. Victor A. Thompson, *Modern Organization: A General Theory* (New York: Alfred A. Knopf, 1961), p. 100.

4. Cf. Thomas R. Dye, Charles S. Liebman, Oliver P. Williams, and Harold Herman, "Differentiation and Cooperation in a Metropolitan Area," *Midwest Journal of Political Science,* VII (1963), 145–155, and V. Stanley Vardys, "Select Committees of the House of Representatives," *Midwest Journal of Political Science,* VI (1962), 247–265.

Some old units do die, and it would be interesting to research this carefully. Under what conditions is a unit dropped from a clearance circuit or a comprehensive budget? What happens to the personnel of disbanded units? Cf. Charles Tilly, "Clio and Minerva," mimeo., July 1968.

5. See Thompson, *op. cit.,* p. 105; Karl W. Deutsch, *The Nerves of Government: Models of Political Communication and Control* (New York: The Free Press, 1963), pp. 225–226; Robert R. Blake and Jane Srygley Mouton, "Comprehension of Own and of Outgroup Positions Under Intergroup Competition," *Journal of Conflict Resolution,* V (1961), 304–310.

6. For an argument that "a felt need for joint decision making, and that the existence of differences in goals or differences in perceptions or both, are necessary for intergroup conflict," see James G. March and Herbert A. Simon, *Organizations* (New York: John Wiley and Sons, Inc., 1958), p. 135,

and the rest of Chapter 5. For an illustration of these tendencies, see Robert C. Wood, *1400 Governments* (Cambridge, Mass.: Harvard University Press, 1961), pp. 128–131, and Vincent Ostrom, Charles M. Tiebout, and Robert Warren, "The Organization of Government in Metropolitan Areas: A Theoretical Inquiry," *American Political Science Review,* LV (1961), 838–842.

There is a special case in which jurisdictional conflicts and other entropic results may be postponed, though, I would argue, not eliminated. This is the creation of a new unit to advance the interests of a newly mobilized clientele (that is, one whose members have been excluded from other clienteles), by providing rewards specialized to that clientele. The initial results may be encouraging. The long-term results are likely to fade as the new unit is integrated into larger organizational structures, but not as fast as in the typical case.

7. Cf. James W. Fesler, "Administration in the Federal Government," *Yale Papers in Political Science,* No. 6, 1963: ". . . The interrelatedness of everything, and often the poor fit of long-established definitions of department functions to the kinds of policy problems that now arise, take much decision-making out of the department head's own hands. As in the national security area, many problems must be moved to the agenda of interagency committees, be referred through the Executive Office of the President to other agencies for consideration or be taken up with a presidential assistant. The department head thus becomes more an advocate, negotiator, and committee member than the master of a major segment of policy and administration."

On difficulties in feedback processes from outside the system, see especially David Easton, *A Systems Analysis of Political Life* (New York: John Wiley and Sons, Inc., 1965), Chapter 24.

8. This and the following two propositions are developed in a somewhat different way by James Q. Wilson, "Innovation in Organization: Notes Toward a Theory," a paper delivered at the 1963 annual meeting of the American Political Science Association. Wilson hypothesizes that the *proportion* of innovations adopted will decline as organizational diversity increases. I think the absolute number of adoptions would decline.

9. See Dean E. Mann, "The Selection of Federal Political Executives," *American Political Science Review,* LVIII (1964), 88; Sheldon L. Messinger, "Organizational Transformation: A Case Study of a Declining Social Movement," *American Sociological Review,* Vol. 20 (1955), 3–10; Lewis A. Coser, "Social Conflict and the Theory of Social Change," *The British Journal of Sociology,* VIII (1957), 199; and Herbert A. Simon, *Administrative Behavior* (New York: The Macmillan Company, 1957), pp. 117–118.

10. The phrase is David Truman's. See *The Governmental Process* (New York: Alfred A. Knopf, 1960), pp. 353–362.

11. On "veto groups" in the United States, see David Riesman, *The Lonely Crowd* (Garden City, New York: Doubleday and Company, Inc., 1955), pp. 246–251. On the veto propensities of particular governmental institutions, see V. O. Key, Jr., *American State Politics* (New York: Alfred A. Knopf, 1956), Chapter 7; Richard E. Neustadt, *Presidential Power: The Politics of Leadership* (New York: John Wiley and Sons, Inc., 1960), Chapters 1–3; James MacGregor Burns, *The Deadlock of Democracy: Four-Party Politics in America* (Englewood Cliffs, New Jersey: Prentice-Hall, Inc., 1963); Bertram M. Gross, *The Legislative Struggle: A Study in Social Combat* (New York: McGraw-Hill, Inc., 1953), pp. 175–179; Walter F. Murphy, "Lower Court Checks on Supreme Court Power," *American Political Science Review,* LII (1959), 1017–

1031; Jack W. Pelatson, *Federal Courts in the Political Process* (Garden City, New York: Doubleday and Company, Inc., 1955), p. 60; Edward C. Banfield and James Q. Wilson, *City Politics* (Cambridge, Mass.: Harvard University Press and The M.I.T. Press, 1963), pp. 111 and 336ff.

For a suggestion that the proposal-veto sequence may be a self-reinforcing one, see Carl J. Friedrich, *Man and His Government* (New York: McGraw-Hill Inc., 1963), p. 380. On deadlock despite the "reasonableness" of compromise, see Robert A. Dahl, *Modern Political Analysis* (Englewood Cliffs, New Jersey: Prentice-Hall, Inc., 1963).

12. Wilson, "Innovation in Organization," p. 18. For a striking example, see Harry M. Scoble, "Interdisciplinary Perspectives on Poverty in America: The View from Political Science," mimeo.

13. See William R. Dill, "The Impact of Environment on Organizational Development," in Sidney Malick and Edward H. van Ness, eds., *Concepts and Issues in Administrative Behavior* (Englewood Cliffs, New Jersey: Prentice-Hall, Inc., 1962), p. 101. Cf. the invention of "non-negotiable demands" as initiations for negotiation.

14. Aaron Wildavsky summarizes the process by which executive agencies decide "how much to ask for" in the budget process as follows: "The most common conclusion resulted in some range of figures considered to be the most the agency could get; figures, however, which always bore some relationship to the agency's going base plus or minus increments involving a few programs expected to garner support or run into opposition." *The Politics of the Budgetary Process* (Boston: Little, Brown and Company, 1964), p. 31. See also my *Power in Committees* (Chicago: Rand McNally and Company, 1966), Chapter II.

In some cases, those closest to a situation (e.g., a Peace Corpsman in the field) may develop fatalism and apathy due to first-hand awareness of the difficulties of change, in contrast to those in distant headquarters who press for action. Since energy at both points is necessary for results, the outcome is likely to be the same, but for different reasons.

15. The argument here is that incrementalism tends to be conservative in practice, not that it is inherently or inevitably so. Compare David Braybrooke and Charles E. Lindblom, *A Strategy of Decision* (New York: The Free Press, 1963), pp. 106–110, with Jerome S. Bruner *et al.*, *A Study of Thinking* (New York: John Wiley and Sons, Inc., 1956), pp. 87–89, 124, 235–236, and Carl J. Friedrich, *op. cit.*, p. 202. See John T. Lanzetta and Vera T. Kanareff, "Information Cost, Amount of Payoff, and Level of Aspiration as Determinants of Information Seeking in Decision-Making," *Behavioral Science*, Vol. 7 (1962), pp. 459–473; Randall B. Ripley, "Interagency Committees and Incrementalism: The Case of Aid to India," *Midwest Journal of Political Science*, VII (1964), 143–165; Vernon Van Dyke, *Pride and Power: The Rationale of the Space Program* (Urbana: University of Illinois Press, 1964), Chapter 16; Yehezkel Dror, Charles E. Lindblom *et al.*, "Governmental Decision Making," *Public Administration Review*, Vol. XXIV (1964), 154–165.

16. "This tendency of policies once enacted to persevere is no accident in polyarchies. It is related to the process itself. For if there is sufficient agreement on processes and policies to operate polyarchy, there is likely to be enough agreement to make for considerable stability in policy. Conversely, if alternating parties really do adopt widely different policies, agreement is so weak that polyarchy itself is endangered. . . . Neither party can win if its

program is very much different from the other. Hence a high degree of continuity will result; there may be breaks in the continuity, if the center of public opinion shifts abruptly or if there are cumulative changes which, for some reason, neither party exploits; but these take place rather infrequently," Dahl and Lindblom, *op. cit.*, p. 301. Cf. Frank W. Young, "Reactive Subsystems and Structural Differentiation," mimeo., October 1968, p. 17. For example, teachers' strikes averaged 3.7 annually in the period 1950–1965, ranging from 1 to 10. In 1966 there were 33 and in 1967 there were an estimated 70 (*Americana Encyclopedia Annual*, p. 238). Similar contagions are seen in the student sit-ins of Spring 1968, and in the New York City strikes following that of the Sanitation Workers.

18. See Blau and Scott, *op. cit.*, pp. 240 ff.; Thompson, *op. cit.*, p. 86; Michael D. Reagan, "The Political Structure of the Federal Reserve System," *American Political Science Review*, LV (1961), 64–76; John A. Seiler, "Toward a Theory of Organization Congruent with Primary Group Concepts," *Behavioral Science*, Vol. 8 (1963), 190–198; Talcott Parsons, *Societies: Evolutionary and Comparative Perspectives* (Englewood Cliffs, N.J.: Prentice-Hall, Inc., 1966), p. 23.

On the temptation to seek quick success with the easiest cases, see Thomas F. Pettigrew, "Complexity and Change in American Social Patterns: A Social Psychological View," *Daedelus*, Fall 1965, especially pp. 994–996. On the vulnerability of government to special interests, see Stanley S. Surrey, "How Special Tax Provisions Get Enacted," in Randall B. Ripley, ed., *Public Policies and Their Politics* (New York: W. W. Norton and Company, Inc., 1966).

19. For many examples of these tendencies at work, see Henry S. Kariel, *The Decline of American Pluralism* (Stanford, Calif.: Stanford University Press, 1961), Chapters 3–7. Cf. Wood, *op. cit.*, pp. 173–174, on local governments and regional enterprises in the New York region: ". . . These systems . . . strengthen the economic trends in being. They leave most of the important decision for Regional development to the private marketplace. . . . To be sure, the two systems arrive at their positions of negative influence by quite separate routes. That system which we have subsumed under the title 'local governments' . . . is ineffective in the aggregate principally because its parts tend to cancel one another out."

20. On the broadening of agency functions, see Norton Long, *The Polity* (Chicago: Rand McNally and Company, 1962), Chapter Six; Gideon Sjoberg, "Contradictory Functional Requirements and Social Systems," *Journal of Conflict Resolution*, IV (1960), 198–208.

21. Cf. Robert J. Merton, "The Environment of the Innovating Organization: Some Conjectures and Proposals," in Gary A. Steiner, ed., *The Creative Organization* (Chicago: University of Chicago Press, 1965), p. 58: "For individual organizations, the recruitment of men of talent and the rate of innovation tend to be mutually reinforcing. The innovative organization recruits men of creative potential and helps them convert that potential into productive innovation by providing them with an effective environment *within* the organization. As the flow of innovation becomes visible to others in the environment *of* the organization, it facilitates the recruitment of new men of talent. The cycle is renewed and amplified in magnitude." Because talent is scarce many posts must be manned by persons who lack the qualities needed. Therefore, rules are proliferated to control the behavior of the semi-competent. See number 11 above.

22. The number of lawyers in government service increased from 25,621 in 1961 to 29,314 in 1964 (*American Bar Association News,* April 15, 1964). See the account of the history and powers of New York City's Board of Estimate, as described by Sayre and Kaufman, *op. cit.,* Chapter XVII. However, fragmentation of budgeting powers can weaken their effectiveness; see Bernard K. Gordon, "The Military Budget: Congressional Phase," *The Journal of Politics,* Vol. 23 (1961), 689–710.

23. Robert A. Dahl's comments on Mayor Lee illustrate this. Lee "was not at the peak of a pyramid but rather at the center of intersecting circles. He rarely commanded. He negotiated, cajoled, exhorted, beguiled, charmed, pressed, appealed, reasoned, promised, insisted, demanded, even threatened, but he most needed support and acquiescence from other leaders who simply could not be commanded. . . (T)he system was like a tire with a slow leak, and the mayor had the only air pump. Whether the executive-centered order was maintained or the system reverted to independent sovereignties depended almost entirely, then, on the relative amount of influence the mayor could succeed in extracting from his political resources." *Who Governs?* (New Haven: Yale University Press, 1961), pp 204–205.

24. Cf. William Kornhauser, *The Politics of Mass Society* (New York: The Free Press, 1959), p. 234. On "the long-run instability of multi-polar systems," see Karl W. Deutsch and J. David Singer, "Multipolar Power Systems and International Stability," *World Politics,* XVI (1964), 404–406.

On loss of authority through inability to produce, see Chalmers Johnson, *Revolutionary Change* (Boston: Little, Brown and Company, 1966), p. 91.

25. Herbert Kaufman, "Organizational Theory and Political Theory," *American Political Science Review,* LVIII (1964), 5–14. Cf. also Alvin W. Gouldner, "Metaphysical Pathos and the Theory of Democracy," in S. M. Lipset and N. J. Smelser, eds., *Sociology: The Process of a Decade* (Englewood Cliffs, New Jersey: Prentice-Hall, Inc., 1961), pp. 80–89.

26. See Irving Louis Horowitz, "Sociology and Politics: The Myth of Functionalism Revisited," *The Journal of Politics,* Vol. 25 (1963).

27. In the sense of Webster's definition: "Presenting themselves simultaneously and being interchangeable in the enunciation of properties. . . ." Cf. also one of his definitions of a college: "specif., a body of clergy living in common on a foundation."

28. To begin with, one might be the Congress of the United States.

29. Chris Argyris, "Some Causes of Organizational Ineffectiveness within the Department of State," Occasional Papers, Number 2, Center for International Systems Research, Department of State. Cf. Chris Argyris, "Today's Problems with Tomorrow's Organizations," *Journal of Management Studies,* Vol. 4, No. 1 (February 1967), 31–55.

From the Transcript

DISCUSSION OF "SOME CONSEQUENCES OF PLURALIZATION IN GOVERNMENT"

PARTICIPANTS

James David Barber
Karl W. Deutsch
Leonard J. Duhl
Matthew Holden, Jr.
Harold Orlans
Harvey S. Perloff
James L. Sundquist
John Voss

DEUTSCH: I'm much impressed by this paper and am especially struck by the combination of delay in making decisions, and then in enacting them, because you must coordinate more and more agencies, and the agencies set up to coordinate require coordination themselves. Since the system as a whole is in the long run conservative, the decisions must be made at high speed just to cope with the emergency. We are geared to react in an ad-hoc way to emergency problems instead of anticipating future problems and planning for their solutions. We now need some administrative inventions for direct channels for getting rapid feedback to the substantive problem. Obviously I cannot say what these inventions will be, but they will come. We know from historical experience that when the need arises, people can invent strategic simplifications.

SUNDQUIST: I struggled with this problem over the years in government service and came to the conclusion that the solution, if there is one, lies in the hierarchical structure: you can have proliferation at a lower level provided there is coordination and direction at a higher level. In the Office of the President, you have a supervisory organization that could reach down into this bureaucracy and pull out the problems that need to be dealt with. The same is true of Congress, but it would be much easier to organize in the executive branch. The Executive Office could be so rationalized, for example, that there would be particular people in charge of issues that cut across various departments of the government. You have to give the President the proper staff to handle these matters and to function in his name.

BARBER: What is the difference between an interagency coordinating committee and your man in the White House who coordinates relations between the Agriculture and the State Departments?

DUHL: None of your suggestions has dealt with the crux of the problem—how to introduce long-range planning into the day-by-day operation of the government. Part of the problem is that all the organizations have different levels of concern—both local and national. I can suggest a new operational structure. Suppose you assumed that American society should be designed entirely from the point of view of agriculture, or of health: everything from housing to education and transportation from the point of view of health. Others would do it from different vantage points.

You would end up with a dozen competing systems covering every aspect of society. Then you could set up a "forum" for negotiating the various points of view, and a workable, comprehensive system could be evolved.

PERLOFF: I'm looking for a criterion of action. Are we worried about lack of coordination? If so, must we eliminate so many units, or do we need new coordinating institutions? Or are we concerned with waste of resources? Then we have to devise techniques by which we can save resources. But first we should identify some major principles or standards.

BARBER: Our standards should be the output of the system, in terms of the happiness of the society. We're very good at cooling things down; we silence dissidents by bringing them into the system, and everything's quiet for a while. But given the resources this nation can draw on, it is not making positive progress. Our government should act to increase happiness.

One example, along Tugwell's lines: a Congress without committees but with an immense staff, a Congress in which people are elected to national bodies in which *all* the members deal with broad national policy and do not waste their time gaining expertise in specializations. They are not divided functionally, and there is no limit on the issues brought before that body. That kind of structure should be used not just for Congress, but for decision-making bodies throughout the system.

VOSS: By pluralization do you mean the multiplicity of governmental units or the multiplicity of all units, public, private, autonomous, or semi-public? I don't know whether you're talking about the pluralization of governmental units at the national, state, and local levels, or whether you're talking about such semi-private organizations as universities.

BARBER: Although it is probably a pervasive problem, I'm dealing with pluralization here from the point of view of government. I agree that groups can be harmless, but I think most Americans consider government an instrument for achieving certain ends beyond itself. Happiness is not just having your own group, but making groups produce for you the products that you want produced.

HOLDEN: Two questions trouble me. You say that pluralization leads to crisis politics, but wouldn't crises arise equally often in a more compact type of government? And are you also opposed to creating new units to accomplish things that would get bogged down in existing units?

BARBER: The creation of the new unit often leads to unanticipated consequences that complicate the system, so the new unit itself cannot effectively perform what it set out to do. It often happens that after an initial burst of action the unit falls into disrepair. No one has paid attention to this unanticipated consequence of adding another clearance channel, another veto point, without destroying the old one. In the aggregate, a complexity grows in the system, and productive action most probably declines.

HOLDEN: There is another option—instead of having things bog down because of so many clearing points, they could very well bog down because we have so few clearing points, because the issues and problems are continually discussed and never acted upon.

BARBER: It has to do with the separateness of new institutions. In part, the pressure for new institutions is due to the work load.

HOLDEN: Work load in an elastic sense. Not just more issues, but issues involving a variety of decisions, motives, preferences, values. This state of affairs is the same whether you have six offices or sixty-six. I'm simply asking why it isn't just as likely that the work load will prevent decisions even if you simplify the system.

BARBER: Just statistically, the odds of a veto occurring multiply with the number of veto points. A great deal of the work that policy makers do is not policy, and if you can delegate the technical and informational tasks, you will cut down on the work load. If, as we have mentioned, every congressman had at his disposal efficient information service, a corps of legislative assistants, and his own council of professional advisers, he would not spend his time on trivia.

DUHL: You are saying that the policy maker is the man who runs one of these hundreds of organizations, but I do not think he is the new policy maker. The new policy makers are the entrepreneurs—people who spend most of their time connecting and linking various parts of our society, reconceptualizing and focusing on creative processes for change. Some of the old-style politicians can't make policy and don't coordinate with anybody. Those who do change style will ultimately be able to participate in policy formulation. This kind of thing is beginning to be used—for example, by John Lindsay and his staff. Johnson, Humphrey, and Nixon do not work that way at all and are thus behind the times, out of touch with a significant new political form.

BARBER: That's why I think pluralization increases the demand for men with extraordinary political talent. I'm not so sure how new that is. But are there enough of these people? Can there be? Is it realistic to think that a system of this sort can be patched together by a platoon of operators?

DUHL: This is the new elite that may develop in the next few years. The universities have trained people, and they are the ones who will come up through the political system.

PERLOFF: Why do you assume that it is irrational to start new operations or units? Let's assume you're trying to get something done within a given set-up and you run into an opposing city council and mayor. Isn't it then rational, given your objectives, to start a new organization to achieve them? Otherwise, you're assuming that people who start new units are really punishing themselves or not achieving their objectives. To effect changes in an existing bureaucracy can be a long, painful, and costly process; the creation of new units may be the better approach.

BARBER: The point is that there is more to social rationality than the sum of individual rationalities, and the two may conflict.

PERLOFF: But to prove your point, you have to show that the basic system simply is not satisfying needs. A wholly different kind of system is required, and small improvements will not be sufficient.

SUNDQUIST: The system is inevitable. The question is how you live with it. It is not new. Big plural organizations were being talked about a long time ago, and they gave rise to a whole science, or pseudo-science, of administration. How do you set up and manage an organization so it doesn't give you all these problems? As organizations grew, so did the science of management. Are you saying that you don't acknowledge the science of administration at all, that it's bankrupt, and that we must start over? If you are, be explicit about it. Isn't it merely a question of refining and applying our managerial techniques?

ORLANS: I think there is a confusion here between the problems of bureaucracy and the problems of pluralization. Most of the problems cited here are part of bureaucracy, and bureaucracy is worse when you have fewer, not more, systems.

BARBER: That's why hierarchy is not the answer here. It seems to me there is a possibility for collegial bodies of a multifunctional character dealing only with policy problems and avoiding diversions. That might be a way out of this, no hierarchy, or government by university-trained new-style policy makers.

PERLOFF: I'm not bothered by your not coming up with a solution, but you're asking us to accept almost everything you've written on face value. You must start with the situation in the year 2000, or something about the nature of our society, or something about the nature of government that makes everything follow logically.

BARBER: I do imply that a great deal more needs to be done by the government to meet the needs of the society, now and in the year 2000.

PERLOFF: Shouldn't we rather start with the assumption that we need a different kind of governmental system than the one devised for an agricultural society?

ORLANS: The historical context is clear at the outset. During the 1930's and the 1940's the pyramidal notion of power in American society was still influential—the Marxian heritage reformulated by C. Wright Mills and Floyd Hunter. In the 1950's, this view was rejected by David Riesman and others, who substituted the idea of countervailing powers—a market system of politics in which no one class was dominant; there were as many powers as consumers, and, if the political price was right, the result was a great progressive democratic consensus. This pluralist theory of community and national power that held sway in political science and sociology during the 1950's and the 1960's rejected the Marxist view of an exploitative society and extolled a democracy in which almost every person and every group was equal. But now, in 1968, the happy pluralistic consensus that once produced a kind of automatic, Victorian political progress has turned into a bog, an unmappable, unworkable nonsystem of messages that enter and never emerge. The government has become a vast Kafkaesque bureaucracy that neither recognizes nor responds to domestic crises: our bureaucrats fiddle while our cities burn. That is the historical, and very useful, context of this paper. But it isn't explicit enough.

V

THE FUTURE OF NATIONAL GOVERNMENTAL INSTITUTIONS

THE SHAPING OF THE CONSTITUTION FOR 2000: AN EXERCISE IN PUTATIVE PROGNOSTICS

Rexford G. Tugwell

I

The year 2000 has been reached, and some explanation should be made of recent changes in the American system of government. These changes have gradually gone into effect since 1993, following the 1992 election, when a new constitution was the issue. The consequent changes can now be weighed.

The Philadelphia Constitution of 1787 had been congealed for over two hundred years. True, there had been thirty amendments, but only a few had affected the structure of government and only a few more its operations.[1] Federalism was nominally intact; the formal tripartite system of branches had not been altered, the assignment of powers not modified. To one studying the Constitution without a commentary, it would seem to have been intended for a small government, with few duties, and those mostly negative. To one living in the latter part of the twentieth century, much of it appeared irrelevant, almost quaint. A government that had grown big and omnipresent drew its authority from an agreement dealing for the most part with its limitations.

Federalism, like the other structural arrangements, had slowly disintegrated. There were now sixty states or associated states; but of these forty-seven could not be said to have had an original sovereignty or to have delegated part of it to the central government, as had the original thirteen. The new associates had joined for the benefits of union, not of separatism.

State sovereignty was an anachronism, kept alive only because of duties requiring large bureaucracies. But even this presented problems, since, as metropolitan areas expanded, these bureaucracies were interposed between federal and city governments. The main separatist sentiment in later years had been cultural, but even these regional characteristics had lost much of their distinctiveness through increasing mobility, nationwide distribution of goods, common services, and sharing in the affluence of the seventies and eighties.

There were many conveniences in national standards for personal and business conduct, and the cost of living was about the same everywhere. The educational and social-security systems had necessarily conformed to similar demands; so had grants for many other services that only the central government could support. Moreover, new sources of power and new kinds of materials had caused industry to be established in new patterns. These had not yet much affected the dozen gigantic and still-growing conurbations; but it could be seen that in time they would. No one knew exactly what the effect would be, but it was being actively explored. It was clear that hardly anyone wanted to move out of the cities except for recreation.

The international situation was reoriented. Like the states, nations might be in their last stages, but they were persistently useful to their politicians and thus dangerous to world peace. Nevertheless, the forces favoring integration were overcoming opposition, particularly in America, where technology had its freest development and boundaries were most irrelevant.

Of course the demand for equality among individuals had been gaining momentum for many years, though it often could not be supported by feeble economies isolated by nationalism. But where standards were low, governments were on the defensive. In the American union it was an accepted principle, but to insure its continuance certain defenses had to be maintained. Democracy was vulnerable to the pride and envy of poorer people. There still had to be a military establishment.

Even in America, although the progress of industry was finally understood to depend on the continued ability of consumers to absorb the goods and services it produced, economic distinctions had only gradually disappeared. Logic demanded that everyone share alike. The conclusion was slowly acted upon; but when everyone did begin to share generously, the news was very soon heard in South America, and not very much later in Africa. The only certain relief for permanent underdevelopment was joining with more efficient economies; but this was the last thing the elite classes of backward nations wanted. If it remained the worst world problem of the late century, it was at least one whose solution was obvious.

In America abundance, equally shared, gradually became characteristic; but there were strains as institutions accommodated themselves with increasing difficulty. There had been more and more occasions in the seventies, when it had become baldly apparent that the seams of the formal governmental web were straining to the bursting point and that extraconstitutional arrangements would no longer do. Looking back, it could be seen that during the early seventies two alternate courses of development might have been entered on. The one would have led to something like disaster, the other to a remarkable achievement of the human spirit. The one was, at the time, as likely to be chosen as the other; it depended on the concurrence—or lack of it—of several technological discoveries and alternate resolutions concerning their use; but it also depended on the willingness of many people to make a deliberate decision.

They could hardly be blamed if they were confused. It could be seen in 2000 that one choice had been the condition of affluence and liberation from old fears and the other a narrowing of opportunities and paralysis of the spirit; but it had not been obvious earlier. On the whole, political leaders had been more often wrong than right and had had to be corrected by events, reluctantly and very nearly too late.

Either course had been bound, in due time, to require constitutional revision; an obsolete superior law was untenable for either development. But how the changes were to be made depended on the course chosen. Each possibility will be discussed as it might have happened.

II

Not until the seventies did business regulation become effective. Before that, corporations had been able to expand at will. Private controls of industrial empires became so centralized that, with no standards of fairness, the strong were increasingly more effective in exploiting the weak. The strengths of some and weaknesses of others in what needed to be a nicely articulated system affected the whole organism, allowing the more aggressive and affluent enterprises to dominate the whole.

Acquisition of some firms by others resulted in vast conglomerates almost immune to the risks of change. Corporate immortality seemed to have been attained, but the working of a machine whose parts made no attempt to accommodate themselves to the whole caused continual imbalance and occasional crisis. The logical end, of course, was one enormous centrally managed complex; but if it did come to that, only government could be the manager. Any other arrangement would have vested the control of people's lives in an elite group responsible to no one but themselves.

Another factor in this development was the organization of workers. Their unions had grown more effective, but their disciplines were hard to enforce, and small but strategically placed groups found it easy to disrupt whole industries and at times the entire economy. They thus exploited the whole for their benefit, even in the public services. Compulsory arbitration was ineffective because compliance was very hard to enforce except by police-state methods. The final anarchy of conflicting claims among thousands of tightly organized business and labor groups became insupportable.

Late in this evolution industries realized that the situation was becoming intolerable and began to reach more rational arrangements among themselves. This did not happen, however, until government had consented to bring them into a loose confederation and had established standards of fairness enforceable by law. The precedent of the National Recovery Administration, abandoned before it had been well established, was useful for the purpose. But if there was to be anything left of the pluralistic enterprise system, something more had to be done. Concordance among competitors and between workers and employers was one thing; but paralysis because of a too-successful domination of the many by the few was quite another.

This condition had developed in an atmosphere of recrimination and sometimes outright conflict. Finally there was general recognition that some order had to be imposed. The most unscrupulous had to be prevented from exercising their advantage over the others. And the consolidation had to be controlled. Because it was not understood that profit is not always a good measure of usefulness, the nation had all but lost its railways.

Organization into industrial groups, administering among themselves the arrangements needed for common existence, was still open to exploitation by the more powerful. They tended to establish a level of efficiency that others either had to meet, or submit to being taken over or discarded. There was a tendency too, among politicians, to make the highest standards statutory: prices came more and more under the control of mutual associations and under the scrutiny of public authorities. The minimum wage was raised time after time; benefits amounting to extra pay multiplied and became compulsory. Economic arrangements finally lost all relation to productivity.

The basic difficulty with this was that a seemingly necessary recognition of mutuality became frozen. The organic integrity of the productive system had to be recognized if it was to operate successfully; but it also had to grow toward recognition of its duty to the whole; and this it had no means of doing and was not required to do.

Before the strains became insupportable, a high level of productivity and living had been reached. It was hardly noticed that the life was going out of the system until it was already well into its decline.

This had been forecast by the British crisis of the sixties. The Labour government had adopted rules of distribution that compelled the economy to undertake more than could be accomplished by an indifferent management and withholding workers. Politicans assumed productivity would increase to meet the demands made on the system. And when commitments in wages, in welfare benefits, in public services, and in enlarged numbers of unproductive consumers grew beyond the capability of the system, they were reluctant to admit that the demands of income recipients had become too heavy a weight to be carried.

In America, without so heavy a welfare commitment, there might have been stabilization at the high level reached in the seventies if it had not been for forces attacking the system. One of these was the human propensity for restless inventiveness together with relatively free striving for advantage. The resulting conflicts led to civil disturbances almost like war. The unions of the fifties had set a bad example.

Another force also had its origin in human restlessness. Technology continued to have an expanding life of its own, but its discoveries often did not fit into old schemes. The monolith being shaped was almost continually under siege, and resistance was not always possible.

The system, perfected with such skill and cooperation, seemed likely to die of its own innate characteristics—and of its ultimate reliance on men, not on things or natural forces.

It was at this juncture that choice was precipitated by crisis. Stability at the high level already reached could be accepted and institutionalized, or new ways to further progress could be looked for. Both were possible. The technological system could be accepted and its policies shaped for forward movement, or it could be stabilized and defended from all disturbing influences and ultimately show the wear of long use.

III

There were further dangers during this time. By 1970 commentators easily predicted the abolition of routine work, and the meaning of "routine" had tended to expand. It was for powered machines to labor and even calculate; it was for men to plan and manage. The work day and the work week were shortened, leaves were lengthened, and retirement was earlier.

However, the high threshold for primary entry into the working group had not been anticipated. Not everyone could "think" better than computers, and those who could were becoming an elite. A smaller and smaller number were useful in the new employments, and the rest were clearly becoming, in any essential sense, nonparticipants. And their numbers were to increase. Faithful machines would support them, but would provide them neither with all the appurtenances available to the wealthy nor with a sense of being needed. But since these nonparticipants could vote, their representatives would strongly influence legislation, and since more and more of the national product would be channeled to their uses, there would be less and less capital for research and development.

This was not the worst: since these people were less and less educable as the scale of intelligence descended, and since there remained a large majority below the level of participation, they were increasingly hostile to the creative members of society.[2]

There had been a period in American history when equality had been actual, or nearly so. Anyone physically fit could use the simple tools needed for clearing land, for planting and harvesting, and even for building modest houses and barns. The operation of small shops and village stores required some managerial ability but not so much that it precluded the eligibility of the majority of society. A man's deficiencies did not keep him from making a living or participating in the common concerns of the community.

This early equality had been written into the political system as universal suffrage and had become impacted there, but it was an idea the original framers of the Constitution would not for a moment have entertained. They had belonged to the elite 5 percent, and their appreciation of educated abilities had been lively; they also had believed that ownership of property was essential to responsible citizenship. Jefferson and Jackson had soon subverted this principle, which was written into the Constitution. Anyone could vote. It was a natural right, also expressed in a laissez faire that assumed all competitors in business would be equal. The American mind had been deeply impressed by these convictions.

As new western states had entered the American union, their pioneer ideas had overwhelmed the elite notion that the rich and wellborn ought to be politically dominant. The Jacksonian belief that if one man was as good as any other he could hold any job was not a conceit that governed American behavior for very long. But it remained latent and it did not stop at equality of opportunity. It emerged again in the demand for common benefits as soon as affluence made them attainable.

True, a new power class arose after the Civil War: the businessmen who believed they were free to do as they liked with their property, and also with their employees. In the attempt to enforce freedom, freedom itself had nearly been abolished.

The consequences of these successive developments were mitigated by immense efforts to restore equality. The most strenuous and costly concerted social effort was made in the system of education, but the results were immensely disappointing. The fact that the system could not do more than enable every child to reach his inborn capacities was hard to accept.

Clearly, the Constitution had been written for a kind of democracy quite different in definition from that of fifty years later. The framers, with no thought of political equality, had left suffrage to the states, where it was already safely restricted. But the federal Constitution was never adapted to Jacksonianism. Representation was the same for the enlarged electorate, as it had been for the exclusive one of 1787. The propertied, and presumably responsible, voters were supplanted by the unpropertied masses.

As the qualifications for participation rose, lack of ability eliminated more and more workers from the occupations of ordinary life. With the change in technology came the migration into cities, already crowded with foreigners, of farmers and farm workers no longer needed on the land. They swelled the ranks of those already displaced by machines in urban employments. The result was a mass of unemployables, seething with resentment, who could still vote.

When the proportion of unemployed grew to more than a third of the population, and continued to grow, wholly new problems arose. Those still working did not at first rebel, but when their situations caused jealousy and belittlement, and when the necessities for their work were given only grudgingly, they began to hit back.

The situation was worst of all for creative individuals. With each successive budget, research was systematically starved. Productivity began to be seriously sacrificed to welfare in the sixties; and in the seventies creative contributors seemed likely to have positions reminiscent of Rome, where the intellectuals and experts were generally slaves. They found themselves suppressed when they generated proposals that threatened the current "established order" so favorable to "the common man."

It was a comparatively prosperous order. But by this time productivity was beginning to decrease. Population had been stabilized, and sharing had been formalized; but so much income had been diverted to the support of noncontributors that enterprisers were contending even for maintainance and replacement funds. There were demands that proposals of potential creators and movers should be restricted. A committee of Congress, similar to the House Un-American Activities Committee of the 1940's and 1950's, was set up to keep them under surveillance. A Civil Disturbances Act was passed, making it a crime to propose the displacement of men by machines or processes; but those already in use had left relatively few at work.

It was inevitably recognized that life was going out of the economy and that paralysis might well follow the peace of stability. Actually, that peace was more seeming than real. What might appear to mythical visitors to be a placid and smoothly operating organism actually seethed with subsurface violence that occasionally had to be controlled. The nonworkers had ample time and audience, and their rabble-rousing threatened to become anarchy. Internal-security officials had only limited funds for the containment of violence.

Only one serious problem of the 1960's had become less threatening: the Communist nations were much less aggressive, and the old European nations had formed the world's third most productive aggregate. Though the industries of Communist nations never reached the effectiveness of those in the West, the present situation seemed to provide them with an advantage: since they did not promote equality, their elite was more favored and their creativity not suppressed.

Their advance as the Americans faltered was another effective argument of the President in his plea for a new constitution. The old fear of Communist aggression, far from having disappeared, was easily revived by xenophobic demagogues in the late 1980's. The President, representing the nation, was the people's surrogate, as he had long been; he was their protector too, as Commander in Chief, from the Communist threat. When he told them their future safety from conquest depended on recapturing their strength, they believed him. Only the fears of mutual destruction kept war from breaking out.

In his effort at conversion, the President pointed out that competition and equality had produced monopoly, or something very like it, by the elimination of inefficient competitors.

The attempt to proceed into the later age of technology with this eighteenth-century apparatus had resulted at first in its use by the strongest businessmen and the cleverest politicians to subvert the system they praised. But the nonparticipating bloc had opposed them. The demand for equal sharing, with universal suffrage to enforce it, had gradually restricted enterprise and drained off its profits for welfare.

The dominant characteristic of the Constitution had been the protection of individuals from a potentially encroaching government. It still did this. But the system of checks and balances established by the framers amounted to stasis. True, as conditions had changed in the years before 1960, all branches had expanded, or had tried to, gradually working out allocations of power among themselves. Patriotic sentiment had succumbed to resentment at fancied injustices, and the President's task in 1991 was one of restoration, a call to old loyalties.

Such abundance had become available before decline had set in that it was not until the reduction had amounted to 15 percent over a period of several years that the situation was generally recognized as critical. The cause of disorientation, the President said, was a frustrating inability to possess the goods and services people had come to regard as their right. But such possession was not a right. The President reiterated that what was not produced could not be distributed. And since it was an educated electorate, it listened.

Ask yourselves, demanded the President, what has gone wrong. The old rules of individualism and equality have resulted in such a tangle of regulation, subsidy, restriction, and claims that the essential elements of progress are being strangled. Must producers continue to be the slaves of users? Is it really sensible to suppress the creators? At one time the Luddites had smashed the machines that threatened their jobs. Now it was the people protecting their incomes as well as job holders protecting their positions. What had to result from present policies was the destruction of enterprise and progress. It was thus essential that the remarkable possibilities of technology be reopened.

There had to be a new constitution—one that defined duties equally with rights and that established institutions for expansion rather than restriction. It had to provide for a government able to act, not one prevented from acting by built-in hostilities. In spite of secure incomes and elaborate recreational facilities, more and more dissatisfaction was being expressed. This was partly because no one felt needed any more. It showed itself in ways that would have resembled the ghetto riots of the 1960's, had there not been immensely enlarged police forces to supplement other efforts at pacification and diversion. An overhaul of institutions was needed to deal with a deepening crisis.

IV

This imagined history written in 2000 might have had a series of more favorable events to record. Instead of being excluded from participation in productive activities, most citizens might have found themselves involved more deeply because of discoveries and technical advances that required an outpouring of energies similar to those that had gone into the conquest of the American continent. Those energies might have been enlarged by being made common. Instead of paralysis there might have been a new era of activity after the seventies, in dealing with the environment, solar forces, the seas, the deserts, the tropics, genetics, and personality control.

In the years between 1970 and 1990 theoretical hints of laboratory experiments had developed into their first operational stages. Gravity waves, new knowledge of magnetic forces, and ways to carry people into far higher altitudes had opened the way to penetration of all the earth's places and much space as well. Nationalism was dying, and racial xenophobia was fading away. The skies were crowded with vehicles, some of immense size, not only transversing the lanes just above the earth, but stationed at strategic intervals for future journeys to other worlds.

The seas, deserts, and tropics had been tamed and transformed, and they contributed hugely to the world's resources. This new abundance had made obsolete a good many old ideas, along with the old techniques of exploitation. Everyone now had access to goods and services, in part because control of the birth rate to accord with death rates had checked mounting claims. No one had to scramble for necessities, at least, and attention could be given to the problems of a civilization relieved of the fears and pressures men had always endured in the past. This made possible a transformation in people themselves.

Urging people to behave better might be the mission of the moralists, but the life scientists were interested in making people more intelligent, more energetic, and more cooperative. These improvements had not been possible until the genetic processes had been understood and particular genes made susceptible to modification. Personalities were being altered, and most of the children being born could be expected to participate in an educational regime suited to their particular propensities and to emerge from it civilized individuals. Now that scientists were discovering new ways to influence behavior, what remained was to adapt public policy to the new knowledge.

A new era had indeed opened, and it was time to shape the institutions suitable for the new prospect. The Americans had been the first to do this, by creating a revised constitution. This was the Magna Carta of the new age.

Looking back from 2000, it could be seen that for the constitution makers of 1991, the problem would have been very similar no matter which course social development had followed: the country had reached a condition of paralysis and decline, or it was advancing into a remarkable age of achievement. Either way, the Constitution would have fallen into complete irrelevancy if the Supreme Court had not from time to time given new meaning to its antique clauses. But a court ought not to be a legislature or a constitution-maker.

The nation, the President said in 1991, had need of a charter made by authentic constitutional processes, not by unchallenged custom or by the Courts of Appeal in adversary actions. People had to give up thinking only of themselves, and the rule of laissez faire had to be abandoned. Experience had shown that every man guided by the interest of the whole and contributing to it would find his own well-being increased by the general product, and that it could be increased in no other way.

With the forces of progress being freed and those of obstruction being diminished, the Constitution had to be adapted to this principle. The old Constitution had no bill of duties to match its Bill of Rights, but there had to be one. Welfare had had only a word in the preamble; it had to have defining clauses.

A constitution embodying new objectives would not only protect the individual from oppression but match this right with a duty to participate. An individual's right to share in the national income had to be clear; but no amount could be guaranteed. His duty to contribute and to encourage others to contribute also had to be acknowledged. Even if his part were restricted, he had to carry its responsibilities without shirking. Those also would serve who could only receive—children, the aged, the incapacitated—but they could not expect more than the economy made available.

If the government was to be recognized as the agent of the people instead of their potential enemy, it had to be organized to do what was required of it, rather than being prevented from acting because it might seem to favor one group over another. The balance of power and the checking advised for the protection of individuals had to be modified to allow for the planning that would produce fair shares for all.

Another formulative principle of the old constitution had to be reconsidered—states' rights. It now had to be recognized that the central government was the creation of the sovereign people, not of sovereign states, and that the states' powers derived from their positions as parts of the whole. The states certainly would have to be abandoned as intervenors in the nation's work. Equality in the legislative branch between Vermont and Texas, Nevada and New York, was absurd. Equal, or substantially equal, regional republics were seen to be more convenient.

The President had asked for ratification of his constitution in 1992, saying that unless 65 percent of the electorate supported him, he would not go forward with the project; but that if that proportion of the voters agreed, he would disregard the amendment procedures in the old constitution and assume the temporary powers needed for putting the new one into effect. His majority was 80 percent; and he did go forward.

The new document had directives for protecting the welfare state, but there were provisions as well for the maintainance of productivity. Citizens were to be not only recipients but also contributors; they were not to demand impossible privileges; welfare services were to be apportioned half, but not more, of the annual gains in productivity. This then was shared out as minimum income without having to be earned.

The structure of government consisted of six branches instead of the traditional three: the Political, the Presidential, the Legislative, the Planning, the Internal Affairs, and the Judicial. The most conspicuous addition was the Political Branch, omitted from the original constitution because its framers had thought statesmen alone would not engage in political contention, and they had distrusted the common man's competence to join in important decisions. There had been no provisions about voting eligibility except those in effect in the states. And political institutions had developed quite outside the law.

So a political branch had been devised to provide meeting places and legitimize candidates. Public funds would be used for election appeals; private funds were forbidden. There would be a system of local and national primaries, followed by conventions, and then by short and orderly campaigns.

Legislators would be elected for longer terms and would serve in one People's House; the other chamber would be a revised Senate, with a duty to the nation as a whole. Its members would renounce any other occupation for life, and would be chosen accordingly. Members would graduate into it from other positions of responsibility or be appointed, some by the President and some by the Chief Justice, from panels selected by their associates; they would be elected, but elected by their colleagues. Their duties would have a national orientation: they would possess the emergency powers; they would act as national watchmen; they would advise the President, and even share some of his power.

The presidency would be relieved of many executive duties so that it could attend to those essential to the nation's wholeness, security, and well-being. The President would be most conspicuously the head of state, and as such, the conductor of foreign policy and disposer of the armed and civil forces. He would still retain the departmental responsibilities necessary to those duties: foreign affairs, finance, and the military. And above all, he would be the public mentor and the legislative leader.

There would be a new Executive for domestic governmental operations, now grown very large and essential, and unforeseen by the drafters of the old constitution. The President had, because of this lack of foresight, seized the emergency powers, as well as those necessary to the conduct of foreign policy, and had become the initiator of practically all legislation.

Planning had been carried on almost clandestinely by all government agencies for half a century, although the use of prognostics was not yet generally accepted. It had been opposed by legislators and executives who felt that it limited their prerogatives and their ability to appeal for support in elections. They had always found it necessary to claim credit for public projects and for favors to their constituents.

The Planning Branch was to assess the nation's capabilities and suggest their distribution in the most equable and productive manner. The Senate could refuse to accept any part of the planners' proposals, but it had to explain its refusals. Thus the nation's capabilities would be mustered for new advances.

There was also an Internal Affairs Branch, provided to supervise the many agencies now in existence. It was not proposed that the traditional pluralism that had been a favorable feature of capitalism be abandoned: it was so obviously the alternative to a monolithic economic system that its revitalization was an important part of the President's plan. Private and semiprivate operations had to have sufficient scope to encourage productivity.

However, public enterprise would not be abandoned, especially the services that had to be carried on as interconnecting parts of a system. Transport, communication, and power were particularly unsuitable for private operation. This was another reason for establishing the new branch, abstracted from presidential responsibility, for performing services and regulating enterprises.

The Judicial Branch was to be modernized by providing subsidiary courts for adversary actions, for settling administrative controversies, and for defining rights and duties. But since it was as necessary as ever that at some place lititgation should come to an end, and since it was equally obvious that interpretation of the Constitution had to be entrusted to some body, the Court was given the power to decide. Under the new provisions, however, the Court could no longer issue broad directives to the Executive or Legislative Branches, who, along with it, had sworn to uphold the Constitution.

The making of constitutional law by the Court, however, was rendered much less necessary by a provision that the Constitution be reviewed or revised in each generation. Thus, most serious questions of adaptation would be settled by procedures proper to the making of fundamental law.

This, then, was the government in outline.

THE REPUBLICS

Republics: groupings of former states, each with a constitution and all the autonomy appropriate in modern circumstances; and with elected Governors General and legislatures.

THE CENTRAL GOVERNMENT

A Political Branch: to organize the democratic dialogue and to oversee the choosing of candidates by parties and their election to office.

The Presidency: the President, and two Vice-Presidents; Departments of Finance, Foreign Affairs, and Military Affairs, together with such subsidiary offices as may be necessary.

A Planning Branch: six- and twelve-year plans, each revised annually, submitted for approval to the Nation's House, not having the force of law but being the agreed intention of the nation; annual budget for legislative approval.

A Legislative Branch: three Houses: a People's House, one-third to be elected at large, having four-year terms; a Republic's House, membership to be elected from the Republics, to originate legislation affecting them; a Nation's House, members having held other public positions or being appointees of the President or Chief Justice from panels elected by recognized national associations; to serve for life, with no other occupation; to possess emergency and watchkeeping powers; to approve or disapprove laws passed by the People's House, but with no final veto; and to advise the President.

Internal Affairs Branch: to administer departments and agencies necessary to governmental responsibilities within the nation, both executive and regulatory.

A Judicial Branch: to administer justice in a system of courts supervised by a Chief Justice with an appropriate organization.

There were sharp departures from the customary concentrations on local interests. The whole was now given first attention, but this allowed much more extensive passing to the Republics and their constituent governments of responsibility for matters within their competence and for much of the administrative work.

By 2000 the central bureaucracy had already been reduced by half, its duties transferred to organizations nearer the level of execution. The President who had asked for and sponsored the new constitution had now given way to his successor and taken his place in the Senate. The reorganization was well under way, and clearly the new spirit had found the institutions it needed. There was a general wish to cooperate and a new impetus in economic affairs. Production was increasing at accelerating rates;

the principle of fair shares was fully accepted; the desire to participate was markedly different as the improved generation came of age. The nation had begun to be one that welcomed creativity and administrative talent.

The farewell address of President Nexus on March 3, 1993, now seven years in the past, had already become as familiar as that of Washington in 1796. The advice for the future was very different. The first President had advised against parties, for instance, and against permanent alliances. The forty-first President had helped to lodge parties firmly in the Constitution and had sponsored a complete network of treaties with other nations. The parties were necessary mechanisms, he had said, for democratic expression in a populous country; the alliances were a recognition that the whole world had become one at the end of the twentieth century. These were policies to be pursued out of national self-interest.

These, however, were themes of less importance than his advice for the future. The nation, he said, had now averted the threat of decline and was on the way to an era of greatness, using its genius, rather than smothering it, realizing its potentialities rather than diverting them to sterile uses. When they were brought to think, men would not be satisfied with goods and services; those were means, not ends. The less substantial but still more real values once talked of but for a time almost forgotten were reemerging: freedom, justice, self-expression, kindness.

These values had been obscured in the contradictions of affluence. Freedom had become destructive competition; justice had become license to exploit others; self-expression had become carping criticism; and even kindliness had become limited caring. These dead-ends had resulted from the use of eighteenth-century political theory in the twentieth century.

The new constitution recognized this and provided a framework for its opposite—a government for a close-coupled society, a disciplined technology, citizens with understood duties and the willingness to meet responsibilities. Affluence of the spirit as well as of the body was now possible.

As for the nation among nations, in a genocidal age there was only one acceptable policy: draw together; make alliances, but make them open; find ways to make friends.

During the years since 1993 there had been reversions, but the nation had held together; it had expanded and had again prospered. It seemed that a way into the future might really have been found.

NOTES

1. The most important, after the first ten (the Bill of Rights), being the fourteenth (equal protection) and the twenty-second (limitation of presidential terms).

2. The outcome of a prolonged controversy—nature versus nurture—was thus in the end concluded. Much could be done through better nutrition, improved education, and sensible human relations to improve behavior; but there were genetic limits not to be exceeded except by selective breeding; and even then the highest expectations were confined by the limits of the breed. The human race was no exception to this biological rule.

From the Transcript

NATIONAL PLANNING AND THE OFFICE OF THE PRESIDENT

PARTICIPANTS

John Dixon
Kermit Gordon
Herbert Kaufman
Richard P. Nathan
Harvey S. Perloff
James L. Sundquist

PERLOFF: Our national governmental system is above all a presidential system, revolving around a chief executive with remarkably extensive responsibilities. Normally, we can hope to develop coherent national policy only when the President can direct a great deal of attention—and talent—to the development of long-range, as well as short-range, strategy. What kind of planning system is necessary to cope with the problems anticipated for the year 2000? Is the presidency set up to do this kind of long-range planning job?

SUNDQUIST: The word planning has so many meanings. At the top level of government, planning has to be very sophisticated, and different from what we usually mean when we use the word. I don't think we want a national economic plan like the Five-Year Plan in Russia. The planning has to deal, to a great extent, with our use of manipulative devices to steer independent economic and social forces along a particular course, and this can't be done by any single unit. It is an aspect of everybody's job, not only of the Office of the President. What is wanted is less a planning mechanism than the introduction of good planning processes, information flows, and decision-making processes into the whole mechanism of the government's business.

NATHAN: It's difficult to consider the subject of planning as distinct from political theory. I think we're going to have more planning even though it may not be referred to as such formally and won't be called a "Five-Year Plan" or a "Three-Year Plan." I think we are going to get multiyear budgeting—the kind of planning that we've done in agriculture, involving goals and price conceptions. The same type may well spread into other sectors of the economy without a regulatory or policy parallel. A higher degree of planning will be essential, but it must be formulated within the context of some useful political theory.

SUNDQUIST: In trying to organize for planning, we should analyze all the tasks that need to be done at the top levels of government. We need not only better planning, but better information resources and better organization of the data so that decisions can be made properly. Perhaps more than anything else, we need more efficient techniques of action after the decisions are made. If we were starting all over again we'd examine the President's job and then determine what specific elements were needed in the Executive Office in order to help the President get the job done. If that were done systematically, we might emerge with a planning unit, a directing unit, and a personnel unit. Or conceivably we might emerge with functional units that embrace both the planning and the directing of responsibility in specialized subject-matter areas. Until now the presidency has never been scrutinized in that way.

PERLOFF: Let me put my question more concretely. The French have national plans. They are concerned, for example, with problems of manpower and the kinds of skills that will be required in the next few years, as well as with questions of unemployment and underemployment. Is this the logical direction for us?

NATHAN: I think it is a necessity. We really have to face up to many issues—the length of the work day in relation to rising levels of G.N.P. and income, problems of the retirement level, and the whole recreation-leisure idea in relation to education, productivity, automation, and levels of income. Also, international issues are going to force us to think about resource allocation. I agree that "planning" is only a part of the process; but we're going to have to do a lot more of it.

PERLOFF: Two issues deserve special attention. First, can Congress play a significant role in this, or will it be increasingly difficult for Congress to be involved in planning processes? Second, to what extent can the people have a say in these things? Planning calls for such a tremendous flow of information and so many delicate decisions about complex components that it may become almost impossible for Congress and certainly for the people generally to play a significant role. Is democratic planning possible?

SUNDQUIST: Isn't it merely different in degree from what's being done now? We certainly have elements of a national plan now, but we have trouble carrying it out because of the division of powers. For example, when President Kennedy decided in 1962 that we ought to have a tax cut in order to get the economy moving and fulfill what amounted to a fiscal plan, it took two years to get it. The British decided they needed a tax cut at the same time, but they had it within six weeks. By the time we got it, we might have actually needed a tax increase. Nobody can do the planning except the Executive Branch. Congress, by its nature, cannot plan. We should develop ways for the Executive to prepare plans freely, subject to some kind of review and ratification by Congress.

DIXON: Do you mean that Congress should establish the values and then leave it to the Executive Branch to operate under these guidelines?

SUNDQUIST: There are different kinds of relationships in different fields. In the case of fiscal policy, we could have the same kind of authority in the Executive Branch that we have in tariff policy. Congress sets the general objective, and the Executive then negotiates the tariff schedules, without going back for ratification. In taxes, Congress would oversee the general workings of the whole system and withdraw the power if necessary.

PERLOFF: What about the necessity for making rapid decisions, not only in international problems but in national ones? In order to get the required information for complex decisions you need a large bureaucracy with a very powerful executive. Unless we develop techniques for making the legislature knowledgeable, powerful, able to take quick action, and able to control the Executive, we may find the whole system thrown out of balance. This is certainly a real issue for our day, not alone for the year 2000.

I think Senator Fulbright has raised a serious issue: on the basis of aid commitment and some other rather minor obligations, we found the President making decisions that were considered congressional prerogatives—involving treaties and allocation of financial resources. More than even in our history, these are now directed from the White House. If you project that thirty years, the imbalance may increase.

SUNDQUIST: We probably don't need to worry about the Executive getting out of hand, because what Congress confers, Congress can take away.

PERLOFF: Can they? Don't you think Fulbright's issue is a real one?

SUNDQUIST: Yes, I think it is. But I don't think Fulbright is speaking for Congress at this particular time. If Congress were dissatisfied with the way that the power to declare war was being used, it would find ways of recapturing that power. But that's the most difficult area to talk about. If you talk about tariffs or taxes, Congress could confer and withdraw much more readily.

KAUFMAN: I would predict that in the year 2000 the presidency will be a remarkably weak office, about what it is today. My basic conclusion is that, because it is weak, there are going to be efforts to strengthen it. A new coordinating unit would help build up the Executive Office of the President. Because it is principally preoccupied with the budget, the Budget Bureau has not been able to give serious attention to programming.

I also predict that the thirty-year trend toward superdepartments will continue, with more and more departments in the future, comparable to HEW and Defense. While this holds promise for at least improving coordination within each department, in thirty years the new supersecretaries are not likely to have much control of their departments. It has taken about twenty years for the Secretary of Defense to assert control over his.

The third problem is the development of a national coalition of public chief executives and general chief executives in the country. The President's problems are not primarily with the legislature. While presidents do have to make a lot of compromises, for two hundred years they have been remarkably successful in getting programs they really wanted enacted. But beyond that, it's hard for them to be operational. To sidestep the bureaucratic roadblocks, our mayors, governors, and the President may enter into an active and self-conscious coalition. This would overcome the problems posed by the specialists in such fields as health, welfare, highways, and so on, who tend to ignore their respective chief executives and to consider only each other. If some kind of bloc grant develops, we are likely to see the chief executives try to strengthen the political executives at the lower levels because they are his natural allies against the bureaucracy.

One other point is the current tendency toward decentralization, as a way of speeding decisions that affect domestic programs nationally. There is pressure to strengthen regional officers of the departments and also to establish presidential regional agents who can coordinate them.

GORDON: I am continually mystified by the difference between the conception of the presidential powers and the reality. This office can be described as the most powerful in the world, but on close observation it appears a strikingly weak office—in domestic affairs. Presidential power in security affairs or foreign affairs is quite different. In our system of checks and balances, certain trends seem to be moving toward an increased capacity on the part of the parties to checkmate each other. If you consider the extent to which Congress is becoming increasingly involved with administration, which is presumably a function of the Executive Branch, and if you project this thirty years ahead at recent rates of change and also project the present increasing role of the president as a legislative leader, you might say that by the year 2000 Congress will be wholly in charge of administration and the president wholly in charge of legislation. Though this is the way they're going, it would not be safe to project these trends thirty years ahead.

PERLOFF: Clearly, there is reason to assume that changes in both the Executive and the Legislative Branches of the national government must be anticipated. Hopefully, we can prepare some essays that will throw light on this matter.

THE EXECUTIVE BRANCH IN THE YEAR 2000[*]

William M. Capron

The title of this essay suggests that we expect no radical change in the basic structure of national government in the last third of this century: there will still be an "executive branch." However, by the end of the present century some relatively drastic changes will have occurred within the federal executive establishment, as well as in the relations with other elements of government—Congress, state and local government, and the international community. These changes will occur because they are needed, and the main question is what form they should take.

I will not attempt to forecast the look and structure of the Executive Branch in 2000. Instead, what follows is my own vision, prescriptive, not predictive, of a possible set of developments that would meet the major requirements for an effective Executive Branch. Other workable patterns and policies may emerge, or we may suffer a serious breakdown in one or more crucial areas, leading to much more radical changes.

The needed changes must be seen against the background of relationships among the various levels of government within the country and relationships among nations outside.

* These words were written three years ago, and are inevitably seriously out-of-date, especially because of the significant reorganization actions and proposals of the Nixon administration. Indeed, many of those changes are along the lines suggested in these paragraphs. Not only has the world changed, but so has my own thinking, and were I to write on this subject today, I would modify some points, and put the emphasis somewhat differently. Nonetheless, the main thrust of the argument would remain. Certainly the basic outline of the challenges facing the Executive Branch has not been modified, but instead has emerged more clearly than ever.

1. Intergovernmental Relations

Domestic: The Working Group has identified three great domestic tasks that we must learn to perform more effectively than we have yet done: (a) protecting individual rights and helping individual development; (b) enhancing the quality of the urban and rural environment; (c) promoting civil order and political cohesion. The federal government generally and the presidency in particular must play a vital role if we are to approach an acceptable level of performance and results in each of these great tasks. By 2000 the responsibility for action in some areas will have been markedly decentralized, and the federal role will be diminished in detailed program implementation. On the other hand, some functions related to some of these broad tasks will have been largely federalized, with the President playing a more crucial and central role than he does today. If these changes are to come about, certain reassignments of responsibility and authority among the various levels of government will be required, some through legislation and others through constitutional change at either the federal or state level.

State and Metropolitan Government: The pace and pattern of urbanization raises serious questions about the future role of state governments in the United States. The role and function of state government are inevitably going to change, but the changes will be in either of two divergent directions: the state may atrophy in some functional areas, or it may become a form of "metropolitan" government. If the former course is chosen, then local governments will take over. The federal government would then bypass the states and design programs that would flow directly from Washington to the cities. This may necessitate some constitutional restructuring: metropolitan government might be raised to the position now held by several states; political subdivisions of the state might be given sweeping and irrevocable powers—in effect, transferring elements of "sovereignty" to local government.

The second possibility would see state government playing a more active role in the delivery of services to the public at the local level. Local jurisdictional boundaries are hard to change;

but the right interrelationships between the central city and the suburbs cannot be overlooked. It may be that "metropolitan government" will develop via direct action by the state government, with the state playing a much greater role in education, housing, urban planning, and the like. If this occurs, the federal government would manage more programs through state governments.

Changes in state and local government structure are urgently needed, for one reason, because present political boundaries in a number of significant places such as metropolitan New York bear no relation to the realities of population and activity location. At the least, in the coming decades, specific interstate agreements will deal with the most important metropolitan areas crossing state lines. We can also expect a growing number of interstate arrangements on such problems as river-basin development and pollution control. The federal government will certainly play a major role in designing and implementing such agreements, and the intergovernmental institutions created to deal with these problems will be granted much more sweeping and final power. In short, either de facto or de jure, the states may give up significant elements of "sovereignty," either voluntarily or by federal "coercion" (in the way federal programs are administered, and possibly through constitutional amendment).

The working out of new arrangements along either of these lines is complicated by serious regional differences. While most people will be urbanized by 2000, most of the nation's area will not. Some states in the Great Plains and the Rockies and in parts of the South will still be without large metropolitan populations—though most of their people will be urban-oriented if not urban-dwelling. In such states a strengthened and more effective state government should meet the needs—in some cases through working arrangements with neighboring states. But for the people-oriented problems and the programs designed to solve them, the state will increasingly seem to be an irrelevant layer interfering with effective federal-urban collaboration. Most significantly, the insistent demands of the citizenry that urgent and pressing social and economic issues be tackled effectively may lead to a new set of governmental institutions: metropolitan governments. As suggested earlier, an alternative to overt creation of metropolitan government is the assumption by the states of metropolitan area-wide functions now performed by the crazy-quilt pattern of local general and special-purpose jurisdictions.

No matter what course is followed, the present split between the center city and suburbia creates cumbersome or intractable problems demanding action. Despite all the built-in resistances to such governments, because they would wipe out historic relationships and boundary lines, the pressure of events will force some such solution. The alternative—much more thorough federalization of programs—is both unpalatable and inefficient, especially because over the next three decades we can expect a growing role for "participatory democracy." This often fuzzy phrase, as used here, points to the demand for effective decentralization of control and management in certain types of community services, which should be an improved feature of government in 2000. But to be effective, it requires stronger state and local government. This apparent paradox means that selective decentralization down to the neighborhood level will require care and skill if it is to avoid chaos and gross inefficiency.

One development is certain: chief executives at each important level of government will have much greater authority than they typically have today. The proliferation of special-purpose agencies, often with different boundaries from the central local government, will have ceased, and these activities will have been consolidated.

The above is not as digressive as it may seem. In coming decades, the major challenge to the Executive Branch of the federal government, particularly the President, will be to take a strong leadership role in creating governmental institutions and intergovernmental relationships that can help realize established national goals. Only the President is in the position to direct the required reorganization, for most other political leaders have a vested interest in maintaining at least some of the status quo. Although these leaders must take part in the bargaining required to develop new institutions and redirect the old, the President's leadership is essential in creating the popular will to force such bargains. We must escape from the straitjacket of institutions established nearly two centuries ago under vastly different circumstances, and this will be a principal task of the presidency in the next decade and beyond.

International: If we survive this century as a nation, a number of profound changes will occur in our foreign relations. Many of these will require significant Executive Branch reorganization and will place new demands—and constraints—on the presidency. Perhaps the most significant is the inevitable increase in the scope, importance, and role of international institutions (in addition to bilateral accords in such fields as arms control). By 2000 economic and social bonds among the peoples of the world will have led to new institutions with supranational powers, going well beyond anything nations have yet been willing to accept. In certain vital areas nations will have agreed to limitations on the exercise of national sovereignty —or, put differently, will have agreed to joint and cooperative discharge of sovereignty—in specified (but probably severely limited) fields, such as ocean and air transport, communication, and the economic and scientific uses of the ocean and the seabeds.

As on the domestic scene, changes on the international front will require considerable Executive Branch strengthening and restructuring, but there are significant differences. The President's primacy in domestic affairs today is much vaguer, less well-grounded in constitutional law, custom, and tradition than his uncontested leadership in foreign affairs. Indeed, the President is much weaker in meeting domestic problems than is generally recognized. Those who would prefer that the nation's problems be neglected are happy to sustain the myth of presidential power; Congress wants a scapegoat for ineffective action, and the presidency is convenient. Any strong and activist President often prefers to encourage the myth of his power, and achieve by cajoling what he cannot compel in any formal sense.

This imbalance in actual versus imagined presidential authority in domestic affairs must be redressed in the coming decades if the government is to meet its massive responsibilities. The idea of a "strong" presidency is often misunderstood; it does not mean a dictatorial presidency, or a weakening of democracy and democratic institutions. It does mean a presidency able to relate effectively, actively, and efficiently to all parts of the Executive Branch and Congress, and, most important, to institutions "above" him in the international field, and to institutions (and their leaders) "below" him in the domestic field—a President who has the authority commensurate with his responsibility as Chief Executive.

2. Executive Branch Reorganization

The Cabinet: In the coming decades a number of forces will produce significant changes in the structure and workings of the major departments and agencies. New programs such as Model Cities have highlighted the requirement for much closer integration among several of the most important departments and agencies. Such coordination is important at all stages, including program development, congressional consideration and action, program initiation, actual delivery (often through state and local agencies), and evaluation and modification based on experience. The interdepartmental committee and/or "task force," the "lead-agency" notion, ad-hoc Executive Office, and White House coordination have all been tried and found wanting. What must inevitably be created is a small number (two, three, or four) of "supersecretaries" overseeing "superdepartments." I assume that the Departments of Defense, State, the Treasury, and Justice will remain more or less as they are. But the functions now lodged in HEW, Labor, Interior, Agriculture, Transportation, Commerce, Housing and Urban Development (HUD), and independent agencies, such as Veterans' Administration (VA) and the Office of Economic Opportunity (OEO), will be consolidated in various combinations.

I assume that we will retain the term "secretary" and continue to have an elected Vice-President playing his traditional role. But the new domestic "senior secretaries" might best be described operationally as "executive vice-presidents," and must be the President's own men. Although politics will influence their selection, a wise President will see that they have a high order of executive and management ability as well as breadth and vision, always alert to innovative ideas for solving the demanding problems in their areas of responsibility.

As for the likely reshaping of today's departments and activities: HUD and HEW, together with many Labor, Commerce, OEO and VA activities, might be put under the direction of a single supersecretary; yet in many respects the urban-related activities of the Department of Transportation should be integrated closely with HUD, which suggests a somewhat different grouping. Since excessive consolidation will render the senior or supersecretary's task impossible, there will inevitably remain significant interfaces between the activities of the reduced number of major departments. As we suggest below, a strengthened Executive Office will be required to discharge this function for the President.

One important criterion for regrouping federal activities in a small number of multiprogram departments is the way the major activities grouped in any one department are carried out. Because many important programs in the future will be urban-oriented, with most of the population in the cities, one department should handle those programs in which the main line of federal action flows directly to the cities. On the other hand, in many programs (interurban highways and waterways; natural-resource development, including river-basin development and control; and environmental pollution), the federal government will still deal with the states and regional groupings of states.

Such superdepartment consolidation will not only improve program coordination in Washington but will facilitate intergovernmental cooperation in the development and implementation of federal programs.

The senior secretaries (or executive vice-presidents) would not take over many of the functions now performed (at least in theory) by secretaries of cabinet departments and administrators of the domestic agencies. Such appointive officials would continue to direct day-to-day operations. The senior secretaries would be presidential men with broad responsibility for overseeing the programs operated by the agencies under their control, possessing a strong analytic and evaluative capability closely tied to program planning and budgeting. In short, the model would be that introduced into Defense in the early 1960's.

Foreign Affairs: By 2000, if not long before then, the foreign-affairs organization of the Executive Branch will be substantially reconstructed. The Secretary of State will become the President's Secretary of Foreign Affairs. The functions now performed by the Department of State, except for some agencies such as Agency for International Development (AID), Arms Control and Disarmament (ACDA) and the Peace Corps, will be directly controlled by an under-secretary. The Secretary of Foreign Affairs will become a "supersecretary," acting for the President and having the overall responsibility for the direction, policy formulation, and program development of all foreign activities of the American government. His own office would be relatively small, with heavy emphasis on a high-level policy and program analytic staff, including specialists in those areas with which the United States is involved overseas. His office would be responsible for United States government relations with international organizations.

The CIA will be split into two agencies: the director of intelligence-evaluation activities will report directly to the President, operating closely with the Secretary of Foreign Affairs and the Secretary of Defense; covert operations will be lodged in a separate agency.

Executive Office of the President: Not only will this office be greatly strengthened, but it will have several additional functions. An Office of Domestic Program Direction will coordinate activities involving two or more departments in Washington and will have a strong field staff with a senior official representing the President in each of the nation's several regions. The director of this office will be closely identified with the President.

All federal agencies and departments will have the same regional boundaries and, with a few special exceptions dictated by operating conditions, will each have regional headquarters in the same cities. The regional directors of the Office of Program Direction will be the senior federal officials in each region, with the authority to make decisions about all programs of the federal government operating through state and local government within their regions (such as approving grant applications). Sophisticated communications equipment, together with rapid air travel from any point in the country to Washington, will facilitate continual personal contact between Washington and the field for resolving conflicts and correcting mistakes.

The Office of Management and Budget will continue to be the President's principal staff arm for federal resource allocation decision and program evaluation. Its analytic and evaluative capability will have been significantly enhanced. At the same time, the senior secretaries, with strong budget review staffs, will relieve the Bureau of the Budget of its current minute review each year of every agency's budget down to the smallest subunit. While the annual budget will remain a principal presidential device for making recommendations to Congress, there will be more emphasis on multiyear program planning and budgeting.

Independent Agencies and Regulatory Commissions: By 2000 the regulatory agencies will be reorganized, and certain important separate agencies such as the VA, OEO, AEC, and NASA will become part of a cabinet superdepartment.

The regulatory commissions will function as specialized courts with basic policy-making and administrative functions carried out by executive departments responsible to the President.

Other new and separate agencies will be created to develop new and innovative programs to tackle new problems, develop new technologies, and solve old problems in radically new ways. They will continue to be a device for shaking up the bureaucracy (which will tend to function along routine lines despite the best efforts of the senior secretaries), and for focusing public attention on major new innovative initiatives and attracting talent to such ventures.

3. Other Changes

Information and Communications Systems to Serve the Presidency: By the year 2000, despite the growth in the size and complexity of federal programs, the technological improvement of the computer, closed-circuit TV, facsimile transmission, and so on, will make it possible for the federal bureaucracy to carry out its functions much more efficiently and effectively than it can today, with no increase in total manpower.

Certain functions of a "business" type, such as postal services, will have been turned over to public corporations and nonfederal agencies, operating where necessary under federal regulation. The pressure for more direct citizen participation at the grass-roots level will contribute to, and be served by, these developments.

Income Distribution and Resource Allocation: By 2000, many of the inefficiencies and inequities in federal, state, and local programs of the 1960's will have been eliminated and many important areas rationalized, largely through an effective income-maintenance program, together with sweeping reform of the tax system, at the federal as well as the state and local levels. The federal income-tax collecting mechanism will be used as a revenue raiser for state and local government.

As a result of these reforms and new income transfer programs, income will be distributed in a more equitable manner than it is today, and it will be possible to reexamine the many federal programs that today make for inequity and inefficiency because they are in part designed to subsidize certain individuals and activities by transfers-in-kind.

Adaptive Flexibility in Executive Branch: Although we cannot predict what the emerging problems of the year 2000 will be, we can be sure that new problems and new possibilities will continue to characterize American life. And an increasing number of these problems and possibilities will require some sort of federal leadership and action. One of the lessons we should have learned from the last three decades is that in the next three we need to develop governmental institutions, and especially Executive Branch institutions, that permit us to respond more quickly and effectively to new tasks demanded by emerging challenges. The President should be given broad powers to reorganize the Executive Branch, with Congress retaining only a veto power over such changes. Also, more sophisticated and powerful analytic techniques will make it increasingly possible for the President to be informed by an "early warning system" before a crisis has developed.

Congress and the Presidency: Of all the institutions and institutional relationships, Congress and its relations to other elements of government seem the most resistant to change. This will continue to be true throughout the twentieth century. But there will be some major changes in the way Congress organizes itself and in the matters to which it devotes major attention. If Congress develops an independent analytic and evaluative capability that can be applied to federal programs and policies, the dialogue between it and the Executive Branch should become more sophisticated and rational. Some of the worst kinds of self- and special-interest action common today may be more difficult if they are illuminated by analysis, particularly since a better-informed Congress means a more enlightened public. Congress, vis-à-vis the Executive Branch, will continue to use its broad investigating powers to ensure that programs are fulfilling their purposes. No administration or bureaucracy can itself do an objective and impartial evaluative job.

In closing, I wish to emphasize that this essay is *not* predictive but prescriptive. Without changes of the sort I have suggested, we may not be able to survive major challenges and grasp the great opportunities for the future.

CONGRESS IN THE YEAR 2000

Representative John Brademas

If Congress did not exist in the year 2000, it would be necessary to invent it, for certain functions essential to responsible and effective government in the United States can be carried out only by such an institution.

The principal functions of Congress three decades from now will be to act as a vehicle of representation and participation, to help formulate public policy, and to monitor its administration. Congress today does all of this to some extent, but much more of each will be indispensable to effective democratic government as the United States enters the twenty-first century. I also think that, contrary to many expectations, certain developments over the next thirty years will strengthen rather than erode the ability of Congress to fulfill its responsibilities.

Congress as Vehicle for Participation

It is important that by 2000 Congress should have a central role in making widespread participation in government both possible and meaningful.

Certain themes about the future of government in America run through most of the essays in this volume: the distinctions between public and private activities will fade; there will be a higher degree of policy making on a nationwide basis, more decentralized operation, and reinvigorated local, state, and regional government. But many of these essays also call for increased participation by the citizen in making decisions affecting his life.

The community action agencies in the antipoverty war, the Model Cities Program, the move to decentralize school systems, student demands for a say in running the universities, the Black Power movement, and the priests' insistence on being heard by their ecclesiastical superiors—these are contemporary instances of the participatory phenomenon. For the year 2000, we shall both require and have a strong central government, and we shall need and have widespread participation by the citizenry in the decisions of government.

I believe that the individual senator and congressman—and Congress as an institution—are ideally situated to help insure this kind of participation, for three reasons:

1. Congressmen and senators represent *local* districts or states and must therefore be sensitive to local feelings about national policy and its administration. Our legislators in Washington are links between locally perceived needs and the formulation and administration of national policy, for they are elected, not appointed.

2. Senators and congressmen are *national* legislators whose laws apply to the entire country, not only their own areas. American government in the early twenty-first century will deal with issues requiring coherent policies for an entire nation, though many will be carried out on a local or regional basis.

3. Senators and congressmen develop unusual skill as brokers among private individuals and groups and officials of every level of government—local, state, and federal. Congressional politicians are nurtured in negotiation and swim in a pluralistic sea. Bargaining among disparate forces is their natural way of life.

There are several reasons for encouraging participation in making decisions on matters that affect people, especially on governmental policies. First of all, real problems, not false ones, are more likely to surface. Second, participation enhances the possibility of developing alternative solutions since more people are thinking and reacting. Third, it reduces the disruptive efforts of those who otherwise are left out. Fourth, it increases the prospect that such policy will be accepted by those whose views did not prevail—or at least that their opposition will be minimized. And fifth, participation reduces the possibility of tyranny—one of the principal reasons the founding fathers created what Richard E. Neustadt calls "a government of separated institutions *sharing* powers."[1]

How then can we encourage genuine participation and stimulate the involvement of citizens at the local level in the shaping of national policy? Perhaps we can systematize dialogue between the legislator and his constituency on those issues most relevant to them. The senator or congressman can lead as well as respond. He can bring information and admonition back to Congress and to the Executive Branch, telling them what he learned back home and urging upon them certain courses of action. He can try to change either the policy itself or the way it is carried out.

He thus provides an entry into the political system for the citizen who wants to be heard, and he can also spark the interest of the far larger number of those who are indifferent to problems of government.

Of course, some senators and congressmen already play this role in varying degrees, but those who do usually operate in a piecemeal and haphazard fashion. Obviously a kind of continuous New England town meeting in which every citizen can debate every issue is impossible.

The 106th Congress, sitting in the year 2000, should continue to be a representative institution, and the corrective function of professional politicians will be more urgent than ever at that time. The more complex our society and its problems are, the more work there is for society's leaders and brokers. For the future, we must see how citizen participation can be made both possible and relevant, and not just token interchange.

One concrete model for this dialogue is the neighborhood advisory council, which could both counsel its congressional representatives and have some operating responsibility as well. Such citizen groups could be organized around certain problems important to that community or state, and they would in time develop a certain expertise on, say, pollution control or mass transit or housing. But this model raises difficulties, such as how to form such organizations and how to insure that they are in fact "representative."

It is difficult to ascertain the degree and kind of authority and influence such groups should wield, legally and politically, vis-à-vis legislators and other public officials and other elements of society, including political parties. To what extent does a senator or congressman feel himself bound by the decisions of such groups?

It would seem sensible to adopt Kenneth Karst's "variable franchise," whereby certain local and special-service units of government allow those chiefly affected by a decision to have a greater voice in matters directly affecting them. We do this now, he notes, with farmers, and we make similar efforts in the community-action and Model Cities programs.

The proliferation of such councils would of course raise many difficulties, but it is better to wrestle with those problems than with the larger dilemma of the estrangement of millions from the decisions of a government they regard as distant and removed. Nor can we wait until 2000. The Harris poll reported in 1968 that 28 percent of adult Americans—over thirty-three million people—"feel largely alienated from the mainstream of society." A Congress carrying out its representative function through mechanisms for participatory dialogue with the citizenry can help make the national government more responsive and responsible.[2]

Congress as Creator of Policy

A second function of Congress in 2000 will be to help shape public policy. Congress is often attacked for being either a rubber stamp of the President or a willful obstructionist of his policies, but it is less well appreciated that Congress has also played a creative role in formulating policy. Congress need not choose between subservience to the President or stubborn opposition.[3] Congress not only can but *should* play an important part in making policy for reasons that, if compelling now, will be all the more so at a time when the federal government will be much more involved in a wide spectrum of activities, and the Executive Branch will need the assistance of Congress in many ways.

First, Congress can help resolve conflicts and formulate consensus on controversial issues. In a nation as diverse as the United States, however, with a vastly increased population by the year 2000, lingering economic specialization in the several regions, and a federal system with national, state and local units of government, not to mention the whole array of nonpublic groupings, the resolution of internal conflict becomes indispensable to the operation of free government.

Major changes of public policy in such a society command widespread support, for, as Kennedy liked to quote from Jefferson, "Great innovations should not be forced on slender majorities."[4] Congress is the institution in the American political system most sensitive to public opinion because least insulated from it. It can, through the give-and-take of the political and legislative process, resolve conflict and muster support for public policy. (Of course it is precisely this sensitivity to public opinion that can lead Congress to make bad policy.)

Congress can explain the purposes and details of policy, justify policy, feed back to the Executive Branch views on the weaknesses and strengths of policy, offer measures for improving it, block policy unacceptable to the citizenry, and often act as broker between the federal executive and state and local government officials and nongovernmental organizations and individuals. All these activities can help make existing policy work and channel new policy into the system—functions essential in the more complex America of the year 2000, when the federal government will be engaged in a multiplicity of programs affecting every citizen and community in the land. Moreover, in carrying out these functions, congressmen and senators store up electoral credit for themselves with their constituents—with whom appointed civil servants or even Cabinet officers are less concerned.

James Sundquist has cited the proposal of the Johnson administration for legislation authorizing a war on poverty as an example of a measure almost wholly initiated in the Executive Branch with little original involvement of Congress.[5] Congressional attacks on the poverty program help substantiate Sundquist's thesis.

Many major legislative enactments in recent years were in large measure the product of substantial congressional initiative and effort in such fields as health, education, pollution control, immigration reform, and economic development. And this function will be still greater in the year 2000.

Not only the Executive but the Legislative Branch has the ability to launch ideas into public view, to give them visibility and the respectability essential to serious consideration by a public much broader than the groups that spawned them. The two branches, however, launch ideas in different ways. The Executive proposes policy by promulgating a legislative program. But crucial executive debate on alternatives takes place largely in private, which contracts the field of alternatives.

In contrast, the natural operation of Congress expands the range of alternatives. In this constant concern with public attention, every member of Congress becomes an instrument for propelling ideas into public view. By introducing bills, holding hearings, making speeches, and conducting floor debates, members can capture public interest. Moreover, congressional involvement, given the multiplicity of views expressed and the visible nature of many proceedings, is likely to produce more intelligent policy than that generated by the Executive alone.

One may complain that the dual legislative process often makes it difficult for government to act decisively. But it is well to remember that the Constitution itself, when coupled with the diversity of American society, is not ideally tailored for decisive governmental action. Nor is the voice with which the American voter speaks always a decisive one, as seen in the slender margins of the 1960 and 1968 presidential elections and the present situation in which the presidency and Congress are each controlled by different parties. Our government, for better or for worse, does not seem so ill-matched either to the nature of our political institutions or to the nature of our society.

In a disciplined system, in which legislators are wed to fixed party positions, they are less effective in bargaining with the Executive. In these circumstances, legislators have less incentive to engage in the interchange with citizens, which, I feel, can bring greater insights to legislators and the Executive, thereby leading to more acceptable policy.

Congress as Monitor: Maintaining the Balance

A third function of Congress in the year 2000, as now, will be that of appraising, criticizing, and overseeing—in a word, monitoring—public policies and their administration.

Politicians elected to Congress are eminently well-qualified to play this role of critic, advocate, and broker for their constituents vis-à-vis the Executive. A senator or congressman is constantly trying to persuade the leaders and citizens whom he represents that their interests as well as those of the state or community are better served with him in office than by any possible opponent.

The legislator's capacity to act as an effective broker and advocate depends in no small part on his constituents' perception of his ability to make or modify policy, to affect its administration, and to be generally effective in his dealings with the executive.

Yet there are those who argue that in another generation's time or less, Congress should surrender its pretensions to making and monitoring policy and confine itself to a task still narrower than overseeing—that of ombudsman, or champion of the causes of individual constituents. What the proponents of this view fail to understand is that the effectiveness of Congress in interceding for constituents, appraising policy, and overseeing its administration, is directly related to its capacity to change, effect, oppose, and propose policy, and to vote money. If senators and congressmen did not have at least some influence in shaping policy administered by the Executive, their ability to intervene for constituents and to monitor policy would be greatly diminished.

It must be remembered that American legislators have far more bargaining power with the Executive than do their English or French counterparts. Nor are American legislators directly dependent for their survival on the Executive.

Only if individual citizens are confident that their grievances will be heard and attended to can the alienation of citizens from the processes of big government in a very large and complicated nation be prevented. Such grievances, moreover, can be an important source of knowledge for shaping new policy.

By its very nature as an institution, Congress can focus on the details of policy administration, rather than its broad outlines. The diffuse, fragmentary organization of Congress lends itself far better to preoccupation with details than the kind of overall, unified consideration of policy goals that characterizes a parliamentary system with centralized parties. It is precisely its pluralistic and decentralized base that defines Congress and enables it to represent the multiplicity of interests that make up the American society and to feed new and different views into the policy-making stream. Though the policies may be national in scope, they must be applied at local levels.

Its capacity as monitor enables Congress to protect the citizen and the community against the dangers of bureaucratic insensitivity and centralism. Those who complain that Congress interferes with the Executive in the administration of the laws seem to imply that if Congress were to retreat from this field, so would the other forces that exercise pressure on the executive agencies. This is foolish.

All things considered, the second session of the 106th Congress, convening in January 2000, will have an even more important responsibility than the 92nd Congress of 1971 in monitoring the myriad activities of an Executive Branch grown greater in size and more potent in its capacity to affect everyone.

The doctrines of separation of powers and of checks and balances are not likely to have disappeared in the world of 2000. On the contrary, when a powerful national government has greater access to far more rapid communications and other technology, these doctrines may prove indispensable both to the preservation and extension of individual rights and freedoms and to the prevention of widespread alienation from government. By vigorously exercising the three functions of representation, policy making, and overseeing, Congress will contribute to the achievement of both objectives.

Emerson called Congress "a standing insurrection," but he concluded that it also "escapes the violence of accumulated grievances." [6] In another generation we shall be in great need of mechanisms that will enable government to resolve grievances that, when accumulated, breed violence.

It is my belief that Congress will have a greater function in the American political system of 2000. But to perform this function effectively and creatively, it will have to be strengthened in important ways.

Sources of Strengthened Congress

There are three major sources from which Congress will draw new strength over the next three decades: changes in the national political environment, internal institutional reform, and greater access to information and intelligence.

I do not think there will be a radical restructuring of American government between 1971 and 2000. The public is not that interested in political institutions, as distinguished from political issues, and any changes in the American Constitution are likely to be piecemeal.

There will be a growth of certain nationalizing forces in American politics, among them a realignment of American political parties. With the further erosion of one-party politics in the South and a continuing rise of two-party politics in the Midwest, Congress will become far more representative of urban and suburban interests, and therefore of the population as a whole.

Mass communications, widespread access to education, greater speed and ease of transport, and the enhanced participatory role of Congress by 2000 will also increase the likelihood that legislators of the same region will be in close touch with public opinion and will come to similar conclusions on needed changes in public policy. Robert A. Dahl points out that because of urbanizing influences, objective differences among voters will account even less for voting patterns and political attitudes than they do now, and such subjective factors as values and ideology will rise in importance. Parties will therefore see voters less in terms of their social, economic, and ethnic backgrounds and will pay greater attention to attitudes and policy views. The consequences will be more unified and less heterogeneous policies and increasingly stable coalitions.[7]

It must be clearly understood, however, that in our system of divided powers, the rise of cohesive parties during the next generation will not mean that Congress, like the British House of Commons, will be subject to an all-powerful executive. The participatory Congress that I have suggested for 2000 will surely be at home with the parties that develop policy by consensus rather than by direction. But the nationalizing of the parties along the lines here suggested will not be characterized by the kind of powerful central control that has classically been the hope of many American political scientists. Not only do the division of powers and the decentralized, fragmented electoral system prevent this control, but the pull of local, state, and regional interests and all the other diversities of American life will—and should—remain powerful forces in the politics of the year 2000 if the system continues to represent itself as responsive to the will of the electorate.

Certain changes in the composition of the electorate will also have an impact on the role of Congress in 2000. The full exercise of the franchise by minorities and its extension to younger citizens will yield a Congress more representative of the actual population than is now the case. Redistricting and reapportionment decisions will also strengthen the representative character of Congress.

As the nation grows younger and levels of education rise, the characteristics of senators and congressmen will change. Better-educated legislators will become more numerous and powerful in both parties, and they will tend to have fundamentally different perceptions of their roles than they do now. They will focus primarily upon issues that cut across lines of geography and economic interest, problems that affect the entire country, and, indeed, the world.

Reform: Strengthening Congress from Within

Congress will also be able to increase its effectiveness through two kinds of reform in its own organization and procedures: measures for strengthening the power of party organization in Congress, and measures for making the operations of Congress more efficient.

Because of its organization and procedures, Congress has on many occasions failed to act even when the President and majorities in both houses agreed that action was necessary. It is easier to keep laws from being passed than it is to pass them.

Three decades from now, certain formal modifications in the rules of Congress will assure greater control over the legislative process by the majority of a congressional party than exists today. Accordingly, the majority party in Congress will be able to insist, as it now cannot, that there be both debate and voting on the legislative proposals of its own majority, and on the proposals of the President.

Another step toward enabling a party majority in Congress to exercise its majority is some modification of the seniority system. The present method of selecting committee chairmen will disappear; committees and their chairmen will become responsive to the party majority and not, as in the 92nd Congress, extraordinarily unrepresentative of the majority.[8] With greater party homogeneity in the country, the prospect that Congress and the President (if both were of the same party) would tend to agree on policy matters would be greatly increased.

Even more important, where the rules and procedures governing the chairman's operation of a committee are such that an arbitrary chairman cannot continue to be arbitrary, such democratic processes may themselves be enough to resolve the adverse effects of the seniority system.[9]

None of this is intended to deny senators and congressmen their freedom to take policy positions as they see fit. Realignment into homogeneous parties with policy developed by dialogue and interchange will produce as much discipline on policy as both the electoral system and the diversity of the nation will permit—or require.

At present Congress is greatly outmanned by the Executive in quantity if not quality of staff, advice, and assistance. Yet the increased responsibility simply to oversee the burgeoning federal programs means that Congress will need to staff itself far more effectively if it is not to be overwhelmed by its tasks. In fact, forces are already in motion that will bring to the 106th Congress a staff both more numerous and qualitatively more capable of helping Congress carry out its functions.

Congress and the Computer

Thus far I have discussed two forces—evolution in the external political and social environment and internal congressional reform—which will contribute to strengthening Congress for the decades ahead. But a third force must be harnessed if Congress is to have any serious chance of coping with the number and complexity of future public-policy issues: the revolution in information technology. The response of Congress to this revolution will determine in large measure its capacity to analyze and evaluate existing programs and proposed policies, as well as to improve communications between individual members of Congress and their constituents.

The process of acquiring, structuring, processing, and retrieving various types of data could be considered another aspect of congressional reform. Yet the opportunities that modern information offers Congress are so extraordinary that they need more detailed attention.

The information systems that Congress employs today will simply not be adequate for the Congress of 2000. They were not even adequate in 1970. During the 91st Congress, more than 24,600 bills were introduced on an enormous variety of subjects. Although most of them were noncontroversial, their serious evaluation demanded much better information than was available, both in quantity and quality, on the most complex questions of policy. Many legislators today feel acutely their lack of information of this kind.[10]

Congress lags far behind the Executive in its use of automatic data processing (ADP), and this disparity both symbolizes and helps explain some of the advantages the Executive now enjoys over Congress in generating and supervising policy. Computers are widely employed in the Executive Branch—by June 1969 the federal Executive was using an estimated 4600 computers [11]—at an annual cost of nearly $2 billion.[12] There can be little doubt as to the importance of their contribution. In the judgment of the Bureau of the Budget, "No single technological advance in recent years has contributed more to effectiveness and efficiency in government operations than the development of electronic data processing equipment." [13]

In contrast, the first bill to provide Congress with ADP support was not introduced until 1966. As the 92nd Congress convened in January 1971, there were only three ADP facilities on Capitol Hill. The most impressive of these, at the Library of Congress, sends every congressional office a bimonthly "Digest of Public Bills," including synoptic and status information on all bills and resolutions in both chambers; a "Legislative Status Report" on two hundred major bills once a month; and selected bibliographical information requested by congressional offices and committees. The House of Representatives has a small computer used only for payroll, and the Senate uses automated data processing only to speed mail delivery.[14]

Will Congress continue to deny itself the tools of modern information technology and permit the Executive virtually to monopolize them? If it does, Congress will ultimately destroy its power both to create policy and to oversee the Executive. For in government, as in every other human activity, information is power.

One important facet of the technology revolution is the radical improvement of communications between legislators and constituents. It promises greater accessibility of senators and congressmen to their constituents, individually and collectively, and vice versa. This development, of course, is fundamental to my thesis that Congress should be a principal instrument for making citizen participation possible in government at the national level. The new technology will make it easier to bridge the gulf between the citizen and his government. "Vote for a computer-competent Congressman!" may well be one of the common campaign slogans of the year 2000. Developments like these will obviously have a great impact on the ability of Congress to meet its responsibilities in the twenty-first century.

There are, of course, some pitfalls implicit in these technological changes. Communications may become too close and constant, and act as a constricting force. For instance, by 2000 it will be easy to have virtually up-to-the-minute polls of the electorate on any given issue. But where does this instant-opinion development leave the senator and congressman? Suppose, as Paul Baran of the Rand Corporation suggests, the newspaper then reports that 85 percent of a congressman's constituents oppose curbs on tourists. If the congressman disagrees, it will be difficult for him, confronted with such unambiguous constituent sentiment, to vote with his best judgment.

Nonetheless, the radically increased flow of timely and relevant data about his constituents should combine with a similar rise in the quality and quantity of information available to the legislator to make possible a significant improvement in the caliber of the participatory dialogue.

Advances in information technology, coupled with the emerging technique of programming-planning-budgeting (PPB), also hold unusual promise for enabling Congress to meet its other two major responsibilities—formulating policy and monitoring the Executive. Congress will no longer be confined to its present prison of considering policies on a largely piecemeal and incremental basis, but will be able to conceive and initiate broad and integrated policy proposals more intelligently than it does today.

The Congress of the year 2000 will be able to respond to the program budget recommended by the President with its own budgetary preferences, its own set of legislative priorities, and its own program choices—and do so on the basis of analyses and evaluations made by its own staff and effective access to adequate data. In another generation Congress will be able to tap the data systems of the Executive and parts of the private sector, and will maintain its own information system, together with its own staff of analysts, to insure that it is not dependent on the data supply of the Executive.

It should be evident that the mere existence of sophisticated machinery, even the fantastic machinery we can imagine for the twenty-first century, is no substitute for the human thought and judgment necessary to ask appropriate questions of the computer.

In fact, a more subtle but nevertheless significant consequence of the great change in information systems is the improvement in the quality of human judgment. Because the effective use of computers requires disciplined human thought, in order to program the computer policy makers must undertake a more exacting analysis of issues than they might otherwise do.

Neither technology nor management embodies a panacea for the problems of the future, yet Congress will need all the help it can get from both, for the growth and survival of the United States depend largely upon the effectiveness of its leaders, on their perception of the problems we face, and on the policies they shape to meet them. In the year 2000, Congress must—and will—exploit the tools that will equip it to cope with its great tasks. I do not despair, as some do, for the American political system or for Congress as part of it. Given our large, complex, restless society, and our deliberately fragmented Constitutional structure, I believe that the best hope for the American democracy in the twenty-first century lies in the pattern of national government I have foreseen for the year 2000—one in which the contributions of Congress will be indispensable.

NOTES

1. Richard E. Neustadt, *Presidential Power: The Politics of Leadership* (New York: John Wiley & Sons, 1961), p. 33. Italics his.

2. For an essay that perceptively sounds the participatory theme, see Richard N. Goodwin, "Reflections: Sources of the Public Unhappiness," *The New Yorker* (January 4, 1969), pp. 38–58. For a thoughtful discussion of both the need for and the perils associated with increasing citizen participation in a large representative democracy like the United States, see Robert A. Dahl, "The City in the Future of Democracy," *American Political Science Review*, vol. 61, no. 4 (December 1967), pp. 953–970.

3. John Brademas, "The Role of Congress in Making of Public Policy," *Proceedings, 1967, Indiana Academy of Social Sciences*, 3d ser., vol. 2, pp. 181–204. I have drawn on this paper for some of the analysis in the present essay.

4. Arthur M. Schlesinger, Jr., *A Thousand Days: John F. Kennedy in the White House* (Boston: Houghton Mifflin, 1965), p. 713.

5. James L. Sundquist, *Politics and Policy: The Eisenhower, Kennedy, and Johnson Years* (Washington, D.C.: Brookings Institution, 1968), pp. 490–495.

6. Ralph Waldo Emerson, quoted in Stephen K. Bailey and Howard D. Samuel, *Congress at Work* (New York: Henry Holt, 1952), p. 1.

7. Robert A. Dahl, *Political Oppositions in Western Democracies* (New Haven, Conn.: Yale University Press, 1966), p. 69.

8. Indeed, some may be astonished to learn that an examination of roll-call votes in the House of Representatives during the 90th Congress reveals that the strongest and most stubborn opposition to the positions of the Democratic administration and against the majority of House Democrats came from a minority of powerful Democrats even more often than it did from House Republicans. See *Congressional Quarterly*, Weekly Report No. 43 (October 25, 1968), pp. 2933–2937.

9. Sundquist, *Politics and Policy, op. cit.*, pp. 522–553.

10. A recent study underscores the conviction of many congressmen that they have inadequate information on which to base their decisions. Each of a group of eighty members of the House, selected at random, was asked to "name any problems which prevented him from carrying out the role he would like to play in the House and all problems which he saw as preventing the House from operating as he thought it should." The problems which were cited most frequently by 78 percent of the congressmen were "complexity of decision making; lack of information." Significantly, the problem cited by the second largest number of congressmen fell within the category of "services for constituents"—an area of congressional activity susceptible to greater streamlining through ADP techniques. See Michael O'Leary, ed., *Congressional Reorganization: Problems and Prospects—A Conference Report* (Hanover, N.H.: Public Affairs Center, Dartmouth College, 1964), pp. 22–23; Roger H. Davidson, in Alfred de Grazia, ed., *Congress: The First Branch of Government* (Garden City, New York: Doubleday, 1966), p. 402.

11. General Services Administration, *Management Information Systems Report 2-J: Government-wide EDPE Systems Purchase/Lease Status (in Place as of 6/30/69)*, Washington, D.C., 1968.

12. General Services Administration, *Management Information Systems Report 5-C: Government-wide ADP Resources*, Washington, D.C., November 1968.

13. Executive Office of the President, Bureau of the Budget, *Report to the President on the Management of Automatic Data Processing in the Federal Government*, Washington, D.C., February 1965, p. 1.

14. Among the best descriptions of both present and possible uses of the new information technology by Congress are Robert L. Chartrand, "Congress Seeks a Systems Approach," *Datamation*, vol. 14, no. 5 (May 1968), pp. 46–49; and Robert L. Chartrand, Kenneth Janda, and Michael Hugo, eds., *Information Support, Program Budgeting, and the Congress* (New York: Spartan Books, 1968).

VI

THE FUTURE OF URBANISM AND OF UNITED STATES FEDERALISM

SOME QUESTIONS ABOUT ENHANCING THE QUALITY OF THE URBAN ENVIRONMENT

Martin and Margy Meyerson

Henry Adams, in his extraordinary book *The Education of Henry Adams,* predicted that the world in the year 2000 would have limitless force. Fascinated by the huge dynamo in the Great Exposition at the turn of the last century, he sensed a future in which vast amounts of energy would be readily available to all to transform their material way of life. At the time, *force* was a colloquial term for electricity, but it was not the only term Adams might have chosen. Perhaps he used it with irony, for he was concerned with violence, and implied that a remade material world might have to be sustained by coercion. "Every generation," he said, has "toiled with endless agony to attain and apply power, all the while betraying the deepest alarm and horror at the power they created." The prospects, in his view, were for accelerating power or force.

In the autobiographical *Education,* Adams posed the dilemma for man of choosing between the Virgin or the Dynamo, between the humane and stable, and the technological and transitory. More than fifty years after the publication of his book, the dilemma Henry Adams posed is not only unresolved but greately heightened. Some retain faith in mechanization and accelerating technology; they see a world in which man could be provided with the bounty of material satisfactions and could be freed to think beyond sustenance and survival. They see a world in which man could be liberated from rote drudgery to perform more humane tasks. All people could live at least in dignity, if not in grace, if provided with the basic necessities of decent shelter, food and clothing, and medical care and education. Others are skeptical or fearful of technology, worried that man will become obsolescent as the machines become more efficient; they fear man's values are already askew from the onslaught of superfluous material belongings. They stress paths for man's well-being in the reestablishment of bonds to family, to fellow-man, and to natural environment. Technology and material satisfactions are seen as a threat and not a blessing.

In the exuberance over an ever-increasing Gross National Product, some even claim that by the year 2000 the characteristics of both the Virgin and the Dynamo will be attainable. Material satisfactions could be maximized, as could also a loving and nurturing society.

The confusion and conflict over relative weights to be placed on the humane or on the technological are evident in the current concern for the environment. There are those in their quest for a more healthful or attractive environment who would ban or restrict actions that others have come to regard as an accustomed pleasure and perhaps even a private right. For example, in the consumer realm, if the use of the private automobile, detergents, electric power for dryers and other appliances were to be limited, presumably pollution would be mitigated.

ENVIRONMENTAL IMPROVEMENT THROUGH COERCION

Ironically, such a future urban environment might have to be sustained to a considerable degree by coercion. To obtain an environment that is less polluted, more orderly, more lavishly endowed with open green spaces may well require more rules and regulations, or a less "humane" (in the sense of less free) behavioral environment. Most of what is generally regarded as qualitative improvements in the environment—air and water pollution control, superior open space and recreational opportunities, improved municipal services, tasteful urban design and aesthetics, more diverse cultural offerings, better transportation, decent housing for all, harmonious race relations, streets safe from crimes and accidents—depends largely on deliberate collective actions, not on the sum total of individual actions.

Moreover, such improvements depend largely on public, not private, collective actions. Furthermore, they require not only the collective public action of taxation and other forms of funding, they require regulation of behavior. Although some of the qualitative improvements could be achieved through judicious use of the public exchequer, many of them must be obtained by requiring individuals or firms or agencies to refrain from previous practices—practices they have come to regard from habitual usage as freedoms.

For example, if the air is to be relatively free of contamination, many people and organizations must change their present ways of manufacturing, heating their homes, and transporting themselves in individual internal-combustion-engine cars. They must find other ways of getting rid of industrial wastes than dumping them into the air. Businesses and homes must be converted to "clean" fuels, and most painful, since the automobile is a prime cause of air pollution, they must substitute mass transportation for private cars (or develop a new source of power). Since many people base their life patterns on cars, they may have to be forced, through high taxation or other means, into giving up what they regard as their right. More people would prefer someone else to give up an accustomed practice than to do so themselves. For example, women who condemn an electric power plant for its smoke and other emissions rarely concur when they are urged, in the interests of pollution control, to hang their wash on the backyard line instead of using an electric dryer.

As in the case of air pollution, so it is in the case of other qualitative improvements in the urban environment—change would bring its costs as well as its benefits. More equity in race relations means that whites must give up the expectation that jobs, prestige educational institutions, well-maintained neighborhoods, and other rewards are reserved for them. Decent housing for all would mean that not only would the better-off economic groups have to pay for housing subsidies for the poor, but the poor themselves would have to pay more for their housing in maintenance, foregone return (many landlords of the poor are poor themselves), and changed family patterns.

Similarly, if a superior overall urban design pattern is to be achieved, individuals and firms will have certain costs to bear besides the monetary. They will have to accept even more regulation in the construction, design, and maintenance of buildings (and vacant lots) than they do now, for health and safety. To achieve such a pattern, individuals may perhaps not be permitted to alter historically or architecturally important buildings; may have to use prescribed materials and even colors in their building schemes;

submit building designs and proposed signs and other graphics for review; landscape and maintain open areas in particular ways; provide underground or aboveground parking facilities; build a specified height or bulk (instead of being given a maximum). If the relationship of design to the total environment is to become truly important, the individual will have less freedom in constructing, using, and maintaining business and residential buildings than he has had up to now. The end result of greater visual satisfaction and more harmonious juxtaposition of buildings and land could be achieved only through constraint on individual action. Although the notion that every man's house (and business) is his castle may be a myth today, not even the myth could persist in the face of much stronger community and other governmental controls.

No one knows whether community residents will be willing to give up some of their present habits for such collective benefits as cleaner air or more beautiful views, or whether they will be willing to accept coercion in one sphere of their lives to obtain anticipated pleasure in another.

No one knows how much members of a community will pay (in money and behavior) for an enhanced environment, because no one knows what people seek most in the urban environment and wish to see improved. There is very little agreement on what constitutes an ideal or even a good urban environment, and without such a definition it is almost impossible to achieve concerted changes. This is the case with all vaguely defined broad goals. For example, one reason the character of institutions of higher learning has changed so little is that few agree on what a good education consists of and how one should obtain it. It is easy enough, of course, to find faults within education about which one can complain and offer some remedies. But it is extremely difficult for markedly different educational activities to be conceived and implemented. Similarly, critics of the urban community abound and the complaints increase, but no previously identified problems are solved. In the conventional wisdom, everyone knows that cities suffer from chronic congestion, pollution, dilapidation and slums, fiscal imbalance, archaic management systems, dearth of open spaces and recreational opportunities, dreariness of outlook, poverty in services. But which of these complaints are *critical* either to individuals within the community or to the community as a whole? To solve which complaints, would individuals be willing to pay more for in taxes or altered habits? More important, what satisfactions do citizens seek which transcend the mere alleviation of urban frictions and malfunctioning?

POPULATION DENSITY AND THE AMENITY OF THE ENVIRONMENT

Perhaps all we know now is that people prefer to live in cities—despite their disabilities. And it is expected that man in the future will be even more of a city dweller than he is now; at present about 70 percent of the nation live in urban places and 80 to 90 percent are expected to live there by 2000. No one who thinks of the future, whether technocrat or humanist, pessimist or optimist, expects American man to live on farms or small villages. Instead, the present pattern of living in or near the metropolis is expected to intensify; the tendency all through the twentieth century has been for larger proportions of persons to migrate to metropolitan areas, and for the suburban rings (in the last three decades particularly) to increase at a faster rate than the central cities.

How large each metropolitan area will become, how densely settled and close to other urbanized areas, is immensely important to the future quality of the environment. No one knows at what point economies of scale—which permit an area to support a symphony orchestra or specialty stores or many jobs in a highly specialized division of labor or numerous religious sects or a complex mass transportation system or specialized education for unusual children—turn into diseconomies of scale with such side effects as a cumbersome bureaucracy, difficult daily transportation, noise, air and water pollution, street dirt, overcrowded parks and other facilities, congestion. At what point do diseconomies of scale seem to foster incivility in daily human encounters and confusion about which agency has which responsibility? At what point of density does a "normal" per-capita crime rate result in an absolute number of crimes so terrifying that residents stay away from evening cultural events?

Moreover, is it possible to determine economies and diseconomies of scale abstractly? Is not one man's meat still another's poison? People differ in their images of the communities they prefer to live in. Some may be repelled by a community full of competitors for the satisfactions they seek; others may enjoy the feeling of crowds and excitement.

Since amenity is geared to life style, those who seek, for example, civic involvement, pleasant homes not too far out in the countryside, easy access, good schools, some cultural distinction, and shopping variety may want to live in a medium-sized metropolis (for example, about a million people). But a community of that scale might be too dull for those who seek a varied commercial entertainment; it might be too confusing and impersonal for those who cherish knowing, or knowing about, many of their neighbors.

The dimly perceived relationship of numbers of people and their density to the provision and maintenance of amenities is critical to planning for an enhanced environment. How can technology and better management either increase the satisfactions of a small-scale city or reduce the distressing side effects of a very large one? Because of these doubts, many options on the size and settlement patterns of future cities ought to remain open.

Most analysts, extrapolating from recent trends, expect the greatest metropolitan growth to clot in geographic bands on the East and West Coasts, along the shores of the Gulf and the Great Lakes, and in the Southwest. In this view, giant megalopolises will congeal, with contiguous urban densities (not uniform densities) joining Portland, Maine, to the South; San Diego to San Francisco and beyond; and Milwaukee-Chicago to Pittsburgh and Toronto. These megalopolises would emerge because of a combination of intensified dependence upon imports, the existing heavy capital investment in industrial and cultural and other facilities, and the attracting power of the areas themselves. Presumably a mobile population would increasingly choose such a megalopolitan pattern in response to perceived and shared self-interest. The urban conglomerates would emerge out of the natural reinforcing tendencies of jobs attracting people and people attracting jobs.

Certainly, the megalopolis in part exists. More people could crowd into existing geographic bands. The distance from Boston to Washington is 450 miles. If the urbanized belt were only 20 miles wide, and the population density were 12,000 per square mile (less than the current density of Boston—14,580—and of Washington—12,442), 108 million people could be accommodated, or the bulk of the entire present urbanized population of the nation. Such a pattern could still include some open space.

But not all people may wish to bunch on the edges of the country, and certainly the national government and the neglected states would find that kind of settlement pattern economically and politically undesirable. Presumably there would be strong countermeasures to hold and attract people to other areas of the country.

Recently, after a generation of advocacy by urban planners, the federal government enacted policies to encourage urban growth in new communities. The Housing and Urban Development Act of 1970 provides for loans, grants, guarantees of bonds and other obligations, and planning-assistance funding for developers of new communities and authorizes planning and carrying out large-scale demonstration projects by the government. Under the Act, new communities are defined not only as those built on undeveloped land, but are also 1) communities within metropolitan areas; 2) additions to existing smaller towns and cities; and 3) major in-town developments to help renew central cities. It is, of course, too early to judge whether new density patterns and settlement patterns will be established, or old ones merely reinforced. Certainly, the sum of roughly one-half billion (some of which would revolve, some of which would be expended) is not munificent. (Governor Nelson Rockefeller campaigned in 1970 on the promise that he would raise $10 billion in bonds for the construction of new communities and transportation in New York alone; he has since abandoned the community-development bond proposal.)

The decision to include under the legislation additions to or renovations of existing cities or metropolitan areas together with new "free-standing" communities was undoubtedly a political one. As Anthony Downs points out, there are no constituents in proposed new cities but there are millions in existing ones, and politicians notice the difference. There may be monumental problems in later years to persuade legislators to fund "free-standing" communities generously.

If there is no agreement on what size and density future cities will or should take for the greatest amenity, clearly any policy to control population settlements will encounter great resistance. No country, even the authoritarian Soviet Union, has successfully limited the size of population-magnet cities, and subsidies or other incentives to redistribute population settlement have had a slow response. If a desired balance between the economies and the diseconomies of scale could be determined, the nation would have to decide whether to coerce people through sanctions or entice them through incentives to fit such a settlement pattern.

If, as we expect, existing communities will have to cope with presently identified urban problems plus continuing obsolescence and new growth, some new prospects may emerge to help achieve better living and working environments.

SERVICE, PARTICIPATION, AND TIME AT WORK

Our evolving society may not require people to spend long hours making things. It is therefore expected that people will be able to spend more time on nonwork activities, either by prolonging their schooling, and thus delaying their entrance into the labor market, by early retirement, or by a shortened work day, week, and year. We are assuming that in the future as in the present, work will still be the major way of relating the self to the world, and that most people will prefer to work and will be asked to do so by society. The time freed from work may be spent in commuting (with a decreased number of work hours has come an increased time getting to work), or in individual development and pleasures, or in community services and participation.

Citizens will in part judge the amenity-value of a community by what it has to offer in the use of time. Does the daily journey to work take them through pleasant vistas or derelict slums? Is it smooth and safe, or beset with interruptions and hazards? Are there recreational and educational opportunities for a wide variety of tastes and aspirations?

On another subject, de Tocqueville's observation that America is a nation of joiners is truer today than when he wrote it, and will become more so. Participation in a neighborhood, or an association, or in the governing of a school requires time, practice, and confidence. In recent years there has been a tremendous surge of participation in groups and governments by people who formerly had no time, practice, or confidence in being heard. Students and blacks and other sizable segments of the population want to participate increasingly in decisions affecting them.

More and more people will be able to afford more and more participation if they choose to use their time and energy this way. The number of opportunities for participation may indeed become one of the greatest amenities of all in the future metropolis, if people prefer the group experience to other uses of their time and energy, and get great satisfaction from a sense that government is close to them.

However, the amenity of participation may severely curtail other amenities, for in a heterogeneous community the more widespread the discussion on controversial issues, the more groups stating their opinions, the less likelihood that any affirmative program will be adopted. One citizen group tends to veto another until maximum participation causes paralysis.

AFFLUENCE

It is foolish to guess the cost of enhancing the urban environment when we have not even defined and quantified the qualities of amenity. But we have suggested that amenity is open-ended, infinitely expansible, intricately linked to community scale. Moreover, one man's amenity may be another man's horror. He or she who seeks order will be repelled by a pulsating mixture of high and low culture, of land uses and architectural styles; he or she who seeks stimulus will be bored with neatness, compartmentalization, and facilities and activities geared only to middle-income middle-brows.

Even when there is consensus, as in pollution control, it is difficult to estimate costs. Our technology is still too underdeveloped; our standards of water and air purity still too vague; and the future patterns of urban living, with their side effects on air and water, still undetermined. One thing is clear: the costs for correcting present levels of pollution, let alone avoiding future pollution, could be extraordinarily high in behavior as well as money.

What will be the potential effect of possible increases in private affluence? As education and incomes improve, people's aspirations toward the community change and their willingness to pay for community goods increases. In the United States, every index in the community changes with higher education, including tastes and attitudes. It is the college graduate who is least racially biased and more willing to tax himself for education and other public services; who takes it for granted that museums, concerts, theaters are needed as a part of urban life; who is more willing to volunteer for a variety of civic enterprises.

A larger base of citizenry may thus take it upon themselves to be patrons of the community in various ways: working for the preservation of historic buildings; volunteering to help the poor obtain education, health, and other services; accepting lower salaries and modest standards of living by choosing careers of community service instead of material advancement. They may be willing to pay for services in even more imaginative ways—for example, a neighborhood may pay for extra recreation assistance or police protection or extra garbage collection.

Affluence, of course, is complex. Indeed, past affluence has usually accelerated the obsolescence rate of the urban physical plant. For example, over the past two-thirds of a century people have been upgrading their per-capita working space requirements, and existing buildings, still physically usable, have become obsolete along with the transportation arteries serving them.

Typically, the aged parent nowadays does not live with grown children; young people over eighteen prefer to live away from home. Ideally, a young child is supposed to have a room of his own. One in thirty families has two homes. At work, not only executives but their secretaries demand a private office; much expansion of office space does not accommodate increased staff but the same staff with upgraded tastes. Universities need more space per student, particularly in graduate education.

Although increasing affluence and education may create new problems for communities by raised personal or community expectations, we believe that the potential for more community-oriented goals is higher now, and in the future, than has ever been possible before.

A CONJECTURE

We began by asking whether most of the actions to improve the quality of the urban environment would require painful changes of behavior and possibly some degree of coercion. Do enough people really want to pay for a desired amenity (such as clarity of the air or purity of the water or architectural harmony or decent housing) in terms of behavioral as well as monetary costs? We suspect that the community residents' willingness to accept expert instead of individual judgments (for example, in the matter of urban aesthetics) and to substitute collective goals for individual ones will be related to the total nature of individual freedom and responsibility in the nation. Most Americans have a low tolerance for bureaucracy and rigid regulations, whether in large-scale government programs or such large-scale activities as labor unions, universities, or business enterprises. If some of the present bureaucratic structures become less bureaucratic, people may be more willing to accept certain kinds of central planning and central community judgment about improving the environment.

Thus, if there is more decentralization in the administration of education; if there is a shift from high-overhead social welfare programs to an income-buttressing scheme; if government programs generally are simplified and reduced, then citizens may be more happy to adjust their behavior in ways that will help achieve selected collective goals. But if bureaucratic structures become more intrusive in everyday lives, and there are more restrictions and more delays in getting things done, citizens will probably hold on most tightly to whatever they believe are their last few areas of privacy and individual freedom. This is the major reason, we believe, that metropolitan government, though advocated for more than half a century by experts, has not appealed to voters. They preferred to keep local governmental decisions close to themselves, and have rejected metropolitanism because it increased their burden of distant, collectivized societal sanctions and coercion. Possibly metropolitan government would become more popular if the total package of national, state, and large-enterprise activity were to be reformulated.

Henry Adams' dilemma, sparked by observations at the beginning of the century, may be unresolved by the end of the century, but the terms will have been altered as will our consideration of them.

From the Transcript

I

THE CONCEPT OF "PROPERTY" AND URBAN DEVELOPMENT; URBAN-RURAL SHIFTS

PARTICIPANTS

John Dixon
Harvey S. Perloff
Henry S. Reuss
James L. Sundquist
John G. Wofford

II

THE ROLE OF THE STATES; LOCAL AND METROPOLITAN GOVERNMENT

PARTICIPANTS

James David Barber
John Brademas
Karl W. Deutsch
Leonard J. Duhl
Matthew Holden, Jr.
Herman Kahn
Harold Orlans
Harvey S. Perloff
Henry S. Reuss
James L. Sundquist

I The Concept of "Property" and Urban Development; Urban-Rural Shifts

PERLOFF: We are facing difficult urban problems that challenge some of our traditional values. For example, it is quite probable that in order for us to arrive at more rational forms for developing cities and solving certain problems stemming from urban dispersal—the high costs of providing water and sewage facilities, roads, and so on—it would be helpful if the government bought a certain amount of land and then leased it to private enterprise under developmental controls. Europe has already gone a long way in this direction. It would play havoc with our ideas about property and private enterprise, but this approach to the property issue is not new to the United States. The railways probably couldn't have been built at a profit if the government had not provided the land, and it may well be that such an approach will be necessary in order to create good cities. As we think ahead thirty years, shouldn't we begin to build up a base of support for public holding of land, encouraging private units of various types to undertake actual construction and development rather than having the government do the building? Now we're at the other end of the spectrum: the federal government is actually involved in local affairs—urban renewal, public housing, and many other projects. Instead, it should be setting up a framework in which private units can function effectively.

REUSS: About the only large collections of land that can be bought are raw lands out in the country, like Columbia, Maryland; building new towns within cities presents tremendous difficulties, which is why the federal government is involved only in very local things like rehabilitation and urban renewal.

PERLOFF: But, even in redeveloping a downtown area, government can set up certain rules for land use and transfer to make it attractive for private enterprise to do a good job. It is probably better to give money to the poor to rent private housing than to concentrate our efforts on public housing.

REUSS: Public housing certainly has not worked very well, and I can't get very enthusiastic about just dishing out the equivalent of food stamps to renters or would-be home owners to bid up the price of existing slums. In terms of property, the government probably ought to embark vigorously on the same kind of program of new towns and land assembly that every western European government has now launched. England is planning approximately 125 new towns. If and when this happens here, the concepts of private property and land would be considerably modified.

PERLOFF: We should remember that we do have a very rich country. We seem to have forgotten how to dream, however, and cannot accept the fact that we can afford to build glorious and wonderful cities. Yet we go ahead and permit people to buy great globs of land for profit, while we go on building in a very haphazard way without dreaming at all. We *could* build great cities today, but I don't think we have the will to do it today.

We tend to make it hard to create better communities. For example, the builders of the new town of Columbia, Maryland, have tried to incorporate various innovative features but have had a hard time convincing public officials to change certain rules so that these features can be brought about. The Columbia effort is important, not only because it is an attractive, planned new community but because it will have a broad spectrum of economic and racial groups. Without the cooperation of local government units this kind of innovation will be impossible.

REUSS: The British method of creating public corporations is pretty radical for a federal government like ours. A more practical method, and one the administration has used, is to remove the financial uncertainty by giving an FHA type of guarantee to a builder who will develop a large complex like Columbia. But that doesn't settle his problem of eminent domain. What we really need to do in the next thirty years is to prolong and augment the new-town program recently adopted by Congress. One feasible way to get new towns is to take care of the land developers' inability to command large-scale finance.

CONCENTRATION OF POPULATION: URBAN-RURAL SHIFTS

PERLOFF: The picture for the future seems to be one of large urban centers with an almost deserted countryside owing to very high agricultural productivity. We already have the phenomenon of the declining country village and town. Between 1950 and 1970, a high proportion of the counties in the United States lost population.

Under those circumstances there are two large issues facing the government: the "governability" of the large metropolitan areas; and what to do with an emptying countryside. The picture of a desolate rural area is as real a problem as an overcrowded city.

SUNDQUIST: We should have a national policy of population distribution. The government has not officially decided that this increasing concentration is a bad thing, but it ought to be dealt with. Most observers feel that both overcongestion of the city and desolation of the countryside are bad. Generally speaking, it is undesirable to have most people stacked up on a tiny portion of the land, not just for those left behind, but also for those who are stacked up. But since the government has never taken this as its concern, people go where the economic opportunities are. We've had no policy to influence the location of economic opportunities, except in the Area Redevelopment Act and the Appalachian Act, which were passed almost absentmindedly.

DIXON: There is a government policy that addresses itself to this issue of relocating industry—the recent decision of the National Science Foundation to pump funds into second-rate colleges. We can assume that business and industry will locate in areas with viable educational establishments so that professional people will have some sense of renewal. But we must remember that basically this is a policy for the redistribution of population.

SUNDQUIST: It's only a fragment of a policy, and its entire effect is offset by the single decision to put the new atomic reactor in a Chicago suburb.

PERLOFF: Does a population distribution policy imply that the government can dictate choices regardless of the individual's desires? In our tradition this approach is questionable. Should we have a population-distribution policy, or can we make sure that those who do prefer a certain kind of life will be able to achieve it?

SUNDQUIST: We can't leave it up to free choice. The distribution of population is beyond popular control, in any event, since people must settle where jobs are available. But I agree that population policies should reflect what the people want.

PERLOFF: Then the only kind of policy the government can have is one of making a variety of choices available and making each of these inherently attractive, whether the choice is a big city, a small city, or a village. It's not just the size that makes your choice desirable but certain features of that village or city.

If this is so, what pattern must be evolved to create economic, technological, and sociological features that would make it possible to create a "good life" in all these various kinds of communities? We must start now to think of ways to establish cultural institutions, recreational facilities, and so on, even in decentralized, thinly populated areas.

SUNDQUIST: I don't think it's as difficult as you suggest. I agree that national population policy should try to provide what the people want, not what somebody thinks is good for them. At present we have no such policy. People do what is decided for them by economic forces over which they have no influence. But with our present communication and transportation facilities, we should be able to decentralize most of the good features of the big cities without much trouble.

I'm not thinking of villages but of middle-sized cities as the nuclei around which you build. Within that regional complex, people should be able to choose a rural, small-town, city, or suburban setting.

WOFFORD: It is the location of industry and jobs that determines where people move. One thing that attracts or repels industry is the quality of the local educational establishment. Another is the local tax structure.

SUNDQUIST: Let me give you a good illustration of that. The Department of Agriculture had a small local program for community water systems, and it was trying to get a bigger one. The Budget Bureau oppposed the request on the ground that these communities were obsolete and had no economic future. Senator Aiken became interested in the issue and forced it on the administration. They now have a very active program to put water into these small communities. Thus they learned that a water system can make the difference between decline and growth by attracting both residents and small industry.

DIXON: Something just slipped by there that has great significance for our discussion—the thought process that enables key people in the Bureau of the Budget to make decisions on the basis of "the trends." The only reason their decision was overridden was that it became a political issue. But who makes the trends? And how do the trends come about? In fact, the trend has been changed because of political intervention. If there is one thing that is important in talking about the future, it is that we have to change this kind of attitude.

II The Role of the States; Local and Metropolitan Government

PERLOFF: What will be the role of the states in the future?

REUSS: We must first decide whether we will have states at all thirty years from now. If we continue as we are, the entire system will be moribund by then. Either we abolish the states entirely or consolidate them into eight or twelve regions, but we can't let them atrophy. My own preference would be not to abolish them but to try to build them up through adapting the Heller system of revenue sharing.

BRADEMAS: I agree with this, but I'd like to mention a few specifics. One problem in the state government system is manpower, getting first-class people involved. Perhaps we might encourage exchanges of federal and state civil servants. If you simply give more money to states, without some systematic way of helping them to spend it rationally and improve their decision-making processes, you'll still have serious trouble. Or there might be some kind of inducement, such as a tax-sharing scheme, for the states to improve their own tax structures, as we do in foreign aid.

REUSS: You could insist that the states have a progressive income tax in order to qualify for federal aid.

BRADEMAS: One thing that worries me about a tax-backed plan that requires little of the states is that they won't change their methods unless you use some coercion.

BARBER: The first problem raised by Mr. Brademas—talent and its distribution—is crucial. Here is a political system set up on geographic lines that has to conduct a national economy and a national society, a representative system dependent on the talent that happens to show up in a particular area. New Haven's success in urban-renewal efforts is due largely to the competent personnel it attracted. Surely we will have a professionalization of politics at the state level (perhaps rather far advanced by 2000), with state legislators and even many city councilmen serving full time and maintaining their own staffs. Where will we find enough talented people to fill these posts?

As for the role of the states, I think the problem is part of a larger one of pluralization in American government and politics. We recognize now that our problem is not a struggle for power between federal and state levels, but rather a proliferation of decision-making centers that have to be coordinated in some way. The real danger of pluralization is entropy, not crisis.

SUNDQUIST: The important thing is that we're beginning to realize, for the first time in our history, that the states are a national problem and that we need a national program to update them. Reformers have been saying for years that the states are archaic and hopelessly weak and had better be abolished. But by now opinion is shifting—people realize that the states won't be abolished, and even if they were things would only be worse, since you'd still need an intermediate administrative level. But if it was seriously recognized that the malfunction of the state governments is a national concern, then we could begin to think about this problem seriously. About the problem of personnel: the Advisory Commission on Intergovernmental Relations has endorsed a bill facilitating the mobility of people between federal and state levels. It also provides for national programs, federally or cooperatively administered, to train state and local personnel.

There are many other ways the national government can take action to upgrade state government. For instance, we have put a lot of federal money into the departments and divisions of state government, thus strengthening the subordinates at the expense of the governor. We should offset this by using federal funds and other influences to strengthen the governor's office. There are promising devices like the Appalachia Regional Commission, where the federal government and the states sit down together and work out a joint program of action. In a few years we ought to be able to evaluate the Appalachia experience and decide if it can be more widely applied.

LOCAL AND METROPOLITAN GOVERNMENT

DEUTSCH: I have been thinking about the problems of metropolitan areas where the suburbs tend to take on the role of small nations defending their sovereignty, thus making cooperation between the city and its suburbs difficult. We've tentatively concluded that the old center city is becoming obsolete as a political unit representing the metropolitan area, that certain jobs cannot be done in the municipal framework because you need much larger frameworks. The biggest one, of course, is tax collection. Whether it be income or sales tax, it still involves nationwide collection, since the community cannot collect the full amount needed for welfare, education, and all the other expenses. Indeed, the question may someday arise whether we need the help of an international organization such as the United Nations to recapture some of the fugitive income. But we cannot have anything much smaller than the national unit for tax collection. Also, the spending units have become much bigger. What we need here is not federation but confederation, an idea the American colonies worked out, in which no one group could be forced to do something, and the common interest in the benefits of union were strong enough to keep it going.

Confederation at the metropolitan level might involve not only municipalities but also other levels of government such as countries and states, even parts of Canada around Detroit. This would be a kind of metropolitan assembly in which each government is represented. One might envisage a situation where each individual is represented in each kind of government—once through his country, once through his state, once through his county, once through his city, and possibly once through a nongovernmental agency like the Urban League. The incentive to group cooperation would come from making certain major federal grants dependent on whether plans have been worked out acceptable to a majority of the unitary representatives in the assembly, with the understanding that for certain plans the minorities who didn't want to go along could opt out, within limits. If we considered this a kind of Marshall Plan for distressed cities, we might get effective cooperation. The key, of course, will be the diffusion of federal grants.

But in some cases you might need diminution. It would be absurd for a city like New York, with some five million people, to have only one school board. The bigger the city the more it has to be treated as a state. Robert Dahl's presidential address to the American Political Science Association this year dealt with the optimum size for a community big enough to be efficient and small enough to be responsive, and he suggested a figure between fifty and two hundred thousand.

ORLANS: The ideal size of the English new town was 60,000, and it may have gone up somewhat.

DEUTSCH: I would say that a city should subdivide itself into school districts of about 80,000, each with a school board and its own elected teachers. A borough system for a city involves a political unit for 150,000 people, plus or minus 50,000, in regard to schools, school boards, welfare administration, and police work. These communities should have a fair degree of autonomy in the letting of municipal contracts and other political activities. Initially, there could be some bad government—Harlem politics for a while might resemble Boston politics under Mayor Curley.

Yet the only way to let populations achieve self-government is to let them practice it. You may have to draw limits where human lives are at stake; the state reserves powers in cases of homicide and epidemics. But except for such crises you would let the local municipalities do whatever they think right. I am sure many of our neighborhoods would be well run. Harlem would be a city and the people could get a feedback from their own decisions.

The net result might then be a strengthening of the three-level government: federalist, confederalist, and eventually perhaps the election of a president of the entire municipal area by a direct vote of all New Yorkers. This man would have to give some visible evidence of leadership and executive experience in supervising those services that cover the whole metropolitan area.

SUNDQUIST: Obviously something must be done about loc ment if our national objectives are to be carried out. W on the local governments to initiate the projects ser national goals and then to execute the programs, and th not set up to do this satisfactorily either in metropolitan in rural areas.

The first thing wrong with local government is that very few of the units are territorially adequate. In the metropolitan areas, there are far too many feuding local governments, and in the rural areas they are just not big enough either to provide a working territorial base or to hire the kind of expert staff needed to do the local part of the federal job.

What we need in every state is a system of substate regions designed to be territorially related to the problems they are dealing with. By 2000 this will be even more crucial than it is now. But the dilemma is that the federal government can't create these structures. Only the states can do it, and the federal government must therefore reverse its thinking. For the last generation or so, we've believed that the federal government ought to move into direct dealings with the local governments and either bypass or ignore the states. But this tends to be self-defeating because the federal government can't create the kinds of local units it wants to deal with. It can't deal effectively with the 20,000 local units there are now—it can't even communicate with all of them.

The federal government must adopt a constructive policy of working with the states to modernize local governments; it needs to work through the states to develop the kind of structure Karl Deutsch was talking about, or some alternative.

PERLOFF: I think you have both been concerned with form and ignoring function. What are we trying to accomplish? Different governmental functions have different scale economies, and it's difficult to arrive at an ideal size.

Even more important, we must give high priority in governmental activities to opportunities for the development of the individual. Which governmental units can do this best? For example, I would argue that national government ought to be concerned with providing the base funds for education. The size of the governmental unit will depend on what it is you are trying to accomplish.

DEUTSCH: I define the function of the metropolitan area as that of agent for the production of contact choices. If I move into town I first consider my mobility, and in this case a metropolitan area is more valuable than even a delightful small town like Princeton. On the other hand, I could be tied up in such a congested area that it might take more than half an hour to get to trees or recreation. We should try to give people the widest range of choices, and since a metropolitan area is unparalleled in this respect, I expect that when you get another hundred million people in the United States, at least two-thirds of them will move into the cities.

We must therefore organize for such cities a silent, rapid-transit subway system. But from history we learn that the public sectors of the metropolitan systems are capitalized, and this is one of our problems.

The other necessary set of functions is responsiveness to people's needs and tailoring services to needs. Almost every ethnic group in the United States has a genuine choice; each has the prerogative of choosing its residential area. One of the functions of the metropolitan area is to give our Negro people the same genuine choice. To make this possible for them now, we must give them the finances, the speed of acculturation, and all the other factors that have been effective.

The other, and huge, function of a metropolitan area is to serve as an engine of acculturation. Since acculturation is both a national goal and a national function, we ought to find federal funds to subsidize needy metropolitan areas.

DUHL: Given the present direction of politics, there is an increasing suburbanization of power, with a corresponding polarization between white and black haves and have-nots. What is to prevent this metropolitanization you envisage from ending up as a new containment for the Negroes in the cities?

DEUTSCH: For one thing, suburbanites want to be close to the central city. If the central cities of 2000 are going to be hell holes, this would be a highly unlikely change in American life.

DUHL: Maybe the world of the future won't need that central city. If so many specialized services will be offered outside the central city, it will lose its attractiveness and utility, and the centers will be left to those who can't get out, the Negroes.

HOLDEN: First, I will simply say that I fundamentally disagree with Professor Deutsch's description of the acculturation process.

Second, I don't think people live in the suburbs because they find central cities unattractive, but because the availability of federally-backed mortgages over the years has allowed them to move to the suburbs when they found central cities residentially unattractive but economically necessary.

There is another aspect of this entire problem. For sixty years in this country people have, on occasion after occasion, with full knowledge, rejected all the opportunities presented to them. That rejection used to be clearly related to social class, but in recent years it has been related to race. Clearly, some preferred values are served by this chaotic pattern of local government, and demolishing these archaic units will not necessarily result in full opportunity, participation, and the accompanying sense of dignity.

We also need more discussion of a most revolutionary political theory—that local government is an instrument for national objectives. Perhaps some of the present controversies come from introducing national issues into local political units that originally had quite different purposes.

BRADEMAS: The suburbanization of politics is not producing the results Professor Deutsch has suggested. For instance, in state aid to local public schools, suburban schools are alloted $40 per capita more than center-city schools, and this is a continuing trend.

KAHN: What's the rationale for this?

SUNDQUIST: The states generally support foundation programs that give a certain amount per capita. They also assist the school building programs, and new construction goes on mainly in the suburbs.

KAHN: Let me make a very optimistic statement. You're not going to have this kind of Negro-white problem by 2000, but rather what a lot of Jews had back in the twenties when they felt kind of neurotic about exclusion from clubs, colleges, or some professions. But on the whole, with education they did fairly well.

HOLDEN: Before we go any further, let us calculate what would happen if Negroes' income rose approximately 20 percent a year for the next ten years, while white incomes rose about 10 percent a year. You have to get very far before this syndrome of country-club neurosis is at all relevant.

KAHN: Let's assume that something like a quarter to a third of the

Negroes will still be living in slum conditions. Although Harlem will still be with us, there will also be a great number of Negroes in the suburbs, because when half the Negroes are making more than $10,000 a year, then at least in the North, something like 10, 20, or 30 percent of the Negroes will be spread out in the suburbs, just as the whites are now.

HOLDEN: But wherever Negroes try to penetrate white residential areas the whites flee. Why should that stop?

KAHN: Because it applies to the poorly educated Negro. No one minds having a college-educated Negro for a neighbor.

HOLDEN: You're wrong there.

KAHN: There are all kinds of integrative patterns today that could have been used five years ago. First, people get used to the idea of living next to upper-middle-class Negroes. Second, there's also reverse discrimination. Many people feel that the situation in this country could get very ugly unless we do something about the race problem.

HOLDEN: We'll be able to test the strength of these feelings soon. An open-occupancy bill is now before the Michigan legislature. Let's see how the suburban "liberal" Democratic senators and representatives vote on this matter.

KAHN: There are many neighborhoods now where a Negro has moved in and the prices have not dropped. People also discover they can live with Negroes.

DEUTSCH: The notion that the central city becomes a mixture of a jungle and a slum and that the suburbanites become the threatened prey of these aggressive people is a recurring fantasy wherever sharp transitory social differences happen to coincide with sharp visible ethnic differences.

Although the suburbanite needs the central city, the central city is not indispensable. No other civilization has ever permanently depended on its cities, and our urban setup may be a passing stage.

Incidentally, one cause of our city-versus-suburbs conflict is the inability of the suburbanites to realize that the central cities are inhabited by people. Yet it is hopeful that the *children* of the suburbanites are now the Vista volunteers.

DUHL: I still think these people will be used, exploited, and contained.

THE YEAR 2000: STATE AND LOCAL GOVERNMENT

Representative Henry S. Reuss

By the year 2000, the area of progress in which Americans took the greatest pride was a new and dynamic federal system in which federal, state, and local government were each able to make a maximum contribution to a democratic and good life for all Americans. Progress dated largely from the passage by Congress of the State and Local Government Modernization Act, enacted by the first Congress after the settlement of the Vietnam war.

The law followed a period of crisis marked by the steady deterioration of state and local governments in their ability, both fiscal and organizational, to solve the pressing problems of the day. The central city had become a cancer on the whole nation; its problems grew while the suburbs had the revenues. At the same time, there was increasing popular resentment against the hugeness of the federal government. But state constitution-making seemed a lost art: witness the 1968 fiasco of such an attempt in Maryland.

The aim of the State and Local Government Modernization Act was to give states an incentive to save their central cities and their impoverished rural areas from bankruptcy, and to improve the efficiency and democracy of state and local governments generally, by providing federal block grants for states that adopted Modern Government Programs.

The Content of Reform

The states were encouraged to include in their Modern Government Programs a plan and a timetable for a whole series of reforms comprehensive enough to demonstrate bona-fide "creative state initiative."

The first set of reforms—those designed to make state and local government more efficient, economical, and responsive—had been recommended over a long period of time by such good-government organizations as the Committee for Economic Development, the United States Chamber of Commerce, the Advisory Commission on Intergovernmental Relations, the Council of State Governments, the National Municipal League, the Mayors' Conference, and the National Association of Counties. These reforms included regional governments of states and interstate compacts for cooperative efforts in health, education, welfare, and conservation; modernized state government, including the short ballot, longer terms of constitutional officers, annual sessions of the legislature, adequately paid legislators, modernized borrowing powers, rationalized boards and commissions, and assistance to local governments; modernized local government, including cutting down the number of unnecessary counties, towns, and other local units, working toward all forms of metropolitan government, providing for true home rule, the short ballot, modern borrowing power, the merit system, and decentralizing local government in order to make it more democratic and humane.

The second set of reforms—those designed to induce states to remove economic disparities between various local governments—was an extension of efforts made in the 1960's by big-city mayors and by the federal government to save the central city. These included revision of state grants-in-aid and sharing of tax revenues to eliminate the preferences so widely given to wealthier communities at the expense of poorer communities: for example, the unfairly large state returns of income-tax revenues to communities where large utility plants or factories happened to be located; of sales tax revenues to still other communities that happened to have shopping centers widely patronized by outsiders. Another reform was the prohibition of local zoning regulations that kept out low-income housing, or in some cases all homes of any kind, and the transfer of the zoning power to the state or to a subregional governmental level. Still another was an inducement to the thirteen states that still lacked an income tax to place on their books one of at least moderate progressiveness.

The Politics of Reform

What made the Modernization Act financially possible was the coming into being of the long-awaited federal "fiscal dividend," resulting from federal budgetary surpluses at current tax rates once the war in Vietnam had ceased to absorb so large a part of the national effort, and full-employment, non-inflationary growth had been restored.

What made the Modernization Act politically possible was the new alliance between big-city mayors and officials of impoverished rural governments on the one hand and state governors on the other. Big-city mayors and the trustees of the deserted villages jumped at the proposal because for the first time the wealthy of the state, living mostly in the suburbs, were compelled to help meet the statewide problems of the big cities and the impoverished countryside. The governors, whose elections depended on a statewide vote, joined the coalition because the voters of the cities and impoverished rural areas represented either a majority or a crucial minority. Powerful support was generated from homeowners everywhere who finally came to realize that large-scale and unrestricted financial aid to local government was needed to prevent endless increases in the local property tax which furnished four-fifths of the tax revenue of local government.

The suburb-dominated legislatures at first tended to drag their feet. But once the Modern Government Programs drawn up by the governors had been presented, and the federal block grants to the states had begun, the legislatures grudgingly began to implement the Programs. The legislatures proved unable to resist either the bait of federal block grants, or the lure of their new political power.

Perhaps most significant of all, the first elections after the Vietnam settlement saw radical changes in the makeup of Congress. New men were sent to Washington, dedicated to the belief that the future of America lay in peaceful development rather than in being world policeman.

The Modernization Act also reflected the ascendancy of those who recognized the need for attention to the public sector over those who favored a massive tax decrease and less government expenditure throughout all levels of government. Nor was the congressional faction that favored a supreme and all-knowing federal government and the withering away of state and local governments victorious either.

How Modernization Came About

The State and Local Government Modernization Act authorized block grants without strings for each of the fifty states in the first year of the program, during which governors, aided by state legislators, local officials and special task forces, drew up Modern Government Programs. In the second year, all fifty governors complied with the string specified by Congress and presented plans and timetables for reform, thus qualifying for three more years of block grants.

Congress initially funded the revenue-sharing program with the states at a rate of $10 billion a year. The program went into effect for a four-year trial period. It produced the desired revolution in all except seven of the state capitals, and hence was renewed for a five-year period for all except the seven states. These soon purged themselves of their lethargy. It was renewed at five-year intervals at increasing annual rates, and by 2000 the annual federal contribution to state and local governments of unfettered funds was $50 billion annually.

The law provided a revenue-sharing formula that channeled about one-half of the funds directly to the states, the remaining one-half to cities, counties, and some deserving townships. Over the years the amount of pass-through by states to local governments increased, and by the year 2000 it had reached approximately 90 percent of the revenue-sharing totals.

Distribution under the act was made on a per-capita basis to each state, with a special distribution to those states that showed responsible self-help in their own taxing powers, and to localities whose low per-capita income demonstrated the need to skew the distribution in their favor. Progressively, income throughout the United States showed a tendency to equalize, with the result that the skewing provision was no longer needed by the 1980's.

The Modernization Act coincided with the coming to fruition of the one-person-one-vote requirement of the Supreme Court for state and local legislative bodies. State and local governments increasingly attracted the best Americans. By 1985, all but four of the states had enacted drastically revised, modernized constitutions, with special emphasis on state permission and incentive for the reform of local government, and the states' assumption of the role of financial equalizer.

By the year 2000, the shape of government in the United States had assumed the following forms.

The Federal Role

The federal government continued to represent the great priorities of national need. In addition to its role as administrator of foreign and defense policies and as guarantor of a full-employment-without-inflation economy, Washington continued to have large and expanding responsibilities in health, education, welfare, city development, conservation, and research. As in the 1960's, it maintained direct relationship with local communities—largely bypassing the states—through categorical grants in these areas. But the block grants to the states provided by the Modernization Act sparked a rebirth of the states as political entities, with the federal government as midwife.

Most important, the federal government played an enlarged role as the residual guarantor of civil liberties, civil rights, and equality of opportunity. The President, with his national constituency, continued to be the chief enforcing officer of the Bill of Rights, and the Supreme Court, with life term members, its chief interpreting authority. A major and continuing concern of the federal government was equality in jobs, education, travel, housing, and voting.

The State Role

State government was strengthened by the willed decision of a Congress that the fifty states ought not to be allowed to wither on the vine.

Politically, Congress could hardly have done anything else. The American citizen had made it clear in dozens of opinion polls that he favored an invigorated state government. The pulses of state governors, legislators, and officials were quickened by the prospect of a federal revenue-sharing force that could not be ignored. Facing a decade of sharp political warfare if the rising expectations of the states were denied, Congress decided instead to use federal per-capita block grants as incentives to state modernization.

Moreover, existing state boundaries seemed to make as sensible regional demarcations as any lines that could have been newly drawn in the 1970's. The states were correctly seen as the regional and metropolitan governments they had increasingly become.

By equalizing their tax-rate differentials, the states managed to discourage their citizens from moving to other communities or from purchasing elsewhere to avoid taxes. By using their taxing, spending, and financial reorganization powers for the benefit of their people at the local levels—mainly in metropolitan areas—the states gave local governments the financial capacity they had lacked for education at all levels, health facilities, welfare, public safety, and clean air and water.

Thus, in the decision not to let the states atrophy, it was recognized that American society needed pluralism. Massive labor unions, large farm associations, huge industrial organizations, and above all big government in Washington were seen to press ever more heavily on the originality and responsibility of the individual. To let a Washington power center replace the states would have been a move in the wrong direction. Initiative and innovation could be encouraged only by a federal system of maximum democracy, maximum solvency, and maximum modernization at all three levels—national, state, and local.

Contrary to the predictions of many political scientists, the number of states in the year 2000 was still fifty. The idea of consolidating neighboring states in the interest of economy and efficiency floundered because of the justifiable fear that a liquidated state would lose its two senators, and in some cases, its minimal one congressman. But North and South Dakota; North and South Carolina; Nevada and Arizona; Maine, New Hampshire, and Vermont; Connecticut and Rhode Island; and Montana, Idaho, and Wyoming all had seized on an ingenious idea to save both money *and* their senators. Each grouping amended their constitutions to provide for single governors, legislatures, and administrators for the group of states, while remaining separate states in their federal representation. Their new unitary state universities were among the nation's foremost.

By 2000 all the states had departments of urban affairs, as opposed to only eleven in 1968. All assisted financially in the construction of local air- and water-pollution control facilities, in public housing, urban renewal, and mass transport, as opposed to only a handful in 1968. By 2000 all state governments had eliminated their "long ballots" and elected only the top state officials. All had achieved substantial reorganization of their executive branches and had moved from the spoils systems of 1968 to a universal civil service based on merit and efficiency. The average salary for a state legislator had become $35,000 a year, for a full-time job with an annual legislative session.

More and more, regressive local property taxes had been replaced by more progressive state taxation. By the early 1980's, all states had adequately progressive income taxes owing to the Modernization Act. State income and sales taxes now accounted for upwards of 90 percent of all state and local governmental revenues. Most of the property-tax levy had shifted from local to state government.

The transfer of most taxing power from the locality to the state and the devolution of tax-equalizing power on metropolitan areas resulted in a much broader tax base and the elimination of discriminatory "tax colonies," which had formerly caused great inequality between municipalities in the same state. State distribution of revenues to the localities, together with state direct expenditure, reflected the general principle of need on a per-capita basis. Deviations from per-capita distribution occurred only in favor of *greater* distributions to poorer localities.

The Role of Local Government

Local government by the year 2000 had become both modern and democratic, as a result of two seemingly contradictory but really complementary trends. It moved toward centralized regional government—at the state or substate level—for purposes of equitable revenue raising and problem solving. At the same time, it decentralized itself back to the neighborhood in order to insure democratic participation to the individual.

Both tendencies were seen in the Modern Government Programs of the states that emerged from the Modernization Act. By giving local government the opportunity and incentive to modernize itself, these state programs offered an escape from the insolvency, the fragmentation, the ultra-localism, the poor services, the unbalanced communities, and the citizen apathy of a generation earlier.

TOWARD CENTRALIZATION

The centralizing and regionalizing revolution in local government was marked by the following.

1. *Fewer local governments.* The number of counties, towns, villages, and special districts was drastically reduced in order to enable local government to obtain adequate geographical powers and revenue sources to solve effectively local problems and eliminate wasteful Lilliputs. By 2000, the 80,000 local governments of the 1970's had been reduced to some 20,000. The 3000 counties had dwindled to 1000, as many rural counties consolidated with their neighbors for regional cooperation. Archaic township governments —17,000 of them—had been substantially abolished. All told, it was the greatest decimation of redundant governments since the mid-twentieth-century consolidation of rural school districts.

2. *Metropolitan government.* Cities and suburbs had metropolitanized themselves by such devices as metropolitan councils of government, which had attained a high degree of cooperation, particularly in taxing, while retaining local sovereignty; by building up county governments in many urbanized areas where the county boundaries were more or less congruent with the metropolitan area; and finally, by full-fledged metropolitan governments in some twenty-five large and medium-sized metropolitan areas, completely replacing existing local governments with their own elected legislators.

Many larger metropolitan governments, such as those centered in New York, Philadelphia, Baltimore-Washington, Pittsburgh-Cleveland, Detroit-Toledo, and Chicago-Milwaukee, crossed state lines and were created by interstate compact.

Metropolitanization would have moved even faster had there been less concentration of Negroes in the large central cities. By 2000, nine major cities were more than half Negro, and another nine more than one-third Negro. But Negroes made up only 10 to 30 percent of their metropolitan-area populations, because segregation by income persisted despite nationwide legal prohibition of segregation by race. Though Negroes often resisted metropolitan government, those that were nevertheless formed in many of these mixed areas gave Negroes a surprising degree of political power. In 1967 a Negro mayor was elected in Cleveland despite a white majority, and by 2000 a number of Negroes had been elected chief executives of their metropolitan-area governments despite the metropolitan minority position of the Negro.

The process of metropolitanization was assisted over the generation by an extension of the federal concern with metropolitan planning that first appeared in the 1960's in the form of highway aids, water-pollution assistance, the Land and Water Conservation Act of 1964, the Model Cities Act of 1966, and the Metropolitan Development Act of 1966.

Metropolitanization was made possible by state laws that liberalized the annexation by municipalities of unincorporated areas and discouraged new incorporations that failed to meet minimum standards of total population and of population density. Zoning authorities in metropolitan areas were restricted to larger municipalities or to counties, in order to prevent "fiscal zoning" by smaller municipalities that had for so long excluded lower-income families, and in some cases people generally. State aid to localities was revamped to treat citizens equally according to need rather than place of residence.

3. *Home Rule.* Adequate home-rule powers were granted to reformed counties and other local governments so that the rationalized local governments were able to govern. Revised state constitutions and statutes markedly eased restrictions on the power of local government to borrow and to utilize nonproperty taxes.

4. *The short ballot.* The number of elected officials of local governments units was greatly reduced, thus giving the voter a chance to know what he was doing and making local office worth the participation of good men and women. By the year 2000, elected policy makers were largely confined to local legislators of the en-

larged governmental units and single appointed or elected chief executives for each unit. The swarm of town trustees, coroners, elected tax commissioners, and flotsam inspectors disappeared.

5. *The merit system.* The spoils system in local governments of the 1960's had been replaced with personnel systems based on merit, competence, and adequate compensation.

TOWARD DECENTRALIZATION

Along with these trends toward centralization came the opposite trend, in order to make local government more democratic and humane. In the 1960's New York City had experimented with "little City Halls"—decentralized offices in the neighborhoods staffed by officials ready to listen to a citizen and to save him a long trip downtown. By the year 2000 all American metropolises had decentralized governmental decisions over schools, city services like garbage collection, and neighborhood activities, to legally autonomous neighborhood boards—the "ward republics" of Thomas Jefferson.

Apart from local autonomy, neighborhood nonofficial groups, operating in fields as diverse as health centers, housing construction and rehabilitation, day-care units, libraries, manpower training, poverty programs, and cultural programs in drama, art, and music, were being endowed with federal, state, and local financial help and given the nonprofit corporate form.

As a further step toward decentralized democracy, almost every local community had its ombudsman—an independent government official whose job was to represent the bewildered citizen in his dealings with the bureaucracy at all levels. Hawaii had set up the first state ombudsman in 1967.

Making Federalism Work

As the twentieth century drew to a close, the American people could take comfort in two parallel developments that greatly affected the course of history for the better.

In 1948, the American people, rich with the resources of a healthy economy, worked out the Marshall Plan to place $5 billion a year at the disposal of the ailing European countries. The major condition, right at the start, was that the European countries themselves prepare programs of self-help and modernization in order to qualify. The Europeans did draw up their reconstruction programs and worked them out with the regional grouping of states, the Organization for European Economic Cooperation. And so the Marshall Plan was launched, and in the late 1940's and early 1950's it contributed vastly to the rebuilding of Europe.

In the 1970's, the American people, again rich with the resources of a healthy economy after the end of the war in Southeast Asia, wanted to cure their sick state and local governments. Using the Marshall Plan analogy, Congress offered to place an initial $5 to $10 billion a year at the service of the states in unrestricted block grants, with one big string—that the states themselves prepare Modern Government Programs for the organizational and fiscal improvement of themselves and their local governments. Congress wisely considered that the drawing up of these programs by the governors aided by citizen groups and reform-minded officials was an act of faith rendering unnecessary more detailed performance standards on the road to modernized state and local government.

The United States in the year 2000 still had many problems, but it seemed, for the first time in its history, to be making federalism work.

INTERGOVERNMENTAL RELATIONS IN THE YEAR 2000

*Richard P. Nathan**

Background on Three Theories of Federalism

Before viewing the intergovernmental scene in the year 2000, it would be useful to consider the theoretical underpinnings of American federalism. There have been three major conceptions of federalism as a means of organizing political power.

Arthur Macmahon of Columbia University, in *Federalism: Mature and Emergent* (1955), defined a federal system as one that "distributes power between common and constituent governments under arrangements that require Constitutional amendment to change."[1] All constituent governments must have "substantial" powers of their own; that is, a system under which only "trivial" powers were assigned to one level would not be considered federal.[2]

Another view rejects this static definition and stresses the *evolutionary* character of federalism. Carl J. Friedrich of Harvard defines federalism principally as "process."[3] Federal systems move through time from loose groupings of sepa-ate states to increasingly more integrated and unified nations. In many respects, the American system bears this out, having become increasingly more integrated politically over the years.

Still a third view of federalism defines it in terms that Professor Friedrich might consider a highly advanced state of this evolutionary process. The late Morton Grodzins of the University of Chicago likened American federalism to a "marble cake, characterized by an inseparable mingling of different colored ingredients, the colors

* The author is presently Assistant Director of the Federal Bureau of the Budget. This essay on the year 2000 was written prior to his assuming office. It does not reflect his experience of administration policy decisions in the equally-difficult-to-predict transition from the 1960's to the 1970's.

appearing in vertical and diagonal strands and unexpected swirls. As colors are mixed in the marble cake, so functions are mixed in the American federal system."[4] Grodzins' essential point was that federalism is *pragmatic*. No powers reside intrinsically here or there. Federal systems consist of relationships among governmental bodies designed to get the job done.[5]

There is therefore a sharp division among the experts as to the nature and goals of American federalism. In effect, the critical problem in projecting to 2000 is to anticipate the type and amount of political change over the next three decades with reference to a continuum that has on one side the more traditional Macmahon view of American federalism and on the other side the most centralist Grodzins view. Now to the year 2000.

American Federalism in the Year 2000

The principal intergovernmental wave of the three decades from 1970 to 2000 has been one of *decentralization*, moving back along Professor Friedrich's continuum from the Grodzins to the Macmahon view. New intergovernmental instruments adopted since 1970 have increasingly reflected a strong concern for state and community solutions to major problems in the public sector. This is in strong contrast to the three decades from the New Deal through the mid-1960's, when centralizing tendencies generally predominated.

As far back as the mid-1960's there were forces at work that represented the forefront of these new intergovernmental directions. The tax-sharing idea, originating as a serious national issue in 1964, is one example. Likewise, the Economic Opportunity Act of 1964 and the Model Cities program were enacted with strong provisions for promoting political participation and decision making at the local level.

Beginning in the mid-1960's, the development of sophisticated public-sector planning techniques was basic to the emphasis, over the past three decades, on state-local decision making. The mass informational output of computer technology made possible the development of systems analysis and policy-program-budgeting (PPB). The social indicators that followed in the early 1970's added a further dimension to microeconomic public planning, now very highly developed.

Although it began in Washington, the most productive frontier for these new planning techniques proved to be state and local government. PPB from Washington was found to have serious limitations, since planning has little meaning if the planner cannot carry it out. The appropriate distinction in the year 2000 is between macroeconomic planning (basically aggregative and Keynesian) at the national level, and the intensive application of microeconomic planning techniques at the state and local levels.

The Budget Plan for Fiscal 2001

This thirty-year movement toward greater political and economic decentralization in American federalism can be understood best by examining federal grants-in-aid in the President's Budget Plan for the fiscal year 2000–2001. The biggest single item is the Metro-Center Aid bill, enacted in 1977.

TABLE I.

Federal Intergovernmental Payments 2000–2001 (estimate)

PROGRAM		BILLIONS
1. Metro-Center Aid		$ 33.2
2. State Overhead Aid (Revenue Sharing)		18.1
3. Functional Bloc Grants		48.2
Education	12.3	
Health	9.2	
Manpower	10.3	
Recreation	3.1	
Transportation	13.3	
4. Residual Itemized Grants in Functional Bloc Grant Areas and Others		13.8
5. Welfare		32.4
6. Other		8.7
	Total	$154.4

"Functional Flexibility Grants"

The term "decentralization" as used thus far is not a sufficient description of recent intergovernmental policy trends. Basically, what has been happening since the mid-1960's is that the federal government, through its major federal-aid instruments, has been *reaching out* to support institutions dealing with domestic social problems. This has been done through both state and local governments and through nonprofit community service and economic-development organizations at the local level.

In the 1960's, there was early reliance on enhancing state and local opportunities for decision making through the consolidation of federal grant-in-aid categories. While there was some initial success in some closely related categories (those of water sewers, education, health, and pollution control), the overall results were fairly limited. It was soon evident that more far-reaching techniques were needed to give appropriate recognition and support to state and local governments capable of creative leadership in major domestic policy areas.

The so-called *functional flexibility* concept for federal grants-in-aid illustrates this point. It offers state and local governments a choice between functional bloc grants and the older and more traditional categorical grants-in-aid.

As shown in item 3 of the budget-plan table above, functional bloc grants are currently offered for education, health, manpower, recreation, and transportation. Functional bloc grants in three of these areas—transportation, manpower, and recreation—can also be provided for *regional* groupings of states. The first area in which the functional-flexibility, or selective-decentralization, concept was applied was manpower training. Under the Comprehensive Manpower Services Act of 1970, states and metropolitan areas were given authority to establish comprehensive manpower programs for which a single, consolidated federal grant-in-aid could be provided.

Functional bloc grants are made to states on the basis of recommendations by the Board of Federal Aid Analysis, approved by the President.[6] The Board, in fact, today has a major role in intergovernmental policy, and it is organized as follows: five federal government officials; two state officials; two representatives of urban governments; and three members selected by the President from other fields (currently an educator, a business executive, and the President of the AFL-CIO). The chairman is named by the President. The Board has a small professional staff for each major functional area.

Most local governments receive allocations under the functional-flexibility-grant programs of their particular state. There is, however, one important way that major cities or jetropolises[7] can participate directly under the functional-bloc-grant concept. With state concurrence and, under special circumstances, even without it, cities or metropolitan regional authorities of over a million can receive their own functional bloc grants.

The criteria used by the Board of Federal Aid Analysis for awarding state and metropolitan area functional bloc grants cover: (1) past program results; (2) budget and system analysis capacity; (3) use of social indicators and related techniques for assessing the effectiveness of social policy; (4) availability of informational and data-processing systems; and (5) ratings of state-agency staffing and procedures.

Unlike the more *pro forma* planning requirements of an earlier day, these criteria are performance-oriented. A number of bloc-grant applications have therefore been rejected. Others have been cancelled after being approved and operative. Several smaller states still prefer grants for specific categorical purposes. The concept of functional flexibility does not carry a connotation that categorical grants are necessarily bad. For some states this is acknowledged as the wisest course.

Overhead Aid for States

General aid (or revenue sharing) is estimated at $18.1 billion in the 2000–2001 budget plan. This aid is provided under the State Government Modernization Act of 1971.[8] Its main purposes are to provide overhead support to the states and to ensure a satisfactory level of progressiveness for the nation's global tax system. Overhead aid can be used for any purpose except highways. It is distributed to the states on a per-capita basis adjusted for tax effort. Since 1975, overhead aid has averaged 11.2 percent of total federal aids. It will rise to nearly 12 percent in the budget plan for fiscal 2000–2001.

Welfare: One Field that Bucked the Trend

Though decentralizing trends have predominated, they have not been the only pattern for new federal-aid policies. Welfare intergovernmental relations is the major area in which federalization can be said to have outpaced the decentralizing tendencies of the past three decades.

Nationwide benefit levels and eligibility standards, and the consolidation of all public assistance into a single uniform-support category, were adopted under the Social Security Act of 1972. The net effect of all income-support programs in 2000–2001 (social security, uniform support, unemployment compensation, and the almost universal availability of public-service jobs for the poor) is to guarantee a minimum living income for all. The negative income tax was not made part of this system, although bills in this area were almost passed in the late 1970's.

Along with welfare, a few other decidedly overlapping functions (such as air and water pollution control) have also been nationalized. But economic spillover is a very limited concept. Only highly fluid interarea services have been nationalized. In the welfare field, particularly, the pull from rural to urban areas exerted by the AFDC (Aid for Families with Dependent Children) system produced strong support for basic reform and the development of a single national policy on benefit levels and eligibility standards. Other functions with less spillover effect are aided in large part via the three broad federal-aid instruments: functional-flexibility bloc grants; overhead aid (revenue sharing); and Metro-Center aid for cities.

Metro-Center Aid for the Core City

The intergovernmental level at which the greatest changes have taken place since the 1970's is in the cities. Metropolitan political consolidation has advanced at a fast pace in the past two decades, for essentially three reasons: white fear of Negro-controlled central cities; Supreme Court rulings requiring metropolitan area-wide school desegregation; and the leavening effect of more federal aid for the cities. The latter is now a full-blown reality. In addition to Model Cities coordination grants and the old urban-renewal program, the nation's city areas now receive aid for general purposes under the Metropolitan Center Rehabilitation Act of 1977.

Metro-Center aid is provided *directly* to city governments. It is appropriated on a five-year basis and is allocated by a formula that the Secretary of Housing and Urban Affairs can adjust by as much as 10 percent on an annual basis. The Secretary's decisions to adjust the grants (generally in recognition of special needs or program innovations) must be approved by the Board of Federal Aid Analysis.

The emphasis of the Metro-Center program is on community control and the rehabilitation of the inner city. Although the results have been impressive, metropolitan area tension levels remain high. In fact, they show signs of growing even more serious in suburban areas this coming summer. Emergency decrees under the Anti-Riot Act of 1971 have already been issued for Chicago; Westchester County, New York; and Fairfax County, Virginia.

Back to Earth in the Present

What are the assumptions about political behavior and American government underlying the preference for decentralization which this essay reflects in its projections for 2000? The author would be flying under false colors if he did not acknowledge the prescriptive implications of this essay. Its roots are the basic values of American federalism: (1) participation by citizens in governmental processes; (2) flexibility in problem solving; and (3) opportunities for innovation at different levels of the political system.

In any consideration of governmental structure in the year 2000, one must specify basic value preferences such as these and examine their political and intergovernmental consequences. This time capsule reflects a strong preference for federalism defined as governmental pluralism, much in line with the Macmahon view. Centralists (of the Grodzins view) hear a different drummer and no doubt anticipate a different future. Their values and their predictions must be examined in juxtaposition to the intergovernmental world of the future here portrayed.

NOTES

1. Arthur W. Macmahon, ed., *Federalism Mature and Emergent* (Garden City, N.Y.: Doubleday, 1955), p. 4.
2. *Ibid.*
3. Carl Joachim Friedrich, *Man and His Government* (New York: McGraw-Hill, 1963), p. 594.
4. President's Commission on National Goals, *Goals for Americans* (New York: The American Assembly, 1960), p. 265.
5. *Ibid.*
6. The President can overrule the Board's rejection of a particular function-bloc-grant application, as has been done thus far on three occasions.
7. The name *jetropolis* refers to very large metropolitan areas with new mass-transit systems using a type of vertical up-craft as yet undiscovered in the 1960's.
8. A related proposal, federal-tax credits for state personal income taxes, came close to adoption in 1975. It was dropped when it was realized that all states had, or were close enough to having, personal income taxes to make the credit unnecessary.

From the Transcript

CITIZEN PARTICIPATION

PARTICIPANTS

John Brademas
Richard P. Nathan
Harvey S. Perloff
Henry S. Reuss
James L. Sundquist
John G. Wofford

BRADEMAS: With the proliferation of federal programs we may well have an excellent opportunity to develop not only national advisory councils (say, on education or social security) but also local advisory councils to help communities understand the local implications of such national policies as health care and pollution control.

REUSS: These advisory councils aren't worth much unless they can actually administer as well. It would be a good idea to have training schools for activists who could then take over and lead neighborhood groups.

BRADEMAS: We're talking here about some way of encouraging the development of local political leadership in the whole country—something we sadly lack at present. It would serve to build support for national policies at the local level and at the same time provide a source for positive, constructive suggestions on local needs.

REUSS: Your suggestion is worth further discussion. We have so many alienated young people who feel they play no vital role in our society. If we could encourage an active participation in the areas of poverty, education, conservation, and renewal, we might not only evolve a whole new set of worthwhile political institutions, but engage the talents and attention of our alienated youth as well.

SUNDQUIST: Increasingly we are going to have the problem of leisure time. Participation in public activity would be a productive solution.

BRADEMAS: There might be a more pressing reason for stepping up this kind of local community action in the year 2000. With the tremendous increase in economic power and the power of the national government, and with most of the citizens engaged in nonproductive, nonpolitical leisure activities, the chance that someone may control all the levers of power at the center will be far greater than it is today.

NATHAN: Undoubtedly, the whole economic, political, social, international structure will be increasingly complex. Also the populace will get substantially better formal education. But to have a better-informed and involved populace we must devise techniques to stimulate involvement. It may well be that we should devote a much greater proportion of television time to public programs. I would guess that over the last twenty-five years, the amount of public discussions through forums—church groups and men's clubs and other forums—has gone down 80 or 90 percent.

PERLOFF: If you were to involve a great many local groups, such as advisory groups on community action, would you be likely to get support for national policy as in the past when you had a coalition of farmers and laborers and other groups? I suspect you're likely to develop nonpartisan groups that would undermine political parties. Moreover, I don't see the relationship between really local issues and many important national policies such as international relations.

BRADEMAS: I was thinking primarily of domestic problems. Since local communities are affected by national policies, I think there should be local participation.

SUNDQUIST: We all agree that there should be a great deal of local participation. The key problem is how to fit local advisory councils into the system. Who do they advise? The local system? Or do they advise the federal people, and in competition with the elected local authority? Is it the role of local groups to decide whether to have a program or to decide how to carry it out? The problem will require quite a bit of creative energy to figure out how to make this very complex system work.

REUSS: International affairs aside, I don't think there is any problem. People live at the local level, and that's where all the health, education, and welfare programs are actually carried out. For all these domestic issues, I firmly believe you need the greatest amount of citizen participation through innovative devices. As for getting people more interested in questions of international affairs and foreign aid, if they became really involved at the local level they would be more responsive to the legislator willing to vote for foreign aid.

PERLOFF: How is local participation likely to affect complex national decision? One example of a conflict between local and national interest is flood control. All over the country today, there are vested land interests in flood-prone areas, with the result that the federal government is literally spending billions to hold back the waters, but people continue to go into the flood plain at an increasing rate. The government spends more billions of dollars, and the result is no overall improvement in the total flood condition. In such a situation local interests are causing poor national decisions. Would more participation help in this case? How do we relate the concept of participation to that of national interests? Do we need to?

NATHAN: There are two issues there. One is the manner of reconciling conflict of interest; the other is how to increase local participation and expand local involvement. I think regional planning will partially solve the conflict-of-interest problem. If federal funds and resources were based on a metropolitan area, or a regional watershed, you would begin to get the local public interest evolving in a manageable pattern. Although it may prove to be contrary to national policies, I think that if you broaden the base of participation, things will gradually tend to come out right. For example, if a certain area of the country with a very small number in agriculture still wants agriculture rather than industry, I'd let them have it for a time. I wouldn't worry too much about the local decisions on many of these issues as long as you get broad enough representation.

Second, we should make a major effort to consider workable techniques for enlarging participation and expanding local involvement. Unless we are able to evolve such patterns, we'll find that with a more and more complex social, political, and economic environment, we'll have less and less participation, and all government in the hands of an elite.

WOFFORD: I suggest we don't want to go too far along the road of participation and involvement without examining our assumptions about who will "participate" and for how long and for what reasons. We have to think about our objectives. Is it education—to develop a consensus for certain national policies in which you try to involve hitherto unconcerned, nonparticipating citizens? Or is it to obtain real participation, to use the opinions of these councils about how things really ought to be done at the local level? It's a glorious image—committees all over the country carrying out federal policies. But my impression is that people participate or want to participate mainly when things are going badly. You don't have a great cry today to "participate" in most areas. You have it in Harlem, where something is wrong. The desire to participate fluctuates with both groups and individuals. There is always a delicate balance between concern for the "public" and concern for the "private," and the balance tends to swing back and forth for each individual. The amount of participation also varies in different historical periods. The 1960's showed a great desire on the part of many people to "participate." The "progressive era" in the early part of this century was another such period. But these fluctuations, in terms of the sweep of history and of the life cycle of an individual, tend to be triggered by situations people feel so strongly about that they leave their firesides and their children for the endless meetings that effective participation requires.

PERLOFF: Given the number of serious problems we've identified as important for the coming years, it seems very likely that we will be having a great many committee meetings.

NOTES ON CONTRIBUTORS

James David Barber, Professor of Political Science at Yale University, has written extensively on the psychological dimensions of political leadership. His publications include *The Lawmakers: Recruitment and Adaptation to the Legislative Life* and *Power in Committees: An Experiment in the Governmental Process.*

Daniel Bell is Professor of Sociology at Harvard University and co-editor of *The Public Interest.* He is the author of *The End of Ideology* and editor of *Toward the Year 2000: Work in Progress.*

John Brademas, United States Representative in Congress from Indiana since 1959, is chairman of the Select Education Subcommittee of the House Committee on Education and Labor. He is a graduate of Harvard and Oxford Universities and a Fellow of the American Academy of Arts and Sciences.

Lester R. Brown, Senior Fellow at the Overseas Development Council, was adviser to the Secretary of Agriculture on foreign agricultural policy from 1965 to 1969 and Administrator of the International Agricultural Development Service, the technical assistance arm of the United States Department of Agriculture, from 1966 to 1969. He is the author of three books, the most recent being *Seeds of Change: The Green Revolution and Development in the 1970's.*

William M. Capron is Associate Dean of the John Fitzgerald Kennedy School of Government at Harvard University. From 1962 to 1965 he served in the Executive Office of the President, first at the Council of Economic Advisors and then as Assistant Director of the United States Bureau of the Budget. Mr. Capron is an economist, most of whose work has been in the field of industrial organization.

Matthew Holden, Jr., is Professor of Political Science and is associated with the Center for the Study of Public Policy and Administration at the University of Wisconsin. His publications include *The Republican Crisis* (forthcoming) and papers on decision making, ethnic politics, the political order, and urbanization.

Herman Kahn, physicist and specialist in public-policy analyses, is Director of the Hudson Institute. Among his major interests are inquiries into alternative world futures and long-run political, economic, technological, and cultural changes, along with research into strategic warfare and basic national security policies. His publications include *On Thermonuclear War, Thinking About the Unthinkable, On Escalation: Metaphors and Scenarios,* and (with Anthony J. Wiener) *The Year 2000: A Framework for Speculation on the Next Thirty-Three Years.*

Kenneth L. Karst is Professor of Law at the University of California at Los Angeles. He is the author of *Latin American Legal Institutions: Problems for Comparative Study* and (with Harold W. Horowitz) *Law, Lawyers and Social Change: Cases and Materials on the Abolition of Slavery, Racial Segregation and Inequality of Educational Opportunity.*

George C. Lodge, Associate Professor at the Harvard School of Business Administration, served as Assistant Secretary of Labor for International Affairs from 1958 to 1962. He is the author of *Spearheads of Democracy* and *Engines of Change: United States Interests and Revolution in Latin America.*

Margy Meyerson has served as a lecturer in the Department of City and Regional Planning at the University of California at Berkeley and as Director of Research at The American Society of Planning Officials. She is co-editor with William L. Wheaton and Chester Rapkin of *Urban Housing.*

Martin Meyerson, President of the University of Pennsylvania, formerly served as Director of the Joint Center for Urban Studies of Harvard and MIT, as Professor of Urban Development at the University of California at Berkeley, and as President of the State University of New York at Buffalo. He is currently serving as Chairman of The Assembly on University Goals and Governance. His books include *Face of the Metropolis* and *Housing, People and Cities.*

Richard P. Nathan is Assistant Director of the United States Bureau of the Budget and a former staff member of the Brookings Institution. He was Chairman of President Nixon's Transition Task Force on Welfare and Federal Aid Policy.

Robert R. Nathan, consulting economist, is the author of several books on economic policy. The firm of which he is President has served as consultant on economic matters to many foreign governments, state and local governments, and industrial corporations and trade unions in the United States.

Harold Orlans, a member of the senior staff of Brookings Institution, has served as consultant to the Research and Technical Programs Subcommittee of the House Committee on Government Operations. His areas of interest include government policy toward university science and governmental use of social science research.

Harvey S. Perloff, Dean of the School of Architecture and Urban Planning at the University of California at Los Angeles, was formerly the Director of the Program of Regional and Urban Studies of Resources for the Future, Inc. He is the author of several volumes on urban planning and regional development and on the problems of the less developed countries. He has served as consultant to the Department of State, the TVA, the Department of Housing and Urban Development, and the United Nations.

Henry S. Reuss has represented Wisconsin in the House of Representatives from the 84th to the 91st Congresses and has served on the Committee on Government Operations, the Committee on Banking and Currency, and the Joint Economic Committee. He is the author of *The Critical Decade* and *Revenue Sharing: Crutch or Catalyst.*

Donald A. Schon is President of the Organization for Social and Technical

Innovation, and Visiting Professor of Urban Studies at the Massachusetts Institute of Technology. His publications include *Invention and the Evolution of Ideas, Technology and Change,* and *Problems of Innovation in American Industry.*

James L. Sundquist, political scientist, is a senior fellow in governmental studies at the Brookings Institution. He has participated in political party affairs as Assistant to the Chairman of the Democratic National Committee and as secretary of the platform committee at two Democratic national conventions. He is the author of *Politics and Policy: The Eisenhower, Kennedy, and Johnson Years.*

Rexford G. Tugwell is Senior Fellow in Political Science at the Center for the Study of Democratic Institutions. He is the author of several publications in both economics and political science, including *How They Became President: Thirty-Five Ways to the White House* and a biography of Franklin D. Roosevelt entitled *The Democratic Roosevelt.*

John Voss, Executive Officer of the American Academy of Arts and Sciences, was formerly Manager of Special Projects for Arthur D. Little, Inc. He was a member of the American Academy's Study Committee on Space Efforts and Society and is the coeditor (with Paul L. Ward) of *Confrontation and Learned Societies.*

John G. Wofford is Director of the Urban Mass Transportation Study at the Harvard Law School, where he is a research associate in Urban Legal Studies. He was formerly at the Institute of Politics of the John F. Kennedy School of Government, first as a Fellow and then as Associate Director, and he has recently been serving as Executive Director of a Transportation Task Force established by the Governor of Massachusetts.

Additional Participants to the Working Party on The Future of the United States Government—the Year 2000

Karl W. Deutsch
Professor of Government
Harvard University

John Dixon
Washington, D.C.

Leonard J. Duhl
College of Environmental Design
University of California, Berkeley

Kermit Gordon
President
Brookings Institution

Herbert Kaufman
Senior Fellow
Brookings Institution

Nicholas Johnson
Commissioner
Federal Communications Commission

John Manley
University of Wisconsin

INDEX